If you can reheat your coffee in it, you can use your microwave like a gourmet!

THE MICROWAVE BIBLE shows how to turn a microwave oven from a coffee-warmer-upper into a precise and remarkable cooking machine that can make truly delicious meals in a fraction of the time of conventional cooking. Here are wonderfully clear and easy recipes for: triple cheese manicotti, glazed short ribs, in-a-hurry spaghetti sauce, finger lickin' Chinese chicken, simple salmon, easy apple crisp, three-minute fudge—and nearly 600 more. Beyond a compendium of recipes, Norene Gilletz takes you every step of the way through understanding, operating, and caring for your microwave oven with the safest, up-to-date information. Use *THE MICROWAVE BIBLE* to:

- Make your own homemade cereals.
- Prepare great Italian, Chinese, French, and Kosher food!
- Defrost food in a fraction of the time.
- Choose the right cut of meat for your microwave.
- Adapt recipes for low-cholesterol and low-calorie dishes.
- Cook fish and vegetables—the healthy way!

"The microwave/convection instructions demystify an area of expertise ignored by most current cookbook writers."

—Montreal Gazette

★

"The Microwave Bible is much more than a collection of recipes. It is a reference book—a wealth of information."

—Baltimore Jewish Times

NORENE GILLETZ is a well-known cooking teacher and food consultant, a member of the International Microwave Power Institute and the International Association of Culinary Professionals. She is the author of the "food processor bible," *The Pleasures of Your Food Processor*.

The MICROWAVE Bible

RECIPES FOR BUSY DAYS, LAZY DAYS, HOLIDAYS, EVERY DAY

(formerly titled *MicroWays*)

Norene Gilletz

WARNER BOOKS

A Time Warner Company

Originally published in Canada by J & N Publishing Ltd.

Warner Books Edition

This Warner Books edition is published by arrangement with the author.

Warner Books, Inc., 666 Fifth Avenue, New York, NY 10103

A Time Warner Company

Printed in the United States of America
First Warner Books Printing: November 1991
10 9 8 7 6 5 4 3 2 1

Library of Congress Cataloging-in-Publication Data

Gilletz, Norene.
The microwave bible / by Norene Gilletz.
p. cm.
Includes index.
ISBN 0-446-39297-9
1. Microwave cookery. I. Title.
TX832.G56 1991
641.5′882—dc20 91-16594
CIP

Cover design by Julia Kushnirsky
Cover photo by Perry Beatton

WELCOME TO *THE MICROWAVE BIBLE*

Yes, you CAN cook in a microwave oven! Once you learn the techniques you need for successful microwave cooking, you'll wonder how you ever lived without one. Microwave ovens do have limitations, but what they do, they do extremely well!

Your microwave oven will help you prepare delicious meals in minutes with less muss and fuss. Cooking is fast, nutritious and easy. You can cook or heat your meal right in the serving dish, saving on clean-ups. Foods don't stick, so little or no additional fat is needed, saving on calories. Foods cook quickly, saving time. Sometimes it will be faster to use your microwave for part of your cooking and to prepare other dishes simultaneously in other appliances.

Your microwave oven won't eliminate preparation time. If you have a food processor, it makes a perfect partner for your microwave. Zip it, zap it, what a great way to cook! You'll spend less time in the kitchen and have more time to enjoy life. However, microwave cooking does require time and attention until you develop "micro-sense". First learn the rules; then you can experiment and know which ones you can break! Start with simple recipes to help you learn quickly.

Learning to cook in the microwave is an ongoing process. It doesn't happen overnight. This book is an evolution of my own learning experiences. I want to share them with you so that you can also experience the marvels of microwave cooking. I've goofed many times. I still make mistakes and I sometimes forget if a particular food is cooked covered or how long it takes to cook. When in doubt, I use common sense. I've had to unlearn many bad techniques, like cooking eggs in margarine containers (a no-no), or cooking potatoes in a plastic bag (it melted)!

As I wrote the recipes, I could hear the questions my students always ask me: "What kind of dish should I use? Do I cover it? With what? Do I have to turn the dish if my oven has a turntable? How can I prepare several dishes and keep them all hot? How do I convert my favorite recipe? How do I double a recipe? If I only need a single serving, how long do I cook it?"

I've tried to answer your questions in *The Microwave Bible*. I hope my book gives you confidence and shows you that a microwave oven CAN do more than just heat and defrost. The recipes have been written to hold your hand while you learn. The instructions are more detailed than in my other cookbooks, but I felt it was the next best thing to having me in your kitchen!

Although recipes may take time to read, they are all quick and easy to prepare. If it takes more than 15 minutes of preparation, I probably didn't include the recipe, unless it was very special. I prefer to cook from scratch, but there are many times when I am too busy or too lazy to do so and use short-cuts.

You don't have to be Jewish to enjoy the recipes in this book! I have included a wonderful selection of recipes from a variety of ethnic cuisines, but have adapted them to follow Jewish dietary guidelines. Availability of Kosher products may vary from area to area, but most products can be found on supermarket shelves.

The recipes in *The Microwave Bible* were tested on 600 to 700 watt microwave ovens, as well as several Convection/Microwave ovens. Cooking times will vary with different brands of ovens.

This cookbook is a collection of recipes, information, tricks and techniques from so many people, it is impossible to name them all! My family, friends and students helped shape this book with their questions and suggestions. Thank you to everyone who helped in any way, from testing, tasting, proof-reading, washing dishes or just being there!

My sincere appreciation goes to Bella Borts, Mimi Brownstein, Seline Malament, Natalie Frankel, Terry Jacobson, Linda Dumas, Rita Polansky, Marilyn Melnick and Perry Beaton for their help. Thank you to Robert Schiffmann for his technical expertise. It all started with Barbara Harris, author of *Let's Cook Microwave*, who first taught me how to use my microwave and started me on the road to develop my own MicroWays.

The Microwave Bible would not have been possible without the tremendous help and support of my son Douglas Gilletz. He shopped for groceries, tested recipes, washed dishes, programmed my computer, proof-read recipes and was my right-hand man. He was indispensable and I couldn't have written this book without him. Thank you also to my dear friends and family, especially my daughter Jodi, son Steven, sister Rhonda and brother Bruce for their support and encouragement. Most important of all, thank you Mom. You're still the best cook I know!

When should you use your microwave? For busy days, lazy days, holidays, EVERY DAY!

MICROWAVE FOR EVERY DAY

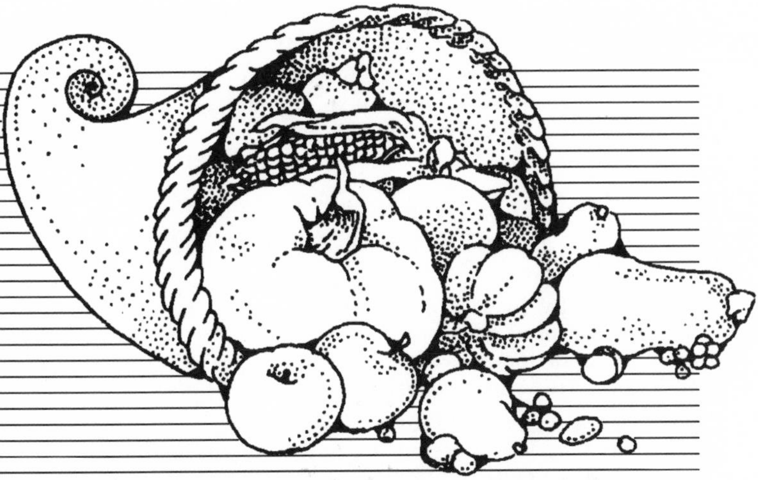

MICRO-WAYS FOR EVERY DAY

YOU KNOW MORE THAN YOU THINK!

Do you only use your microwave oven to reheat coffee? You're probably suffering from **MUG — Microwave Underuser's Guilt!** Forget the guilt. If you know how to reheat coffee, you've had your first lesson in learning how to use your microwave. You're on the way to becoming an expert!

An 8 oz. cup of coffee takes 1 ½ to 2 minutes on HIGH power to heat. Cold coffee takes longer to heat than lukewarm. A full cup takes longer to heat than half a cup. Four cups take longer to heat than one cup. It is faster to heat coffee on **HIGH** than on a lower power level. A low-wattage microwave oven takes longer to heat coffee than a high-wattage microwave oven.

It is important to stir the coffee (or any liquid) before and at least once during heating; the centre will be less hot than around the edges. (Think of the typical middle child who feels ignored!) Stirring helps equalize the temperature. It also helps to prevent the liquid from erupting. A little bit of attention at the right time prevents problems later on!

You have now completed your first lesson in microwaving. Congratulations! Aren't you surprised at how much you already know? This information can be applied to heating most foods.

USING YOUR MICROWAVE OVEN....MORE!

Are you a slave to your microwave? Do you find it easier to cook conventionally instead of trying to learn microwave cooking techniques? Are you confused about how long to cook foods, which power level to use, when to cover foods, what to use as a cover, when to stir, when to turn the dish, what kind of cookware to use? Does it all seem overwhelming?

Don't despair. If I could learn to use my microwave, so can you! I still have to ask my sons for directions on how to record a T.V. program on the VCR. I occasionally get mixed up when I try to open the trunk of my car and unlock the gas tank instead!

We are creatures of habit. It takes time to learn the techniques that guarantee success with microwave cooking. Children learn to cook in the microwave much more easily because they don't have to unlearn old habits; they are used to functioning in a pushbutton world. You CAN learn; practice makes perfect!

Read the manufacturer's instruction manual at least twice to become familiar with the features and functions of your microwave oven. Don't expect to learn everything at once! Learning is an ongoing process. It gets easier and the techniques will become automatic. Try easy recipes at first:- scrambled eggs, cereal, soup, spaghetti sauce, fish, baked apples....they'll help you develop confidence. You may even wish you owned 2 microwaves!

HOW DO MICROWAVES COOK FOOD?

- **When you cook conventionally,** first the heating element gets hot, then the air, then the pan, then the food. When you microwave food, only the food is heated. The microwaves pass through the air and dish; they are absorbed directly by the food.
- **Microwaves are attracted** to the water, fat and sugar molecules in food. It causes them to get excited and vibrate millions of time per second, causing friction within the food. This friction is converted to heat.
- **REFLECTION:** Microwave energy is reflected by metal (e.g. the walls of the oven, metal pots and pans). This is why metal cookware is not usually recommended for microwave cooking.
- **TRANSMISSION:** Microwaves pass through glass, ceramic, paper, porcelain and some plastics the same way that sunlight passes through a window. Because they don't absorb heat, they make good containers for heating &/or cooking foods. However, dishes can get hot from contact with hot food; keep oven mitts on hand.
- **ABSORPTION:** Microwaves are absorbed by the food and penetrate to a depth of ¾ to 1 ½ inches. The heat from the outer edges is conducted towards the middle; the centre of large foods heat &/or cook by conduction.
- **Microwaves heat food from the outside inwards,** not from the inside out!
- **The surface of microwaved foods** is usually cooler than below the surface. This is because the air around the food is not heated as in conventional cooking, so the surface cools slightly.
- **When the microwave oven shuts off,** there are no more microwaves. It is the same principle as when you turn on a light. When you turn it off, there is no more light. Don't worry — you can't eat a microwave!
- **The molecules** (not the microwaves!) will continue to bounce around in the food at the end of the cooking cycle. It's similar to when you work out at an exercise class. You need time to cool down afterwards! In microwave cooking, this time is called standing time. This is part of your cooking time.
- **Microwave energy is safe.** It is contained within the metal walls of the oven. You may not see the metal; the walls may be acrylic-coated. There is a perforated metal shield in the glass door; you can see through, but the microwaves can't get through. There is a special seal around the door frame to keep the microwaves inside when the oven is operating.
- **If you open the microwave oven door during cooking,** it shuts off instantly. Wipe around the door frame with a damp cloth after cooking to prevent grease build-up.
- **You may prefer the taste** of certain foods when they are cooked conventionally. That's okay; our tastes are acquired. It reminds me of the young bride who tried to please her husband with her cooking. He would say "It's delicious, but it's not quite like my mother's cooking. It's missing that certain flavor." This went on for 6 months. One day a terrible disaster happened; she burned his dinner. Fed up, she served the meal to him anyways. He exclaimed "THAT'S the flavor I've been missing!"
- **Microwaves won't give a burnt taste to foods.** They will taste "just-made" and be moist and juicy. Enjoy!

MICROWAVE TERMS

ARCING: Sparks and flashes of light, accompanied by sharp, crackling sounds. It is caused by improper use of metal in the microwave (e.g. metal twist ties, dishes with gold or silver trim, aluminum foil which is too close to the walls of your microwave oven). Arcing can damage your microwave oven.

ARRANGE: To place food so that it will cook evenly, usually in a circle or donut shape, or with thicker parts towards the outside of the cooking dish.

BROWNING DISH: A microwave dish which has been treated with special substances that absorb microwave energy. The empty dish becomes very hot when preheated in the microwave oven. It becomes a microwave skillet and will quickly sear the surface of the food. It can also be used as a regular microwave cooking casserole if it has not been preheated.

COMBINATION OVEN: A microwave oven which also has convection or conventional heating capability in the same cavity. It may also have a broiling feature. Various cooking modes may be used, either alone or in combination with other cycles. (e.g. microwave; combination convection/microwave; convection or conventional cooking.)

COMBO-COOKING: Cooking foods first with microwave energy, then completing or browning them with conventional heat, or vice versa.

CONVECTION COOKING: Similar to cooking in your conventional oven, but hot air is circulated throughout the oven by a fan. Temperatures are usually lowered 25 to 50°F to prevent overbrowning before the centre of the food is cooked.

DUAL-USE COOKWARE: Containers or casseroles which are transparent to microwave energy as well as ovenproof.

ELEVATE: To raise food or casserole in the microwave oven for more efficient and even heating/cooking. See **RACK OR TRIVET.**

FOIL DONUT: A circle of aluminum foil with the centre cut out so that it resembles a donut or bagel. This helps the centre of food to cook while shielding the outside edges from overcooking.

GLASS, CERAMIC & GLASS/CERAMIC COOKWARE: Casseroles and containers which are heatproof as well as transparent to microwave energy. Glassware which is not heatproof can break from the heat of the food which is transferred to the cookware during microwave cooking. See Dish Test (p. 21).

HOT SPOT: This is definitely not the newest disco or night club! A hot spot is where there is a concentration of energy in a microwave oven. To test if your microwave has a hot spot, place a layer of sliced white bread over the floor of the oven, with the crusts touching. **MW on HIGH for 5 to 7 minutes.** Brown spots = hot spots.

MAGNETRON: The microwave power generator which converts electricity into microwave energy.

MICROSAFE or MICROWAVABLE: Cookware, containers, utensils, coverings or food which can be safely used in the microwave oven without danger to the cookware, microwave oven or YOU.

MICROWAVE COOKWARE: Containers or casseroles which are transparent to microwave energy and safe to use for defrosting, heating and cooking in your microwave oven.

MICROWAVE THERMOMETER: A specially designed thermometer which can be left in the microwave oven during cooking. **DO NOT** use a regular mercury thermometer inside the microwave. However, you can use an instant-read thermometer outside of the microwave to check the internal temperature of a particular food.

MW: An abbreviation for the verb **"microwave".** To cook, heat or defrost food in a microwave oven. (e.g. **MW on HIGH for 2 minutes.)**

OVEN COOKING BAGS: Special transparent bags which can be used for microwave, convection, combination or conventional cooking. These are **NOT** plastic storage or sandwich bags, or the bags your grocery store uses to pack your fruits and vegetables!

OVERCOOKED: Foods which seem done when they have completed their cooking cycle in the microwave, but are overdone after standing time. Also refers to thin or bony ends of foods, or outside edges of foods which cook before the centre of the food. See **FOIL DONUT, SHIELD, STANDING TIME.**

PIERCE: To puncture the membrane or skin of a food to allow steam to escape and prevent bursting (e.g. egg yolks, potatoes, squash).

PLASTIC COOKWARE: Dishes which are transparent to microwave energy and which won't melt or release toxic substances into the food. Check the label before using to ensure that cookware is microwavable. Some plastic cookware is heat-resistant up to at least 400°F and can be used as **DUAL-USE COOKWARE.**

PROBE: A temperature sensor supplied by some oven manufacturers. It plugs into your microwave oven and is inserted into the food to measure the internal heat. The oven turns off automatically when the desired temperature is reached; on some microwave ovens, the probe holds foods at serving temperature. See **MICROWAVE THERMOMETER.**

RACK OR TRIVET: A microsafe accessory available in kitchenware shops which is used to elevate food. Various designs are available. I prefer a rack with deep grooves or wide spaces. This allows adequate air circulation under and around the food and helps avoid condensation. The rack should also elevate the food out of any cooking juices to prevent steaming or uneven cooking.

REARRANGE: To change the position of foods in the microwave oven partway through defrosting, heating or cooking for more even results. Foods can also be turned over. Rearranging is used for foods which cannot be stirred or mixed.

ROTATE: To turn a casserole, container or food ¼ or ½ turn in a microwave oven for more even cooking. This technique is used when the food cannot be stirred, rearranged or turned over.

SHIELD: To cover part of a food with small, flat pieces of aluminum foil for part of the cooking to reflect microwave energy and prevent overcooking. Foil must be kept at least 1″ away from the walls and doors of the oven to prevent **ARCING.**

STANDING TIME: This is part of cooking time. After a food has completed its cycle in the microwave, it should stand for a few minutes (either inside or outside of the oven) to complete its cooking and to equalize the temperature. If properly used, standing time will help you keep food hot until serving time. Standing time is usually ¼ of the cooking time.

STARTING TEMPERATURE: The temperature of the food before cooking or heating. The colder the food, the longer its cooking time. Temperature of foods in this book are based on where they are normally stored. Meat, dairy products and most vegetables (e.g. carrots, celery) are at refrigerator temperature; potatoes, onions and canned foods are stored at room temperature.

STIR: To mix a food in order to equalize the temperature, help cook the centre and prevent overcooking around the outer edges.

STIR-SHAKE: To mix pieces of food (e.g. vegetables) by shaking the covered casserole back and forth with a slight tossing motion. Hold on tightly to keep the lid on. Do not use this technique for liquids.

TURNTABLE: An accessory which rotates the food or cooking dish constantly to help it cook more evenly. Some manufacturers provide a built-in turntable in their oven. Other manufacturers use alternate methods of ensuring even microwave cooking. If your microwave has an uneven cooking pattern, you can always purchase a separate turntable. If you use a turntable, it is not necessary to rotate the casserole dish during cooking. However, stirring or rearranging may be necessary to help cook the centre of foods more evenly.

VARIABLE POWER SETTINGS: The settings on your microwave oven which are used to cook different types of foods. They can be compared to the settings you use when you cook conventionally (e.g. **HIGH, MEDIUM-HIGH, MEDIUM, MEDIUM-LOW and LOW**). Your microwave oven is usually on **HIGH** power unless you choose another setting. Different manufacturers use different names or numbers for their settings. Refer to your manufacturer's manual for further information. See Power Level Chart (p. 16).

VENT: To fold back microwavable plastic wrap at one corner to allow steam to escape and prevent the plastic wrap from splitting during microwave cooking.

THE RIGHT CONNECTIONS

- **Your microwave oven should be plugged** into its own electrical circuit. If other appliances share the same circuit, your microwave will cook more slowly if any of the other appliances are operating at the same time. You may even blow a fuse or trip the circuit breaker. **Please note:- different outlets do not mean separate circuits!**
- **If you don't want to go to the expense** of having an electrician install a separate circuit, plug your microwave oven into the outlet on your electric stove if it is convenient. (If you have a gas stove, sorry!)
- **Make sure your microwave** is plugged into a grounded 3 prong wall outlet. **NEVER** cut or remove the third ground prong from the electrical cord; you risk a potentially serious electrical shock.
- **Don't use an extension cord.**

COOKING TIMES

- **As a general rule,** most foods cook in ¼ to ⅓ of the conventional cooking time. Porous foods heat &/or cook more quickly than dense foods. When cooking a recipe for the first time, choose the minimum time suggested in the recipe. Check occasionally.
- **Use your nose as a guide.** Foods usually "smell done", just like in conventional cooking!
- **Most foods cook in 6 to 7 minutes per lb. on HIGH.** Foods high in fat heat faster. Cooking times for specific foods are covered throughout this book in the appropriate chapters.
- **My recipes have been developed and tested** for 600 to 700 watt microwave ovens. Your cooking times may differ from those I have indicated. This is why I have given time ranges, as well as what to look for in each recipe. (e.g. **MW on HIGH for 3 to 4 minutes,** or until boiling and thickened.)
- **Foods which require rehydrating** (e.g. rice, grains) take almost the same time to cook in the microwave as conventionally. However, they can be cooked, served and stored in the same dish.
- **Even though foods may not look done,** they will continue to cook during standing time. It is better to undercook; you can always add more time.
- **When cooking large quantities of food,** it may be faster to cook them conventionally. For family-sized servings, the microwave oven is usually quicker and cleaner.
- **Be sure to set your timer correctly.** Small quantities of foods with low moisture content (e.g. bread) may dry out or become hard if heated or cooked too long.

FACTORS AFFECTING YOUR COOKING TIME

- **Quantity of food.** More food takes more time.
- **Amount of liquid added.** Extra liquid slows down cooking time.
- **Starting temperature of food.** Refrigerated foods take longer than foods at room temperature.
- **Size &/or shape of food.** Smaller pieces cook faster than big pieces. Thinner pieces cook faster than thick pieces.
- **Density of food.** A dinner roll heats faster than a potato.
- **Freshness.** Fresh vegetables cook faster than those which have been hanging around in your refrigerator for a week.
- **Shape of casserole dish.** Food cooks faster in a shallow casserole than in a deep one. Food cooks faster in microsafe plastic cookware than in glass or ceramic cookware.
- **Personal taste.** Everybody has their own preference as to what they consider "cooked enough".
- **Length of standing time.** Foods continue to cook after microwaving. Cover to retain heat. Undercook foods slightly if they will be ready before you are! Uncover foods and serve them immediately if they start to overcook during standing time.
- **Time of day you are cooking.** Your microwave oven may cook faster at some times, slower at others, especially during peak periods of electrical consumption.
- **Wattage output of your oven.** A 700 watt microwave oven cooks faster than a 500 watt microwave oven.

QUICK TIME CONVERSION

- **If your microwave oven has 400 to 500 watts,** add 1 minute for every 3 minutes cooking time (e.g. 3 minutes = 4 minutes).
- **If your oven has 500 to 600 watts,** add 1 minute for every 5 minutes (e.g. 5 minutes = 6 minutes).

"WATT'S" YOUR COOKING TIME?

Refer to your owner's manual or cookbook for the wattage output of your oven. However, several factors will influence its **ACTUAL WATTAGE OUTPUT.** Even two identical microwave ovens will perform differently, depending on electrical power variations in your community and the time of day you are cooking.

TIME TO BOIL TEST

This will help you judge the heating &/or cooking time required for most recipes in this book. Test your microwave oven at the time you usually do most of your cooking (e.g. 6:00 p.m., peak cooking time) as well as a time of low usage (e.g. 1:30 P.M.)

Measure 1 cup (8 oz.) of cold water into a glass measuring cup. Temperature should be about 65°F. **MW water uncovered for 3 minutes on HIGH.** Note how long it took to reach a full rolling boil. **A 600 to 700 watt microwave oven boils 1 cup of water on HIGH in 2 ½ to 3 minutes.** If your oven takes longer, it has a lower wattage output and your cooking times will be longer than mine. If it takes less time, your cooking times will be shorter.

POWER LEVEL	WATTAGE OUTPUT	TIME TO BOIL
HIGH	**600 — 700 watts**	**2 ½ — 3 minutes**
MEDIUM-HIGH (70%)	**425 — 500 watts**	**3 ½ — 4 minutes**
MEDIUM (50%)	**300 — 350 watts**	**5 — 6 minutes**
MEDIUM-LOW or DEFROST (30%)	**200 — 225 watts**	**8 — 10 minutes**

On low-wattage ovens, DEFROST is usually 50% (200 to 250 watts).

A METRIC TRICK

Here is a quick trick I discovered to help calculate how long it takes liquid to boil. Pour liquid into a Pyrex™ measuring cup which has metric and standard measurements. **Allow 1 minute for each 100 ml.** Two cups (500 ml) take about 5 minutes on **HIGH** to boil. 700 ml takes 7 minutes. 350 ml takes 3 ½ minutes. Easy!

WATTAGE & TIME CONVERSION CHART

My cooking times are based on 600 to 700 watt microwave ovens **(one cup of water boils in 2 ½ minutes on HIGH)*.** If you have a lower wattage oven, use the times given in the appropriate column.

600 — 700 WATTS	**500 — 600 WATTS** Increase time by about 20% (⅕)	**400 — 500 WATTS** Increase time by about 33 ⅓% (⅓)
15 sec.	18 sec.	20 sec.
20 sec.	24 sec.	27 sec.
25 sec.	30 sec.	33 sec.
30 sec.	35 sec.	41 sec.
45 sec.	54 sec.	1 min.
1 min.	1 min. 10 sec.	1 min. 25 sec.
2 min.	2 min. 30 sec.	2 min. 45 sec.
***2 min. 30 sec.**	**3 min.**	**3 min. 30 sec.**
3 min.	3 min. 30 sec.	4 min.
4 min.	4 min. 45 sec.	5 min. 30 sec.
5 min.	6 min.	7 min.
6 min.	7 min. 15 sec.	8 min. 30 sec.
7 min.	8 min. 30 sec.	9 min. 45 sec.
8 min.	9 min. 30 sec.	11 min.
9 min.	10 min. 45 sec.	12 min. 30 sec.
10 min.	12 min.	14 min.
15 min.	18 min.	20 min.
20 min.	24 min.	27 min.
25 min.	30 min.	33 min.
30 min.	35 min.	41 min.
45 min.	54 min.	1 hr.

- **ALWAYS CHECK FOOD** shortly before estimated cooking time is completed. Add more time if necessary. Cooking times can vary from oven to oven. Always allow for standing time.

GOOD TIMES WITH YOUR MICROWAVE!

DOUBLE THE RECIPE	=	½ to ⅔ more cooking time.
HALF THE RECIPE	=	⅓ less cooking time.
4 ITEMS	=	Triple the time of 1 item.
HIGH POWER	=	Less time; foods cook faster.
LOWER POWER LEVEL	=	More time; foods cook slower.

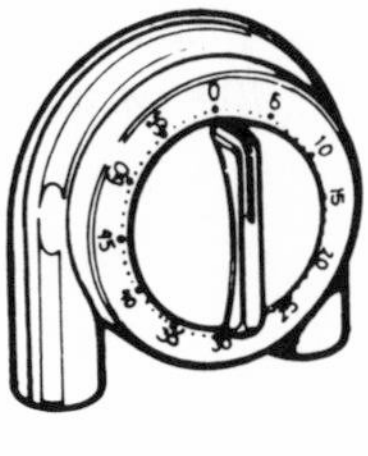

THE WEIGH TO COOK™!

A scale is the best guide in helping you estimate the time it takes to cook a particular food. If you don't own one, I highly recommend you purchase one. It makes microwave cooking a breeze!

As a general rule, most foods cook in **6 to 7 minutes per lb. on HIGH,** after trimming. There are several exceptions. **Fish takes 3 to 4 minutes per lb.,** because of its high water content. Smaller pieces will cook more quickly than big pieces. Cooking times for each type of food are given throughout this book.

A quick and easy way to calculate the cooking time is to weigh the empty casserole and note its weight (e.g. 1 lb.). Then weigh the filled casserole (e.g. 5 lb.). Deduct the weight of the empty casserole (5 − 1 = 4 lb. of food.) Multiply the answer by **6 to 7 minutes per lb. (4 lb. will take 24 to 28 minutes to cook in the microwave on HIGH.)**

EVERYBODY'S ON DIFFERENT WAVE LENGTHS!

The power levels which I have used for the recipes in this book are listed below. They are the settings suggested by the International Microwave Power Institute. However, all microwave oven manufacturers do not use the same terms or settings. To determine the setting for your microwave oven, check the manufacturer's instruction manual or cookbook. You can also do the Time to Boil Test (p. 14) at different power levels. Mark the corresponding names on the Power Level Chart below.

POWER LEVEL CHART

POWER LEVEL SETTING	PERCENTAGE OF POWER	WATTAGE OUTPUT	MY OVEN'S SETTING
HIGH (#10 or #9)	100%	600 – 700 watts	____________
MEDIUM-HIGH (#7)	70%	425 – 500 watts	____________
MEDIUM (#5)	50%	300 – 350 watts	____________
MEDIUM-LOW or DEFROST (#3)	30%	200 – 225 watts	____________
LOW or WARM (#1)	10%	60 – 75 watts	____________

On low-wattage ovens, **DEFROST** is usually 50% (200 to 250 watts).

Microwave energy pulses on and off when you use lower power levels. You can hear it if you listen carefully. Percentage of Power refers to the amount of **"on"** time. For example, on 30% power, the magnetron is **"on"** full strength 30% of the time and **"off"** 70% of the time, even though the light and fan are on.

WHICH POWER LEVEL TO CHOOSE

- **Use HIGH power to cook most foods** (fresh or frozen vegetables, meat, poultry, fish, soups, fruits). I reheat most foods on **HIGH,** unless they are delicate or very dense.
- **Use MEDIUM-HIGH (70%) to cook dense casseroles,** to slow down cooking, to reheat more delicate foods (e.g. lasagna).
- **Use MEDIUM (50%) for more delicate foods** (e.g. cheese, eggs), to develop flavor and tenderize tougher cuts of meat (e.g. stews), to slow down cooking, to prevent boil-overs. If your oven has a hot spot, use **MEDIUM (50%)** to melt chocolate.
- **Use MEDIUM-LOW or DEFROST (30%) to thaw frozen foods,** to soften foods that will melt (e.g. butter, ice cream), or to simmer foods to help develop flavor and prevent boil-overs.
- **Use HIGH power to defrost or soften foods** when it doesn't matter if they start to melt (e.g. frozen orange juice).
- **Use LOW or WARM (10%) to rise yeast dough, defrost cheesecake.**
- **If milk is heated on HIGH power,** watch carefully to prevent boilovers (e.g. cocoa). Stir occasionally to prevent a skin from forming on top and to prevent uneven heating. Foods containing cream (e.g. cream soups) should be heated on **MEDIUM (50%).**
- **Baby's formula should be heated uncovered on MEDIUM (50%)** to prevent uneven heating. If you use **HIGH** power, shake the bottle well and test the milk on your wrist before feeding baby in case of uneven heating.

ROUND WE GO!

- **The outer edges of food** cook more quickly than the centre. If food is in a square dish, the corners will usually overcook before the rest of the food is completely cooked.
- **Use round dishes** rather than square or rectangular ones. Oval dishes also work well. A ring-shaped pan is the ideal choice.
- **If you don't have a ring-shaped pan,** either depress the centre of the food slightly or place a heatproof glass open-end up in the centre of a round microsafe casserole or bowl.

IT'S ALL IN THE ARRANGEMENT!

- **For more even cooking,** arrange foods in a circle, leaving the centre empty, or place smaller pieces in the centre.
- **Arrange larger, thicker pieces towards the outside edge of the casserole dish** and thinner, more delicate parts towards the centre. You can also overlap thin ends of foods, or fold them under.
- **Arrange longer-cooking,** denser foods towards the outside of the dish and shorter-cooking, more porous foods towards the centre.
- **More information is given on specific foods** in the appropriate chapters.

TRICKS & TECHNIQUES

- **To help foods cook more evenly** in the microwave, use the following techniques: **1.** Stir. **2.** Rearrange &/or turn food over. **3.** Rotate the plate or casserole dish ¼ turn. **4.** Reduce the power level.
- **Rotate dishes which can't be stirred** (e.g. baked apples, meat loaf, lasagna).
- **If you have a turntable,** you don't have to rotate the dish. However, you do have to stir, rearrange or turn foods over if directed.
- **Don't panic if you were supposed to stir or turn a food over at half time** and you forgot. Do it when you remember; chances are it will probably be okay unless it is a very delicate food.
- **If your recipe tells you to cook a particular food for 10 minutes on HIGH** but to stir it at half time, set your microwave timer for **5 minutes on HIGH** so you won't forget.
- **If your oven** has several stages of cooking, program it for **5 minutes on HIGH, then another 5 minutes on HIGH.** It will beep at half time as a reminder.
- **Stir soups, sauces and liquids** from the outer edges towards the centre to help equalize the temperature.
- **Stir liquids before microwaving** and again at half time to prevent them from erupting. Keep a microwavable spoon inside; it's convenient for stirring.
- **Stir liquids that have been heated, then cooled down,** before you reheat them in the microwave to prevent liquid from erupting.
- **If you add instant coffee or tea to hot water** that you have heated in the microwave, it can erupt. Stir a few grains of instant coffee or tea into liquid before microwaving.
- **Does your microwave oven get all steamed up after cooking?** This is condensation from cooking foods which are very high in water content. No problem; just wipe walls dry with a cloth.
- **To avoid condensation on food,** place it on a microsafe rack, or cover or wrap the food with microsafe paper towels.
- **Your microwave oven can get hot** from the heat which is released from food during long periods of cooking. The air from the vents will become warm.

DON'T....

- **Don't block the vents.** Leave 2″ or 3″ around the microwave oven for proper air circulation.
- **Don't operate your microwave oven empty.** If you have young children who like to push buttons, keep a cup of water in your microwave at all times when it is not in use.
- **Don't microwave Angel Food or Sponge Cakes,** Yorkshire Pudding, soufflés, popovers, cream puffs, crisp pastry, puffed dough or eggs in the shell. Don't deep-fry foods in the microwave.
- **Don't do canning in the microwave** (unless you have a special microwave canner). P.S. Paraffin wax won't melt in the microwave.
- **Don't dry newspapers, mittens,** socks or underwear in your microwave. Don't use twist ties. They can cause a fire.
- **Drying herbs can be dangerous;** fires have occurred. Instead, see my method for freezing and defrosting herbs on p. 265.
- **Paper products can burn** if they are recycled and contain metal particles.
- **Cracked or chipped dishes** can break in the microwave from the heat of the food.
- **Yeast doughs are best** when baked conventionally.
- **Don't reuse microwavable packaging from convenience foods** (e.g., microwave popcorn bags). Chemical migration from the packaging into the food can occur.
- **When using plastic wrap to cover food during the microwaving,** the container should be deep enough to allow an air space between the plastic wrap and the food.

IN CASE OF FIRE

- **Don't open the oven door.** Shut off the oven or pull out the plug immediately. Cover the top vent with a heavy towel to block the oxygen flow. Wait until the fire is completely out before opening the door.

CLEAN-UPS

- **Keep your microwave oven clean.** Microwaves don't know the difference between the food in the casserole dish and the spills on the walls and floor of your oven; it will cook them all! This can affect the cooking time of your foods.
- **Moisten a dishcloth,** squeeze a drop of detergent on it if you wish, and heat it on **HIGH** for 15 to 20 seconds. Then wipe out your oven with the warm, damp cloth.
- **Make sure to wipe the door seal clean.** It only takes a moment!
- **Don't use ammonia, scouring pads or abrasive cleaners.**
- **To remove odors from your microwave:** Combine ½ cup lemon juice with 2 cups of water in a glass measure. (You could also use the rind of a lemon plus water.) **MW uncovered on HIGH for 8 to 10 minutes.** Your oven will smell lemon-fresh.
- **Another way to deodorize your microwave:** Place ½ cup vinegar in a glass measure. **MW uncovered on HIGH for 2 minutes.**

WHAT COOKWARE CAN I USE?

- **OVEN-SAFE GLASS** (e.g. Pyrex™); **GLASS-CERAMIC** (e.g. Corning Ware™, Visions™): Excellent for microwave, conventional &/or convection cooking. Large casseroles may not fit mid-size or compact ovens. Glass **MUST** be heat resistant or it will break from the heat of the food. Don't broil in Pyrex™ dishes. (Corning Ware™ is fine.) Not recommended for cooking sugar syrups which reach high temperatures (e.g. peanut brittle).
- **PORCELAIN, POTTERY:** The type of clay or ingredients used in the glaze will determine if the dish is microsafe. Do the Dish Test (p. 21). Do not use under the broiler. Can go from the microwave to the conventional or convection oven. Avoid temperature extremes to prevent breakage.
- **DINNERWARE:** Many brands are microwavable. If your dinnerware is not marked microwave-safe, do the Dish Test (p. 21). Do not use dishes with gold or silver trim, delicate glassware, crystal or melamine.
- **BROWNING DISHES:** These can be preheated uncovered according to manufacturer's directions and used to brown foods. Be careful, they get very hot. Use pot holders to prevent burns. They can also be used without preheating as a regular microwavable casserole. Do not use in the conventional or convection oven.
- **CLAY BAKERS:** Excellent for less tender cuts of meat such as brisket, stews. Soak 15 minutes before using; then discard water.
- **MICROSAFE PLASTIC COOKWARE:** (e.g. polysulfone, filled thermoset polyester.) Cooks 20% faster than glass because it doesn't absorb heat from the food. High temperature-resistant plastic cookware (safe to at least 400°F) can also be used in the conventional or convection oven. Some plastics can only be used for short-term microwave heating; they warp or melt if they get too hot from the food, particularly from fats and sugars.
- **PLASTIC STORAGE CONTAINERS:** These should be marked **"microwavable".** Otherwise they can warp or melt in the microwave. If they are dishwasher-safe, they can usually be used for short-term heating.
- **PLASTIC MARGARINE OR DELI CONTAINERS:** Don't use! Toxic materials can be released from the container into the food.
- **STYROFOAM:** Don't use! It is a hazard to our environment.
- **METAL COOKWARE:** Microwaves are reflected by metal; therefore metal is not suitable as a cooking container. Also, arcing could occur if the pan gets too close to the walls of the oven. Sometimes aluminum foil is used to shield parts of food to prevent overcooking. (P.S. My bachelor brother Bruce suggests that you empty soup out of the metal can and into a bowl before heating it in the microwave!)
- **PAPER PLATES:** Can be used to reheat foods or for brief periods of cooking (3 or 4 minutes). Do not used recycled paper as it could ignite.
- **WOODEN SPOONS OR CHOPSTICKS:** Use to stir foods. They can be left in the microwave during cooking for short periods of time.

THE DISH TEST

Measure ½ cup of cold water into a glass measuring cup. Place it in your microwave. Place the empty dish you wish to test next to the measuring cup, but not touching it. **MW on HIGH for 1 minute.** If dish is cool or slightly warm and the water in the cup is hot, the dish is microsafe. If dish is warm and the water is warm, the dish can be used for reheating. If the dish is hot, do not use it for microwaving. Your cooking container may be microsafe when you test it, but it will get hot from heat transferred from the food.

THE RIGHT DISH

- **Many of the dishes** in your cupboard can be used for microwave cooking. Use round or oval microsafe dishes for best results.
- **Use deep glass bowls for liquids, soups and sauces.** Ceramic or glass soufflé dishes can be used for rice, potatoes and soups.
- **Deep round casseroles** with a lid are handy for a variety of foods. I have several sizes. Custard cups are also very useful.
- **Glass measuring cups** are excellent for cooking soups, sauces and gravies. I have several sizes, from 1 to 8 cups. Glass pie plates and ceramic quiche dishes are also useful.
- **Use a microsafe ring mold** for foods which can't be stirred. A 12 cup microsafe Bundt pan (not metal) can be used for cakes. A microsafe muffin pan can be used for muffins, cupcakes and eggs.
- **Shallow oblong or oval casseroles** in various sizes are used for foods cooked in a single layer (e.g. chicken, fish). A clay baker is great for tenderizing less tender cuts of meat. Long foods (e.g. corn on the cob) should be cooked in oblong dishes.
- **An 8 cup glass measure,** 2 quart deep round casserole and a 7″ x 11″ casserole all hold 2 quarts of food. However, food cooks more quickly in the shallow casserole because more surface is exposed to microwave energy.
- **Use straight-sided casseroles and dishes** for more uniform cooking. If a casserole has sloped sides, it won't cook evenly; you will get overcooking on the edges.
- **A 12″ round microsafe platter** is ideal for hors d'oeuvres.
- **A microsafe roasting rack** is essential for cooking poultry, meats, baked potatoes, elevating foods for more even cooking.

FOIL IN THE MICROWAVE

- **Aluminum foil is used to shield foods** in the microwave to prevent areas from overcooking (e.g. chicken wing tips, narrow edges of roasts, fatty or bony areas which cook more quickly, square corners). Pieces of foil should be smooth and should be at least 1″ away from the microwave oven walls and door.
- **Use foil to keep foods hot after cooking.** It doesn't matter whether the shiny side is up or down. The shiny side was in contact with the polished steel rollers when the foil was manufactured; the dull side wasn't.
- **Shallow foil T.V. dinner trays** can be used to thaw and heat food, but I prefer to thaw, heat and serve the food on a dinner plate. The food heats faster and it is much more elegant.

COVER-UPS

- **Foods are covered to retain moisture and heat,** as well as prevent spatters. If no covering is mentioned, cook uncovered.
- **Your first choice of covering** should always be the casserole lid. A dinner plate can be used to cover a soufflé dish.
- **If your casserole or bowl doesn't have a cover,** use microsafe plastic wrap (e.g. Saran Wrap). Use a casserole that is deep enough so that wrap does not touch the surface of food, or place a sheet of waxed paper or parchment between food and plastic wrap. Turn back one corner ¼″ to ½″ to allow steam to escape. (Even casserole lids have a slight space to let some steam escape.) Don't pierce the plastic wrap; it could split during cooking. A wooden chopstick can be inserted through the vented opening so you can stir the food during microwaving without removing plastic wrap. Always remove plastic wrap with the vented opening away from you to prevent steam burns.
- **Parchment paper** makes an excellent cover. In addition to being microsafe, it can be used for conventional, convection and combination cooking.
- **A domed plate cover** (available in kitchen boutiques) stops spatters. A glass pie plate can be inverted and used to cover a dinner plate of food.
- **Oven cooking bags** can be used instead of a covered casserole for microwave, conventional, convection or combination cooking. Follow package directions. Cooking bags are handy to use when you don't have the casserole size called for in a recipe; they also save on clean-ups. Place the bag into a second cooking bag or casserole to catch any juices that might leak out during cooking. This will avoid a mess in your microwave.
- **Don't use plastic grocery bags or cover food with plastic sandwich or storage bags** when microwaving. They can melt &/or release toxic substances into the food.
- **There are special bags** which can be used to freeze, store and cook food in the microwave oven. These meal-sealing bags are labeled microwavable. Always pierce bag before microwaving.
- **Don't use plastic lids** from storage containers to cover foods in the microwave. They will warp unless they are microsafe.
- **Waxed paper is used where a loose covering is needed** to retain heat but release some steam. Wrap loosely around the food or dish, tucking it underneath. Waxed paper may weaken and tear from the steam if it is used for long periods of cooking time.
- **Microwavable paper towels** can be placed under running water and gently squeezed to remove any excess water. Use to cover or wrap foods that are steamed (e.g. fish, vegetables) in the microwave. Bounty™ Microwave Paper Towels are available in the U.S. and are excellent. Other brands can be used, as long as they are white and are not made from recycled paper.
- **Non-recycled paper towels or napkins** are used to prevent spatters, to retain heat and to keep the surface of foods dry. Use to cover bread, rolls or as a cover for breaded foods. They should only be used for brief periods of cooking time.
- **Food is cooked uncovered** when a dry surface is required, or if a lot of stirring is needed.
- **If foods have a natural covering** (e.g. potatoes, squash), they require venting to release steam. Therefore pierce them all over with a knife or fork before microwaving. Cook uncovered.

- **If food is cooked covered,** it generally should be kept covered during standing time. Foods that are cooked uncovered can be covered during standing time to keep them hot. A large casserole that doesn't have a lid can be covered with a cookie sheet, plastic wrap or foil.
- **Browning dishes are preheated uncovered.** They can be covered once the food has been browned.
- **If you have removed the plastic wrap** to stir or rearrange food, it may be difficult to cover again. You will probably have to replace it with a fresh piece of plastic wrap.

COOKING SEQUENCE FOR MEAL PREPARATION

- **First cook or prepare any foods that need refrigeration** (e.g. dessert, salad).
- **Then cook those that have a long standing time** (e.g. meat, chicken, rice). Cover tightly to retain heat (or cool and refrigerate until serving time).
- **At mealtime, reheat or microwave any foods that were prepared in advance and refrigerated.** Cover tightly after microwaving to retain heat.
- **Microwave any quick-cooking foods that have a brief standing time** (e.g. vegetables).
- **Heat rolls and/or any foods** that have cooled too much.

SOME LIKE IT HOT!

- **I like to use the stacking system to keep foods hot.** Stack casseroles of cooked foods one on top of the other as they are ready. Always place the hottest casserole on the bottom. This method takes up very little space and the heat rises upwards, keeping everything hot! If the casseroles don't quite fit, try using dinner plates as a covering. It's an easy way to warm plates for serving!
- **Soups, stews and sauces are okay if they "overstand".** Some vegetables can overcook (e.g. asparagus) if the standing time is too long.
- **My general rule is:** If I want to plan a long standing time so I can cook several dishes in my microwave, I undercook each food slightly and keep the food tightly covered to retain heat. If I want to serve the food right away, I cook it the full amount of time, then uncover and serve it immediately so it will not aftercook.
- **Foods cooked in the serving dish retain their heat better** than those which are transferred to another dish. The heat from the food is transferred into the cool plate; therefore your food cools off faster.
- **Don't forget about your conventional oven.** It will help you maximize your time if you use it in conjunction with your microwave. Place cooked foods in a 200°F oven to keep several dishes warm for a period of time. Remember to use heatproof casseroles and to remove plastic wrap!

COOKING & HEATING WITH A SHELF

- **Some manufacturers provide a shelf with their microwave ovens.** You can also buy a meal rack. To cook or heat several foods at a time, add up all the cooking times.
- **The food on the top shelf usually heats faster than the food on the bottom.** Dishes may have to be switched halfway through cooking or heating.
- **Place dense foods on the top shelf** and more delicate or quicker cooking foods on the bottom shelf. Always follow manufacturer's guidelines on how to place foods for best results.
- **Check for doneness.** Remove foods as soon as they're ready.
- **I usually find it easier to microwave foods in sequence because most foods require a standing time anyways.**

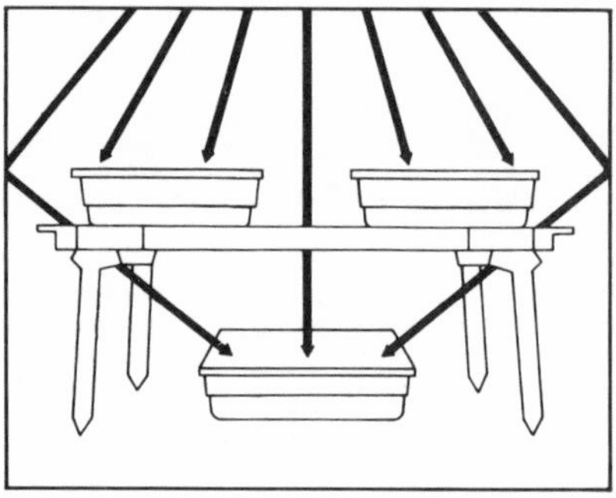

MICROWAVE COOKING AT HIGH ALTITUDES

- **In high altitude areas,** the air weighs less and exerts less pressure on everything. This affects microwave cooking times.
- **Water and other liquids boil at lower temperatures,** so longer microwave time is usually necessary. Increase cooking time slightly; foods don't get as hot because of lower boiling point. Make careful note of your microwave cooking time on the recipe for future reference.
- **Liquids evaporate faster,** so you'll probably have to use more. Add 1 to 3 tbsp. extra liquid when cooking vegetables.
- **Use larger cooking dishes.** Don't fill more than half full.
- **Watch for boil-overs.** Put a microsafe pie plate under the cooking bowl to catch spills.
- **For fruits, vegetables, large or less tender cuts of meat, soup and grains,** longer microwave time is usually needed.
- **Hot foods will cool faster.** You may have to cover or reheat.
- **Contact food manufacturers for high altitude** microwave directions for cake mixes. There is usually a toll-free phone number on the package. Elevate cakes on a rack to help them cook more evenly.
- **When reheating, sprinkle foods with a few drops of water** to prevent them from drying.
- **Contact your local Department of Agriculture** representative or newspaper food editor for further information.

TRIMMING CALORIES

- **Foods don't stick to the casserole,** so little or no fat is needed. A few drops of water can be used to "sauté" vegetables.
- **The microwave steams fish, chicken and vegetables beautifully.** You can bake an apple in 2 or 3 minutes! The major problem is that you can also reheat all the leftovers in your fridge in just moments, and goodies from the freezer thaw very quickly. Also, when you first get your microwave, you will be so busy experimenting, you will also be tasting much more than usual!
- **It's so easy to microwave single portions** when you're watching your weight. Your meal is ready in moments and tastes so good.
- **Foods cooked in the microwave** retain more vitamins and minerals.

SUGAR MIXTURES IN THE MICROWAVE OVEN

Glass-ceramic cookware (e.g. Corning Ware™, Visions™) may be used for sugar solutions that don't exceed 250°F (thread, soft ball and firm ball stages, e.g. fudge, soft caramels). **Don't use Pyrex™ or similar heat-resistant glassware for any high temperature sugar cooking.**

At temperatures above 250°F (hard ball, soft and hard crack stages, e.g. popcorn balls, peanut brittle), the glass container could splinter or break.

- **The above information** was provided by Wendy Sanford, Manager, Consumer Relations & Marketing Services, Corning Canada Inc.
- **Robert Schiffmann, President of R. F. Schiffmann Associates,** a Microwave Consultant, suggests that the consumer could use high temperature-resistant plastic cookware (over 450°F) in the microwave oven to cook sugar mixtures which reach extremely high temperatures.
- **Don't use the probe to measure the temperature of sugar mixtures** when making candy in the microwave. It cannot register the high temperatures necessary. Either use a special microwave candy thermometer (which is difficult to find) for mixtures inside the microwave oven, or an instant-read thermometer for mixtures removed from the microwave oven. Temperature of sugar mixture rises about 15°F when you remove it from the microwave, so always undercook slightly.

HIGH TEMPERATURE-RESISTANT COOKWARE

Although many microwave cookbooks call for using glass and glass-ceramic cookware for recipes where the sugar must be carmelized, doing so could result in chipping or breakage. However, you can use plastic cookware which has been specially tempered to tolerate high temperatures without shattering. It should be microwavable, as well as heatproof up to at least 400°F.

N.B. Don't use plastic cookware or storage containers which aren't heatproof at high temperatures for candy-making. The container can warp &/or melt.

DO MICROWAVE OVENS BROWN FOOD?

Yes, but not always. It depends on the amount of fat in the food, as well as the length of time it is in the microwave oven. Poultry and roasts will brown, but not as much as you are used to seeing, because they are in the microwave for a shorter period of time. The fat in the food must be carbonized in order to brown. Cakes (unless they are chocolate) don't brown in the microwave because the cooking time is too short.

In a regular oven, food browns and crisps because of its contact with the hot air. In a microwave oven the only heat is within the food itself. The air around the food is relatively cool.

To create a brown appearance on foods, the following techniques are useful: marinate in a teriyaki or soya sauce mixture; sprinkle with paprika; use a preheated microwave browning dish; sauté foods conventionally in a hot skillet before microwaving; sprinkle with toasted bread crumbs after cooking; place microwaved food in a **400 to 425°F oven for 10 to 15 minutes,** or under the broiler for a few minutes.

BABY FOOD

- **ALWAYS remove nipple and cap** before microwaving baby's milk.
- **Room temperature milk or food** takes less time than if refrigerated.
- **MW 4 oz. room temperature milk uncovered on HIGH for 15 to 20 seconds. If refrigerated, it will take 30 to 40 seconds. Double the time if using MEDIUM (50%).**
- **MW 8 oz. room temperature milk uncovered on HIGH for 30 to 40 seconds. If refrigerated, it will take 45 to 60 seconds. Double the time if using MEDIUM (50%).**
- **Cover and shake;** test on your wrist. **ALWAYS SHAKE MILK OR STIR BABY FOOD AND TEST TEMPERATURE BEFORE FEEDING BABY.**
- **Milk should be lukewarm,** not hot (95°F). Overheated or unevenly heated milk can burn an infant! It may feel cold on the outside but there can be hot spots inside.
- **Bottle manufacturers** do not recommend heating formula in plastic lined baby bottles.
- **Heat baby food in a small microsafe dish,** using just the amount baby will eat. Heat just until lukewarm.
- **MW 4 oz. of room temperature baby food uncovered on HIGH for 15 to 20 seconds. If refrigerated, it will take 30 to 40 seconds. Double the time if using MEDIUM (50%). Stir well.**
- **Refrigerate remaining food.** Once baby has eaten from a dish of food, throw away any portions baby did not finish to prevent bacterial contamination.
- **It is not recommended to heat baby food in the jars** in which they are sold. Testing has proved there can be superheating, causing hot spots that are far in excess of boiling. This can cause the jar to break. It can also burn baby.
- **Freeze baby food in ice cube trays.** Each cube holds 2 tbsp. food. **1 cube takes 20 to 30 seconds on HIGH to thaw; 4 cubes take 1 to 2 minutes.** Break up at ½ time. Stir before serving.

HOW TO CHOOSE A MICROWAVE OVEN

If you buy an oven which is too small or not powerful enough for your needs, you'll regret it later on. The size of your family, where and how much space you have available, your eating habits and lifestyle all affect your choice.

My personal preference is for a full size 700 watt microwave oven. A mid-size oven with at least 600 watts is also a good choice. It should be large enough to hold a 3 quart oblong or oval casserole (e.g. 9″ x 13″). Variable power levels are important to defrost and cook a wide range of foods successfully.

The microwave oven should be made by a reputable manufacturer and should have a good warrantee. Automatic features are handy, but not essential. I don't believe in a lot of "whistles and bells". Keep it simple! A turntable helps cook food evenly, but most manufacturers have features which compensate for uneven cooking. You lose space with a turntable. A probe will help you cook foods to the desired temperature. A sensor will terminate the cooking cycle when the heat or humidity inside the oven reaches a certain level. Read Convection/Micro Ways (p. 28) for information on combination ovens. Read Cooking and Heating with a Shelf (p. 24).

CONVERTING RECIPES FOR THE MICROWAVE

- **Select a recipe you like** when cooked conventionally. Most recipes will cook in ¼ to ⅓ of the conventional time. Foods that are cooked covered conventionally convert well, especially those that are poached or steamed.
- **Don't sprinkle salt** on foods before cooking. Add salt to cooking liquid or salt foods just before standing time.
- **Foods cooked for short periods of time** do not usually brown because there is no dry heat touching the surface of the food. If desired, transfer to a hot oven for a few minutes to brown and crisp. Use heatproof/microsafe cookware.
- **Covering retains moisture and heat.** Leave food uncovered for a drier surface.
- **Use round microsafe containers** wherever possible. Arrange foods with the thicker, larger pieces towards the outside.
- **Foods should be thawed before cooking.** Cold foods take longer to cook that those that are at room temperature.
- **Foods that could bubble up and boil over** (e.g. cereals, sauces) should be cooked in a container that is twice the volume of the food being cooked.
- **Reduce liquids by at least half.** There is almost no evaporation in microwave cooking.
- **Remember to stir,** rearrange or turn foods over halfway through cooking. If food can't be moved, then turn the dish.
- **Always allow for standing time to complete cooking.** If food is cooked covered, it should be covered during standing time. If it was cooked uncovered, leave it uncovered during standing time.
- **Refer to the hints** throughout this book for more details.
- **For a quick everyday guide for most foods,** refer to the "MicroBuddy" on p. 36.

CONVECTION/MICRO WAYS

In a **CONVECTION/MICROWAVE** oven, you have several choices of cooking cycles: **MICROWAVE, CONVECTION** and **COMBINATION** (or **CONVECTION/MICROWAVE**). Some models also have a **BROIL** setting.

MICROWAVE CYCLE

In a combination oven, the **MICROWAVE CYCLE** functions just like a regular microwave oven. Use microsafe cookware. Food usually cooks in ¼ to ⅓ of the conventional time. I use my microwave for 90% of my cooking needs, from appetizers to desserts.

CONVECTION CYCLE

This is very much like cooking in your conventional oven, except the hot air produced by the heating element is circulated around the food by a high-speed fan. **CONVECTION** cooking produces a crisp, brown exterior on foods.

To adapt your conventional recipes, reduce temperature by 25°F for small items and 50°F for large items. Place food on the rack or shelf (the same as cooking conventionally). Reduce cooking time by 25% and check at minimum time. Add more time if needed. If food is cooking unevenly, turn casserole or pan around (the same as conventionally). Leave at least 1″ of space all around the pan to allow for maximum heat flow. I prefer to preheat when baking, or for foods which take less than 15 minutes to cook. Preheating for meat or poultry is optional.

Let the oven cool down completely before using it on the **MICROWAVE CYCLE** to prevent plastic microwave cookware from melting and paper products from catching on fire. Take care not to burn yourself when checking foods during cooking. Oven walls, door, shelf and cookware get hot! Use long oven mitts. When the oven is cool, remove the metal rack or shelf before using the **MICROWAVE CYCLE**.

The **CONVECTION CYCLE** is used for appetizers, fish sticks, pastry, cream puffs, yeast breads and rolls, pizza, cookies, squares, muffins, cakes and soufflés.

Use metal pans for best results. Dark pans are used for yeast breads and pastry to create a crisp, brown crust. Aluminum pans are used for cakes, muffins and cookies. Light pans will reflect heat; dark pans absorb heat. If you are using an ovenproof glass or porcelain casserole, place an aluminum or tin cookie sheet underneath to help conduct heat more evenly. Add a little more time if food isn't cooked in the suggested time. If the top is brown but the food isn't cooked through, cover with foil and cook a few minutes longer. Another trick is to leave the food in the oven for a few minutes after the timer has shut off to "aftercook". If you are still having problems, write or call the oven manufacturer for further advice.

BROIL CYCLE

On **BROIL**, the oven temperature is usually 450 to 475°F. It's not as powerful as the setting in your regular oven, so cooking time is longer and foods won't brown as much. Use **BROIL** for meats, fish, poultry or to brown casseroles. Preheating is usually necessary. Place foods on broiling rack close to top of oven. Use oven mitts to prevent burns. Oven must cool down completely before you can use the **MICROWAVE CYCLE.** Remove shelf when cool. Wipe oven clean after each use to prevent grease build-up.

CONVECTION/MICROWAVE CYCLE

The **CONVECTION/MICROWAVE CYCLE** usually uses preset programs on a power-sharing basis. It alternates between microwave energy and convection heat. Brother International recently introduced a combination oven that cooks on both cycles simultaneously.

The advantage of combination cooking is that food is moist and juicy inside, crisp and brown outside. Cooking time is ¼ to ½ of conventional cooking time; roasts and poultry shrink less. Manufacturers use different power-sharing combinations of microwaves and convection heat. That's why recipes from other oven manufacturers may not work in your oven.

ADVANTAGES & DISADVANTAGES

People who learn to use their combination oven properly swear they couldn't live without it! It's great if you need a second conventional oven and it's portable. It takes up the same amount of space as a regular microwave oven, but offers more options.

However, it is more expensive. You must be careful not to burn yourself when using the **CONVECTION** or **COMBINATION CYCLE.** The oven must cool down and the rack or shelf must be removed before you can use it for microwaving. It's more difficult to clean because splatters bake on from the heat.

It takes more time to learn how to use a combination oven to its maximum potential. More thought is needed in choosing proper cookware. The **COMBINATION CYCLE** usually takes longer than if you microwave the food first, then finish cooking it conventionally or on the **CONVECTION CYCLE.** Because the **COMBINATION CYCLE** takes longer, your oven is not available for quick microwave tasks.

If you already own a combination oven, take advantage of its features. It takes time to learn to use it to its maximum, but learning is an ongoing process. Take the cooking course offered by the oven manufacturer. If you are thinking about buying one, evaluate your needs carefully. If you find electronic equipment complicated and confusing to use, you probably won't use the multi-functions of a combination oven to its full potential.

CHOOSING THE RIGHT SETTING

To date, all manufacturers of **CONVECTION/MICROWAVE** ovens have not followed the same set of standards for automatic combination programs. Because manufacturers may have one or several different automatic programs, it is extremely difficult to give a single set of rules which will apply to all brands of ovens. On some ovens it is possible to overide the automatic program and set your own combinations of heat &/or microwave levels.

Always follow the guidelines given by the manufacturer of your convection/ microwave oven. When in doubt, find a similar recipe in the cookbook that came with your oven and adapt your recipe, setting and cooking time accordingly. Your manufacturer's Use and Care Manual and cookbook always take precedence over any information and cooking times given in this cookbook.

Read Convection/Micro Tips (p. 31) for further information.

CONVECTION/MICRO WAYS WITH COOKWARE

- **Casserole dishes** should be heatproof as well as microsafe (e.g. Pyrex™, Corning Ware™, ceramic, porcelain) when cooking on the **COMBINATION CYCLE.** Oval or round dishes are excellent.
- **There are also heat-resistant** plastic cooking containers that are dual purpose. They can be used on the **COMBINATION, CONVECTION** or **MICROWAVE CYCLE.** Check the cookware manufacturer's recommendations for maximum temperature that can be used to prevent dual purpose cookware from melting, warping or breaking.
- **Do not use paper or plastic products on the COMBINATION CYCLE.**
- **Wait for the oven to cool** down completely from **CONVECTION** or **COMBINATION** cooking before using microsafe-only products (e.g. plastic wrap, paper towels, plastic cookware).
- **Food may take longer to cook** in light-colored or shiny pans. You can use dark ovensafe glass casseroles or baking pans on the **CONVECTION** or **COMBINATION CYCLE** for better heat absorption. This will help cook the bottom and centre of food.
- **On the CONVECTION cycle,** use the same cookware you do when cooking or baking in your conventional oven. Light colored pans may not cook as evenly (see Convection Cycle, p. 28).
- **On the BROIL setting,** use the metal broiling pans which come with your oven. Pyrex™ should not be used under the broiler; Corning Ware™ can be.
- **Microwave thermometers** are not heat-resistant and conventional mercury thermometers are not microwavable. Do not use either one for cooking on the **COMBINATION CYCLE.**
- **Use microwave thermometers** for microwave cooking; use conventional mercury thermometers for convection cooking. Otherwise, test temperature of food outside the oven with an instant-read thermometer.

CONVECTION/MICRO TIPS

- **Choose the appropriate COMBINATION CYCLE** suggested by your oven manufacturer as suitable to cook a particular food category.
- **Cooking times are given** as guidelines, as well as a descriptive phrase indicating doneness. Always check at minimum time; add more time if necessary. Your own judgment is the best guide.
- **Remember to push the "start"** button again after checking food! If the food is done before anticipated, remember to cancel any remaining time left on the timer.
- **When in doubt,** choose a **COMBINATION CYCLE** with a temperature of 350 to 375°F for appetizers, casseroles, most poultry, meat loaf and fruit pies. Use a lower temperature (325°F) for roasts (beef, veal or lamb), turkey and custard pies.
- **Elevate foods** on the rack or shelf for maximum circulation of hot air on the **CONVECTION** or **COMBINATION CYCLE.**
- **Cooking time on the COMBINATION CYCLE** will be ½ to ¾ of your conventional recipe, depending on your oven, but on some recipes there will be very little, if any time savings.
- **Remove food** from oven immediately after the **CONVECTION** or **COMBINATION CYCLE** has completed. Even though the oven has shut off, there is still residual heat and food can overcook. (I know from experience!)
- **To conserve energy,** food can be undercooked slightly, then left in the oven with the door closed for a few minutes after cooking cycle is completed. It will finish cooking from the hot air remaining in the oven. Remove it as soon as it tests done.
- **Metal shelf** must not touch walls of oven on the **COMBINATION CYCLE.** Always follow your manufacturer's guidelines for proper use of the metal shelf.
- **Some recipes** call for using the probe (if your oven has one) during the last half of the **COMBINATION CYCLE.** Probe should be inserted into the centre of the food and should not touch bone, fat or any metal.
- **Foods are generally cooked** uncovered on the **COMBINATION CYCLE** so they will crisp. Glass casserole lids or parchment paper can be used to prevent splatters &/or keep food moist.
- **Foods can be started on the MICROWAVE cycle,** then completed on **CONVECTION.** Use microsafe/heatproof casseroles (e.g. Pyrex™, porcelain). Remove any paper or plastic coverings, insert the rack or shelf into the oven and elevate food on the rack on the **CONVECTION** cycle.
- **When using the BROIL setting,** place food on top rack near the top of the oven so food is as close as possible to the heat.
- **Be sure to use oven mitts** or pot holders when removing hot pans or casseroles from the oven.
- **Let oven cool completely;** then wipe clean with a soft cloth and non-abrasive stainless steel cleaner. There are soft cleansers that clean like powdered cleansers, but don't scratch. Always follow microwave manufacturer's cleaning recommendations.
- **I have not included any recipes for baking cakes or breads on the COMBINATION CYCLE** because of the variations in different brands of ovens. Refer to the recipes in you manufacturer's cookbook.

NICE TO KNOW

- **To defrost 1 lb. of frozen butter, MW uncovered on DEFROST (30%) for 3 minutes.**
- **To soften ¼ lb. butter, MW uncovered on DEFROST (30%) for 30 to 40 seconds.** If you use **HIGH** power, butter may start to melt.
- **To melt ¼ lb. butter, MW uncovered for 1 minute on HIGH.** (I always melt butter on **HIGH.** There is no sense to use a lower power level; it just takes longer.) Use a microsafe container large enough to prevent spatters.
- **Unsalted butter** takes longer to melt than salted; margarine melts faster than butter.
- **Overheating makes bread and rolls tough.** Sugar toppings and fillings will get very hot (e.g. jelly donuts). Take care. Heat bread products just until **WARM,** not hot.
- **One square** of soggy matzo will be crisp after **30 seconds on HIGH.**
- **Crackers can be crisped** easily in the microwave. Place in a napkin in a wicker basket. (No staples, please!) **MW on HIGH for 30 to 60 seconds.** Let stand for a few minutes to crisp.
- **Don't heat foods** in narrow-necked bottles (e.g. maple syrup); pressure can build up and they can boil over. Transfer to a microsafe serving pitcher to heat. **Allow 1 minute on HIGH per cup.**
- **To toast sesame seeds, coconut or almonds:** Spread ½ c. sesame seeds, shredded coconut or slivered or sliced almonds in a thin layer in a 9″ glass pie plate. **MW uncovered on HIGH for 2½ to 4 minutes,** or until lightly toasted, stirring every minute. Let stand for a few minutes to complete toasting. Careful; plate will be very hot!
- **To shell walnuts, pecans, filberts, almonds or Brazil nuts:** Combine 2 cups of unshelled nuts with 1 cup of water in a microsafe bowl. Cover with vented plastic wrap. **MW on HIGH for 2½ to 3 minutes,** until water boils. Let stand for 1 minute. Drain, dry well and cool before shelling. Chestnuts should be slashed crosswise through shell before microwaving. Increase standing time to 5 to 10 minutes.
- **To melt jam or jelly:** Remove lid. **MW ½ cup on HIGH for 45 to 60 seconds.**
- **To soften brown sugar:** Place a slice of bread or half an apple, cut-side up, on top of the sugar in a microsafe dish. Cover with vented plastic wrap. **MW on HIGH for 30 to 60 seconds,** until softened. Let stand for 1 minute; stir.
- **Egg whites can be quickly warmed** to room temperature. **MW on HIGH, allowing 4 to 5 seconds per egg white.** They will whip to a greater volume.
- **Leftover egg yolks or whites** need not be hidden in the back of the refrigerator and then pitched out weeks later! Place in a small microsafe dish, pierce yolks with the point of a knife, and cover tightly with microsafe plastic wrap. **Two egg yolks will take 1 minute on MEDIUM (50%); two egg whites will take 1½ minutes.** Let stand covered for 1 minute. Use as a garnish, or in chopped egg salad or potato salad.
- **To extract more juice from a lemon: MW on HIGH for 15 to 20 seconds for 1 lemon.**
- **To make a hot compress** for your headache, wet a washcloth and wring out excess water. **MW on HIGH for 15 seconds.** The same trick can be used to heat a dishcloth to clean your microwave oven. I usually put a few drops of detergent on it first.

- **To warm finger towels** for your next dinner party, place terrycloth washcloths in water; press out excess. Roll up and place in a microsafe dish. **MW on HIGH until warm, allowing 15 seconds each. Four will take about 1 minute.** So elegant!
- **To shorten cooking time on the BBQ,** partially cook chicken, ribs, potatoes, etc. in the microwave. Then transfer immediately to the preheated BBQ grill to sear and brown.
- **Wooden toothpicks or wooden skewers** can be used to test for doneness. Wooden spoons or chopsticks can be used for stirring.
- **Non-stick sprays** can be used instead of oil or butter to grease casseroles, but you will find greasing is usually not necessary because foods don't stick when microwaved. Greasing is usually necessary if you are completing the cooking conventionally.
- **Defrost frozen foods before cooking.** Food should still be icy in centre after defrosting. Let stand to complete defrosting.
- **Spices are not as strong** when food is frozen. You can adjust seasonings when reheating.
- **Always remember to clear any time remaining** on the timer if you remove the food from the oven before the end of the cooking cycle.
- **A plate of refrigerated food will reheat in 1 ½ to 2 minutes on HIGH.** Feel bottom of plate; it should be hot in the centre.
- **Gelatin dessert** (e.g. Gel-Dessert, Jello): Combine 2 cups of water plus a 3 oz. package of flavored gelatin in a 4 cup glass measure. **MW uncovered on HIGH for 5 to 6 minutes,** stirring once or twice. Gelatin will clear once it comes to a boil. (Kosher gelatins are more rubbery and may require more water.)
- **If you are making a mold** and have to partially set the gelatin before adding fruit, don't worry if the gelatin oversets. **MW on MEDIUM (50%) for a minute at a time,** until the consistency of unbeaten egg whites. Stir in fruit.

HOME-MADE KID DOUGH

My friend Dona teaches creative art to young children. She shared this easy recipe with me for you to enjoy with your children. Easy and inexpensive! She makes up batches in different colors for the kids to use.

food coloring
1 ½ c. water
2 c. flour
1 c. salt
4 tsp. cream of tartar
¼ c. vegetable oil

1. Dissolve food coloring in water. Blend flour with salt and cream of tartar in a large microsafe bowl; mix well. Add oil; gradually add water a little at a time to make a soft, pliable dough. **MW uncovered on HIGH for 3 to 4 minutes,** until thick.

2. Knead dough while it is still warm. Store in a sealed plastic bag or airtight container in the refrigerator. Dough will keep about 6 months.

CASSEROLE KNOW-HOW

- **Most casseroles** are a combination of cooked foods that are heated together to blend flavors. **A 1 quart casserole takes about 6 to 8 minutes on HIGH to heat. A 2 quart casserole will take 10 to 12 minutes,** until bubbling hot.
- **A 3 quart casserole should be microwaved on MEDIUM-HIGH (70%) for 15 to 18 minutes** to help the centre heat evenly and prevent the corners from overcooking.
- **Elevate large casseroles** on a microsafe rack or inverted pie plate to help the centre cook evenly.
- **Crumb toppings** should be added at the end of the cooking time; otherwise they become soggy.
- **Cheese topping** should be added at the end of the cooking time; otherwise cheese can become tough. It will melt from the heat of the casserole. If necessary, **MW on HIGH for 2 to 3 minutes,** until cheese is melted.
- **Casseroles** can be microwaved until heated through, then **baked at 400°F for 10 to 15 minutes,** until golden brown.
- **To reheat** a 2 or 3 quart refrigerated casserole, **MW covered on HIGH for 5 minutes.** Rotate dish ¼ turn. **Then MW for 10 to 12 minutes on MEDIUM (50%),** until heated through.
- **To thaw a frozen 2 quart casserole** (e.g. lasagna), elevate on a microsafe rack. **MW covered on HIGH for 5 minutes.** Rotate ¼ turn. **MW on MEDIUM (50%) for 35 to 40 minutes,** rotating dish ¼ turn every 10 minutes. (If edges are overcooking, stop the microwave and let food stand for 5 minutes. Shield corners with foil.) When ready, centre bottom of casserole dish will feel hot.

MORE PLEASURES FROM YOUR FOOD PROCESSOR!

- **Test if your processor bowl** is microsafe (Dish Test, p. 21). I use mine to melt chocolate or butter for Brownies or to thicken sauces that have been prepared in the processor.
- **Remove the Steel Knife** from the processor bowl when putting the bowl in the microwave. One of my students melted the plastic base on the **Steel Knife** when melting butter and chocolate in the microwave; the blade fused to the bowl!
- **Don't know which blade to use?** If you are not slicing or grating, then you probably need to use the **Steel Knife**. I call it the "do-almost-everything blade".
- **When chopping on the Steel Knife,** cut food in 1″ pieces and place in a single layer in the bottom of the bowl. Process with quick on/offs, just until desired texture is reached. Stop and check. You can always process a little longer, but if overprocessed, you will have mush.
- **When mincing or grinding foods,** use quick on/offs to start, then let machine run until food is finely minced.
- **Process hard ingredients first;** then add soft ingredients to prevent overprocessing.
- **Process dry ingredients first;** then process wet ingredients to save on clean-ups.

- **Instead of processing each ingredient separately** on the **Steel Knife**, it is more practical to process two or three foods at the same time (e.g. chopping onions and peppers).
- **For a more uniform appearance** for your chopped vegetables, first slice them on the **Slicer**. Then insert the **Steel Knife** and process with 2 or 3 quick on/off turns or pulses, until desired texture is reached.
- **If shredded or grated foods** are too coarse (e.g. cabbage for cole slaw), process with 3 or 4 quick on/offs on the **Steel Knife**, until desired texture is reached.
- **Purées are smoother** (e.g. soups, baby foods, fruits) if you process the solids on the **Steel Knife** first, then slowly add the liquid through the feed tube while the machine is running.
- **A quick trick:** To clean the **Steel Knife** easily when making cakes, squares, purées, etc., first empty the contents of the processor bowl. Then put the bowl and **Steel Knife** back on the base, put on the cover and turn the processor on for 2 or 3 seconds. Centrifugal force will spin the blade clean!
- **To avoid "ring around the counter",** remember to turn the dirty cover upside down before placing it on your countertop.
- **Some food processors have a standard feed tube** with an opening about 3″ wide. Others may have a large feed tube nearly 5″ wide with a smaller feed tube inside the large tube. For small veggies (e.g. a stalk of celery or one carrot), use the small feed tube. For large vegetables and fruits (e.g. potatoes, apples, tomatoes), use the large feed tube.
- **Cut one end flat** from foods which are to be sliced or shredded. Place food flat end down in the feed tube. Let gravity pull the food down. Use the pusher to guide food through the tube. Adjust pressure to the texture of the food being processed. Use lighter pressure for softer foods, firmer pressure for firmer foods.
- **Uneven pressure** results in uneven slices or shreds.
- **For long shreds** when grating carrots or zucchini, cut them to fit crosswise in a standard or large feed tube. Grate, using medium pressure. So pretty when added to cooked spaghetti or linguini; just **MW them covered on HIGH for 45 to 60 seconds.**
- **Sometimes it is faster to chop or slice** just one onion with a knife rather than use your processor. However, you can use your processor to chop large quantities; refrigerate or freeze the extras in plastic bags for future use.
- **An easy trick:** Cut ends off onions, then make a cut through the peel from one end to the other. It will peel off just like a jacket!
- **If you have a lot of onions to chop,** peel them and cut in quarters (or wedges for larger onions). Insert **Slicer** or **French-Fry Blade**. Place onions flat end down in feed tube. Slice, using medium pressure. Voila! A whole bowl of chopped onions!
- **When grating soft cheeses** such as Mozzerella, chill or freeze cheese for 15 minutes before grating.
- **Harder cheeses** which are to be added to a sauce (e.g. Swiss, Cheddar) can be either shredded on the **Grater**, or cut in 1″ chunks and processed with on/off turns on the **Steel Knife**.
- **If a small amount of food** still remains on top of the **Slicer** or **Grater** after processing, turn the machine on and off quickly several times. The food will usually pass through the blade. If not, it becomes a nibble for the cook!

MICROBUDDY

A QUICK MICROWAVE GUIDE FOR EVERY DAY

DEFROSTING

Remember to remove foil wrapping. Stir to break up food; turn over solid foods at ½ time. Foods complete thawing process during standing time. Do not cover unless directed. If edges start to overcook, stop oven for 5 minutes, then continue.

	SETTING	TIME
BREAD PRODUCTS *To defrost and warm, cover with paper towel.*		
1 roll, muffin, danish, bagel	HIGH	20 - 25 sec.
1 pancake, waffle (uncovered)	HIGH	20 - 30 sec.
1 loaf bread	HIGH	1 - 1 ¼ min.
BUTTER/MARGARINE *Remove wrapping.*		
¼ lb.	DEF	1 - 1 ¼ min.
CAKES/BROWNIES/PIES		
8″ or 9″ cake	DEF	2 - 4 min.
Baked Frozen Pie	DEF	8 - 12 min.
FROZEN CASSEROLES/DINNERS/SNACKS *To Defrost and Heat:*		
2 - 3 quarts	MED	15 min.
stir; then	HIGH	5 - 10 min.
1 Frozen Dinner	HIGH	6 min.
1 pre-cooked Chicken Piece	HIGH	3 - 4 min.
1 Mini Pizza	HIGH	2 min.
FROZEN FISH/MEAT/POULTRY *Remove portions as they defrost. Stack steaks, chops, fish fillets for more even defrosting.*		
Fish	DEF	4 - 6 min./lb.
Beef, Poultry, Veal, Lamb	DEF	5 - 7 min./lb.
Ground Beef, Hot Dogs	DEF	4 - 6 min./lb.
1 Hot Dog	DEF	45 - 60 sec.
1 Hamburger	DEF	1 - 2 min.
FROZEN JUICE *(Remove from container)*		
6 oz. can	HIGH	1 min.
FROZEN PASTA/RICE *To Defrost and Heat:*		
1 cup	HIGH	2 min.
FROZEN SOUP/SPAGHETTI SAUCE *To Defrost and Heat:*		
4 cups	HIGH	15 - 18 min.
FROZEN VEGETABLES *To Defrost and Heat: Place package on a plate; pierce 2 — 3 times with a knife.*		
10 - 12 oz. pkg.	HIGH	6 - 8 min.

COOKING

Vent plastic wrap to allow steam to escape. Standing time completes cooking. Waxed paper prevents spatters. Stir or turn at ½ time.

	SETTING	TIME
CAKES/BROWNIES/PASTRY		
8″ Layer Cake	HIGH	4 - 6 min.
6 Cupcakes/Muffins	HIGH	2 - 2 ½ min.
9″ Crumb Crust	HIGH	2 min.
COOKED CEREALS *Large bowl prevents boil-overs.*		
1 serving	HIGH	1 ½ - 2 min.
EGGS *Don't cook eggs in shell! For poached or fried egg, pierce yolk to prevent popping. Cover with plastic wrap, except scrambled eggs which require stirring. If oven cooks unevenly, use MEDIUM and double the time.*		
1 egg	HIGH	30 - 35 sec.
2 eggs	HIGH	1 - 1 ¼ min.
FISH/MEAT/POULTRY		
Fish (cover with plastic wrap)	HIGH	4 min./lb.
Beef, Veal, Lamb	HIGH	6 - 7 min./lb.
Ground Beef	HIGH	5 - 6 min./lb.
1 Hamburger Patty	HIGH	2 min.
Meatloaf (1 lb.) (shape in a ring)	HIGH	6 - 8 min.
Spaghetti Sauce/Chili (4 - 6 servings)	HIGH	20 - 25 min.
Poultry	HIGH	6 - 7 min./lb.
RICE *Cover with casserole lid.*		
1 cup uncooked	HIGH	5 - 6 min.
then	MED	12 min.
FRESH VEGETABLES *Plastic wrap retains steam. Stir or turn over at half time. Vegetables cooked in their skins should be pierced.*		
Asparagus (tips inward)	HIGH	5 - 6 min./lb.
Green/Wax Beans (+ ½ cup water)	HIGH	7 - 8 min./lb.
Broccoli/Cauliflower (heads inward)	HIGH	6 - 7 min./lb.
Brussel Sprouts/Cabbage	HIGH	6 - 7 min./lb.
Carrots (+ ¼ cup water)	HIGH	7 min./lb.
Corn	HIGH	2 ½ min./ear
Mushrooms/Tomatoes (uncovered)	HIGH	4 - 5 min./lb.
Onions/Peppers	HIGH	2 - 3 min./one
Baked Potatoes/Squash (uncovered on rack)	HIGH	6 - 7 min./lb.
1 Baked Potato (7 oz.)	HIGH	4 - 5 min.
Spinach/Greens	HIGH	3 - 4 min./lb.
Zucchini/Eggplant	HIGH	5 - 6 min./lb.
FRUIT DESSERTS *Cover with waxed paper.*		
Apple Sauce (6 - 8 apples)	HIGH	7 - 10 min.
1 Baked Apple	HIGH	2 min.
4 Baked Apples	HIGH	4 - 6 min.
Stewed Fruit (1 - 1 ½ lb.)	HIGH	10 min.
Fruit Crisps (uncovered)	HIGH	10 - 12 min.
SAUCES & GRAVY		
1 cup	HIGH	3 - 4 min.

HEATING

	SETTING	TIME
BABY FOOD/MILK/JUICE *Uncover before heating. Stir or turn at ½ time; test temperature before feeding baby!*		
FROM ROOM TEMPERATURE		
4 oz. milk/juice/food	HIGH	15 - 20 sec.
8 oz. milk/juice/food	HIGH	30 - 40 sec.
FROM REFRIGERATOR		
4 oz. milk/juice/food	HIGH	30 - 40 sec.
8 oz. milk/juice/food	HIGH	45 - 60 sec.

BEVERAGES/SOUP	HOT		BOILING	
1 cup	HIGH	1 ½ - 2 min.	HIGH	2 - 3 min.
4 cups	HIGH	6 - 7 min.	HIGH	8 - 10 min.

	SETTING	TIME
BREAD & PASTRY *Cover with paper towel.*		
1 roll, muffin, danish, bagel	HIGH	10 - 15 sec.
1 pancake, waffle (uncovered)	HIGH	15 sec.
1 slice apple pie	HIGH	20 - 30 sec.
BUTTER/MARGARINE *Remove wrapping.*		
2 tbsp.	HIGH	30 - 45 sec. to melt
¼ lb. (1 stick)	HIGH	1 min. to melt
¼ lb. (1 stick)	DEF	30 sec. to soften
CHOCOLATE/CHOCOLATE CHIPS *If oven cooks unevenly, use MEDIUM and increase time by 50%. Stir every minute. Uncovered.*		
1 - 2 oz. square	HIGH	1 ½ - 2 min.
6 oz. pkg.	HIGH	1 ½ - 2 min.
FRUIT *To release more juice:*		
½ grapefruit	HIGH	30 sec.
1 lemon/orange	HIGH	15 - 20 sec.
SAUCES & SYRUPS		
½ cup	HIGH	30 - 45 sec.
SNACKS & LEFTOVERS *Wrap bread products in microsafe paper towel. Cover leftovers with waxed paper. When hot, bottom center of plate should feel warm.*		
1 Hot Dog & Bun	HIGH	30 - 40 sec.
1 Sandwich or Hamburger	HIGH	30 - 40 sec.
1 slice Pizza	HIGH	45 - 60 sec.
2 Pieces Chicken	HIGH	2 - 3 min.
1 Whole Chicken	MED-HIGH	7 - 10 min.
Dinner Plate for 1	HIGH	2 min.
2 cups canned Vegetables	HIGH	3 - 4 min.
1 qt. Casserole	MED-HIGH	4 - 6 min.
2 qt. Casserole	MED-HIGH	10 - 12 min.
1 cup Rice/Pasta	HIGH	1 min.
1 serving Soup	HIGH	2 - 3 min.

QUICK MICRO-WAYS

- **For maximum speed, HIGH** power (600 to 700 watts) is used unless otherwise indicated. If your oven has only 500 watts, increase time by ¼ to ½.
- **If food is overcooking on edges,** reduce power to **MEDIUM (50%)** and double the time. MicroBuddy is a quick time guide. Timing may vary with different ovens as well as electrical power variations in your community.
- **Starting temperature affects time.** Room temperature foods take less time than refrigerated foods to heat.
- **Allow ¼ of microwave time** as standing time to complete cooking and/or equalize heat. Cover to retain heat.
- **ALWAYS check foods before full time** to prevent overcooking. Add more time if necessary.
- **When DOUBLING quantity,** add ½ to ⅔ more time. When making **HALF** the amount, decrease time by ⅓.
- **Arrange foods in a circle,** or use round or oval casseroles; cooking will be more even. Place thicker, meatier parts towards the outside of the dish. Stir or turn foods once or twice during cooking.
- **Cooking containers and coverings** must be microsafe (e.g. heat-resistant glass and ceramic casseroles and lids; microsafe plastics; non-recycled paper plates, paper towels and napkins; microsafe plastic wrap; waxed paper.)

THE KOSHER COOK

The recipes in this book have been developed using Kosher dietary guidelines for food preparation. There is no mixing of milk and meat products; there are no shellfish or pork recipes.

Availability of Kosher products varies from area to area. Most products called for in my recipes can be found on supermarket shelves. There are Kosher grocery stores, bakeries and health food stores in large cities. New Kosher products are constantly becoming available. When in doubt, consult with your Rabbi for which processed foods and/or ingredients require Kosher certification.

On the Emergency Substitutions chart (p. 40-41), I have also included substitutions for products which may not have Kosher certification. The final taste may be slightly different, but will still be good. Use pareve margarine and instant soup mix where necessary. Matzo meal can be used to replace bread or cracker crumbs for Passover. Potato starch is used instead of cornstarch.

EMERGENCY SUBSTITUTIONS OR EQUIVALENTS

This list will help you if you're missing an ingredient or if you have difficulty finding certain specialty products called for in recipes. It provides some low-cholesterol alternatives; Kosher and vegetarian substitutions are also included. Liquid soy milk product, available in health food stores, can be used for those with lactose intolerance.

For	Use
1 tbsp. butter	1 tbsp. margarine or oil. Soft or tub margarines are more unsaturated; solid margarines contain more saturated fat. Don't use whipped margarine in baking.
½ c. butter	1 stick butter (¼ lb.)
1 c. milk (for cooking)	1 c. water plus 1 tsp. instant chicken soup mix or 1 c. liquid soy milk.
1 c. milk (for baking)	1 c. orange juice, apple juice, water, coffee or liquid soy milk. Skim milk can be used for low-fat diets.
1 c. sour cream	1 c. yogurt.
1 c. buttermilk or yogurt (in baking)	1 tbsp. lemon juice or vinegar plus enough milk to measure 1 cup.
2 c. whipped cream	(For low-cholesterol diets.) Combine ⅓ c. ice water, 2 tsp. lemon juice and ½ tsp. vanilla in a deep bowl. Blend in ⅓ c. skim milk powder plus 2 tbsp. sugar. Whip 5 to 10 minutes, until stiff.
1 tsp. vanilla extract	1 tsp. coffee, orange or almond flavored liqueur. (I usually add a little more!)
1 envelope unflavored gelatin (7 grams or 1 tbsp.)	5 sheets of leaf gelatin 2 ⅞″ x 8 ½″. Soak for ½ hour in cold water to soften. Squeeze out water; dissolve gelatin in 2 c. hot liquid.
1 envelope non-Kosher unflavored gelatin (7 grams or 1 tbsp.)	1 envelope (1 tbsp.) Eficol unflavored Kosher gelatin or 4 tbsp. Rokeach Jel or Carmel Kosher Gel Dessert. Agar-Agar, vegetable-based gelatin, can also be used.
1 c. brown sugar, packed (light or dark brown)	1 cup granulated sugar plus 4 tbsp. molasses.
1 c. sugar	Reduce liquid in recipe by ¼ cup; use ¾ c. honey, ¾ c. maple syrup or 1 ¼ c. molasses.
1 c. all-purpose or unbleached flour	Whole wheat flour can be substituted, but texture will be slightly heavier. Try half and half.
1 whole egg	2 egg whites (in baking). For 3 eggs, substitute 1 whole egg plus 4 whites.
1 square (1 oz.) unsweetened chocolate	3 tbsp. cocoa plus 1 tbsp. oil or shortening.
1 square (1 oz.) semi-sweet chocolate, melted	¼ c. semi-sweet chocolate chips, melted.
3 squares (3 oz.) semi-sweet or bittersweet chocolate	1 oz. (1 square) unsweetened chocolate plus 3 ½ tbsp. sugar plus 1 tbsp. shortening.
1 c. chocolate chips	1 c. coarsely chopped semi-sweet chocolate.

For	Use
1 c. chicken broth	1 c. water plus 1 tsp. instant chicken soup mix (may be more salty).
Oriental sesame oil	Tahini (sesame seed paste). If possible, use the oily portion which has separated from the paste. Flavor is not as intense.
¼ tsp. Chili oil	6 to 8 drops Tabasco sauce, or chili powder to taste.
Rice wine vinegar	White vinegar plus a pinch of sugar.
Chili Paste with Garlic (1 tsp.)	Combine 1 tsp. chili powder, 15 drops Tabasco sauce, 1 tsp. vinegar, 1 clove minced garlic and a pinch of sugar.
Mirin or Chinese cooking wine	cooking sherry.
2 c. tomato sauce	5 ½ oz. can tomato paste plus water to equal 2 cups.
1 c. fresh mushrooms	10 oz. can mushrooms, drained.
1 clove garlic	⅛ tsp. garlic powder or ½ tsp. minced garlic.
1 tsp. dried herbs	1 tbsp. fresh herbs.
2 tbsp. flour	1 tbsp. cornstarch or potato starch (for thickening).
1 c. bread crumbs	1 c. matzo meal, cracker or corn flake crumbs.

METRIC CONVERSIONS

VOLUME — APPROXIMATE REPLACEMENTS

1/4 tsp.	— 1 ml	1/3 cup	— 75 ml
1/2 tsp.	— 2 ml	1/2 cup	— 125 ml
1 tsp.	— 5 ml	1 cup	— 250 ml
1 tbsp.	— 15 ml	4 cups (1 qt.)	— 1 litre
1/4 cup	— 50 ml		

WEIGHTS — APPROXIMATE REPLACEMENTS

1 oz.	— 28.5 grams	kilograms x 2.2 = lb.
3 1/2 oz.	— 100 grams	grams x 0.035 = ounces
8 oz.	— 225 grams	lb. x 0.45 = kilograms
1 lb.	— 454 grams	ounces x 28 = grams
2.2 lb.	— 1 kilogram	

APPROXIMATE METRIC SIZES FOR CASSEROLES & DISHES

8″ square pan x 2″ deep	— 20 cm x 5 cm
7″ x 11″ x 2″ oblong casserole	— 30 x 20 x 5 cm (2 litres)
9″ x 13″ x 2″ oblong casserole	— 33 x 22 x 5 cm (3 litres)
9″ pie plate	— 22 cm
10″ quiche dish	— 25 cm
1 quart casserole	— 1 litre casserole
2 quart casserole	— 2 litre casserole
3 quart casserole	— 3 litre casserole

2.5 centimetres = 1 inch   30 centimetres = 12 inches

TEMPERATURE - APPROXIMATE CONVERSIONS

32°F	= 0°C	350°F	= 180°C
65°F	= 18°C	375°F	= 190°C
100°F	= 38°C	400°F	= 200°C
212°F	= 100°C	425°F	= 220°C
275°F	= 140°C	450°F	= 230°C
300°F	= 150°C	475°F	= 240°C
325°F	= 160°C	500°F	= 260°C

To convert Fahrenheit to Celsius, subtract 32, multiply by 5, then divide by 9. To convert Celsius to Fahrenheit, multiply by 9, divide by 5, then add 32.

METRIC COOKING TIMES

6 to 7 mins/lb.	=	13 to 15 mins/kg
5 to 6 mins/lb.	=	11 to 13 mins/kg
4 to 5 mins/lb.	=	9 to 11 mins/kg

APPETIZERS

MICRO-WAYS WITH APPETIZERS

- **Appetizers can be prepared** in advance and placed on a microsafe serving dish. When your company arrives, just pop the plate into the microwave and heat. Cool convenience!
- **Use HIGH power** for most appetizers. Small items heat quickly and evenly; if they have been frozen, they usually do not require defrosting before reheating.
- **Prepare toppings** for canapés ahead of time, but place on crackers or toasted bread just before heating to prevent soggy bottoms!
- **Quick appetizers** can be made by spreading crisp crackers with a dab of tomato sauce or Taco sauce and sprinkling with grated Swiss, Cheddar or Mozzerella cheese. **MW on MEDIUM (50%) for a minute or two.**
- **To help prevent soggy bottoms,** heat canapés and crackers on a paper towel or napkin; a microsafe rack also works well to keep a drier, crisper texture.
- **To refresh chips** or crackers that are soggy, place a double layer of microsafe paper towels or napkins in a microsafe serving bowl. Add chips or crackers. **MW on HIGH for 30 seconds.** Remove from microwave, uncover and let stand for 3 to 4 minutes. They will crisp as they stand.
- **Frozen baked miniature quiches** can be taken from the freezer, arranged in a circle on a paper towel-lined plate and heated without defrosting. **One dozen will take about 1 to 2 minutes on HIGH** to thaw and heat. Let stand for a minute to crisp.
- **If serving broccoli, cauliflower** or green beans with a dip, rinse veggies under cold water and shake off excess; place them in a Pyrex™ measuring cup. Partially cook them in the microwave until tender-crisp. Allow **45 to 60 seconds per cup of vegetables**, then immediately place under cold running water to stop the cooking. They will be easier to digest.
- **One cup of vegetable dip** will serve 6 to 8, depending on how many other hors d'oeuvres you are serving. Any leftovers can be thinned with a little milk, if necessary, and used as a salad dressing.
- **Fried foods** (e.g. potato pancakes) generally do not reheat well in the microwave; they require the dry heat of a conventional oven to crisp them.
- **Filled filo** triangles may become tough on the pointed ends if reheated in the microwave. I find that filo dough requires the heat of the conventional oven for proper crisping. However, I use the microwave to help me prepare fillings quickly (e.g. sautéeing or cooking vegetables, meat or chicken).
- **Cover foods** according to the amount of moisture you wish to retain. All coverings prevent spatters, but lids and plastic wrap trap moisture while paper towels absorb it. Be sure to use microwavable plastic wraps and paper towels.
- **Arrange food in a circle** for even heating.
- **Deep-frying foods** in your microwave is not recommended by microwave or cookware manufacturers. It is unsafe.
- **Breaded products** won't come out as crispy in the microwave as they do from a conventional oven.

NOTES ON MEATBALLS

- **Because meatballs freeze well,** I usually make 2 pounds at a time. Basic Meatballs (p. 46) can be used as a guideline when converting your own favorite recipe.
- **Ground beef or veal are interchangeable.** No oil is necessary because microwaved meatballs never stick. Excess fat should be drained off after cooking and before adding sauce.
- **For more flavor,** add ¼ cup of the sauce plus 2 tbsp. bread crumbs for each pound of ground meat. Combine with remaining ingredients and mix well.
- **Make meatballs uniform** in size for even cooking.
- **Meatballs should be arranged** in a single layer in an ungreased casserole. A shallow 2 or 3 quart oval casserole is an excellent cooking container.
- **A shallow 3 quart oval casserole** will fit in a full-size microwave oven with a turntable. If you have a mid-size oven without a turntable, place the casserole diagonally.
- **The 10″ square browning dish** that comes with a lid also makes an excellent cooking container and fits in most microwaves. It can be used as a regular microwave casserole if you don't preheat it. Make sure the meatballs in the corners don't overcook.
- **If your casserole has a lid,** use it when covering is required. Wax paper or vented microsafe plastic wrap can be used when the casserole does not have a lid. Covering prevents spattering.
- **For one pound of meat, cook meatballs uncovered on HIGH for 6 to 7 minutes** in a 2 quart casserole, stirring once. **For 2 pounds of meat, cook for 10 to 12 minutes** in a 3 quart casserole, stirring once or twice. Move those that are more cooked to the centre of the casserole.
- **Add desired sauce** to drained meatballs, **cover and MW on HIGH 5 to 10 minutes longer,** until piping hot, stirring at half time.
- **If you are not in a hurry,** meatballs and sauce can be microwaved covered on **MEDIUM (50%) for 15 to 20 minutes** to absorb more flavor.
- **Standing time for meatballs** is 5 minutes. When cooked in a sauce, they taste even better when reheated.
- **MIX & MATCH MEATBALLS:** Prepare Basic Meatballs (p. 46) and microwave as directed. Do not add any sauce. When meatballs are cool, freeze. Prepare batches of different sauces and freeze in separate containers. When you need a meal, thaw a container of meatballs and a container of desired sauce. Combine and **microwave covered on HIGH for approximately 10 minutes** to blend flavors.

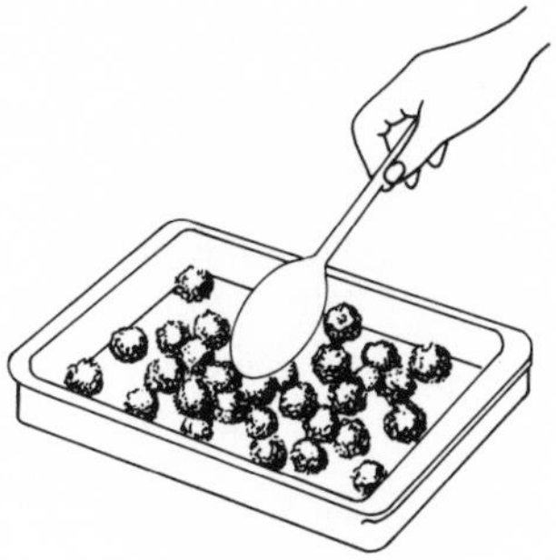

BASIC MEATBALLS

2 lb. ground beef or veal
2 eggs
6 tbsp. bread crumbs
1 tsp. salt
freshly ground pepper
2 cloves garlic, minced or ½ tsp. garlic powder
Desired sauce (see recipe variations that follow)

1. Combine meat, eggs, crumbs and seasonings. Prepare desired sauce and blend ¼ cup into meat mixture. Shape into 1″ meatballs. Arrange in a single layer in an ungreased 3 quart oval or rectangular casserole.

2. MW uncovered on HIGH for 10 to 12 minutes, rearranging at half time. Meatballs should lose their pink color. Let stand 3 to 4 minutes. Drain pan juices from meat.

3. Add desired sauce to cooked meatballs and mix well. (Can be prepared in advance up to this point and refrigerated until needed.)

4. MW covered with casserole lid or waxed paper on HIGH for 5 to 10 minutes, until piping hot. Stir once or twice. (If refrigerated, it will require the longer cooking time.)

Yield: 12 servings as an appetizer or 6 to 8 servings as a main dish. Freezes and/or reheats very well. Serve over rice or noodles.

* For one pound of meat, cook meatballs **uncovered on HIGH for 6 to 7 minutes** in a 2 quart casserole, rearranging at half time.
* Matzo meal or cracker crumbs can be substituted for bread crumbs. You can also use your own favorite meatball recipe, using the cooking method described above.
* Cooked meatballs can be frozen with or without sauce. See Mix & Match Meatballs (p. 45).
* **SZECHUAN ORANGE MEATBALLS:** Prepare Basic Meatballs. Prepare Szechuan Orange Sauce (p. 91), but thicken sauce with cornstarch mixture as directed. Add to cooked meatballs and complete as directed.
* **SWEET'N'SASSY MEATBALLS:** Prepare Sweet'n'Sassy BBQ Sauce (p. 91). Prepare Basic Meatballs, increasing bread crumbs to ½ cup. Add ½ cup of Sweet'n'Sassy BBQ Sauce and ½ tsp. basil to meatball mixture. Shape into 1″ balls. Continue as directed in basic recipe.
* **SWEET & SOUR MEATBALLS:** Combine a 5 ½ oz. can tomato paste, 19 oz. can tomatoes, ⅓ c. brown sugar, packed and 2 tbsp. vinegar or lemon juice. Mix well. Prepare Basic Meatballs, increasing bread crumbs to ½ cup. Add ½ cup of the sauce and ½ tsp. basil to meatball mixture. Shape into 1″ balls. Continue as directed in basic recipe.
* **EASY PARTY MEATBALLS:** Combine 9 oz. jar grape jelly, 2 tbsp. lemon juice and 1 ½ c. chili sauce in a 4 cup Pyrex™ measure. **MW uncovered on HIGH for 6 to 7 minutes,** until bubbling hot, stirring once or twice. Prepare meatball mixture and shape into 1″ balls. Continue as directed in basic recipe.
* **ORIENTAL MEATBALLS:** Refer to recipe on p. 193, but omit onion and peppers.

COCKTAIL HOT DOGS

"Frankly" speaking, this recipe is as easy as they come. It may not be gourmet, but it's good. It can be made with beef, veal or chicken hot dogs.

½ c. grape jelly
¾ c. chili sauce or bottled barbecue sauce
1 tbsp. lemon juice
1 lb. hot dogs, sliced ½″ thick

1. Combine grape jelly, chili sauce and lemon juice in a 2 quart microsafe casserole. **MW uncovered on HIGH for 3 minutes,** until bubbling hot, stirring once. Add hot dogs; cover with waxed paper.

2. MW 3 to 4 minutes longer, stirring once, until hot dogs are heated through. Serve on toothpicks.

Yield: about 4 to 5 dozen slices.

CHICKEN FINGERS

Although these are not crisp like the ones that are fried, I find them easy, delicious and lower in calories. They certainly disappear quickly enough!

1 lb. boneless, skinless chicken breasts
1 egg
1 tbsp. oil
¾ c. seasoned bread crumbs

1. Cut fillet portion from underside of chicken breast. Cut remaining chicken in fingers the same size as the fillet portion (about 2″ long). Rinse well; pat dry with paper towels. Blend egg with oil. Dip chicken pieces first in egg, then coat with crumb mixture. Arrange on a microsafe platter with the larger pieces towards the outside edge of the dish. Cover with paper towelling.

2. MW on HIGH for 4 to 5 minutes, until tender. It is not necessary to turn them over. Let stand covered for 2 minutes. Serve with Oriental Sauce (p. 92), Chinese Sweet & Sour Sauce (p. 93) or Sweet'n'Sassy BBQ sauce (p. 91).

Yield: 4 servings (20 fingers).

* Chicken Fingers are ideal as an appetizer at your next party. **Two lbs. take 8 to 10 minutes on HIGH.** (Or prepare 2 batches. While you are serving the first batch, the second one will be cooking in the microwave and will be piping hot just when you need it!)
* Sometimes I save just the fillet portion of the chicken breast to make chicken fingers. They're perfect if you have young children or you want to make a quick snack. I dip them in bottled salad dressing or a little oil, then in seasoned crumbs. **Four strips will cook in about 2 minutes on HIGH.** Kids love them plain, with ketchup or Chinese plum sauce (duck sauce).

HORS D'OEUVRES CHICKEN KABOBS

1. Follow recipe for Chicken Kabobs #1 or #2 (p. 167). Place each piece of chicken on a 1″ square of red or green pepper. Skewer onto wooden toothpicks. Arrange on 2 serving plates. Brush with marinade; sprinkle lightly with sesame seeds. Cover with wax paper.

2. **MW one plate at a time on HIGH for 4 to 5 minutes.** Cook the second batch while serving the first one. Serve hot or cold.

SZECHUAN ORANGE CHICKEN WINGS

Spicy & Wonderful!

¼ c. fresh orange juice
rind of an orange
4 cloves garlic
1 slice ginger, about 1 tbsp. minced
2 green onions
¼ c. Hoisin Sauce*
1 tsp. Chili Paste with Garlic*
¼ c. soya sauce
¼ c. honey
½ tsp. Oriental Sesame Oil*
¼ c. orange marmalade
2 lb. chicken wings
1 tbsp. cornstarch
3 tbsp. cold water

1. Squeeze juice from orange and set aside. Remove rind carefully with a sharp knife, being careful not to take any of the bitter white part.

2. **Steel Knife:** Drop garlic, ginger, green onions and orange rind through feed tube while machine is running. Process until minced, about 10 seconds. Add Hoisin, Chili Paste, soya sauce, honey, sesame oil, marmalade and reserved orange juice; process for a few seconds to blend.

3. Cut wing tips from chicken and discard, or save to use in chicken soup. Cut wings in two. Place in a plastic bag. Add sauce and marinate 30 minutes at room temperature or refrigerate and marinate overnight. Turn once or twice to coat with sauce.

4. Remove wings from marinade and arrange in a single layer on an ungreased 12″ round microsafe plate. Arrange the meatier parts towards the outside edge of the dish. Reserve marinade. **MW covered with waxed paper on HIGH for 10 to 12 minutes,** turning wings over and brushing them with additional marinade at half time. Let stand covered while preparing sauce.

5. Dissolve cornstarch in cold water in a 2 cup Pyrex™ measure. Stir in reserved marinade and any cooking juices from chicken. **MW sauce uncovered on HIGH for 3 minutes,** until bubbling and thickened, stirring 2 or 3 times. Serve as a sauce with wings.

Yield: 24 wings. Serves 4 as a main course or 6 to 8 as an appetizer. Freezes well.

* Chinese products are available in Oriental grocery stores.

* **Chili Paste with Garlic Substitute:** Combine 1 tsp. chili powder, 15 drops Tabasco sauce, 1 tsp. vinegar, 1 clove minced garlic and a pinch of sugar.

CHINESE CHICKEN WINGS

2 lb. chicken wings
¼ c. soya sauce
¼ c. honey
2 cloves garlic, crushed
½ tsp. dry mustard
1 tbsp. lemon juice
1 tbsp. ketchup
¼ tsp. Oriental sesame oil
1 - 2 tbsp. sesame seeds

1. Cut wing tips from chicken and discard, or save to use in chicken soup. Cut wings in two. Place in a plastic bag. Combine remaining ingredients except sesame seeds and mix well. Add to wings and marinate 30 minutes at room temperature or refrigerate and marinate overnight. Turn bag once or twice to coat wings with sauce.

2. Remove wings from marinade and arrange in a single layer on an ungreased 12″ round microsafe plate. Arrange the meatier parts towards the outside of the dish. Reserve marinade. Sprinkle wings with sesame seeds.

3. MW covered with waxed paper on HIGH for 10 to 12 minutes, brushing wings with reserved marinade at half time. Let stand covered for 3 to 4 minutes.

Yield: 24 wings. Serves 4 as a main course or 6 to 8 as an appetizer. Freezes well.

BBQ CHICKEN WINGS

2 lb. chicken wings
Sweet'n'Sassy BBQ Sauce (p. 91) or bottled barbecue sauce

Follow recipe for Chinese Chicken Wings, substituting Sweet'n'Sassy BBQ Sauce for marinade. Sesame seeds are optional.

CHICKEN SALAD

3 eggs
1 lb. boneless, skinless chicken breasts (about 3 single breasts)
4 green onions
1 stalk celery
⅓ c. mayonnaise
salt & pepper, to taste

1. Crack eggs into ungreased individual custard cups or a microsafe muffin pan. Pierce yolks with a fork. (It doesn't matter if the yolk runs into the white.) Cover tightly with plastic wrap. **MW on MEDIUM (50%) for 3 minutes,** until eggs are firm. Rotate pan halfway through cooking. Let stand covered for 2 minutes. Uncover and let cool.

2. Place chicken in a single layer in a microsafe casserole with the thicker parts towards the outside of the dish. Cover with casserole lid or vented plastic wrap. **MW on HIGH for 5 to 6 minutes,** turning chicken over at half time. Let stand covered for 2 minutes. Uncover and let cool.

3. Chop vegetables, chicken and eggs. (If using the food processor, use the **Steel Knife.** Chop green onions and celery, about 10 seconds. Add cut-up chicken and eggs; process with quick on/off turns, until coarsely chopped.) Mix in mayonnaise and seasonings. Chill.

Yield: 6 servings. Do not freeze.

HOT & SPICY NUTS

A variation of a recipe shared with me by an ardent microwaver. Barbara's guests love these — you will too!

2 tbsp. butter or margarine
1 ½ tsp. chili powder
½ tsp. celery salt
1 tsp. Worcestershire sauce
½ tsp. salt
½ tsp. garlic powder
⅛ tsp. each of basil, onion powder & cayenne
1 ½ c. almonds or pecans
1 tbsp. coarse (Kosher) salt

1. Place butter in a 9″ Pyrex™ pie plate. **MW uncovered on HIGH for 45 seconds,** until melted. Remove from microwave and stir in all seasonings except coarse salt. Add nuts and mix well.

2. **MW uncovered on HIGH for 6 to 7 minutes,** stirring once or twice, until nuts are toasted. Toss with coarse salt. Cool. Store in an airtight container.

Yield: 1 ½ cups nuts.

CHOPPED CHICKEN LIVERS

So quick and easy! Onions and eggs are cooked in the same casserole, saving on cleanup. If you observe the Jewish dietary laws, livers must be broiled instead of microwaved.

1 lb. chicken livers
2 onions, chopped
3 tbsp. oil
2 eggs
salt & pepper, to taste
2 tbsp. chicken broth or red wine, if needed*

1. Either broil livers conventionally or cook them in the microwave. (To microwave, arrange livers in a single layer in a casserole and pierce with a fork to prevent popping. Cover with waxed paper. **MW on 50% (MEDIUM) for 10 to 12 minutes,** until livers are firm and no longer pink, stirring once or twice. Let stand covered for 5 minutes.) Refrigerate livers until cold.

2. Onions can be chopped with quick on/off turns on the **Steel Knife** of the food processor. Place onions and oil in a microsafe 1 quart bowl. **MW uncovered on HIGH for 5 minutes,** until onions are tender.

3. Add raw eggs to onion and beat lightly to blend. **MW uncovered on HIGH for 1 to 1 ½ minutes,** stirring once or twice. Eggs should be set but slightly moist. Let stand uncovered for 2 or 3 minutes.

4. **Steel Knife:** Process liver until minced, about 10 to 12 seconds. Add remaining ingredients and process to desired texture, about 10 seconds longer. Mixture will be somewhat moist but will firm up when refrigerated.

Yield: 6 servings. May be used as an appetizer, as a spread with crackers or as a sandwich filling.

* Juices from chicken livers cooked by microwave method may be used instead of chicken broth or wine to moisten chopped liver.
* Eggs may be "hard-cooked" in the microwave, if you prefer. See p. 130 for method.

MOCK "CHOPPED LIVER"

An excellent vegetarian dish.

½ lb. fresh green or wax beans*
½ c. water
4 eggs
2 medium onions
3 tbsp. oil
12 walnut or pecan halves
salt & pepper, to taste
1 to 2 tbsp. mayonnaise

1. Trim beans and cut into 1″ pieces. You should have about 2 cups. Place beans and water in a 1 quart microsafe casserole. Cover and **MW on HIGH for 5 minutes,** until tender. Let stand covered for 2 minutes. Drain; refrigerate until cold.

2. Break eggs into a microsafe muffin pan or individual custard cups. Pierce yolks with a fork to make an "x". (It doesn't matter if the yolks run.) Cover tightly with plastic wrap. **MW on MEDIUM (50%) for 4 to 5 minutes,** or until firm, rotating the eggs once or twice during cooking. Let stand covered while you prepare the onions.

3. **Steel Knife:** Chop onions, using quick on/off turns. Combine with oil in a small microsafe bowl. **MW uncovered on HIGH for 5 minutes,** until tender. (For a browner color to this dish, you may prefer to sauté the onions in a skillet on top of the stove.)

4. **Steel Knife:** Place all ingredients in food processor and process, using on/off turns, until finely chopped. Season to taste. Refrigerate.

Yield: 4 to 6 servings. Do not freeze.

* Substitute a 10 oz. package of frozen beans, if desired. Refer to cooking directions on p. 244. Recipe also works with drained canned wax or green beans.

MOCK KISHKA

2 medium onions
2 carrots, peeled & trimmed
1 stalk celery
½ green pepper
2 eggs
½ c. oil
2 c. cracker crumbs (Tam Tams are delicious)
3 tbsp. water or chicken broth
¾ tsp. salt
¼ tsp. pepper, garlic powder & paprika

1. **Steel Knife:** Cut vegetables in chunks. Process until fine, about 15 seconds. Add eggs and process 5 seconds longer. Add remaining ingredients and process until well mixed.

2. Empty mixture into a 9″ Pyrex™ pie plate or 10″ ceramic quiche dish. Shape mixture into a ring about 3″ in diameter, wetting your hands for easier handling. Cover with waxed paper, tucking ends under the dish.

3. **MW on HIGH for 6 to 8 minutes,** until dry to the touch. Let stand covered for 2 or 3 minutes. Slice into 12 to 16 pieces. Serve with gravy from roast brisket or chicken.

Yield: 12 to 16 slices, making 6 to 8 servings. (Everyone goes back for seconds!) Reheats and/or freezes well.

MINI PIZZAS

3 English muffins or French rolls, split
1 c. pizza or tomato sauce
½ green &/or red pepper, chopped
2 green onions, sliced
3 to 4 mushrooms, sliced
1 ½ c. grated Mozzerella cheese

1. Toast muffins conventionally. Spread with sauce. Top with peppers, green onions and mushrooms. Sprinkle with cheese. Line a large microsafe platter with a double layer of paper towels. Place pizzas 1″ apart on platter.

2. **MW uncovered on HIGH for 2 to 3 minutes,** rotating plate ¼ turn halfway through cooking. Cheese should be melted and pizzas should be hot. (**Calculate 25 to 30 seconds on HIGH for each mini-pizza.**)

Yield: 6 miniature pizzas.

* If you only want to make 1 or 2 as a quick snack, **MW on MEDIUM (50%), allowing 45 to 60 seconds per mini-pizza.**
* Lower power level prevents cheese from running off the pizzas when cooking small quantities!
* For those who don't observe the Jewish dietary laws, sliced pepperoni, salami or thinly sliced cooked chicken can be added to the toppings.
* **TO FREEZE:** Assemble mini-pizzas and freeze unbaked on a cookie sheet. Wrap with plastic wrap. To cook, unwrap (do not thaw) and place on a paper towel lined plate. **MW uncovered on HIGH, allowing 1 minute per pizza.** Rotate the plate ¼ turn halfway through cooking.
* To reheat slices of leftover commercial or home-made pizza, place on a paper towel lined plate and **MW uncovered on HIGH about 30 to 45 seconds per slice.** Let stand about 1 minute to equalize the heat, then serve.

CALIFORNIA-STYLE MINI PIZZAS

3 French rolls, split & toasted
1 c. tomato sauce
½ red pepper, chopped
½ c. canned artichoke hearts, chopped
2 tbsp. chopped red onion
¼ c. sliced black olives
¾ c. grated Swiss cheese
¾ c. grated Mozzerella cheese

Assemble and microwave as directed for Mini Pizzas (above).

MEXICAN-STYLE MINI PIZZAS

Top toasted rolls with bottled salsa, chopped coriander (Chinese parsley), onions, chopped tomatoes and canned green chilis. Top with grated Monterey Jack cheese or a combination of Cheddar and Mozzerella cheeses. Microwave as directed for Mini Pizzas (above).

PITA PIZZAS

Split miniature or regular pitas in half. Toast conventionally. Place split-side up on paper towel lined platter, top and cook as directed for Mini Pizzas (p. 52). **Calculate 25 to 35 seconds per pizza**, depending on size. **If making only 1 or 2 as a snack, MW on MEDIUM (50%) and allow 45 to 60 seconds per pizza.**

QUICK & EASY PIZZA CRACKERS

Prepare as for Mini Pizzas (p. 52), but use 24 crisp crackers as the base. Use about 1 scant teaspoon of sauce on each cracker. Assemble pizzas just before microwaving to keep them from becoming soggy. Arrange on a paper towel lined platter. **MW on MEDIUM (50%) for 3 minutes**, or until cheese is melted.

Yield: 24 pizza crackers.

* Do not use HIGH power or the cheese and sauce may run off the crackers!
* **Six pizza crackers will take about 1 minute on MEDIUM; 1 dozen will take about 2 minutes.**

NACHOS

This is an excellent appetizer to serve to unexpected company. All the ingredients can be kept on hand and assembled quickly. It tastes like pizza, Mexican style!

7 oz. pkg. tortilla or corn chips
1 c. grated Monterey Jack or Mozzerella cheese
1 c. grated strong Cheddar cheese
½ c. bottled Taco sauce (Salsa)

1. Spread chips in a single layer on a large microsafe platter. Sprinkle with cheese; drizzle Taco sauce over cheese.

2. MW uncovered on HIGH for 2½ to 3 minutes, or until cheese melts.

Yield: 10 to 12 servings.

* If you make half the recipe, it will take about **2 minutes in the microwave.**
* Clean-up is a snap if you make and "mike" Nachos on a plastic or wax-coated paper plate. If plate is uncoated, cheese will stick to the plate!

PIZZA NACHOS

Prepare as for Nachos (above), but omit Cheddar Cheese and use 2 cups grated Mozzerella cheese. Substitute pizza sauce for Taco sauce. (Once I was desperate and used potato chips! Just be sure to use the thick kind because the thin ones break.)

STUFFED MUSHROOMS FLORENTINE

A perfect low-calorie hors d'oeuvre. They are so delicious that I ate the whole recipe for my lunch the day I tested this recipe!

24 large mushrooms
10 oz. pkg. frozen spinach
4 green onions
1 tbsp. fresh dill or 1 tsp. dried dill
½ c. Ricotta or dry cottage cheese
¼ c. grated Parmesan cheese
1 egg yolk
salt & pepper, to taste
2 to 3 tbsp. additional Parmesan cheese

1. Clean mushrooms. Gently twist out stems and reserve for another use.
2. Pierce package of spinach in 2 or 3 places with a sharp knife. Place package on a dinner plate and **MW on HIGH for 5 minutes.** Let stand in package for 5 minutes. Unwrap and squeeze very dry.
3. **Steel Knife:** Mince green onions and dill. Add spinach, Ricotta, ¼ cup Parmesan, egg yolk and seasoning. Process just until mixed. Fill mushroom caps, mounding filling slightly. Sprinkle with remaining Parmesan cheese.
4. Layer a round microsafe plate with a double layer of paper towels. Arrange half of the mushrooms in a circle, placing smaller mushrooms in the centre. Repeat with remaining mushrooms on a second plate. (Can be prepared in advance up to this point and refrigerated until serving time.)
5. Cover loosely with a paper towel. **MW one plate at a time on HIGH for 2½ to 3 minutes,** until cheese is melted and filling is piping hot.

Yield: 2 dozen. 6 to 8 servings.

* Roll excess filling into small balls and freeze. When unexpected company drops in, just drop frozen balls into mushroom caps and **MW as directed above.** Cooking time will be a few seconds longer. Voilà — instant hors d'oeuvres!
* Feta cheese can be used instead of Ricotta or cottage cheese. Omit salt. Crumble feta cheese first for easier mixing.

CHERRY TOMATOES FLORENTINE

Follow recipe for Stuffed Mushrooms Florentine (above) but substitute 24 hollowed-out cherry tomatoes for the mushrooms. **Cooking time will be slightly less, about 2 minutes on HIGH for 1 dozen.**

NATALIE'S STUFFED MUSHROOMS

Excellent!

1 lb. medium mushrooms
4 tbsp. butter or margarine
1/3 c. bread or cornflake crumbs
1/3 c. grated Parmesan cheese
dash of salt & pepper
1/4 tsp. garlic powder
1 c. grated Mozzerella cheese

1. Clean mushrooms. Gently twist out stems, setting caps aside. Finely chop stems.

2. **MW butter on HIGH** in a 1 quart microsafe bowl until melted, **about 45 seconds.** Add stems and crumbs. **MW uncovered on HIGH for 3 to 4 minutes,** or until golden and toasted, stirring once or twice. Add Parmesan cheese and seasonings; mix well. Fill mushroom caps with crumb mixture. Top with Mozzerella cheese.

3. Layer a round microsafe platter with a double layer of paper towels. Arrange half of the mushrooms in a circle, placing smaller mushrooms in the centre. Repeat with remaining mushrooms on a second platter. Cover loosely with wax paper. (Can be prepared in advance up to this point, covered and refrigerated until serving time.)

4. **MW one plate at a time on HIGH for 2 minutes,** until hot.

Yield: 4 dozen. 12 servings.

CHEESE FONDUE

1 1/2 lb. Swiss cheese, grated
1/4 c. flour
1 clove garlic, halved
3 c. dry white wine
1/4 c. Kirsch
2 tbsp. fresh lemon juice
dash salt & nutmeg
freshly ground pepper
French bread, cut in 1/2″ chunks

1. Combine cheese and flour in a bag and shake well. Rub bottom and sides of a ceramic cheese fondue pot or 2 quart microsafe casserole with cut clove of garlic. Discard garlic. Add wine, Kirsch and lemon juice.

2. **MW uncovered on HIGH about 6 to 7 minutes,** just until bubbles start to appear; do not boil. Stir in cheese and seasonings. **MW uncovered on MEDIUM (50%) about 4 to 5 minutes longer,** until smooth, whisking every 2 minutes.

3. Serve with chunks of French bread, Caesar Salad and a bottle of your favorite wine.

Yield: 6 servings.

* Leftover cheese fondue makes a delicious topping for boiled or baked potatoes, cauliflower or broccoli.

ASPARAGUS CHEESE ROLLS

24 aparagus tips*
1 clove garlic
2 tbsp. fresh parsley &/or dill
2 green onions
½ lb. cream cheese or dry cottage cheese
2 tbsp. sour cream or plain yogurt
dash salt & pepper
dash basil & oregano
12 slices white or whole wheat bread, crusts trimmed

1. Rinse asparagus tips in cold water; shake off excess. Stand asparagus with the tips pointing upwards in a 2 cup Pyrex™ measure. Cover with vented plastic wrap. **MW for 1 ½ to 2 minutes on HIGH,** until tender-crisp. Let stand covered for 1 minute. Uncover and let cool.

2. **Steel Knife:** Mince garlic, parsley and green onions. Add cheese, sour cream and seasonings; process a few seconds longer, just until smooth. Spread each bread slice with cheese mixture. Place 2 asparagus tips along one edge of each bread slice, with the tips pointing outwards. Roll up like miniature jelly rolls and cut in half.

3. Chill tightly covered until serving time. Delicious served cold. Rolls may also be brushed with melted butter and broiled 3 to 4 minutes.

Yield: 2 dozen.

* Break off and discard the woody base from the asparagus stems where they snap off most easily. Reserve stem portion for Asparagus Vichysoisse (p. 74) and use tips for this tasty hors d'oeuvre. Pencil-thin asparagus are best.
* Recipe may be halved, if desired. **1 cup of asparagus tips will take 1 to 1 ½ minutes on HIGH.**
* The cheese mixture is delicious as a spread on bagels. Also scrumptious with **¼ cup chopped lox added to the filling.**

GREEN GODDESS DIP

This delicious dip is similar to a creamy Caesar dressing. It is wonderful as a dip with veggies or can be used as a salad dressing over Romaine lettuce or raw spinach leaves. Although it requires no microwaving, I have included it because it makes a wonderful topping for Simple Salmon (p. 121).

2 cloves garlic
4 green onions, cut in chunks
¼ c. fresh parsley
½ can anchovies, drained
¾ c. Mayonnaise (p. 88)
¾ c. sour cream or yogurt
3 tbsp. lemon juice
freshly ground pepper

1. **Steel Knife:** Drop garlic through feed tube while machine is running. Process until minced. Discard any peel. Add green onions, parsley and anchovies and process until finely minced, about 10 seconds. Add remaining ingredients and process until blended, scraping down sides of bowl once or twice. Refrigerate.

Yield: about 1 ½ cups. Do not freeze. Will keep about 10 days in the refrigerator.

EMERALD DIP

You'll flip over this dip — it's a real gem to have in your collection!

10 oz. pkg. frozen chopped spinach
½ onion
½ c. parsley
1 c. Mayonnaise (p. 88)
1 c. sour cream, yogourt or Crème Fraîche (p. 88)
½ tsp. salt
freshly ground pepper

1. Slash package of unwrapped spinach in several places with a sharp knife. Place on a microsafe plate. **MW on HIGH for 4 to 5 minutes,** until completely thawed and heated through. Unwrap and cool. Squeeze very dry.

2. Steel Knife: Process onion with parsley until finely minced, about 8 to 10 seconds. Add remaining ingredients and process until blended, about 10 seconds. Chill 2 or 3 hours (or overnight) to blend flavors.

Yield: 2 ½ cups. Serves 16 to 20.

* When I tested this recipe, I used Crème Fraîche that I had in the fridge from a testing I had done several days before. The taste was incredible! Make your own mayonnaise for the ultimate in taste.
* If you must trim calories, use "light" mayonnaise and yogourt.
* A pretty way to serve this is to cut 1″ off the top of a round pumpernickel bread. Hollow out the inside carefully, leaving a wall of bread about ½″ thick. Cut bread you have removed into bite-sized chunks. Fill bread shell with dip. Place on a serving platter and serve with chunks of bread and assorted veggies.

CUCUMBER YOGURT SAUCE (TZATZIKI)

Although the microwave is not used for this Greek favorite, it makes an excellent sauce for microwaved fish fillets or topping for baked potatoes or broccoli. It's also perfect as a dip for crudités and makes a great salad dressing.

1 clove garlic
2 tbsp. fresh dill
1 large cucumber, peeled & seeded
salt & pepper
½ c. Mayonnaise (p. 88)
½ c. yogurt (sour cream can be substituted)

1. Steel Knife: Drop garlic and dill through feed tube while machine is running. Process until minced. Transfer to a mixing bowl.

2. Grater: Grate cucumber, using medium pressure. Transfer to a colander and sprinkle with ½ tsp. salt. Let stand for 20 minutes. Rinse with cold water and press out liquid. Combine with remaining ingredients. Chill.

Yield: 1 cup sauce. Do not freeze.

Note: To remove seeds from cucumber, cut in half lengthwise and scrape out seeds with a teaspoon.

EGGPLANT SPREAD

1 eggplant (about 1 ¼ lb.)
½ small onion, minced (omit if freezing)
1 clove garlic
½ green pepper
1 small tomato, optional
1 to 2 tbsp. oil (to taste)
2 tsp. lemon juice or vinegar
salt & pepper, to taste
pinch of sugar
2 or 3 drops liquid smoke, if desired

1. Wash eggplant and dry well. Pierce skin in several places with a fork. Weigh to determine cooking time. Calculate 5 to 6 minutes per lb.

2. Place eggplant on a microsafe rack and **MW uncovered on HIGH. One pound will take 5 to 6 minutes; 1 ¼ lb. will take 7 to 8 minutes.** Turn eggplant over halfway through cooking time. At the end of the cooking time, it will be nearly tender when pierced with a fork. It will continue to cook while it stands. Let stand 10 minutes, or until cool enough to handle. Cut in half and scoop out pulp.

3. Steel Knife: Mince onion and garlic. Add chunks of green pepper and tomato; process with quick on/off turns, until coarsely chopped. Add remaining ingredients; process with quick on/offs, just until mixed. Adjust seasonings to taste. Refrigerate or freeze. Serve with crackers or corn chips as a spread or dip.

Yield: 8 servings (about 1 ½ cups).

> * Liquid smoke is available in gourmet specialty food shops. It gives a smoky flavor to the eggplant so it will taste like it was cooked over charcoal.

BABA GANOUJ

This Middle-Eastern spread can be used as a dip for assorted veggies. Mayonnaise can be used instead of Tahini.

1 ¼ lb. eggplant
2 cloves garlic
½ small onion
3 tbsp. Tahini (sesame seed paste)
2 to 3 tbsp. lemon juice
salt to taste
2 to 3 tbsp. olive oil
2 tbsp. chopped green onions
black olives to garnish
toasted pita bread wedges

1 Wash eggplant and dry well. Pierce skin in several places with a fork. Calculate 5 to 6 minutes per lb. Place eggplant on a microsafe rack.

2. MW uncovered on HIGH (1 ¼ lb. will take 7 to 8 minutes). Turn eggplant over at half time. At the end of the cooking time, it will be nearly tender when pierced with a fork. It will continue to cook while it stands. Let stand 10 minutes, or until cool enough to handle. Cut in half and scoop out pulp.

3. Steel Knife: Mince garlic and onion. Add eggplant pulp, Tahini, lemon juice and salt. Process with 6 or 8 quick on/offs, until smooth. Spread on a serving plate. Drizzle with oil and top with green onions. Arrange a border of olives around the outer edge of the dish. Serve with toasted wedges of pita bread.

Yield: about 1 ½ cups (8 servings).

CAPONATA

If you like Ratatouille, you'll love Caponata!

1 ½ lb. eggplant, unpeeled
1 tbsp. salt
2 cloves garlic, minced
2 onions, chopped
1 stalk celery, chopped
6 tbsp. olive or corn oil
2 c. tomato sauce
2 tbsp. tomato paste, optional
2 tbsp. wine vinegar
1 tbsp. sugar
¼ c. raisins
2 tbsp. capers
½ c. pitted green olives, sliced
½ c. pitted black olives, sliced

1. Cut eggplant into 1″ chunks. Place in a colander and sprinkle with salt. Let stand for 15 to 20 minutes. Rinse under cold running water. Press firmly to remove bitter juices. Pat dry with paper towels.

2. Combine garlic, onions and celery with 4 tbsp. of the oil in a 2 cup Pyrex™ measure. **MW uncovered on HIGH for 5 minutes,** until tender, stirring once.

3. Combine eggplant with remaining 2 tbsp. oil in a 2 quart microsafe bowl; mix well. **MW uncovered on HIGH for 6 to 7 minutes,** until tender, stirring once or twice. Drain well.

4. Add remaining ingredients except olives; mix well. Cover with plastic wrap, turning back one corner slightly to vent. **MW covered on HIGH for 10 to 12 minutes,** until tender, stirring once or twice through the vented opening with a wooden chopstick. The eggplant should be tender but still retain its shape. Let stand covered for 5 minutes.

5. Add olives. Adjust seasonings to taste. Delicious hot or cold. Serve cold as an appetizer with crackers or hot as a side dish with meat or poultry. Will keep about 10 days in the refrigerator.

Yield: Serves 6 to 8.

* A nice variation on this dish is to add a 7 oz. can of solid white tuna, drained & broken into chunks, to cooled Caponata. Serve chilled as an appetizer or light lunch on a bed of mixed salad greens.
* If desired, omit raisins. Add 2 or 3 chopped anchovy fillets to cooled Caponata.

GUACAMOLE

2 cloves garlic, minced
1 medium onion, chopped
2 tsp. oil
2 avocados, peeled & pitted
¼ c. red pepper, chopped
1 tbsp. finely chopped coriander leaves, optional
1 tbsp. mayonnaise
2 tbsp. lime juice
¼ c. sour cream or yogurt
¾ tsp. salt
dash chili powder, cayenne or Tabasco sauce

1. Combine garlic, onion and oil in a 1 cup Pyrex™ measure. **MW uncovered on HIGH for 2 minutes,** until tender.

2. Coarsely mash avocado with a potato masher or use on/off turns on your food processor. Do not overprocess; avocado should be chunky. Add remaining ingredients and mix just until combined. Transfer to a serving bowl; add avocado pit to mixture to prevent discoloration. Place plastic wrap directly on the mixture to prevent discoloration. Refrigerate.

Yield: 2 cups. Serve as a dip with tortilla chips or assorted veggies. Also delicious as a topping for salads. (Don't forget to remove the avocado pit before serving!)

* Avocados are sometimes called "alligator pears" because of their leathery skin and pear shape. The Hass avocado has a heavier, darker skin which turns almost black as it ripens. Plan ahead when buying avocados so they are ready when you are!
* To test if an avocado is ripe, hold it in the palm of your hands and squeeze gently. It should yield to gentle pressure like a peach.
* For thick-skinned avocados, stick a toothpick into the stem end. If toothpick slides in easily, the avocado is ready to eat. Once ripe, avocados can be stored in the fridge about a week.
* To speed up ripening of an avocado, place it in a brown paper bag with an apple or banana; leave at room temperature until ripe.
* A quick method to soften (but not ripen) an avocado is to microwave it on **HIGH for 1 minute.**
* Did you know that 1 tbsp. mashed avocado contains only 19 calories? Half an avocado contains twice the potassium of a medium banana, is high in unsaturated fat and low in sodium.
* Avocado purée makes an excellent facial!

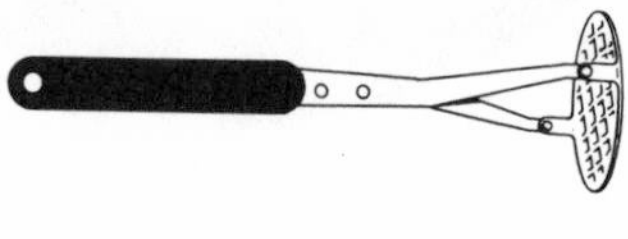

SMOKED SALMON MOUSSE

Since smoked salmon is so expensive, this marvelous mousse is a wonderful way to stretch a small amount to feed a large group!

1 envelope unflavored gelatin*
½ c. cold water
10 oz. pkg. frozen spinach
1 c. whipping cream (35%)
½ lb. cream cheese
½ c. sour cream
¼ c. fresh dill
½ lb. smoked salmon (lox)
2 tbsp. lemon juice
½ tsp. pepper
1 tsp. paprika

1. Sprinkle gelatin over cold water in a Pyrex™ measuring cup. Let stand 5 minutes to soften. **MW uncovered on HIGH for 1 minute,** until clear. Stir to dissolve gelatin. Let cool.

2. Pierce top of package of spinach 3 or 4 times. Place package on a plate and **MW on HIGH for 5 minutes.** Cool. Squeeze very dry.

3. Whip cream until soft peaks form. Refrigerate.

4. MW cream cheese uncovered on MEDIUM (50%) for 30 seconds, until softened.

5. Steel Knife: Process cream cheese with sour cream until blended. Add dill and cut-up smoked salmon; process with several quick on/off turns, until lox is coarsely chopped. Add lemon juice, paprika, pepper and dissolved gelatin. Process for a few seconds to mix. Blend in whipped cream with quick on/off turns.

6. Pour slightly less than half of mixture into a lightly greased 6 cup ring mold or loaf pan* and spread evenly. Pour most of remaining mixture into the bowl you used to whip the cream; leave about 1 cup in the processor bowl. Add spinach to processor bowl and blend well. Pour spinach mixture into mold. Top with remaining salmon mixture. Cover with plastic wrap and refrigerate until set, about 3 hours, or overnight.

7. To unmold, loosen edges with a knife, dip mold ¾ of the way into very hot water, count to 5 and invert onto a lettuce-lined serving plate. (It may be necessary to jiggle the pan slightly to allow air to get under the mousse so it will release.)

8. Garnish with lemon and cucumber slices, pimento and olives. You can also roll narrow strips of lox to make "roses". Use fresh dill sprigs as the leaves for the lox roses. Serve with crackers and thinly sliced pumpernickel bread.

Yield: 12 to 16 servings. Mousse will keep 3 to 4 days in the fridge or 2 weeks in the freezer. Texture is smoother if not frozen.

* If you observe the Jewish dietary laws, use pareve unflavored gelatin. See Emergency Substitutions (p. 40).
* A fish-shaped mold also makes an elegant presentation.

SALMON MOUSSE

1 envelope unflavored gelatin*
½ c. cold water
¾ c. whipping cream
½ c. Mayonnaise (p. 88)
4 green onions, minced
¼ c. fresh dill, minced or 1 tbsp. dried dill weed
2 - 7 ¾ oz. cans salmon, drained & flaked
1 tbsp. lemon juice
6 drops Tabasco sauce
¼ tsp. paprika
¾ tsp. salt
dash pepper

1. Sprinkle gelatin over cold water in a Pyrex™ measuring cup. Let stand 5 minutes to soften. **MW uncovered on HIGH for 1 minute,** until clear. Stir to dissolve gelatin. Let cool.

2. Whip cream until soft peaks form. Refrigerate.

3. Combine mayonnaise with green onions and dill. Mix in gelatin. Add remaining ingredients and mix just until blended. (Can be done in the food processor.) Pour into a lightly greased 6 cup mold. Cover and refrigerate until set, about 4 hours.

4. To unmold, loosen edges with a knife, dip mold ¾ of the way into very hot water, count to 5 and invert onto a lettuce-lined serving plate. (It may be necessary to jiggle the pan slightly to allow air to get under the mousse so it will release.)

5. Garnish with lemon and cucumber slices, pimento and olives. Serve with crackers and thinly sliced pumpernickel bread.

Yield: 12 to 16 servings. Mousse will keep 3 to 4 days in the fridge or 2 weeks in the freezer. Texture is smoother if not frozen.

* If you observe the Jewish dietary laws, use pareve unflavored gelatin. See Emergency Substitutions (p. 40).
* ½ cup drained capers can be added to the mousse, if desired.
* Substitute 1 ½ to 2 cups fresh cooked salmon or halibut or two 7 oz. cans drained flaked tuna for the canned salmon.
* When I am too lazy to unmold the mousse, I pour mixture into a large glass fish-shaped plate and garnish as directed above once it has set.

SOUPS, SAUCES & BEVERAGES

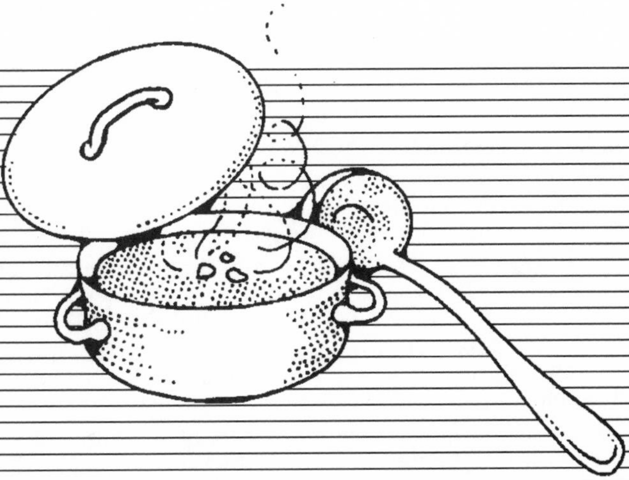

MICRO-WAYS WITH SOUPS, SAUCES & BEVERAGES

- **Since microwaved soups and sauces** don't stick to the pot, clean-ups are ever so easy!
- **To convert** your favorite soup, sauce and gravy recipes, remember there will be less evaporation of liquid. You may need to reduce the amount of liquid slightly.
- **Soups are cooked covered.** Either choose a container which has its own cover, or use plastic wrap (e.g. Saran Wrap).
- **If using plastic wrap** to cover soup, remember to turn back one corner about ½″ to vent.
- **An easy way to stir soups** is to use a wooden chopstick or the handle of a wooden spoon. Just insert through the vented opening in the plastic wrap and stir. This avoids the problem of trying to put the plastic wrap back in place again!
- **Use a large cooking container** to prevent boil-overs. An 8 cup glass measuring cup (known as a 2 quart batter bowl) is ideal for many of the soups in this book. It has a handle for easier handling. You may also use the glass bowl from your electric mixer or a 3 or 5 quart Corning Ware™ casserole. There are also deep casseroles made from microsafe plastic called simmer pots.
- **If you have a soup tureen** which is microsafe, it is great to use as both a cooking and serving casserole.
- **Place a microsafe pie plate** under the cooking container to catch boil-overs and eliminate messy clean-ups.
- **Soups are started on HIGH**, then are simmered either on **MEDIUM (50%) or DEFROST (30%)** once they start to boil. Using lower power levels prevents soups from boiling over and develops flavor.
- **Quick soups based on vegetables** can be cooked completely on **HIGH** power. Cook until veggies are tender and flavors are blended, about **25 to 30 minutes.**
- **If soup seems too thin**, either purée part of the vegetables or add some instant mashed potatoes for a quick thickener.
- **I use my food processor** to chop, slice or grate vegetables quickly, and to purée soups. Without a processor, preparation just takes a little longer. Use a sharp knife to chop and a food mill or strainer for purées.
- **Leftover cooked veggies**, rice or noodles make tasty additions to soups.
- **Many of my soup recipes** call for instant chicken soup mix. For those who observe the Jewish dietary laws, there are Kosher powdered soup mixes which are pareve (i.e. containing no meat or dairy products) and can be used in recipes which also include milk, cream or butter.
- **Packaged dry soup mixes** (6 oz. size) such as bean & barley or split pea soup will take nearly the same amount of time to cook in the microwave as cooking conventionally, but they never stick or scorch! Reduce cooking time by 25% and adjust cooking time after taste-testing.
- **Add your own chopped vegetables** such as carrots, celery and onions to packaged soup mixes for improved flavor.

- **Save the bones** when the recipe calls for boneless chicken breasts and freeze them; use to make a tasty soup.
- **Pour boiling water over beef or chicken** before combining with remaining soup ingredients. This helps eliminate the scum that usually forms on meat-based soups.
- **Beef takes about 2 hours to tenderize** in microwaved soups, plus a standing time of 20 to 30 minutes.
- **Use pot holders** when removing soup from the microwave as the cooking container will get very hot.
- **Allow 5 to 10 minutes standing time** for flavors to blend.
- **Since soups stay piping hot** for at least ½ hour if they are tightly covered after cooking, use this time to prepare the rest of your meal.
- **Be careful not to burn yourself** with the steam build-up when uncovering soup. Lift covering away from you.
- **Soups freeze very well.** Leave 1″ at the top of the container to allow for expansion during freezing.
- **Large batches of soup** can be cooked conventionally and then divided into family-size batches. Freeze until needed; then defrost and reheat in the microwave.
- **Ideal freezing containers** are microsafe so that you can thaw and heat soup in the same container you used for freezing.
- **Never reheat foods in disposable plastic containers** (e.g. margarine, ice cream or salad containers from the deli). When heated, these containers may release toxic plastic by-products into your food.
- **If your freezing container** is not microsafe, loosen contents by placing container under hot water. Transfer to a microsafe bowl.
- **Defrost soup on HIGH power** until partially thawed. Cover if desired. When partly thawed, break it apart with the tines of a fork. Stir often.
- **One quart (4 cups) of soup will defrost** and be hot enough to eat in **15 minutes on HIGH.**
- **Stir soups and beverages** before and during reheating to prevent them from erupting and for even heating. Outer edges heat more quickly than the center.
- **One serving** (8 to 10 oz.) of refrigerated soup (or any other liquid) **takes 2 to 3 minutes to reheat on HIGH.** If you wish, cover loosely with wax paper. (I usually don't bother.)
- **If you have a temperature probe**, set it at 160 to 170°F for reheating soups and beverages.
- **Bowls may get very hot** when reheating because they can absorb heat from the soup or sauce. Place bowl on a serving plate before reheating for ease in removing from the microwave. Soup can also be reheated in mugs.
- **Sauces are cooked uncovered** so they will thicken.
- **Use a wooden spoon or chopstick** for stirring sauces and gravies. You can leave them right in the sauce in the microwave; the wood won't get hot!
- **Milk-based sauces and beverages** can boil over, so watch carefully. Stir at least once for even heating.
- **Beverages can be heated and served** directly from a microsafe pitcher or mug. Don't forget that the container can get hot from heat transfer, so although glass is transparent to microwave energy, it must be heatproof to prevent breakage.

SOUPS

CONDENSED CANNED SOUPS

Combine a 10 oz. can of soup with 1 can of water or milk in a 4 cup Pyrex™ measure. **MW uncovered on HIGH for 5 to 6 minutes,** until piping hot, stirring once or twice.

Yield: 2 servings.

DRY SOUP MIXES

CHICKEN NOODLE, ONION SOUP, ETC.

Using an 8 cup Pyrex™ measure, combine 1 envelope (4 serving size) of soup mix with the amount of hot water called for on the package. Cover with plastic wrap, turning back one corner slightly to vent. **MW on HIGH for 5 to 8 minutes,** or until boiling. Time will depend on quantity of water used. **Reduce power to MEDIUM (50%) and simmer 6 to 7 minutes longer**, until fully rehydrated, stirring once.

Yield: 3 to 4 servings.

* For 1 serving, bring 1 cup water to boiling (**about 2½ minutes on HIGH**). Add 1 tsp. instant soup mix or the contents of a single serving size package and mix well. Let stand for 2 to 3 minutes.

BEAN & BARLEY, MINESTRONE, SPLIT PEA SOUP MIX, ETC.

Packaged dry soup mixes (6 oz. size) such as bean & barley, minestrone or split pea soup take nearly the same amount of time to cook in the microwave as conventionally, **about 1½ to 2 hours**. However, they don't stick or burn. Reduce cooking time called for on package by 25% and add more time as needed after taste-testing. Soup thickens during standing time.

For more flavor, add 1 chopped onion, 2 stalks chopped celery, 2 chopped carrots and 1 tsp. dried dill or a bay leaf to soup before cooking. Increase water to 8 cups. Using hot water speeds up time. Cook covered in a 3 quart microsafe bowl. One large diced potato or ⅓ cup of uncooked long-grain rice or pearl barley can also be added to ingredients at the beginning of cooking time for a heartier version.

Yield: 6 to 8 servings.

CHICKEN SOUP

I love to cook my chicken soup in the microwave! Although not much time is saved, there are many advantages. All the ingredients are added at once, skimming is not necessary and there is almost no evaporation. The chicken and vegetables never fall apart — boiled chicken never tasted so good! My grandmother would have been impressed!

3 ½ lb. chicken, cut up
boiling water
4 or 5 large carrots, peeled
2 or 3 stalks celery
1 large onion
4 sprigs dill
1 tbsp. salt
¼ tsp. pepper
7 to 8 c. hot tap water

1. Pour boiling water over chicken. Trim off excess fat. Place in a 5 quart Corning Ware™ casserole or microsafe bowl. Cut carrots and celery in chunks. Add to chicken along with remaining ingredients and stir well. Water should come no higher than 1½″ from the top of the casserole to prevent boil-overs.

2. Cover and MW on HIGH for 30 to 35 minutes, or until soup is boiling. Stir. Simmer on **50% (MEDIUM) for 25 to 30 minutes.**

3. Let stand covered for 15 to 20 minutes. Strain soup and serve chicken and vegetables separately. Serve soup with noodles, rice, kasha or Matzo Balls (p. 369). Enjoy!

Yield: 8 servings. Freezes well.

* Very little scum forms on top of the soup and it will disappear as it cooks.
* Other vegetables can be added, if desired. (e.g. parsnip, turnip, parsley, etc.)
* If you refrigerate the soup, the fat will rise to the surface and congeal. Leave fat on as a protective cover and use the soup from underneath. Soup will keep about 1 week in the fridge.
* The fat from the chicken soup gives a wonderful flavor to mashed potatoes! Use it like you use schmaltz (rendered chicken fat). It also makes the best fried onions. (Throw it out if you are on a diet or are watching your cholesterol!)

EASY CHICKEN DUMPLING SOUP

See recipe on p. 370.

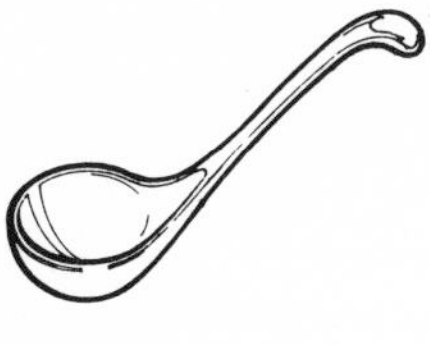

HOT & SOUR SOUP

- 4 or 5 dried Chinese mushrooms*
- 1 c. water
- ½ c. canned bamboo shoots, drained & rinsed with cold water*
- 1 single chicken breast
- ½ lb. tofu (bean curd)*
- 4 tbsp. soya sauce
- 4 tbsp. white vinegar
- ½ tsp. salt (to taste)
- ½ tsp. pepper
- 2 tsp. sugar (to taste)
- 4 c. home-made chicken broth (canned may be used)*
- 4 tbsp. cornstarch dissolved in 4 tbsp. cold water
- 2 eggs, lightly beaten
- 2 tsp. Oriental sesame oil
- ¼ tsp. chili oil (to taste)
- 2 green onions, sliced

1. Rinse mushrooms. Combine with water in a 2 quart microsafe bowl. **MW uncovered on HIGH for 2 minutes**, until steaming hot. Let soak for 15 minutes. Remove mushrooms from bowl, reserving soaking liquid. Cut off tough stems. Shred mushrooms.

2. While mushrooms are soaking, cut drained bamboo shoots and chicken into shreds. Place in a bowl; add shredded mushrooms. Shred tofu; place in another bowl. Combine soya sauce, vinegar, salt, pepper and sugar in another bowl.

3. Add chicken stock to reserved soaking liquid. **MW uncovered on HIGH for 10 minutes**, or until boiling. Add mushrooms, bamboo shoots and chicken. **MW uncovered on HIGH for 5 minutes**, until chicken turns white. Meanwhile, prepare remaining ingredients and line up ready to add to soup.

4. Add tofu to soup; stir in soya sauce mixture. **MW on HIGH for 3 minutes**, until simmering. Slowly stir in cornstarch mixture; **MW on HIGH 3 minutes longer**, or until thickened, stirring once.

5. Remove soup from microwave. Pour in beaten eggs in a thin stream, stirring gently to break into shreds. Stir in sesame and chili oils. Taste; if you wish, add more seasonings. Garnish with green onions.

Yield: 6 servings. If reheating soup, do not boil.

* Chinese Mushrooms are available in Oriental grocery stores. Store in a tightly closed dry jar. Your hands must be dry when removing mushrooms from jar or mushrooms will spoil.
* 4 Tiger Lily Buds and 4 Tree Ears (Cloud Ears or black fungus) may be added to soup. Soak in warm water for 20 to 30 minutes first. Drain well and shred. Discard soaking liquid.
* Leftover bamboo shoots will keep for a month in the fridge once they are drained and rinsed. Cover with cold water; change water daily.
* Chinese tofu (bean curd) is preferable to Japanese tofu as it is firmer and shreds better. Store leftovers in refrigerator covered with water; change water daily. Drain before using.
* If you do not have home-made broth, substitute two 10 oz. cans condensed chicken broth plus 1 ½ cups water.

CHINESE CHICKEN & CORN SOUP

Whenever I go to a Chinese restaurant, this is my first choice when ordering soup. This recipe is a microwave version of one taught by my friend Arlene Stein.

2 - 14 oz. cans cream style corn
4 c. home-made chicken broth (canned may be used)
2 tbsp. cornstarch dissolved in 2 tbsp. cold water
1 tbsp. soya sauce
½ tsp. sugar
2 eggs, lightly beaten
½ - ¾ tsp. Oriental sesame oil
¼ tsp. Oriental chili oil
salt & pepper, to taste
1 green onion, choppped

1. Combine corn with chicken broth in a 2 quart microsafe bowl. **MW uncovered on HIGH for 15 minutes**, until boiling, stirring at half time. Stir in cornstarch mixture, soya sauce and sugar. Mix well. **MW uncovered on HIGH 3 minutes longer**, until thickened, stirring once.

2. Remove soup from microwave. Pour in beaten eggs in a thin stream, stirring gently to break into shreds. Stir in sesame and chili oil to taste. Taste; season with salt and pepper. Garnish with green onions.

Yield: 6 servings. Do not freeze.

CONSOMMÉ

1 lb. stewing beef or veal
boiling water
8 c. hot water
2 tsp. salt
½ tsp. pepper
2 onions
3 carrots, cut in chunks
2 stalks celery, cut in chunks
¼ c. fresh parsley

1. Cut meat in ½″ pieces. Pour boiling water over meat; drain well. Place in a 5 quart Corning Ware™ casserole or large microsafe bowl with remaining ingredients.

2. Cover with casserole lid or vented plastic wrap. **MW covered on HIGH about 25 to 30 minutes**, until boiling. **Reduce power to MEDIUM (50%) and simmer 1½ hours**, or until meat is tender. Let stand covered for 20 to 30 minutes. Strain soup through cheesecloth. Serve clear soup with rice or noodles.

Yield: 8 servings. Freezes well.

* Leftover cooked vegetables may be added to soup. If they are puréed first, you will have a thick soup.

QUICK SOAKING OF DRIED PEAS, BEANS & LENTILS

No need to soak overnight when you use this method! Although some cookbooks tell you that lentils and split peas do not require soaking, all legumes will be tastier and much easier to digest if they are presoaked before cooking. There will be no appreciable time saved in cooking peas, beans and lentils in the microwave, but you will also have no scorching or sticking to the pot. The choice is up to you.

1. Rinse beans, peas or lentils under cold running water in a colander, discarding any shriveled or discolored ones. Combine with water in a large microsafe bowl, cover with vented plastic wrap and **MW on HIGH** until boiling:

1 c. dried legumes + 3 c. water	**7 to 8 minutes**
2 c. dried legumes + 6 c. water	**12 to 15 minutes**

2. **Reduce power to MEDIUM (50%) and simmer for 2 minutes.** Let stand covered for 1 hour.

3. Discard any beans that are floating. Cut through one bean with a sharp knife. The interior should be the same color and texture throughout. Otherwise, soak a few minutes longer. Drain and rinse well.

4. Cook in fresh water according to your favorite recipe. (If you use the soaking water to cook them, you may suffer from flatulence!)

LENTIL SOUP

This is a variation of a recipe from my friend Desirée, who learnt it from her Egyptian grandmother. Add 1 cup cooked pasta or rice to the cooked soup, if you wish. My son Doug likes to add a little Parmesan cheese.

1 c. lentils
4 cloves garlic, minced
1 large onion, chopped
2 tbsp. olive or corn oil
1/4 c. fresh parsley, minced
1 stalk celery, chopped
28 oz. can tomatoes
1 bay leaf
4 c. water
2 tsp. salt
1/2 tsp. pepper
1 tsp. dried basil (or 1 tbsp. fresh, minced)
juice of 1/2 lemon

1. Presoak lentils for 1 hour as directed above. Drain and rinse well; discard soaking liquid.

2. Combine garlic, onion and oil in a 4 or 5 quart microsafe casserole or bowl. **MW uncovered on HIGH for 4 minutes**, until tender. Add remaining ingredients except lemon juice; mix well. Cover with casserole lid or vented plastic wrap.

3. **MW covered on HIGH for 1 1/2 hours**, until lentils are tender; stir once or twice during cooking. If soup becomes too thick, add some boiling water. If soup is boiling too much, reduce power to **MEDIUM (50%)**.

4. **MW lemon on HIGH for 15 seconds.** Squeeze lemon juice into soup. Cover and let stand at least 10 minutes for flavors to blend. Adjust seasonings to taste. (Soup tastes better the longer it stands; it's even better the next day.)

Yield: 8 hearty servings. Freezes well.

VEGETABLE BARLEY SOUP

This soup takes over 3 hours to cook conventionally. No skimming is required in the microwave! Use your food processor to make quick work of preparing the vegetables.

1 ½ lb. flanken (short ribs), stewing beef or veal
boiling water
¼ c. fresh parsley, minced
2 onions, chopped
1 potato, chopped
3 carrots, sliced
3 stalks celery, sliced
6 c. hot water
28 oz. can tomatoes
1 tbsp. salt
½ tsp. pepper
½ tsp. thyme
½ c. pearl barley

1. If using short ribs, cut in pieces. If using stewing meat, cut in ½″ pieces. Trim excess fat from meat. Pour boiling water over meat; drain well. Place meat in a 5 quart Corning Ware™ casserole or large microsafe bowl.

2. Add all ingredients except barley to meat. Break up tomatoes with a spoon. Cover with casserole lid or vented plastic wrap. **MW on HIGH until boiling, about 30 to 35 minutes.** Add barley.

3. **Reduce power to 50% (MEDIUM) and simmer 1 ½ hours longer**, until meat and barley are fairly tender. Stir once or twice during cooking. Let stand covered for ½ hour. (Meat will become more tender as it stands.) Adjust seasonings if necessary. Flavor is even better the next day.

Yield: 8 to 10 servings. Freezes well.

MUSHROOM BARLEY SOUP

Follow recipe for Vegetable Barley Soup (above), but add 2 cups sliced mushrooms along with the barley. Canned tomatoes can be omitted, but increase hot water to 8 cups.

EASY VEGETABLE SOUP

I teach this recipe in my classes and my students can't wait to "mike it" at home. One of my students didn't have any fresh dill, so he used ¼ cup of dried dill! The soup got the nickname of "Greg's Green Soup."

1 medium onion
3 tbsp. butter or margarine
¼ c. fresh dill (or 1 tsp. dried dill weed)
2 stalks celery, with leaves
2 carrots, peeled & trimmed
2 medium potatoes, peeled
1 zucchini, ends trimmed
4 c. water
4 tsp. instant chicken soup mix (pareve)
1 tsp. salt
pinch of pepper and basil

1. Using the **Steel Knife** of the food processor, coarsely chop onion. Combine with butter in a 2 or 3 quart microsafe bowl. **MW uncovered on HIGH for 3 minutes**, until tender.

2. Process dill with celery leaves until minced, about 10 seconds. Cut remaining vegetables in large chunks. Process in 2 batches, using on/off turns, until coarsely chopped. Add to onions along with remaining ingredients. Cover bowl with vented plastic wrap.

3. **MW on HIGH for 25 minutes**, or until vegetables are tender. Let stand covered for 5 minutes. Correct seasonings if necessary. If too thick, thin with a little broth, water or milk.

Yield: 6 to 8 servings. May be frozen.

* For a different flavor, omit zucchini and add 1 cup of any frozen vegetable (e.g. broccoli, cauliflower, green beans, peas or corn) during the last 5 minutes of cooking.
* If you add frozen vegetables, their cooking time will be brief since they only require thawing and heating. Remember to stir once or twice to break them up.
* You could also add any leftover cooked vegetables to your soup during the last 4 to 5 minutes of cooking.
* For a thicker soup, purée about ⅓ of the vegetable mixture on the **Steel Knife** of the processor. Stir purée back into soup. For extra richness and flavor, add 1 tbsp. butter and 1 cup milk to the finished soup.
* For a tomato-flavored soup, reduce water to 3 cups and add a 19 oz. can of tomatoes. Use a 3 quart microsafe casserole. If desired, substitute basil for dill.

GARDEN NOODLE SOUP

1 onion, quartered
2 tbsp. butter or margarine
¼ c. parsley, loosely packed
2 medium potatoes
1 large carrot
4 or 5 broccoli stems
½ zucchini
1 stalk celery
5 c. water
5 tsp. instant chicken soup mix (pareve)
1 tsp. salt
freshly ground pepper
¼ tsp. basil
½ c. fine noodles
1 tbsp. butter or margarine
½ c. milk or cream, optional

1. Using the **Steel Knife** of the food processor, coarsely chop onion. Combine with 2 tbsp. butter in a 3 quart microsafe bowl. **MW uncovered on HIGH for 3 minutes**, until tender.

2. Mince parsley. Peel remaining vegetables except zucchini. Cut potatoes into chunks. Slice remaining vegetables. Add all ingredients except noodles, 1 tbsp. butter and milk to onions. Cover with vented plastic wrap. **MW on HIGH for 15 minutes**, or until boiling. Add noodles carefully through the steam vent and stir with a chopstick.

3. **MW on MEDIUM (50%) 12 to 15 minutes longer**, until noodles and vegetables are tender, stirring once. Let stand covered for 5 minutes. Stir in additional butter and milk; adjust seasonings if necessary.

Yield: 6 to 8 servings. May be frozen.

CABBAGE SOUP

2 lb. short ribs (flanken) or stewing veal
boiling water
1 large onion, chopped
4 c. grated cabbage
28 oz. can tomatoes
4 tbsp. tomato paste*
½ c. brown sugar, lightly packed*
2 tbsp. lemon juice
2 tsp. salt
½ tsp. pepper
6 c. hot water

1. Cut meat into pieces. Trim excess fat from meat. Pour boiling water over meat; drain well. Place meat in a 5 quart Corning Ware™ casserole or large microsafe bowl. Add remaining ingredients. Cover with casserole lid or vented plastic wrap. **MW on HIGH for 30 to 35 minutes, until boiling.**

2. **Reduce power to MEDIUM (50%) and simmer 1 ½ hours longer**, until meat is fairly tender. Stir once or twice during cooking. Let stand covered for ½ hour. (Meat will become more tender as it stands.)

Yield: 8 to 10 servings. Freezes well.

* Leftover tomato paste can be dropped in mounds from a tablespoon onto a foil-lined plate and frozen. Transfer to a covered container and store in the freezer. Use as needed.
* Artificial sweetener can be used instead of brown sugar. Add at end of cooking time to prevent it from becoming bitter.

ASPARAGUS VICHYSSOISE

During asparagus season, from April to June, use fresh asparagus for this recipe. I use the tender tips to make Asparagus Cheese Rolls (p. 56) and reserve the stems for this delicious soup.

1 lb. fresh asparagus (or
2 - 14 oz. cans asparagus, drained, reserving liquid)
2 cloves garlic, minced
1 onion or leek, chopped
2 tbsp. butter
2 medium carrots, in chunks
4 medium potatoes, in chunks
1 tsp. salt
freshly ground pepper
1 tsp. basil
¼ tsp. tarragon
4 c. hot water
1 tbsp. instant chicken soup mix (pareve)
1 c. milk or light cream
chopped parsley to garnish

1. If using fresh asparagus, break off and discard the woody base from the stems at the point where they snap off most easily. Peel stems to within 1″ from tips. Rinse well. Cut in 1″ pieces. Reserve tips as a garnish for soup. (If using canned asparagus, measure liquid and use to replace part of water called for in the recipe.)

2. Combine garlic, onion and butter in a 3 quart microsafe bowl or casserole. **MW uncovered for 3 to 4 minutes**, until tender.

3. Add remaining ingredients except milk. (If using canned asparagus, add during the last 10 minutes of cooking.) Cover with vented plastic wrap or casserole lid. **MW on HIGH for 25 minutes**, until vegetables are tender.

4. Using the **Steel Knife** of the food processor, purée soup in batches.* Add milk and correct seasonings to taste. Garnish each serving with chopped parsley or reserved cooked asparagus tips.

Yield: 6 to 8 servings. Freezes well.

* If you don't peel the asparagus, cooked soup will have to be strained through a food mill or fine wire strainer to remove the woody fibres.

* If you want to use the asparagus tips as a garnish, rinse them under cold running water and shake off excess moisture. Place with stems pointing upright in a 1 cup Pyrex™ measure. **MW covered on HIGH for 1 to 2 minutes**, until tender-crisp. Use to garnish soup or reserve for another use.

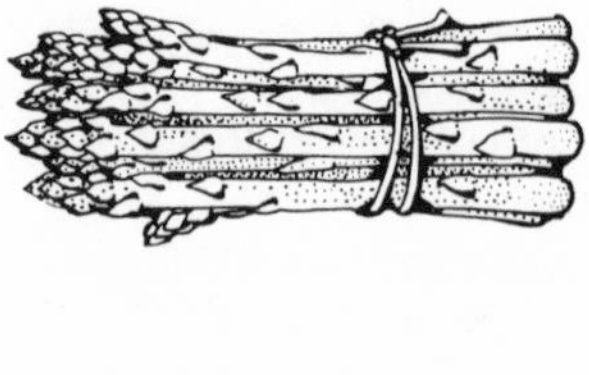

ADELE'S BEET BORSCHT

My Aunt Adele made the most wonderful beet borscht! Her recipe has been adapted for the microwave. Recipe may be halved, if desired, and cooked for 30 to 35 minutes in a 2 quart microsafe bowl.

2 lb. beets, peeled
1 onion
6 c. hot water
19 oz. can tomato juice
¾ c. sugar*
2 tbsp. lemon juice or 3 pieces of sour salt
1 ½ tsp. salt
a few sprigs of fresh dill

1. **Grater:** Grate beets and onion, using medium pressure. Combine with remaining ingredients in a 3 quart microsafe bowl or casserole. Cover with vented plastic wrap or casserole lid.

2. **MW covered on HIGH for 40 to 45 minutes**, until beets are tender. Let stand covered for 10 minutes. Adjust sugar and lemon juice to taste. Discard dill. Serve chilled with a dollop of sour cream or yogourt, or hot with a boiled potato. Keeps 2 to 3 weeks in the fridge in tightly closed jars.

Yield: 10 to 12 servings.

* Artificial sweetener may be used instead of sugar, but it should be added at the end of the cooking time.
* To peel beets without staining your hands, wear rubber gloves.

AVOCADO CUCUMBER SOUP

The low calorie cucumber balances out the higher calorie avocado!

2 medium onions, chopped
2 tbsp. margarine
2 cucumbers, peeled, seeded & diced
2 tbsp. minced parsley
2 cloves garlic, minced
4 c. chicken broth
1 tsp. salt
freshly ground pepper
¼ tsp. basil
¼ tsp. oregano
6 drops Tabasco sauce (to taste)
3 ripe avocados, peeled & pitted

1. Combine onions and margarine in a 2 quart microsafe bowl or casserole. **MW uncovered on HIGH for 3 to 4 minutes**, stirring at half time. Add cucumbers, parsley and garlic. Cover with vented plastic wrap or casserole lid. **MW on HIGH for 5 minutes**, until cucumbers are fairly soft.

2. Add chicken broth along with seasonings. Cover and **MW on HIGH for 15 minutes**. Purée avocado on the **Steel Knife** of the food processor until smooth. Strain cucumber mixture, reserving liquid in a large bowl. Add cucumber mixture to processor and process until smooth. Blend with reserved liquid. Adjust seasonings to taste.

Yield: 6 servings. Delicious hot or cold.

CREAMY CARROT SOUP

If you've never tasted Carrot Soup, try this one. You won't be disappointed!

2 cloves garlic, minced
2 medium onions, chopped
¼ c. butter or margarine
1 stalk celery, in 1″ chunks
1 lb. carrots (3 cups), cut in 1″ chunks
1 small potato, peeled & quartered
4 c. boiling water
4 tsp. instant chicken soup mix (pareve)
2 tsp. salt
¼ tsp. pepper
½ tsp. thyme
¼ tsp. dried dill weed
1 ½ c. milk or light cream
chopped parsley to garnish

1. Place garlic, onions and butter in a 3 quart microsafe bowl or casserole. **MW uncovered on HIGH for 4 to 5 minutes**, until tender.
2. Add remaining ingredients except milk and parsley. Cover with vented plastic wrap. **MW on HIGH for 25 minutes**, until vegetables are tender.
3. Remove vegetables from liquid with a slotted spoon. Process on the **Steel Knife** of the food processor until smooth and puréed, about 25 to 30 seconds. Return mixture to cooking liquid. Add milk. Serve hot, garnished with chopped parsley, if desired.

Yield: 6 servings. May be frozen.

NUKED CUKE SOUP
(HOT CUCUMBER SOUP)

This recipe was inspired by a delicious soup we tried at a Yugoslavian restaurant. Its correct name is "Oogookrah", although I doubt if that is the correct spelling! No problem — you'll find the taste is just right!

2 cloves garlic
2 tbsp. fresh dill (or ½ tsp. dried dill weed)
2 medium onions, peeled & quartered
3 tbsp. butter or margarine
3 medium cucumbers, peeled
2 potatoes, peeled
1 carrot, peeled
4 c. hot water
2 tsp. salt
¼ tsp. pepper
½ tsp. basil
1 c. milk
chopped parsley to garnish

1. **Steel Knife:** Drop garlic and fresh dill through the feed tube while machine is running. Process until minced. Add onions; process with several quick on/off turns, until coarsely chopped. Place in a 3 quart microsafe bowl or casserole along with butter.
2. **MW uncovered on HIGH for 3 to 4 minutes**, until tender, stirring once. Meanwhile, cut cucumbers in half and scrape out seeds with a spoon. Cut cucumbers, potatoes and carrot in chunks; add to onions along with hot water and seasonings. Cover with vented plastic wrap or casserole lid. **MW on HIGH for 25 to 30 minutes**, until vegetables are tender.
3. Remove vegetables from liquid with a slotted spoon. Process on the **Steel Knife** of the food processor until smooth and puréed, about 25 to 30 seconds. Return mixture to cooking liquid. Stir in milk. Serve hot, garnished with chopped parsley, if desired.

Yield: 6 servings. May be frozen.

BROCCOLI & CHEDDAR CHEESE SOUP

1 onion, chopped
4 tbsp. butter, divided
1 bunch broccoli, trimmed
3 c. hot water
2 tsp. salt
¼ tsp. pepper
¼ tsp. basil
¼ tsp. dried dill weed
2 tbsp. flour
1 c. milk
1 c. grated Cheddar cheese

1 Combine onion with 2 tbsp. of the butter in a 3 quart microsafe bowl or casserole. **MW uncovered on HIGH for 3 minutes, until onion is tender.**

2. Peel broccoli stems. Reserve 1 cup florets to garnish soup. Cut remaining broccoli in chunks. You should have about 4 cups. Add broccoli chunks, water and seasonings to onions; mix well. Cover with vented plastic wrap. **MW on HIGH for 20 to 25 minutes**, until tender, stirring halfway through cooking.

3. Place remaining 2 tbsp. butter with flour in a 4 cup Pyrex™ measure. **MW uncovered on HIGH for 45 seconds**, until melted. Gradually stir in milk. **MW on HIGH for 2 ½ to 3 minutes**, until bubbling and thickened, stirring twice during cooking. Stir cheese into sauce mixture. Set aside.

4. Process cooked broccoli with part of the cooking liquid on the **Steel Knife** of the food processor until smooth and puréed, about 25 to 30 seconds. Return puréed mixture to cooking liquid. Add sauce mixture and stir until blended. Adjust seasonings to taste.

5. Rinse reserved broccoli florets under cold water and drain well. Do not dry. **MW covered on HIGH for 1 ½ to 2 minutes**, until tender-crisp. Garnish soup.

Yield: 6 servings. Freezes well.

N.B. Reheat on MEDIUM-HIGH (70%). Do not boil or cheese will toughen.

CREAM OF BROCCOLI OR CAULIFLOWER SOUP

2 tbsp. butter
1 onion, chopped
2 carrots, peeled & trimmed
1 bunch broccoli or 1 cauliflower (about 1 ½ lb.)
4 c. hot water
4 tsp. instant chicken soup mix (pareve)
1 tsp. salt
¼ tsp. pepper
1 tbsp. fresh dill
1 ½ c. milk or light cream

1. Combine butter and onion in a 3 quart microsafe bowl or casserole. **MW uncovered on HIGH for 3 minutes**, until tender. Cut carrots and broccoli in chunks. If using cauliflower, break into florets. Add to onions along with remaining ingredients except milk.

2. Cover with vented plastic wrap or casserole lid. **MW on HIGH for 25 minutes**, or until vegetables are tender, stirring once during cooking. Remove vegetables from liquid with a slotted spoon and transfer to the food processor.

3. **Steel Knife:** Process vegetables until puréed, about 25 seconds, scraping down sides of bowl as necessary. Return purée to cooking liquid; add milk or cream and correct seasonings.

Yield: 6 servings. May be frozen.

FISH CHOWDER

If fish is frozen, thaw before adding to chowder. One lb. of fish fillets will take about 4 minutes on DEFROST (30%).

2 onions
2 stalks celery
2 carrots
2 tbsp. butter or margarine
1 tbsp. flour
2 or 3 medium potatoes
2 c. water
2 tsp. salt
¼ tsp. pepper
1 tbsp. chopped parsley
¼ tsp. thyme
1 lb. fish fillets, cut in 1″ pieces (sole, cod or haddock)
1 ¼ c. light cream or milk

1. Cut onions, celery and carrots in chunks. Process on **Steel Knife** of the food processor with several on/off turns, until coarsely chopped. Combine with butter in a 3 quart microsafe bowl or casserole. **MW uncovered on HIGH for 5 minutes**, stirring once or twice. Stir in flour.

2. **Steel Knife:** Process potatoes with on/off turns, until coarsely chopped. You should have about 2 cups. Add to cooked vegetables along with water and seasonings. Cover with vented plastic wrap or casserole lid. **MW on HIGH for 10 minutes**, until potatoes are barely tender.

3. Add fish to chowder. Cover and **MW 4 to 5 minutes longer on HIGH**, just until fish flakes. Add cream or milk; adjust seasonings to taste. If necessary, reheat briefly for **1 or 2 minutes uncovered on HIGH**. Do not boil.

Yield: 6 servings. Serve with crusty French bread and a salad as a light lunch or supper. May be frozen.

* If you cook a lot of fish dishes, save cooking liquid instead of discarding; freeze in ice cube trays. "Fish cubes" may replace part of the liquid called for in this recipe. Each cube equals about 2 tbsp. (1 oz.) liquid.
* The broth from Gefilte Fish (p. 102) is ideal to use as the cooking liquid for this Chowder.
* To reheat refrigerated soup, do not boil. Reheat uncovered on **MEDIUM-HIGH (70%), allowing about 2 to 3 minutes per cup.** Stir once or twice.

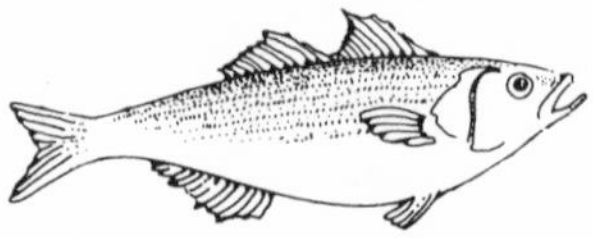

LETTUCE EAT PEA SOUP!

1 clove garlic
1 large onion, quartered
2 tbsp. butter
1 medium Romaine lettuce
2 c. frozen green peas
3 potatoes, peeled & cut in chunks
3 c. hot water
2 tsp. salt
¼ tsp. pepper
¼ tsp. basil
¼ tsp. thyme
pinch of sugar
1 ½ c. light cream (or milk plus 2 tbsp. butter)

1. **Steel Knife:** Drop garlic through feed tube while machine is running. Process until minced. Add onion and process with several quick on/off turns, until coarsely chopped. Combine in a 2 quart microsafe bowl along with butter. **MW uncovered on HIGH for 3 to 4 minutes**, until tender,

2. **Slicer:** Trim and wash lettuce. Slice lettuce, using medium pressure. You should have about 4 cups. Add to onions along with frozen peas, potatoes, hot water and seasonings. Cover with vented plastic wrap.

3. **MW on HIGH for 20 minutes**, until vegetables are cooked. Remove vegetables from liquid with a slotted spoon. Process on the **Steel Knife** until smooth and purеéd, about 25 to 30 seconds. Return mixture to cooking liquid. Stir in cream. Correct seasonings. Serve hot.

Yield: 4 servings. Freezes well.

CREAMY MUSHROOM SOUP

1 medium onion, chopped
3 tbsp. butter or margarine
1 pint mushrooms (½ lb.), sliced
¼ c. flour
1 tbsp. instant chicken soup mix (pareve)
3 c. hot water
salt & pepper, to taste
¼ tsp. thyme
freshly grated nutmeg
½ c. light cream or milk, if desired

1. Combine onion with butter in a 2 quart microsafe bowl. **MW uncovered on HIGH for 3 minutes**, until tender.

2. Add mushrooms to onions and **MW uncovered on HIGH for 4 minutes**, until mushrooms are tender, stirring at half time. Blend in flour. Gradually stir in soup mix, water and seasonings. Cover with vented plastic wrap.

3. **MW covered on HIGH for 15 minutes**, until flavors are blended. Add cream or milk, if desired. Correct seasonings to taste.

Yield: 4 servings. Freezes well.

MUSHROOM CHEDDAR CHOWDER

Prepare Creamy Mushroom Soup (above) as directed, but reduce flour to 2 tbsp. Add 1 large potato, peeled & chopped, along with the chicken broth and seasonings. At serving time, stir ½ cup grated Cheddar cheese into hot soup. Stir to melt. Garnish each serving with a spoonful of sour cream or yogourt.

FRENCH ONION SOUP

This soup makes an excellent lunch or light supper when served with Caesar Salad and garlic bread!

4 slices French bread, ¾″ thick
¼ c. butter or margarine
4 onions, sliced
1 tsp. sugar
2 tbsp. flour
1 pkg. onion soup mix (pareve) (4 serving size)
4 c. hot water
1 tsp. salt
¼ tsp. pepper
1 bay leaf
1 tsp. Worcestershire sauce
1 c. grated cheese (a combination of Mozzerella & Swiss)*
¼ c. grated Parmesan cheese

1. Place bread slices on a microsafe rack. **MW uncovered on HIGH for 3 minutes**, until dry and crisp. Watch carefully to prevent bread from burning.* Set aside.

2. Place butter in a 2 quart microsafe bowl. **MW on HIGH for 1 minute**, until melted. Add onions and sugar. Cover with vented plastic wrap. **MW on HIGH for 10 minutes**, until tender, stirring at half time. (Use a chopstick to stir the onions through the vented opening.)

3. Uncover and blend in flour. Add soup mix, water and seasonings. **Cover and MW on HIGH for 15 minutes**, until flavors are blended. (Can be prepared in advance up to this point and refrigerated until needed. Reheat soup before topping with bread and cheese.)

4. Combine cheeses; mix well. Divide soup among 4 microsafe bowls. Top each with a dried slice of bread. If necessary, trim bread to cover top of soup almost completely. Sprinkle with cheese. **MW uncovered on HIGH until cheese is melted, about 2 to 3 minutes.**

Yield: 4 servings. Soup may be frozen, but omit bread and cheese.

* When drying bread in the microwave, watch carefully and check at minimum time. I have burnt bread (actually, it turned black and started to smoke!) in the microwave by overdrying it! The general guidline is **45 to 60 seconds per slice.**
* Grated Edam cheese can be added to the combination of cheeses for a delicious flavor!
* If you like very cheesy Onion Soup, increase cheese from ¼ lb. to ½ lb. Add an extra minute to final cooking time to allow for additional cheese.
* For a crusty cheese topping, soup can be placed under a hot broiler for about 5 minutes, until bubbling and golden.

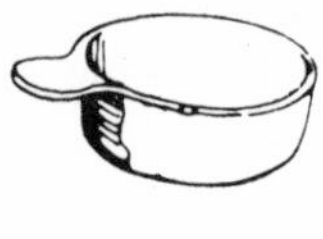

CREAM OF PUMPKIN SOUP

2 tbsp. butter
1 medium onion, chopped
2 ¼ c. water
2 c. canned or fresh pumpkin purée (p.279)
2 tsp. instant chicken soup mix (pareve)
¾ tsp. salt
freshly ground pepper
½ tsp. dill weed
1 ¾ c. milk
1 tbsp. additional butter

1. **MW butter and onion** in a 2 quart microsafe bowl uncovered on **HIGH for 3 to 4 minutes**, until tender. Add water, pumpkin, soup mix and seasonings. Cover with vented plastic wrap.

2. **MW on HIGH for 15 minutes**, stirring at half time. Uncover; stir in milk and additional butter. Adjust seasonings to taste. **MW uncovered on HIGH 2 to 3 minutes longer**, until heated through. Serve hot or cold.

Yield: 4 servings. Freezes well.

* **CREAM OF SQUASH SOUP:** Any cooked squash can be used instead of pumpkin purée in the above recipe.
* Cut a lid from the top of a well-washed pumpkin. Scoop out seedy insides with an ice cream scoop. Fill shell with boiling water and let stand for a few minutes to heat through. Empty out water. Pour in hot soup and cover with lid. Soup will keep hot for quite a while; if it cools, just heat the whole thing in the microwave for a few minutes! Miniature pumpkins are attractive for individual servings.
* Refer to Pumpkin Purée (p. 278) and Pumpkin Seeds (p. 279).

OLD-FASHIONED POTATO SOUP, NEW WAY!

With the help of the food processor and the microwave, this soup is quick as can be to make! Grandma would have been impressed!

2 onions
3 tbsp. butter
4 potatoes, peeled & quartered
3 c. hot water
1 tbsp. instant chicken soup mix (pareve)
2 tsp. salt (or to taste)
½ tsp. pepper
⅛ tsp. dried dill weed
1 c. milk

1. **Steel Knife:** Process onions with several quick on/off turns, until coarsely chopped. Combine with butter in a 3 quart microsafe bowl or casserole. **MW uncovered on HIGH for 5 minutes**, until tender.

2. **Slicer:** Slice potato chunks, using medium pressure. Add to onions along with remaining ingredients except milk. Cover with vented plastic wrap or casserole lid. **MW on HIGH for 20 minutes, or until potatoes are tender**.

3. **Steel Knife:** Purée about half the soup for 25 seconds, until smooth. Combine with remaining soup and milk; mix well. Correct seasonings to taste.

Yield: 6 servings. May be frozen.

POTATO CHEESE SOUP

Hearty, filling and so easy, using ingredients you usually have in the house. Add a big, tossed salad and fresh crusty rolls for a perfect lunch or supper. Kids like the Cheddar cheese version; adults might prefer Parmesan cheese (or use a combination of both, if you wish!)

3 tbsp. butter or margarine
3 medium onions, chopped
3 large potatoes, peeled & cut in chunks (about 3 cups)
2 carrots, peeled, trimmed & cut in chunks
¼ c. fresh dill, minced or 2 tsp. dried dill
1 ½ tsp. salt (to taste)
½ tsp. pepper
3 c. hot water
1 c. milk
1 c. grated Parmesan or 2 c. grated Cheddar cheese
croutons and fresh dill, to garnish

1. Combine butter with onions in a 3 quart microsafe bowl or casserole. **MW uncovered on HIGH for 6 to 7 minutes**, until tender, stirring at half time.

2. Add potatoes, carrots, seasonings and water. Cover with vented plastic wrap or casserole lid. **MW on HIGH for 20 to 25 minutes**, until vegetables are tender.

3. Remove vegetables from cooking liquid with a slotted spoon and transfer to the food processor. Add about ½ cup of cooking liquid. Process on the **Steel Knife** about 25 to 30 seconds, until fairly smooth. Return purée to cooking liquid.

4. Add milk and cheese and stir until cheese is melted. Adjust seasonings to taste. If necessary, **reheat uncovered on HIGH for 1 to 2 minutes** if cheese has not melted completely. Do not boil. Garnish each serving with croutons and a sprig of fresh dill.

Yield: 6 servings. Can be frozen, but add cheese after thawing and reheating.

* If soup is too thick, add a little more milk. Do not boil soup once cheese is added or it will toughen.
* Also delicious with grated Swiss cheese. Omit dill and add ⅛ tsp. grated nutmeg.

ZUCCHINI POTATO SOUP

One of my favorite soups. Youll love it too!

2 cloves garlic, minced
2 onions, chopped
2 tbsp. butter
6 medium potatoes, peeled & quartered
2 medium zucchini, cut in chunks (do not peel)
2 tsp. salt
freshly ground pepper
1 tsp. dried dill weed
½ tsp. basil
3 c. hot water
1 tbsp. instant chicken soup mix (pareve)
1 to 1½ c. milk
1 tbsp. additional butter
croutons to garnish

1. Combine garlic and onions with butter in a 3 quart microsafe bowl or casserole. **MW uncovered on HIGH for 4 to 5 minutes**, until tender.

2. Add potatoes, zucchini, seasonings, water and chicken soup mix. Cover with vented plastic wrap or casserole lid. **MW on HIGH for 20 minutes**, or until vegetables are tender.

3. Remove vegetables from liquid with a slotted spoon. Process on the **Steel Knife** of the food processor until smooth and puréed, about 25 to 30 seconds. Stir puréed vegetables back into the cooking liquid. Add milk and butter. Garnish with croutons at serving time.

Yield: 6 to 8 servings. May be frozen.

PURÉE OF RED PEPPER SOUP

Arlene Ward, a dynamic cooking teacher from New York, shared her recipe with me over dinner at a convention of the International Association of Cooking Professionals in St. Louis. The other teachers at the table added bits and pieces, and I converted the recipe for the microwave!

4 tbsp. margarine
2 cloves garlic, minced
2 leeks (white part), sliced
2 lb. red peppers, halved, seeded & cut into chunks
3 c. chicken stock
salt & pepper, to taste
½ tsp. sugar
5 to 6 drops Tabasco sauce
dash of cayenne pepper

1. Place margarine in a 2 quart microsafe bowl or casserole. **MW uncovered on HIGH for 1 minute**, until melted. Stir in garlic, leeks and peppers. **MW uncovered on HIGH for 6 to 7 minutes, until tender-crisp**, stirring at half time.

2. Add remaining ingredients; cover with vented plastic wrap or casserole lid. **MW on HIGH for 15 minutes**, until peppers are tender. Purée through a food mill or strainer to remove skins from peppers. Adjust seasonings to taste.

Yield: 4 servings. May be frozen.

* For special company, make one batch of soup with red peppers and another with yellow peppers. Cut a strip of heavy-duty foil the diameter of your soup bowl, folding it so it is strong enough to stand upright on its own. Place in bowl. Pour red pepper soup on one side of the foil and yellow pepper soup on the other side. Remove the foil before serving, of course!

BELLA'S FRESH TOMATO SOUP

This tasty soup is mmm-good when made with fresh tomatoes during the height of the gardening season, but you can use canned tomatoes with excellent results.

2 cloves garlic
2 onions, quartered
1 stalk celery, cut in chunks
2 tbsp. butter
2 lb. fresh tomatoes*
or 28 oz. can tomatoes
3 tbsp. tomato paste*
1 ½ c. water
2 tsp. instant chicken soup mix (pareve)
1 tbsp. brown sugar
1 tsp. salt
¼ tsp. pepper
1 tsp. dried basil (or 2 tbsp. minced fresh basil)
½ tsp. dried dill weed (or 1 tbsp. minced fresh dill)
¼ c. butter
¼ c. flour
2 c. milk

1. **Steel Knife:** Drop garlic through feed tube while machine is running. Process until minced. Add onions and celery; process with several on/off turns, until coarsely chopped. Combine with 2 tbsp. butter in a 3 quart microsafe bowl or casserole. **MW uncovered on HIGH for 5 minutes**, until tender, stirring once.

2. Add tomatoes, tomato paste, water, soup mix and seasonings. Mix well. Cover with vented plastic wrap or casserole lid.

3. **MW on HIGH for 25 minutes**, stirring halfway through cooking. Let stand covered for 5 minutes. Process mixture on the **Steel Knife** of the food processor until purééd, about 25 seconds. (It may be necessary to do this in two batches.)

4. Place remaining ¼ c. butter in a 4 cup Pyrex™ measure. **MW uncovered on HIGH for 45 seconds**, until melted. Stir in flour. Gradually stir in milk. **MW uncovered on HIGH for 5 to 6 minutes**, stirring 2 or 3 times, until sauce is thick and bubbling. Stir sauce into tomato mixture; mix well. Taste and correct seasonings.

Yield: 6 servings. Freezes well.

* **How to Peel & Seed Fresh Tomatoes:** Cut out the stem end using the point of a sharp knife. Plunge tomatoes into a pot of boiling water. Cook for 20 seconds. Pour out boiling water; immediately add cold water to cover tomatoes completely. Skins will slip off easily. Cut in half and squeeze gently to remove seeds. Coarsely chop tomatoes on the **Steel Knife** of the food processor, using several quick on/off turns.

* Do you hate recipes that call for a couple of tbsps. of tomato paste? Leftovers can be dropped in mounds from a tablespoon onto a foil-lined plate and frozen. Transfer to a covered container and keep in the freezer until needed. You can also purchase tomato paste in a tube in gourmet shops and squeeze out just the amount you need. Store the tube in the refrigerator.

SAUCES

BECHAMEL (WHITE SAUCE)

2 tbsp. butter or margarine
2 tbsp. flour
½ tsp. salt
⅛ tsp. pepper
1 c. milk

1. Place butter and flour in a 2 cup Pyrex™ measure. **MW on HIGH for 30 to 45 seconds,** until butter is melted. Add seasonings. Slowly blend in milk.

2. **MW uncovered on HIGH for 3 to 4 minutes**, stirring twice, until bubbly and thick.

Yield: 1 cup sauce. Can be frozen.

* **To double the recipe**, double all ingredients. Use a 4 cup Pyrex™ measure. **Butter will take about 1 minute to melt. Sauce will take 5 to 6 minutes to come to a boil and thicken.** Stir 2 or 3 times during cooking.

* Reheat on **HIGH, allowing 1 to 2 minutes per cup of sauce**. Stir every minute. Refrigerated sauce takes longer to reheat than room temperature sauce. Sauce keeps 3 days in the fridge.

SAUCE VELOUTÉ

Follow recipe for Bechamel (White Sauce), but substitute chicken stock for milk and use margarine instead of butter. Reduce salt to ¼ tsp.

CHEESE SAUCE

Prepare Bechamel (White Sauce) as directed, adding a pinch of dry mustard. Stir 1 cup grated Cheddar cheese into hot sauce and stir until melted. (Swiss or other similar cheeses can be substituted, but use nutmeg instead of dry mustard to season sauce.)

PARMESAN SAUCE

¼ c. butter
¼ c. flour
2 c. milk
dash salt & pepper
¼ tsp. nutmeg
½ c. grated Parmesan cheese

1. Place butter and flour in a 1 quart microsafe bowl. **MW uncovered on HIGH for 1 minute**, until butter is melted. Stir well. Blend in milk and seasonings.

2. **MW uncovered on HIGH for 5 to 6 minutes**, until thick and bubbling, stirring every 2 minutes. Blend in Parmesan cheese. Serve over pasta.

Yield: 2 ½ cups sauce.

PROCESSOR/MICROWAVE METHOD FOR SAUCES

1. **MW liquid uncovered on HIGH** until steaming, about **2 minutes** for each cup of liquid.

2. **Steel Knife:** Process butter or margarine with flour and seasonings until blended. (For cheese sauce, 1″ chunks of cheese should also be processed at the same time.) Pour hot liquid through feed tube while machine is running. Process until smooth and blended.

3. Remove cover and **Steel Knife**. Place processor bowl (if microsafe) in microwave. **MW on HIGH until bubbling, about 30 to 60 seconds**, stirring once. Return bowl to processor base and process a few seconds, until smooth.

* To check if your processor bowl is microsafe, test as described on p. 21.

ALFREDO SAUCE

A delicious sauce to serve over pasta!

½ c. unsalted butter
2 cloves garlic, crushed
1 c. whipping cream (35%)
½ tsp. sugar
freshly ground pepper
dash each of nutmeg & basil
1 ¼ c. grated Parmesan cheese

1. Place butter and garlic in a 4 cup Pyrex™ measure. **MW uncovered on HIGH for 2 minutes**. Stir in cream and seasonings.

2. **MW uncovered on HIGH for 2 to 3 minutes**, until bubbling. Stir in Parmesan cheese and **MW 2 to 3 minutes longer**, until thick and smooth. (Add salt only if necessary.)

Yield: 2 ½ cups.

Variation: Refer to recipe for Pasta Primavera (p. 220).

* Sauce can be refrigerated for 2 or 3 days. Delicious over fettucine, spaghetti or Cheese Tortellini (available in the freezer section of your supermarket or in gourmet stores).
* You will have enough sauce to combine with 1 lb. noodles, enough for 4 servings.
* Noodles can be cooked conventionally on the stove while you prepare the sauce in the microwave.

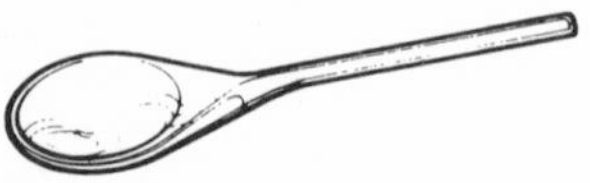

PROCESSOR HOLLANDAISE SAUCE

This gourmet sauce is so simple with the help of your processor and microwave oven! It will give a gourmet touch to broccoli, asparagus, fresh salmon or any fish of your choice.

1 lemon or lime
3 egg yolks, room temperature*
½ c. butter (1 stick)
dash of salt
¼ tsp. pepper
⅛ tsp. cayenne

1. **MW lemon or lime on HIGH for 20 seconds** to release the juice easily. Measure 2 tbsp. juice into processor bowl. To bring yolks to room temperature, **MW uncovered on HIGH for 12 to 15 seconds.**

2. Place butter in a 2 cup Pyrex™ measure. **MW uncovered on HIGH for 1 to 1 ½ minutes**, until bubbling.

3. **Steel Knife:** Process yolks with juice and seasonings for 5 seconds. Pour bubbling butter through feed tube in a thin but steady stream while machine is running. Process about 10 seconds longer.

4. If sauce is not thick enough, remove **Steel Knife** and place processor bowl, if microsafe, in microwave. (Otherwise, pour mixture into 2 cup measure.) **MW on MEDIUM (50%) 30 seconds at a time**, until thick, stirring often. Serve immediately or cover tightly to keep warm. (Can also be stored in a thermos for an hour or two.)

Yield: ¾ cup.

* It is not necessary to pierce yolks or cover them if you are bringing them to room temperature in the microwave.
* **To prepare in advance:** Pour sauce into a microsafe serving bowl. Cover and refrigerate until serving time. (Can be made up to 2 days in advance.) Stir in a few drops of hot water. **MW uncovered on MEDIUM (50%) for 1 to 1 ¼ minutes**, until warm, stirring every 30 seconds.
* If Hollandaise is overheated, the eggs will become scrambled and the sauce will lump and curdle. Try whisking in a tablespoon or two of hot water and beat until smooth.
* Leftover egg whites can be covered with vented plastic wrap and microwaved. **Three egg whites will take 2 to 2 ½ minutes on MEDIUM (50%).** Cool. Press through a sieve and use to garnish vegetables or fish.

CLARIFIED BUTTER

1. Place 1 cup butter in a 2 cup Pyrex™ measure. **MW uncovered on HIGH for 1 ½ to 2 minutes**, until melted and bubbling. Let stand until milk solids settle to the bottom. Skim foam from the top and pour clear yellow mixture into a clean container. Discard milk solids.

Yield: about ¾ cup.

CRÈME FRAÎCHE

Crème Fraîche is wonderful because it never separates when heated, whereas sour cream might. Do not use ultra-pasteurized whipping cream for this recipe (read the label on the carton) because the Crème Fraîche will not thicken properly.

⅓ c. sour cream
2 c. heavy cream (35%)

1. Blend sour cream and heavy cream in a microsafe bowl. **MW uncovered on HIGH about 1 minute**, until barely warm (about 85°F).

2. Cover and let stand at room temperature overnight, or until thickened. This may take up to 24 hours in cold weather. Stir well, cover and refrigerate. It will keep about 2 weeks in the refrigerator.

Yield: about 2 cups.

* The tart, delicious taste goes great with buttered vegetables or fish; season with your favorite herbs.
* Spoon Crème Fraîche over fresh berries; add a little brown sugar to sweeten. You can also whip it like whipping cream. Add a little granulated sugar to cut the tartness.

MAYONNAISE

1 egg
½ lemon
1 tsp. Dijon mustard
¼ tsp. salt
dash white pepper
1 c. vegetable or corn oil

1. To bring egg to room temperature quickly, crack it into a microsafe bowl and **MW uncovered on HIGH for 5 seconds. MW lemon on HIGH for 15 seconds** to release the juice easily. Measure 2 tbsp. juice.

2. Steel Knife: Place all ingredients except oil in processor bowl. Process for 5 seconds. While machine is running, add oil through the feed tube in a very slow, steady stream. You can increase the speed towards the end, once the mayonnaise begins to thicken. Total time is about 45 seconds.

Yield: 1 cup. Will keep about 2 weeks in a tightly covered container in the refrigerator. Do not freeze.

TARTAR SAUCE

1 c. Mayonnaise (above)
2 tbsp. relish or 2 gherkins
¼ tsp. dry mustard
1 tbsp. parsley
2 green onions

1. Prepare Mayonnaise as directed. Do not empty processor bowl. Add remaining ingredients and process for 8 to 10 seconds, until blended. Serve with fish. Tartar sauce will keep about 1 week in the refrigerator.

Variation: Use ½ cup mayonnaise and ½ cup yogourt or sour cream.

Yield: about 1 cup. Do not freeze.

DILL SAUCE FOR FISH

- 1 tbsp. lemon or lime juice
- 2 tbsp. fresh dill
- ½ c. Mayonnaise (p. 88)
- ½ c. sour cream
- salt & pepper

1. Combine all ingredients and blend well. Chill. Delicious over fish.

Yield: 1 cup sauce. Do not freeze.

FRESH TOMATO SAUCE

This is a wonderful recipe to make when the garden is overflowing with its harvest! The processor makes quick work of the vegetable preparation.

- 2 cloves garlic
- 2 onions
- 1 stalk celery
- 1 green pepper
- 2 tbsp. oil
- 4 lb. ripe tomatoes, peeled & seeded (see p. 84)
- 5 ½ oz. can tomato paste
- 1 tsp. basil
- 1 tsp. oregano
- 1 tbsp. sugar
- 2 tsp. salt
- ¼ tsp. pepper

1. **Steel Knife:** Drop garlic through feed tube while machine is running. Process until minced. Cut onions, celery and green pepper in chunks. Process with several quick on/off turns, until coarsely chopped. Place in a 3 quart microsafe casserole along with oil. **MW uncovered on HIGH for 5 minutes**, until tender, stirring once.

2. Peel and seed tomatoes as directed on p. 84. Process in 2 batches on the **Steel Knife** using on/off turns, until coarsely chopped. Add to casserole along with remaining ingredients. Cover casserole with wax paper. **MW covered on HIGH for 30 to 35 minutes**, until slightly thickened and vegetables are tender.

Yield: about 1 ½ quarts sauce. Sauce keeps about 10 days in the refrigerator. Freezes well.

Variation: Add 1 tbsp. Pesto (p. 90) for each cup of cooked sauce. Delicious over spaghetti, linguini, fettucine, cheese tortellini, etc.

QUICK TOMATO SAUCE

A quick and delicious sauce. Try it over breaded veal cutlets, fish, as a pizza sauce or serve it with pasta. Leftover sauce will keep up to 10 days in the refrigerator.

- 28 oz. can tomatoes
- 5 ½ oz. can tomato paste
- 2 cloves garlic, crushed
- ¼ tsp. each salt, basil, oregano & sugar
- freshly ground pepper

1. Combine all ingredients in a 2 quart microsafe bowl, breaking up tomatoes with a spoon. Cover with wax paper and **MW on HIGH for 7 to 8 minutes**, until bubbling, stirring once.

Yield: 4 cups sauce.

PESTO

Pesto is ready "Presto" with the help of your food processor! Although Pesto requires no cooking, it is an excellent addition to many microwaved dishes.

4 to 5 large cloves garlic, peeled
2 c. fresh basil leaves
½ c. fresh parsley
1 c. pignoli (pine nuts)*
1 c. grated Parmesan cheese
1 c. olive oil (approximately)
½ tsp. salt
dash pepper

1. **Steel Knife:** Drop garlic through feed tube and process until minced. Add basil, parsley, nuts and Parmesan. Process until fairly fine, about 15 seconds. Drizzle oil in through feed tube while machine is running and process until blended. Texture should be fairly creamy. If too thick, add up to ¼ cup extra oil. Add seasonings. Store in refrigerator in a glass jar.

Yield: about 2 ½ cups. Freezes well.

* For an interesting variation of this recipe, use fresh spinach or coriander (also called cilantro or Chinese parsley) instead of basil.
* If pine nuts are not available, use walnuts.
* Pesto will keep about 2 months in the refrigerator if you cover it with a thin layer of oil.
* Use a tablespoon or two of Pesto to season pasta dishes. Mama Mia!
* Add a spoonful of Pesto to your favorite tomato sauce or Ratatouille (p. 260). Add it to Alfredo Sauce (p. 86) for a delightful dish. Guaranteed to "wake up" the flavor!
* Try a spoonful of Pesto in your favorite Vinaigrette Salad Dressing. Instant gourmet!
* Brush on fish fillets and top with mayonnaise. Either microwave or broil. Mmmm!
* Add a little Pesto to make dips with zesto!
* **Great Garlic Butter:** Blend 2 tbsp. Pesto into ¼ lb. softened butter. (**MW butter uncovered for 30 to 45 seconds on DEFROST (30%) to soften.**) Use for garlic bread, or to season baked potatoes, rice, noodles or fish.

CRANBERRY SAUCE

12 oz. fresh or frozen cranberries
1 ¼ c. sugar
½ c. water or orange juice
1 tsp. grated orange rind

1. Combine all ingredients in a 3 quart microsafe casserole. Mix well; cover with wax paper. **MW on HIGH for 5 minutes.** Stir well. Cover and **MW 5 to 7 minutes longer**, until cranberries pop and sauce has thickened. Let stand covered until cool. Transfer to a serving bowl and chill for 3 to 4 hours.

Yield: about 2 cups.

SWEET'N'SASSY BBQ SAUCE

This recipe was shared with me by my neighbor Nina one day when I just didn't know what to do with the chicken in my fridge. I microwaved the sauce, then partially cooked the chicken in the microwave, allowing 5 minutes per lb. I finished cooking the chicken on the barbecue, basting it often with this tasty sauce. It was fabulous!

1 c. apple sauce
½ c. ketchup
2 c. brown sugar, lightly packed
6 tbsp. lemon juice
½ tsp. each salt, pepper, paprika & garlic powder
½ tsp. cinnamon

1. Combine all ingredients in an 8 cup Pyrex™ measure and **MW uncovered on HIGH for 5 to 6 minutes**, until boiling and thickened.

Yield: about 3 cups sauce. Use on ribs or chicken.

* Leftover sauce will keep about 1 month in the refrigerator.
* Recipe can be halved and microwaved in a 4 cup microsafe bowl. **Cooking time will be 3 to 3½ minutes on HIGH.**

SZECHUAN ORANGE SAUCE

¼ c. fresh orange juice
rind of an orange
4 cloves garlic
ginger the size of a quarter
2 green onions
¼ c. Hoisin sauce*
1 tsp. Chili Paste with Garlic*
¼ c. soya sauce
¼ c. honey
¼ to ½ tsp. Oriental sesame oil*
¼ c. orange marmalade

1. Squeeze juice from orange and set aside. Remove rind carefully with a sharp knife, being careful not to take any of the bitter white part.

2. Steel Knife: Drop garlic, ginger, green onions and orange rind through feed tube while machine is running. Process until minced, about 10 seconds. Add remaining ingredients and process for a few seconds to mix.

Yield: about 1¼ cups sauce. Delicious on chicken, meatballs, fish, spare ribs or beef.

* Chinese products are available in Oriental food markets. For a less spicy taste, reduce Chili Paste with Garlic to ½ tsp.
* For a thicker sauce, dissolve 1½ tbsp. cornstarch in ¼ cup cold water. Add cornstarch mixture to sauce and **MW uncovered on HIGH for about 3 minutes**, until thick and bubbling. Stir 2 or 3 times during cooking.

SZECHUAN PEANUT BUTTER SAUCE

This fabulous sauce is traditionally served with boiled dumplings in Szechuan restaurants. Now you can make it at home! Excellent hot or cold!

2 cloves garlic
¼ c. smooth peanut butter or tachina (sesame butter paste)
2 tsp. Oriental sesame oil
2 tbsp. light soya sauce
3 tbsp. cold water
½ to 1 tsp. chili oil (beware, its very spicy!)
2 tbsp. sugar
1 tbsp. rice wine (Mirin) or sherry

1. **Steel Knife:** Drop garlic through feed tube while machine is running. Process until minced. Scrape down sides of bowl, add remaining ingredients and process until smooth.

Yield: ¾ cup sauce.

* Sauce will keep up to 2 months in the refrigerator in a tightly closed container. If desired, double the recipe.
* Do not boil sauce or it will curdle. **To reheat sauce, allow 30 to 60 seconds per cup of sauce on HIGH**, stirring every 30 seconds.
* **To serve with noodles:** Cook 1 lb. noodles or Lo Mein until tender. Drain, rinse with cold water and drain again. Mix with 1 tbsp. sesame oil. Mix noodles with sauce. Serve hot or cold.
* **SECHUAN PEANUT BUTTER CHICKEN:** Cut 1 ½ lb. boneless, skinless chicken breasts in 1″ chunks. **MW covered with waxed paper for 6 to 7 minutes**, until cooked, stirring at half time. Drain off juices. Mix chicken with 1 tbsp. sesame oil. Add warm sauce and mix well. Serve with rice and Oriental Green Beans Vinaigrette (p. 248).

ORIENTAL SAUCE

⅓ c. bottled Teriyaki sauce
¾ c. pineapple juice
⅓ c. brown sugar or honey
2 cloves garlic, crushed
2 tbsp. cornstarch
¼ tsp. ground ginger

1. Combine all ingredients in a 2 cup Pyrex™ measure. Stir well. **MW uncovered on HIGH for 3 to 4 minutes**, stirring 2 or 3 times, until thick and bubbling. Use as a glaze for spare ribs, chicken, London Broil. Also excellent as a sauce over fish.

Yield: about 1 ¼ cups sauce.

CHINESE SWEET & SOUR SAUCE

½ c. ketchup
½ c. vinegar
¾ c. water
2 tbsp. lemon juice
1 ¼ c. granulated sugar
½ c. brown sugar, lightly packed
¼ c. cornstarch dissolved in ¼ c. cold water

1. Combine ketchup, vinegar, ¾ c. water, lemon juice and sugars in an 8 cup Pyrex™ measure and stir well. **MW uncovered on HIGH for 6 to 7 minutes**, until boiling, stirring at half time.

2. Stir cornstarch mixture into sauce. **MW on HIGH 2 minutes longer**, until bubbling and thickened.

Yield: 3 cups sauce. Sauce will keep about 1 month in the refrigerator. Delicious with fish or chicken.

CHINESE PLUM SAUCE

(DUCK SAUCE)

Follow recipe for Chinese Sweet & Sour Sauce (above), but substitute canned pumpkin purée for the ketchup.

PINEAPPLE SWEET & SOUR SAUCE

1 tbsp. lemon juice plus enough white vinegar to equal ½ cup
½ c. sugar (white or brown)
2 tbsp. light soya sauce
2 tbsp. ketchup
½ c. pineapple juice
2 tbsp. cornstarch dissolved in 2 tbsp. cold water

1. Combine all ingredients except cornstarch mixture in a 4 cup Pyrex™ measure. **MW uncovered on HIGH for 3½ to 4 minutes**, until boiling, stirring at half time.

2. Blend in cornstarch mixture. **MW 1 to 1½ minutes longer**, until bubbling and thickened, stirring once or twice. When cool, refrigerate. Sauce will keep 1 month in the refrigerator.

Yield: 2 cups sauce.

BEVERAGES

HOW TO BOIL WATER

If you know how long it takes to boil water in the microwave, you can judge heating times for most liquids. Use cold tap water, about 60°F. This is the temperature at which most people drink water.

The times indicated are to bring water to a full rolling boil on **HIGH** using a 700 watt microwave oven. Lower wattage ovens will take longer. Stir before heating to prevent liquid from erupting.

A quick guideline I teach my students is: **1 minute for each 100 ml of water (3 ½ oz., a scant half cup), or 2 ½ minutes per cup**. Most measuring cups have Metric and Imperial measurements marked on the cup.

1 cup water (250 ml)	**HIGH**	**2 ½ to 3 minutes**
2 cups water (500 ml)	**HIGH**	**5 to 6 minutes**
3 cups water (750 ml)	**HIGH**	**7 ½ to 8 ½ minutes**
4 cups water (1 litre)	**HIGH**	**9 to 10 minutes**

If you use lower power levels, the time will take longer. **One cup of water on MEDIUM (50%) takes twice as long, 5 to 6 minutes**, to come to a full rolling boil.

If you only want to heat water, not boil it, allow 2 minutes for 1 cup (8 oz.) on HIGH.

FROZEN ORANGE JUICE

1. Remove cover from one end of orange juice. Place open-end up in microwave oven.* **MW on HIGH according to time below.** Juice should still be frosty in the centre. Do not let it get warm. Transfer to a pitcher and stir in required amount of cold water according to package directions. Serve.

6 oz. can	**HIGH**	**1 minute**
12 oz. can	**HIGH**	**1 ½ - 2 minutes**

* If there is a foil wrapping on the orange juice container, transfer juice to a microsafe pitcher to defrost. Time may be slightly shorter.
* **HIGH** power is used because it is faster than the Defrost cycle. You want to melt the frozen juice, not soften it!
* Many people are amazed that they can put the container from frozen orange juice into the microwave oven because they think you can't put foil in the microwave. The general rule is: "As long as there is more food than metal, there should be no problem." The microwaves will penetrate through the open top and cardboard sides of the container. Keep metal 1″ away from walls of oven.

FRESH ORANGEADE

4 c. water
1 c. sugar
juice of 8 oranges
juice of 2 lemons

1. Combine sugar and water in an 8 cup microsafe pitcher or measuring cup. **MW uncovered on HIGH until boiling, about 8 to 10 minutes**. Stir to dissolve sugar. **MW 3 minutes longer**. Cool completely.

2. Stir juices into sugar syrup. Refrigerate. Serve over ice and garnish with thinly sliced oranges.

Yield: 6 to 8 servings.

COCOA

1. Combine 1 tsp. cocoa and 1 to 2 tsp. sugar in each mug. Fill with milk. Arrange mugs in a circle. **MW uncovered on HIGH for 2 to 2½ minutes per cup**, until hot (170°F on a probe). **Stir at half time or cocoa may boil over.**

2. If desired, put a marshmallow in each cup and **heat 20 to 30 seconds longer per cup**, or until marshmallows are puffed.

* Make sure mugs are microsafe. Do not use mugs with gold or silver trim because you will have "arcing and sparking" in your microwave!
* Use 1 tbsp. Chocolate Fudge Sauce (p. 340) instead of cocoa and sugar if you want to indulge yourself!

INSTANT COFFEE

1. Place 1 tsp. instant coffee in a mug. Add cold water and stir. **MW uncovered on HIGH for 2 minutes**, or until piping hot, stirring at half time.* Do not boil. Stir in cream (or milk) and sugar (or sweetener), if desired.

* If you heat the water first and then add the instant coffee, it will form a foamy layer on top. Also, the coffee may overflow like a volcano!
* Heating time will depend on the size of the mug. **8 oz. of water will be piping hot in 2 minutes.** Smaller mugs take less time, **larger mugs take about 2½ minutes.**

REHEATING COFFEE

Allow 1½ to 2 minutes to reheat 1 cup of coffee. Percolated coffee will taste "just made". Stir at half time.

CAPPUCINO

No need to buy an expensive Espresso machine. The microwave heats the milk and the food processor makes it foam beautifully. Be sure to use whole milk for maximum foaming.

1. Prepare espresso coffee as usual; meanwhile, measure 2 oz. milk for each serving. **MW milk uncovered on HIGH until steaming**. (Can be done in the processor bowl, if microsafe.) **One cup of milk** (enough for 4 servings) **takes about 2 minutes. Two oz. milk takes about 40 to 45 seconds.**

2. Process milk on the **Steel Knife** of the food processor for 25 to 30 seconds, until foamy. Fill cups half full with coffee, then top with foaming milk. Sprinkle with a light dusting of cinnamon or grated semi-sweet chocolate. So good!

TEA

If you have a microsafe tea pot, you can boil the water right in the pot in your microwave! Measure 4 cups water into pot. **Cover and MW on HIGH for 8 to 10 minutes**, until at a full, rolling boil. Add tea and let steep.

For one serving, boil water in a microsafe mug. **One cup of water will boil in 2 to 3 minutes on HIGH.**

BRANDY OR COGNAC

To warm brandy or cognac: Pour 2 ounces into a glass snifter. **MW uncovered on HIGH for 15 seconds.**

To ignite brandy or cognac: Warm 2 tbsp. in a 1 cup Pyrex™ measure **for 15 seconds on HIGH.** Remove from microwave, turn out lights and ignite.

FISH, EGGS & CHEESE

MICRO-WAYS WITH FISH, EGGS & CHEESE

PURCHASING & STORAGE

- **When buying whole fish**, make sure that its eyes are clear. Fish merchant should display fish which still has a skin on a layer of ice, covered with another layer of ice. For skinned fillets, there should be a layer of protective plastic between the fish and the ice. There should be drainage underneath so that the melted ice can drain away.
- **Calculate 1 lb. per serving** for uncleaned whole fish. One lb. of ready-to-eat fillets serves 2 or 3.
- **When you arrive home**, rinse fish thoroughly and pat dry with paper towels. Wrap in plastic wrap and refrigerate. Use within 24 hours for best results.
- **If fish has an odor**, soak for 20 minutes in milk before cooking.

FISHFUL THINKING — DEFROSTING

- **Fish should be completely defrosted** before cooking. Remove from package and defrost on paper towels or on a microsafe rack in a casserole. **Allow 4 to 6 minutes per lb. on DEFROST (30%)**, depending on thickness of fish. Turn fish once or twice during defrosting. Whole fish should be turned over at half time.
- **Shield thinner edges with pieces of aluminum foil** to prevent them from beginning to cook. Be sure to keep foil at least 1″ from walls of oven.
- **Check fish at minimum time** when defrosting. There should be a few ice crystals remaining.
- **Complete defrosting** by placing fish in cold water for a few minutes, just until ice crystals disappear.
- **Do not refreeze fish** once it has thawed. Cook immediately or refrigerate up to 24 hours.
- **To freeze fish**, place it in a milk carton with cold water and freeze. When defrosted, it will be just as if it were fresh.
- **Freeze fatty fish (e.g. salmon) no longer than 2 months** and lean fish (e.g. sole) no longer than 3 months.

COVER-UPS

- **Fish is usually cooked covered.** Microsafe plastic wrap, waxed paper, a damp paper towel or the casserole lid can be used.
- **Wrap fish in lettuce leaves** for excellent results. The lettuce keeps the fish moist and imparts a delicate flavor. Discard lettuce after cooking.
- **To steam fish**, little or no additional liquid is needed. Cover casserole with vented plastic wrap.
- **Salmon steaks** can be cooked between 2 layers of moistened white paper towel in a microsafe casserole. Paper towelling will absorb the white juices of coagulated protein which usually appear on the surface of the salmon.
- **Place paper towelling** under cold running water and squeeze out excess moisture. Cover fish completely with damp paper towel. This is an ideal way to "micro-poach" any fish!
- **Turbot is a very moist fish** and is best if covered with a dry microsafe paper towel during cooking to absorb excess juices.

CONVERTING FISH RECIPES

- **To convert conventional fish recipes** for the microwave, reduce liquid by ¼ to ⅓ since very little evaporation takes place in the brief time it takes to microwave fish.
- **If you are a calorie counter**, omit fat. Fish will remain moist. Avoid heavy sauces. Skim milk can replace whole milk or cream in sauces. Herbs, steamed veggies and dry white wine keep calories down and flavor high.
- **It is not necessary** to grease the casserole when cooking fish because it does not stick.
- **Pat fish fillets** or steaks with paper towels to remove excess moisture before cooking.
- **When arranging fish** in a casserole, remember, **THIN IS IN!** Place the thicker parts towards the outside edge. Fold the thinner ends under, or overlap the fish so that it is the same thickness.
- **Fillets can also be rolled** and arranged in a circle around the casserole so that they will cook evenly.
- **Use salt sparingly** to season fish.

TIMES & TIPS

- **Fish is fabulous** in the microwave. It is fast, flaky, flavorful and healthy.
- **Watch carefully — fish cooks in approximately 4 minutes per lb. on HIGH power,** almost half the time of most foods.
- **A single serving** of fish (about 6 to 8 oz.) will take about **2 ½ to 3 minutes on HIGH** to microwave. An easy guideline is to weigh it on a metric scale and estimate about **1 minute for each 100 grams (3 ½ oz.)**
- **Fish steaks should be cooked 3 minutes per lb.,** turned over and cooked **1 minute per lb. longer.** This helps cook the centre more evenly by taking advantage of the liquid which is released by the fish and collects at the bottom of the dish during cooking.
- **Sauces and vegetables** which require longer cooking should be microwaved first. Then add fish and complete cooking. Microwave cooking time will increase with the addition of sauce &/or vegetables.
- **If stuffing fish fillets** with a vegetable or crumb stuffing, make sure that the vegetables are cooked first as fish requires a very brief cooking time.
- **When cooking whole fish,** shield head and tail with aluminum foil. Make sure that eye is shielded in order to prevent it from popping!
- **When cooking several small whole fish, cook on MEDIUM (50%) for 8 minutes per lb.**
- **Breaded fish** should be cooked covered with microsafe paper towelling on a microsafe rack. Otherwise, moisture will be released from the fish into the dish, making a soggy coating. My opinion is that breaded fish tastes best when pan-fried conventionally in a combination of butter and oil.
- **Never deep-fry fish** in the microwave!
- **Combo-cooked fish:** Microwave fish for half the required time, then place it under a preheated broiler or in a preheated conventional oven to brown and crisp. The casserole dish should be microsafe and heatproof.
- **Save drained juices** from cooked fish. Use as part of the cooking liquid when making a sauce to serve over fish. Juices can also be frozen in ice cube trays for future use. Each ice cube will contain about 2 tbsp. fish liquid. **Allow 30 to 45 seconds on HIGH** to melt one ice cube.

READY OR NOT?

- **If fish doesn't flake** when pressed with a fork (or your fingertips), add 30 seconds and retest. Adding one minute could mean the difference between delight and disaster, since 1 minute in the microwave is equal to 4 minutes of cooking conventionally.
- **Allow about half the cooking time** as your standing time.
- **It is best to microwave fish just before serving.**

REHEATING & LEFTOVERS

- Use **MEDIUM-HIGH (70%)** for reheating. Since fish takes almost as long to cook as to reheat, check often as fish might overcook.
- **When reheating fish,** cover it with a layer of lettuce leaves to keep it moist and prevent it from drying out. Do not use this technique if fish has a bread-crumb topping!
- **Fish which is** covered with a sauce reheats well.
- **QUICK FISH SALAD:** Leftover fish can be mashed and mixed with a little mayonnaise, minced onion, green pepper and celery. Season with salt and pepper. Chopped hard-cooked egg can also be added.

SAY CHEESE, PLEASE!

- **Cheese dishes** adapt very well to microwave cooking, but if cooked for too long or on too high a power level, cheese can become tough and stringy.
- **Power level used** depends on the individual recipe and quantity. Larger quantities take more time, so cheese usually melts more evenly and **HIGH** power can be used. For small quantities, **MEDIUM (50%)** works better.
- **Cheese recipes that microwave well** are sauces, fondues, sandwich fillings, casseroles, desserts and cheesecakes.
- **Cheese usually melts without additional microwaving** when stirred into a hot white sauce. Grated cheese melts faster than chunks of cheese.
- **For sandwich fillings and toppings, MEDIUM (50%)** is usually used, especially for small quantities.
- **If topping a casserole with cheese,** sprinkle it on the cooked hot casserole. Heat of the casserole will help the cheese melt during standing time. Some recipes may call for returning the casserole to the microwave briefly to melt the cheese.
- **For cheese or vegetable soufflées,** the basic sauce mixture &/or vegetables can be microwaved, but once all the ingredients are combined, it must be baked conventionally to set its structure.
- **To soften cream cheese,** remove wrappings and place in a microsafe bowl. Microwave uncovered on **MEDIUM (50%)**. Cheese will hold its shape. Do not use high power as cheese could melt and/or curdle.

  ¼ lb. (4 oz.) will take 30 seconds.
  ½ to 1 lb. will take 1 to 1½ minutes.
  1½ lb. will take 1½ to 2 minutes.

- **To bring Cheddar cheese** (and other similar cheeses) to room temperature, place on a microsafe serving plate. **MW ½ lb. cheese uncovered on MEDIUM (50%) for 30 to 45 seconds,** until no longer cold to the touch.
- **A quick way to grate a small amount of cheese** is to use a potato peeler.

EGGS & EGG DISHES

- **Egg whites and egg yolks** cook at different rates. Scrambled eggs can be cooked on **HIGH** power because the white and yolk are mixed together. Other types of eggs may do better on **MEDIUM (50%),** especially if your microwave oven cooks unevenly.
- **Never cook an egg in its shell!** It could burst.
- **Always puncture egg yolk gently** with the tines of a fork or the point of a sharp knife for poached, fried, soft or "hard-cooked eggs". Cook eggs tightly covered, except for scrambled eggs or omelets, which require stirring during microwaving.
- **Scrambled eggs** should be shiny and glistening after microwaving. They will finish cooking during standing time.
- **If using a browning dish** to fry eggs, preheat it first according to manufacturer's recommendations, usually 2 minutes.
- **Leftover French toast, pancakes or waffles** can be refrigerated or frozen. **If refrigerated, allow 15 to 20 seconds each on HIGH to reheat. If frozen, allow 20 to 30 seconds. Four will take 1 to 1 ½ minutes uncovered on HIGH to thaw and heat.**
- **To reheat pancake syrup,** transfer to a microsafe serving pitcher. **MW 1 cup of syrup for 1 minute uncovered on HIGH.**
- **Crêpes:** Fillings and/or sauces for crêpes can be prepared easily in the microwave. Crepes (p. 128) must be prepared conventionally.
- **To defrost cheese blintzes or filled crêpes, allow 2 to 2 ½ minutes uncovered on DEFROST (30%) for two. Six will take about 5 minutes on DEFROST.** Let stand for 3 or 4 minutes to complete thawing. Then reheat on **MEDIUM (50%), allowing 40 to 60 seconds each.** Thawed blintzes can be fried conventionally in a skillet in melted butter until golden brown.

GEFILTE FISH

Two hours of cooking conventionally? Never again!

Fish Stock:

2 onions
2 carrots, peeled & trimmed
5 c. hot water
1 tsp. salt
1 tsp. sugar

1. Slicer: Slice onions and carrots, using medium pressure. Combine with hot water, salt and sugar in a 5 quart Corning Ware™ casserole (or the glass bowl from your electric mixer). **MW covered on HIGH for 20 minutes.** Meanwhile, prepare fish mixture.

Gefilte Fish Mixture:

2 onions, cut in chunks
1 or 2 medium carrots, peeled, trimmed and cut in chunks
2 lb. ground fish (pike, whitefish & doré*)
4 eggs
¼ c. matzo meal
¼ c. water
2 tsp. salt
1 tsp. pepper
1 tbsp. sugar (to taste)

2. Steel Knife: Process onions and carrots until finely minced, about 15 seconds. Add remaining ingredients and process until well mixed, about 1 minute. Scrape down sides of bowl as necessary.

3. Moisten your hands with cold water to facilitate shaping of fish. Shape into balls and add to fish stock. Fish should be completely covered with liquid; otherwise add additional hot water. Cover casserole.

4. Simmer on MEDIUM (50%) for 15 to 18 minutes. Let stand covered for 10 to 15 minutes. Carefully remove fish from broth and transfer to a large platter. Garnish with the cooked carrot slices. Serve hot or cold with horseradish.

Yield: 12 to 14 balls.

* Fish markets often sell a gefilte fish mixture or you can grind your own. I like a mixture of whitefish, pike and pickerel (doré). You can use other combinations, depending on what is available at your local fish market.
* If frozen, fish may become watery. Simmer thawed gefilte fish in boiling water to cover on **MEDIUM (50%) for 10 minutes.** It will taste freshly cooked.
* Leftover fish can be sliced ½″ thick, dipped in egg and seasoned bread crumbs or matzo meal, and pan-fried conventionally in hot oil on the rangetop.
* Reserve leftover cooking liquid from fish and use when making Fish Chowder (p. 78). Cooking liquid can be frozen until needed.

GEFILTE FISH RING

1 carrot, peeled
4 green pepper rings
Gefilte Fish Mixture (p. 102)
(omit Fish Stock)

1. Wrap carrot in waxed paper, leaving one end open to vent. **MW on HIGH 1 minute,** until slightly softened. Let stand 1 minute. Cut 4 round slices ¼″ thick from the large end of the carrot. Arrange carrot rounds in the bottom of a well-greased microsafe Bundt pan; arrange them like the points on a compass: North, South, East and West.

2. Place green pepper rings so that a carrot is in the centre of each ring. (If green pepper rings are very firm, **MW for 30 seconds on HIGH** to soften slightly.) Cut another piece of carrot 2 ½″ long, then slice it into 4 matchsticks. Arrange carrot sticks between pepper rings.

3. Prepare fish mixture as directed. Spread evenly in Bundt pan. Bang pan on counter so fish mixture fills in spaces between carrots and peppers. Cover with microsafe plastic wrap, turning back one corner slightly to vent.

4. **MW on HIGH for 10 to 14 minutes,** rotating pan ¼ turn at half time. Top of fish will be firm to the touch and edges will begin to pull away from the sides of the pan when done. If you insert a wooden skewer into the fish halfway between the centre and the outside edge, the skewer will come out clean.

5. Let stand covered for 15 minutes. Carefully drain any excess liquid. Loosen fish with a long, narrow spatula and cover pan with a serving plate. Invert and shake gently to unmold. Chill. Fill centre with horseradish and garnish serving plate with tomato and cucumber slices.

Yield: 12 servings. Do not freeze.

* If you don't have a microsafe Bundt pan or ring mold, use a deep 9″ round baking dish; insert a custard cup, open end up, in the centre of the dish. Moisten hands with cold water to facilitate shaping of the fish.

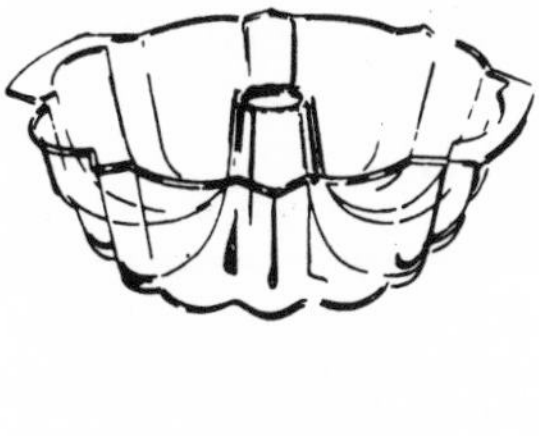

SIMPLE SOLE FOR A SINGLE SOUL

1 large sole fillet (about ⅓ — ½ lb.)
1 tsp. lemon juice
salt, pepper, basil & paprika

1. Place sole on a microsafe dinner plate. Sprinkle with lemon juice and seasonings. Moisten a paper towel by placing it under running water. Squeeze out excess moisture. Place over sole, making sure to cover fish completely.

2. MW on HIGH for 2½ minutes, rotating plate ¼ turn at half time. Let stand covered for 1 minute. Fish should flake when lightly pressed.

Yield: 1 serving. Do not freeze.

* If you are cooking for 2, purchase 1 lb. fish. Allow 4 minutes per lb. cooking time and 2 minutes per lb. standing time.
* If you have a mini oven (less than 1 cubic foot) or a 500 watt oven, fish will take about 6 minutes per lb. to cook. One serving will take about 4 minutes.
* Fish can be enhanced by serving it with melted butter, tomato sauce or toasted almonds.

SOLE AMANDINE

Sure to be a favorite!

¼ c. sliced or slivered almonds
2 tbsp. butter or margarine
1½ lb. sole fillets (or any fish fillets of your choice)
1 tbsp. lemon juice
salt & pepper
garlic powder & paprika
2 tbsp. chopped parsley

1. Place almonds and butter in a 7″ x 11″ Pyrex™ casserole. **MW uncovered on HIGH for 3 minutes,** or until golden, stirring every minute to prevent burning. Be careful, casserole will become very hot! Let stand 2 minutes. Remove almonds from plate with a slotted spoon and set aside.

2. Place fish in casserole. Turn fish over to coat both sides with melted butter remaining in casserole. Sprinkle with lemon juice, seasonings and parsley. Cover with microsafe plastic wrap, turning back one corner slightly to vent.

3. MW covered on HIGH for 6 minutes, rotating casserole ¼ turn halfway through cooking. Let stand covered for 2 or 3 minutes. Fish should flake when lightly pressed. Top with almonds. Serve with Rice Pilaf (p. 214) and buttered green beans (p. 244).

Yield: 4 servings. Do not freeze.

* Cook Rice Pilaf first; cover tightly to retain heat. It keeps hot for ½ hour.
* Cook green beans as directed. Rinse under cold water to stop cooking and keep them bright green. To reheat, add a pat of butter or margarine and **MW covered on HIGH for 2 minutes** (during the standing time for fish). Season with salt & pepper.

SOLE ITALIANO

Quick, easy and perfect if you're watching your weight! With the help of your food processor and microwave, this tasty dish can be ready to serve in 20 minutes.

2 carrots
½ green pepper
½ red pepper
4 green onions
1 medium zucchini
1 lb. sole fillets
salt, pepper, garlic powder & basil
½ c. tomato sauce
½ c. grated Mozzerella cheese
¼ c. grated Parmesan cheese

1. Coarsely chop vegetables. (This can be done in batches on the **Steel Knife** of the food processor, using quick on/off turns.) Place in an ungreased 2 quart oval casserole. Cover with vented plastic wrap. **MW on HIGH for 4 to 5 minutes,** until tender-crisp.

2. Place fish fillets over vegetables, arranging thicker portions towards the outside edge of the casserole. Sprinkle with seasonings and top with sauce. Cover with vented plastic wrap. **MW on HIGH for 5 to 6 minutes,** rotating casserole ½ turn at half time. Fish will flake if you press it lightly. Let stand covered for 2 or 3 minutes.

3. Drain excess watery liquid from casserole through the vented opening. Uncover carefully and sprinkle cheeses over fish. **MW uncovered on HIGH for 2 minutes,** until cheese is melted. Serve on a bed of spinach fettucine.

Yield: 3 to 4 servings.

* Any lean fish fillets can be substituted for the sole.
* Cook fettucine conventionally while you prepare the fish in the microwave.
* **For 6 to 8 servings:** Double all ingredients, but use only ¾ cup tomato sauce. Use a 3 quart oval microsafe casserole. In Step 1, cover and **MW vegetables on HIGH 5 to 6 minutes,** until tender-crisp. In Step 2, **MW fish and vegetables covered on HIGH for 9 to 11 minutes.** In Step 3, **MW uncovered on HIGH for 2½ to 3 minutes,** until cheese is melted.

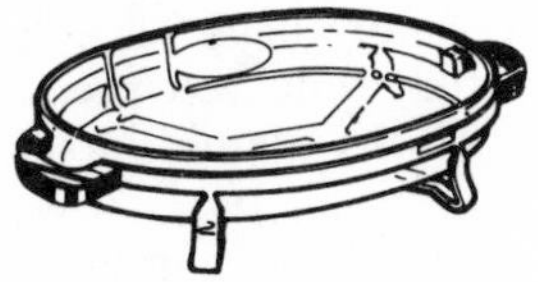

VERA'S QUICK PIZZA FISH

1 lb. sole fillets
dash pepper, garlic powder, basil & oregano
½ c. Marinara or meatless spaghetti sauce
½ c. grated Mozzerella cheese
2 tbsp. grated Parmesan cheese

1. Place fish in a single layer in an ungreased oblong casserole with the thicker pieces towards the outside edge of the dish. Sprinkle with seasonings. Top with sauce. Cover with microsafe plastic wrap, turning back one corner slightly to vent.

2. **MW covered on HIGH for 4 minutes,** until fish barely flakes when pressed with your fingertips. (Casserole should be turned ¼ turn halfway through cooking.) Let stand covered for 2 or 3 minutes.

3. Drain excess watery liquid from bottom of casserole through the vented opening. Carefully remove plastic wrap. Sprinkle cheeses over fish. **MW uncovered for 2 to 3 minutes,** until cheese is melted. Serve with buttered noodles and a salad.

Yield: 2 to 3 servings. Do not freeze.

* **For 4 servings:** Increase fish to 1 ½ lbs. Top with seasonings and sauce. **MW covered on HIGH for 6 minutes.** Let stand covered for 3 minutes. Drain excess watery liquid. Top with ¾ c. grated Mozzerella and 3 tbsp. Parmesan cheese. **MW uncovered on HIGH 2 to 3 minutes longer.**

FISH IN WINE SAUCE

1 ½ lb. fish fillets
salt, pepper & thyme
3 tbsp. white wine
2 tbsp. butter or margarine
2 tbsp. chopped parsley
1 tbsp. cornstarch
¾ c. milk
1 small tomato, peeled, seeded & chopped (optional)

1. Place fish in a single layer in an ungreased 1 ½ quart microsafe casserole, arranging the thicker pieces towards the outside of the dish. Sprinkle lightly with salt, pepper and thyme. Drizzle wine over fish. Cover with vented plastic wrap.

2. **MW covered on HIGH for 6 minutes,** rotating casserole ¼ turn halfway through cooking. Fish should barely flake when gently pressed with your fingertips. Let fish stand covered while you prepare the sauce. Drain and reserve cooking juices from fish. You should have about ¼ cup.

3. **MW butter uncovered** in a 2 cup Pyrex™ measure **on HIGH for 45 seconds,** until melted. Add cornstarch and a dash of salt & pepper. Gradually blend in milk and cooking juices from fish. **MW uncovered on HIGH for 3 to 4 minutes,** until thick and bubbling. Stir 2 or 3 times during cooking. Stir in tomato. Pour sauce over fish. Garnish with chopped parsley.

Yield: 4 servings. Do not freeze.

DEAN'S TIPSY SOLE

Dean St. Germain was responsible for introducing me to the food processor in 1974. We were both inexperienced and had a marvelous time turning apples and carrots into purée! I've come a long way since that day and have Dean to thank. She's very special and I toast our friendship with this recipe!

1 ½ lb. sole fillets
salt & pepper
2 tbsp. Triple Sec or Cointreau
2 tbsp. minced parsley
1 tsp. orange zest
grapefruit &/or mandarin orange sections, to garnish

1. Arrange fish in a single layer in a large microsafe casserole, with the thicker parts towards the outside of the dish. Overlap or fold thinner ends under. Sprinkle lightly with salt & pepper. Drizzle liqueur over fish. Sprinkle with parsley and orange zest. Cover with vented microsafe plastic wrap.

2. MW on HIGH for 6 minutes, rotating casserole ½ turn at half time. Fish should barely flake when lightly pressed with your fingertips. Let stand covered for 2 to 3 minutes. Garnish with a few grapefruit and mandarin orange sections. Serve with Snow Pea & Mandarin Salad (p. 280) and rice.

Yield: 4 servings. Do not freeze.

* Orange and grapefruit sections can be warmed slightly before serving. Place in a microsafe dish and **MW uncovered on HIGH for 20 to 30 seconds.**

ROLL YOUR SOLE

Prepare as for Sole Florentine (p. 108), but instead of spinach, spread fish fillets with any of the fillings below, or any cooked, lightly seasoned vegetables you wish. Roll up and arrange fish seam-side down in casserole. Drizzle with butter, lemon juice and paprika. Cover with vented plastic wrap; ***MW on HIGH, allowing 4 minutes per lb.*** *Let stand covered for 2 to 3 minutes.*

You can make "fish sandwiches" if you are too lazy to roll! Just place half the fish fillets in the bottom of the casserole, spread with desired filling and top with remaining fillets.

Broccoli Filling: Slash a 10 oz. pkg. frozen chopped broccoli in several places with a sharp knife. **MW on HIGH for 5 minutes.** Drain well. Sprinkle with salt, pepper & thyme.

Vegetable Filling: Prepare ¼ c. each of chopped onions or shallots, celery & green pepper. **MW uncovered in 1 tbsp. butter or margarine on HIGH for 3 to 4 minutes.** Sprinkle with salt, pepper & basil.

Zucchini Filling: Grate 1 zucchini; press out excess moisture. Mince half a small onion. **MW zucchini and onion in 1 tsp. butter on HIGH for 2 to 3 minutes,** until tender-crisp. Sprinkle with salt, pepper & dill.

Mushroom Filling: Drain a 10 oz. can of sliced mushrooms. **MW in 1 tsp. butter on HIGH for 2 minutes.** Sprinkle with salt, pepper & nutmeg.

If desired, serve with any of the starred suggestions in Create-A-Fish-Dish (p. 109).

SOLE FLORENTINE

10 oz. pkg. frozen
chopped spinach
1 ½ lb. sole fillets
(4 large fillets)
½ tsp. salt
pepper to taste
¼ tsp. basil
1 tbsp. melted butter
1 tbsp. lemon or lime juice
paprika
Hollandaise Sauce (p. 87) or
Cheese Sauce (p. 85) or
Toasted Crumb Topping
(p. 109)

1. Place package of frozen spinach on a dinner plate. Slash top of package in 2 or 3 places with a sharp knife. **MW on HIGH for 5 minutes.** A knife should pass easily through the centre of the package. Let cool 5 minutes. Drain well, squeezing spinach to remove excess liquid.

2. Spread spinach on fish fillets. Sprinkle with salt, pepper and basil. Roll up and arrange seam-side down in an ungreased 9″ round microsafe casserole (or make "fish sandwiches"; see below*). Drizzle with butter and lemon juice (omit if topping cooked fish with sauce or crumb topping). Sprinkle with paprika. Cover with vented plastic wrap.

3. **MW on HIGH for 6 minutes,** rotating the dish ¼ turn halfway through cooking time. Fish should be opaque and flake when pressed with a fork. Let stand 2 or 3 minutes before serving. Drain juices from fish. Top with desired sauce or crumb topping. Serve with rice and buttered carrots.

Yield: 4 servings.

* To melt butter, **MW on HIGH for 30 seconds.** To release juice easily from lemon, **MW on HIGH for 15 seconds.**
* **"Fish Sandwiches":** Place half of fillets in the bottom of the casserole, spread with spinach and top with remaining fillets. Arrange thicker parts of fish towards the outside edge of the casserole.
* Hollandaise or Cheese Sauce or Crumb Topping can be prepared during standing time for the fish.
* If fish has been topped with Hollandaise, it cannot be reheated because the sauce will turn to scrambled eggs! I make a delicious spread from the leftover fish, spinach and Hollandaise by processing them together using the **Steel Knife** of the food processor. Add salt & pepper to taste and serve with crackers. Everyone will want the recipe!

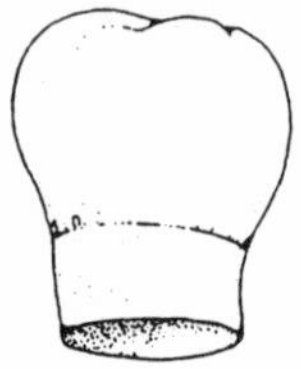

CREATE-A-FISH-DISH

1. Weigh fish fillets or steaks (whatever kind you like). Place in an ungreased casserole, with the thicker parts towards the outer edge of the dish. (You can also place fish on a layer of lightly cooked vegetables; fillets can be rolled or made into "sandwiches" as directed in the recipe for Roll Your Sole, p. 107). Sprinkle with your favorite seasonings. Cover with vented plastic wrap, damp paper towels or lettuce leaves.

2. **MW on HIGH, calculating 4 minutes per lb.**; rotate casserole ¼ turn halfway through cooking. Fish should barely flake when lightly pressed with your fingertips. Let stand covered for 2 to 3 minutes. If you used lettuce leaves to cover fish during cooking, discard them; they will be too wilted to use.

3. Serve fish with any of the suggestions below. Refer to Index for page numbers. Garnish with lemon, parsley, chives, chopped red or green peppers, etc.

*** Lemon Butter**
*** Garlic Butter**
*** Great Garlic Butter**
*** Tartar Sauce**
*** Bechamel Sauce**
*** Cheese Sauce**
*** Oriental Sauce**
*** Dill Sauce for Fish**
*** Chinese Sweet & Sour Sauce**
*** Pineapple Sweet & Sour Sauce**
*** Alfredo Sauce**
*** Fresh Tomato Sauce**
*** Quick Tomato Sauce (or bottled Tomato, Pizza or Marinara Sauce)**
*** Cucumber Yogurt Sauce**
*** Hollandaise Sauce**
*** Toasted Almonds**
*** Toasted Crumb Topping**

LEMON BUTTER: **MW 2 tbsp. butter on HIGH for 30 to 45 seconds,** until melted. Stir in 2 tbsp. lemon juice and ½ tsp. minced parsley. Serve over fish or vegetables.

GARLIC BUTTER: **MW ¼ lb. butter uncovered on DEFROST (30%) for 30 to 45 seconds to soften.** Blend in 2 cloves minced garlic and 1 tbsp. finely chopped parsley.

GREAT GARLIC BUTTER: **MW ¼ lb. butter uncovered on DEFROST (30%) for 30 to 45 seconds to soften.** Blend in 2 tbsp. Pesto (p. 90). Serve over fish, vegetables or use to make garlic bread.

TOASTED CRUMB TOPPING: Combine 1 tbsp. butter or margarine with ¼ cup seasoned bread crumbs or cracker crumbs. **MW uncovered on HIGH for 1 to 1 ½ minutes,** until toasted, stirring once or twice. Sprinkle over cooked fish, vegetables or casseroles.

TOASTED ALMONDS: Place ¼ cup sliced or slivered almonds in a 9″ Pyrex™ pie plate. (If desired, add 1 tbsp. butter, margarine or garlic butter.) **MW uncovered on HIGH for 3 to 4 minutes,** until golden, stirring once or twice during cooking to prevent burning. Be careful, plate will become very hot! Let stand uncovered for 2 or 3 minutes. Almonds will darken during standing time. Sprinkle over cooked fish or vegetables.

CREAMY STUFFED SOLE AU GRATIN

Filling must be cooked first before stuffing the fish fillets. This dish is easy to prepare and is excellent as a family meal or makes fine fare for company. Mushrooms can be replaced by finely chopped broccoli or spinach.

2 c. mushrooms, sliced
1 medium onion, chopped
3 tbsp. butter
¼ c. seasoned bread crumbs
4 tbsp. grated Parmesan cheese
1 ½ lb. fish fillets
salt, pepper & basil, to taste
½ c. sour cream or Crème Fraîche (p. 88)

1. Combine onions and mushrooms with 2 tbsp. of the butter in a microsafe bowl. **MW uncovered on HIGH until tender, about 3 to 4 minutes,** stirring once.

2. Combine 1 tbsp. butter with bread crumbs in a small microsafe bowl. **MW uncovered on HIGH for 1 minute.** Stir in 1 tbsp. Parmesan cheese.

3. Place half of fish fillets in the bottom of an ungreased 10″ ceramic quiche dish. Sprinkle with seasonings. Spread drained mushroom/onion mixture over fish. Top with remaining fillets to make "fish sandwiches". Thicker parts should be towards the outer edges of the casserole. Sprinkle once again with seasonings. Cover with vented microsafe plastic wrap. (Can be prepared in advance up to this point and refrigerated until mealtime.)

4. **MW covered on HIGH for 4 minutes.** Carefully drain excess juices through the vented opening. Remove plastic wrap.

5. Combine sour cream or Crème Fraîche with remaining 3 tbsp. Parmesan cheese; spread evenly over fish. Top with crumb mixture. **MW uncovered on HIGH for 3 to 4 minutes longer.** Fish should flake when lightly pressed. Let stand for 2 or 3 minutes. Serve with rice or mashed potatoes and a green salad.

Yield: 4 servings. Do not freeze.

FISH FILLETS WITH CUCUMBER YOGURT SAUCE

Cucumber Yogurt Sauce (p. 57)
1 ½ lb. fish fillets
salt & pepper
2 tbsp. lemon juice
paprika

1. Prepare sauce as directed and refrigerate until serving time.

2. Place fish fillets in a single layer in an ungreased microsafe casserole, with the thicker parts towards the outside of the dish. Sprinkle lightly with salt and pepper. Drizzle with lemon juice and sprinkle with paprika. Place paper towelling under cold running water. Gently squeeze out excess moisture. Cover fish completely with paper towels.

3. **MW on HIGH for 6 minutes,** or until fish barely flakes when pressed with your fingertips. Casserole should be turned ¼ turn at half time. Let stand covered for 3 minutes to complete cooking. Arrange on individual serving plates. Garnish with a dollop of Cucumber Yogurt Sauce; garnish with parsley and lemon wedges. Serve with a tossed salad and baked potatoes (the sauce also makes a wonderful topping for the salad and potatoes!)

Yield: 4 servings. Do not freeze.

FISH FILLETS WITH BROCCOLI AU GRATIN

10 oz. pkg. frozen chopped broccoli
1 ½ lb. fish fillets
1 tbsp. lemon juice
salt & pepper, to taste
2 tbsp. butter or margarine
2 tbsp. flour
1 c. milk
½ tsp. salt
freshly ground pepper
1 c. grated Norwegian, Cheddar or Gruyere cheese
paprika to garnish

1. Place unwrapped package of broccoli on a microsafe plate. Pierce top of package in several places with a sharp knife. **MW on HIGH for 5 to 6 minutes,** turning package over at half time. Let stand 2 or 3 minutes. Drain broccoli thoroughly. Place in the bottom of an ungreased 7″ x 11″ Pyrex™ casserole.

2. Pat fish dry with paper towels. Place fish over broccoli, with the thicker parts of fish towards the outer edge of the dish. Sprinkle with lemon juice and seasonings.

3. Place butter in a 2 cup Pyrex™ measure. **MW uncovered on HIGH for 30 to 45 seconds,** until melted. Stir in flour. Gradually add milk and seasonings. **MW uncovered on HIGH for 3 to 4 minutes,** stirring 2 or 3 times, until sauce is bubbly and thick. Stir cheese into sauce.

4. Pour sauce over fish and sprinkle with paprika. Cover with microsafe plastic wrap, turning back one corner slightly to vent. (May be prepared in advance up to this point and refrigerated until needed.)

5. **MW covered on HIGH 7 to 9 minutes,** rotating dish ¼ turn halfway through cooking. Fish should flake when lightly pressed. Let stand covered for 3 to 4 minutes. Serve with Stuffed Baked Potatoes (p. 270).

Yield: 4 servings. Do not freeze.

* Potatoes can be prepared first and reheated during the standing time for the fish.
* 1 lb. chopped fresh broccoli can be substituted for frozen broccoli. Place in ungreased 7″ x 11″ casserole and sprinkle with 2 tbsp. water. Cover with vented plastic wrap and **MW on HIGH for 5 to 6 minutes.** Drain well. Continue as directed above in Step 2.

ORIENTAL FISH & VEGETABLES

This recipe is very quick to prepare with the help of your processor and microwave. It almost takes longer to read it than cook it!

2 cloves garlic
1 slice ginger, the size of a dime (or ¼ tsp. powdered ginger)
1 small onion, halved
½ each red pepper & green pepper
1 stalk celery
1 c. broccoli florets
2 tbsp. peanut or corn oil
1 ½ lb. fish fillets
4 tbsp. soya sauce
1 tbsp. cornstarch
2 tsp. brown sugar
2 tsp. lemon juice
¼ c. cold water
½ tsp. sesame oil
3 c. cooked rice (p. 214)
chow mein noodles to garnish

1. **Steel Knife:** Drop garlic and fresh ginger through feed tube while machine is running. Process until minced. Do not empty bowl.

2. **Slicer:** Slice onion, peppers and celery. Combine contents of processor bowl with broccoli and oil in an 8 cup microsafe bowl. Cover with microsafe plastic wrap, turning back one corner slightly to vent. **MW on HIGH for 4 to 5 minutes,** until tender-crisp. Shake bowl at half time to mix vegetables. Let stand covered while you cook fish.

3. Arrange fish in a single layer in an ungreased oblong microsafe casserole, with the thicker parts towards the outside of the dish. Drizzle with soya sauce. Cover with vented microsafe plastic wrap. **MW covered on HIGH for 6 minutes,** rotating dish ¼ turn halfway through cooking. Fish should barely flake when lightly pressed. Let stand covered while you prepare sauce.

4. Combine cornstarch, brown sugar, lemon juice and cold water in a 1 cup Pyrex™ measure. Stir well. Add fish juices (and powdered ginger if you are using it). **MW uncovered on HIGH for 1 ½ to 2 minutes,** until bubbling and thickened, stirring once. Add sesame oil; pour sauce over cooked vegetables; mix well.

5. Spoon vegetable mixture over fish. Serve immediately on a bed of fluffy white rice. Garnish with chow mein noodles.

Yield: 4 servings.

* First cook rice. Cover casserole with a dinner plate to keep cooked rice hot. Cook vegetables. Stack covered veggies on top of rice. Cook fish. Stack on top of veggies. Your meal will stay hot while you microwave the sauce ingredients.

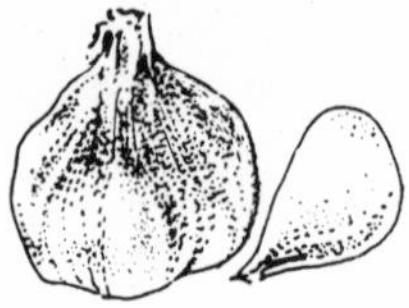

ORIENTAL FILLETS & SNOW PEAS

Snow peas cook tender-crisp in the same amount of time as the fish, so they can be cooked together. The carrots must be partially cooked before adding them to the fish since they have a longer cooking time.

1 lb. snapper or sole fillets
½ lb. snow peas
1 clove garlic, minced
1 tbsp. butter or margarine
1 c. julienned carrots
½ tsp. minced ginger
¼ tsp. pepper
2 tbsp. soya sauce
1 tbsp. cornstarch
⅔ c. cold water

1. Pat fish dry with paper towels. Place in a single layer in an ungreased microsafe casserole. Tuck thin ends under so fish is fairly uniform in thickness. Remove ends and stringy part from the seam-edge of snow peas. Rinse under cold running water; pat dry. Place on top of fish.

2. Combine garlic and butter with carrots in a 2 cup Pyrex™ measure. Cover with vented microsafe plastic wrap. **MW on HIGH for 2 to 3 minutes,** until tender-crisp. Spoon butter and carrots over fish. Sprinkle with ginger, pepper and soya sauce. Cover with vented plastic wrap.

3. **MW on HIGH for 6 minutes,** or until fish barely flakes when gently pressed with your fingertips. (Rotate casserole ¼ turn halfway through cooking.) Let stand covered while you prepare the sauce.

4. Dissolve cornstarch in water in a 2 cup Pyrex™ measure. Add cooking juices from fish and mix well. (Pour the juices into the cup through the vented opening in the plastic wrap. If sauce seems light in color, add a little more soya sauce.) **MW uncovered for 2 to 2½ minutes,** until thickened and bubbling. Stir once or twice during cooking. Pour sauce over fish and vegetables. Serve over rice or noodles.

Yield: 3 servings. Do not freeze.

* **For 4 servings: Use 1½ lb. fish fillets and increase cooking time for fish and vegetables to 8 minutes.**
* Any firm fish fillets can be used.
* If serving with noodles, cook them conventionally while you cook the fish in the microwave. If serving with rice, cook it first in the microwave, then cover it tightly. Rice will stay hot for half an hour.

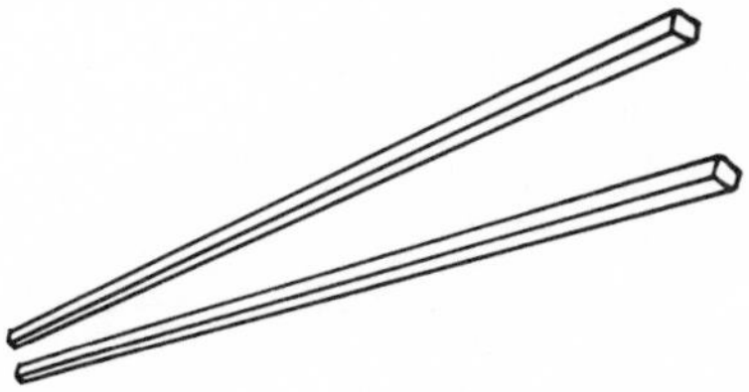

SOLE MORNAY WITH MUSHROOM STUFFING

A great company dish!

1 onion, sliced
½ lb. mushrooms, sliced
3 tbsp. butter or margarine
1 tsp. lemon juice
salt & pepper, to taste
⅓ c. seasoned bread crumbs
2 lb. sole fillets (or any thin fish fillets)

Sauce:
2 tbsp. butter or margarine
2 tbsp. flour
1 c. milk
½ tsp. salt
⅛ tsp. pepper
⅛ tsp. nutmeg
1 c. grated Gruyere cheese

1. Combine onion and mushrooms with 2 tbsp. of the butter in a 9″ x 13″ Pyrex™ casserole. **MW uncovered on HIGH for 5 minutes,** until tender, stirring at half time. Let cool slightly. Drain well. Sprinkle mushrooms with lemon juice, salt & pepper. Push to one side of casserole.

2. Combine 1 tbsp. butter with crumbs in a 1 cup Pyrex™ measure. **MW uncovered on HIGH for 1 minute,** until golden, stirring once. Set aside.

3. Pat fish fillets dry with paper towels. Place half the fish in a single layer in the bottom of the casserole. Sprinkle lightly with salt & pepper. Spread mushrooms evenly over fish. Top with remaining fillets, arranging fish so that thicker parts are towards the outside of the casserole.

4. Sauce: Place butter in a 2 cup Pyrex™ measure. **MW uncovered on HIGH for 30 to 45 seconds, until melted.** Stir in flour. Gradually add milk and seasonings. **MW uncovered on HIGH for 3 to 4 minutes,** stirring 2 or 3 times, until sauce is bubbly and thick. Stir cheese into sauce. Pour sauce over fish; cover with vented microsafe plastic wrap. (Can be prepared in advance up to this point and refrigerated.)

5. MW covered on HIGH 9 to 10 minutes (10 to 12 minutes if refrigerated), rotating dish ¼ turn halfway through cooking. Fish in centre of casserole should flake when lightly pressed. Let stand covered for 3 to 4 minutes. Top with reserved crumbs. Garnish with parsley and lemon. Serve with rice and buttered carrots.

Yield: 6 servings. Do not freeze.

* **To prepare in advance:** Cook rice and carrots early in the day; chill until serving time. Prepare fish up to the end of Step 4. First, reheat rice; **6 servings will take about 5 minutes on HIGH.** Cover tightly to retain heat (or place in 200°F oven). Begin cooking of fish 15 minutes before serving time. Reheat carrots during standing time for fish. Enjoy!

STUFFED RAINBOW TROUT

4 oven-ready rainbow trout (about 2 lb.)
salt, pepper & basil
juice of ½ lemon
2 tbsp. fresh parsley
2 tbsp. fresh dill
1 onion, quartered
1 stalk celery, in chunks
2 tbsp. butter or margarine
1 c. bread crumbs or cooked rice
¼ c. sliced almonds
julienned red & green pepper, to garnish

1. Wash trout and pat dry with paper towels. Sprinkle cavity lightly with salt, pepper, basil & lemon juice. Arrange in a single layer in an ungreased 9″ x 13″ Pyrex™ casserole.

2. **Steel Knife:** Drop parsley and dill through feed tube while machine is running. Process until minced. Add onion and celery; process with several on/off turns, until coarsely chopped. Combine with butter in a microsafe bowl. **MW uncovered on HIGH for 4 minutes,** until tender.

3. Combine vegetables with bread crumbs or rice, almonds, ½ tsp. salt, ¼ tsp. pepper, and a dash of basil. Mix well. Spoon stuffing into each trout cavity. Cover fish with waxed paper. (Can be prepared in advance up to this point and refrigerated.)

4. **MW covered on HIGH, calculating 4 to 4½ minutes per lb.** Four average trout will take about **8 to 10 minutes to cook on HIGH.** (If your oven has an uneven cooking pattern, **MW on MEDIUM (50%). Cooking time will be 15 to 18 minutes.)** Rotate casserole ½ turn at half time. If necessary, shield ends of fish with smooth pieces of foil for the last half of cooking in order to prevent them from becoming overcooked.

5. Let stand covered for 3 to 4 minutes before serving. Fish should flake when lightly pressed. Garnish with red & green peppers. Serve with buttered cauliflower and Caesar salad.

Yield: 4 to 6 servings. Do not freeze.

> * Bread crumbs can be made by processing slightly stale or dried bread on the **Steel Knife** of the food processor until fine. Corn flake crumbs, matzo meal or any cracker crumbs can be substituted. If crumbs are salty, adjust seasonings accordingly.

STUFFED FISH FILLETS

1. Follow recipe for Stuffed Rainbow Trout (above), but substitute 2 lb. sole or any thin fish fillets for the trout. Arrange half the fillets in the bottom of an ungreased 9″ x 13″ Pyrex™ casserole. Sprinkle lightly with seasonings.

2. Prepare stuffing as directed in Steps 2 & 3, using bread crumbs. Set aside ½ cup stuffing. Spread remaining stuffing evenly over fish. Top with remaining fish, placing thicker parts towards the outside edge of the casserole.

3. **MW covered on HIGH for 8 to 9 minutes,** rotating casserole ½ turn at half time. Let stand covered for 3 minutes. Fish should flake when lightly pressed. Uncover and sprinkle reserved crumb mixture over fish. Garnish with red & green peppers.

Yield: 6 servings. Do not freeze.

FISH FILLETS IN PARCHMENT

Parchment paper is available in specialty kitchen shops. It retains the heat very well, and also makes an elegant presentation.

4 fish fillets, ½″ thick (1 lb.)
2 tbsp. butter or margarine
4 green onions, chopped
2 tbsp. lemon or lime juice
1 tsp. grated lemon rind, if desired
2 tbsp. chopped fresh parsley or dill
salt & pepper
basil & thyme
8 thin slices of tomato

1. Cut four 12″ squares of parchment paper. Place a fish fillet on the centre of each square of paper.

2. MW butter and green onions uncovered on HIGH for 2 minutes. Spoon over fish. Sprinkle lightly with lemon juice, rind, parsley and seasonings. Fold thin ends of fillets under so fish is the same thickness all over. Top each fillet with two tomato slices.

3. Bring edges of parchment together and fold over twice along the long edge to make an airtight seal. Twist ends like party favors to close. Arrange packages seam-side up on a 12″ microsafe platter. (Can be prepared in advance up to this point.)

4. MW packages on HIGH for 5 to 7 minutes, or until paper is puffed up. Open one package and check to see if fish flakes when lightly pressed. Let stand for 2 to 3 minutes before serving. Place each package on an individual serving plate. Serve with Quick Potato & Carrot Scallop (p. 275) or Rice Pilaf (p. 214).

Yield: 4 servings. Do not freeze.

* If desired, substitute 1 c. thinly sliced zucchini or cucumber for the tomatoes.
* Chopped carrots &/or celery can be added to the green onions. **MW uncovered in 2 tbsp. butter for 3 minutes,** until tender. Spoon over fish and continue as directed in Step 2.
* Fish fillets are also delicious when coated with Dijon mustard. Use about 1 tsp. mustard for each fish fillet.
* **A single serving (¼ to ⅓ lb.) will take 2 to 2½ minutes on HIGH to cook. Two servings will take 4 to 5 minutes.**

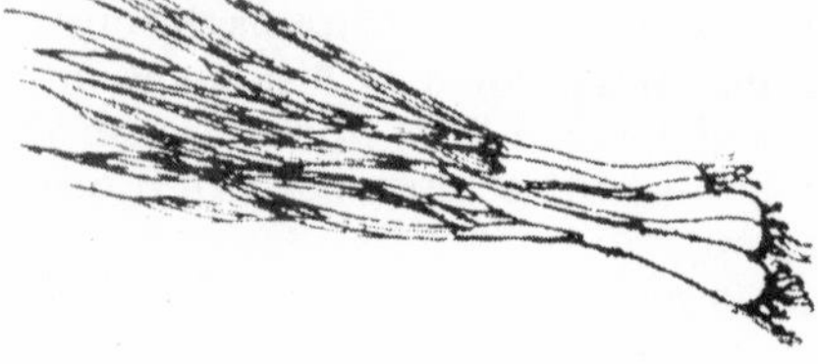

LETTUCE COOK FISH FOR DINNER!

½ head Iceberg or Romaine lettuce
1 lb. fish fillets or steaks
salt, pepper & thyme
juice of ½ lemon or lime
paprika to garnish

1. Wash lettuce well. Shake off excess water. Arrange a layer of lettuce in the bottom of a shallow microsafe casserole large enough to hold the fish in a single layer. Place fish with the thicker parts towards the outside edge of the casserole. Fold under any thin ends. Sprinkle with seasonings and lemon juice. Top with another layer of lettuce. (The lettuce will act as a cover.)

2. MW on HIGH for 4 to 4½ minutes, or until fish is no longer opaque. (Remember to rotate casserole ¼ turn at half time.) Let stand covered for 2 minutes. Fish should flake when lightly pressed. Discard lettuce leaves. Garnish fish with thinly sliced lemon, chopped parsley and tomato slices. If desired, drizzle fish with melted butter or margarine. Serve with green peas and Stuffed Baked Potatoes (p. 270).

Yield: 2 to 3 servings.

* You can vary the seasonings; some suggestions are tarragon, dill, parsley, basil or oregano. If using fresh herbs instead of dried, use triple the amount.
* **If using 2 lb. fish, (4 to 6 servings) MW for 8 minutes on HIGH.**
* **If cooking a single serving (⅓ to ½ lb.), MW 2½ to 3 minutes on HIGH.**
* **Timetable for Preparation:** Bake and stuff potatoes early in the day. Prepare fish. **MW a 10 oz. pkg. of frozen peas covered on HIGH for 5 minutes.** Keep peas covered while you cook the fish. Reheat stuffed potatoes during standing time for fish.
* **FISHERMAN'S PITA POCKETS:** Flake any leftover fish with a fork and add a little mayonnaise and chili sauce to moisten. Add 1 hard-cooked chopped egg, celery, onion, green pepper, salt & pepper. Stuff into pita pockets. Top with lettuce and tomato slices. Use for lunch the next day. Much tastier than the usual tuna sandwich!

PAPER-POACHED FISH

Prepare Lettuce Cook Fish for Dinner! (above), but omit lettuce leaves. Moisten microsafe paper towels under running water and squeeze gently to remove excess moisture. Place on top of fish to cover completely. Cook as directed above. Discard paper towelling before serving.

SNAPPER FILLETS IN A SNAP

2 tbsp. oil
1 medium onion, chopped
1 clove garlic, crushed
3 medium carrots, julienned
2 medium zucchini, julienned
4 red snapper fillets (about 1 ½ lb.)
2 tbsp. dry white wine or lemon juice
½ tsp. salt
freshly ground pepper
¼ tsp. basil
chopped parsley to garnish

1. Combine oil with onion, garlic, carrots and zucchini in a microsafe 2 quart oval or rectangular casserole. Cover with vented plastic wrap. **MW covered on HIGH 4 to 5 minutes,** until tender-crisp, stirring at half time.

2. Uncover; place fish fillets in a single layer over vegetables, arranging thicker parts towards the outside edge of the casserole. Overlap fish if necessary. Sprinkle with wine or lemon juice and seasonings. Cover with vented plastic wrap.

3. MW covered on HIGH for 7 to 8 minutes, until fish flakes when lightly pressed with your fingertips. Rotate dish ¼ turn halfway through cooking. Let stand covered for 3 to 4 minutes. Garnish with chopped parsley. Serve with rice.

Yield: 4 servings. Do not freeze.

EMMA'S FISH

This quick and easy recipe was given to me by a lovely lady from California I met at the airport in Florida while waiting for our planes! Orange roughy is a firm-fleshed, mild-tasting white fish which is becoming available in many areas.

4 thick fish fillets or steaks (halibut, sole, orange roughy or grouper)
4 tsp. Dijon mustard
4 tbsp. mayonnaise
1 med. zucchini (or cucumber)
2 cloves garlic
1 c. drained, canned plum tomatoes
salt & pepper, to taste

1. Weigh fish. Place in an ungreased shallow 2 quart microsafe casserole, with the thicker parts towards the outside of the dish. Coat top surface of fish with mustard and mayonnaise.

2. Grater: Grate zucchini or cucumber. (Cucumber should be peeled first; zucchini does not require peeling.) Pat dry with paper towels. Spread over fish. Wipe processor bowl dry with paper towels.

3. Steel Knife: Drop garlic through feed tube while machine is running. Process until minced. Add tomatoes and process with 4 or 5 quick on/off turns, until coarsely chopped. Add salt and pepper to taste. Spread over zucchini. Cover casserole with vented microsafe plastic wrap. (Can be prepared in advance up to this point.)

4. MW on HIGH, calculating 4 ½ to 5 minutes per lb. (Remember to rotate casserole ¼ turn at half time.) Fish should flake when lightly pressed. Let stand covered for 3 minutes. Serve with Rice Pilaf (p. 214).

Yield: 4 servings. Do not freeze.

HALIBUT JARDINIERE

2 carrots, peeled & trimmed
4 green onions
1 medium zucchini (do not peel)
4 halibut steaks (about 2 lb.)
salt & pepper, to taste
dash of basil & garlic powder
juice of half a lemon
1 tsp. grated lemon rind
2 tomatoes, diced
2 tbsp. chopped parsley

1. **Steel Knife:** Cut carrots, green onions and zucchini in chunks. Process with quick on/off turns, until coarsely chopped. Transfer to a 4 cup Pyrex™ measure. Cover with microsafe plastic wrap, turning back one corner slightly to vent. **MW on HIGH for 4 to 5 minutes,** until tender-crisp, stirring once. (Insert a wooden chopstick through the vented opening to stir vegetables.)

2. Arrange fish in a single layer in an ungreased microsafe casserole, with the thicker parts towards the outside of the dish. Sprinkle with seasonings, lemon juice and rind. Top with cooked vegetables, tomatoes and parsley.

3. Cover with vented plastic wrap and **MW on HIGH for 9 to 10 minutes,** rotating casserole ¼ turn at half time. Let stand covered for 5 minutes. Fish should flake when you press it lightly. Serve with Cheesy Scalloped Potatoes (p. 274).

Yield: 4 servings.

* Cook Cheesy Scalloped Potatoes first. Place a dinner plate on top of the casserole to trap the heat. They will keep hot up to ½ hour.

HALIBUT PIZZA STYLE

1 c. mushrooms
½ red pepper
½ green pepper
4 green onions
1 tbsp. oil
4 halibut steaks (about 2 lb.)
¾ c. pizza sauce
¼ lb. Mozzerella cheese (1 c. grated)

1. **Steel Knife:** Process vegetables with several quick on/off turns, until coarsely chopped. Combine with oil in a 9″ x 13″ microsafe casserole. **MW uncovered on HIGH for 3 to 4 minutes,** until tender-crisp, stirring once.

2. Push vegetables to one side of casserole. Arrange fish in a single layer in the same casserole, with the thicker parts towards the outside of the dish. Spoon vegetables over fish. Top with pizza sauce. Cover with plastic wrap, turning back one corner slightly to vent. (May be prepared in advance up to this point.)

3. **MW covered on HIGH for 8 to 9 minutes (calculate about 4½ minutes per lb. of fish),** rotating casserole ½ turn halfway through cooking. Fish should barely flake when pressed with your fingertips. Let stand covered for 3 or 4 minutes.

4. Drain excess watery liquid from bottom of casserole through the vented opening. Carefully uncover. Sprinkle cheese over fish. **MW uncovered on HIGH for 2 to 3 minutes,** until cheese is melted. Serve with rice or noodles.

Yield: 4 servings. Do not freeze.

SALMON TERIYAKI

4 salmon steaks, about ½″ thick (about 2 lb.)
2 tbsp. light soya sauce
1 tbsp. water
1 tsp. lemon juice
1 ½ tsp. sugar
1 clove garlic, crushed
1 or 2 green onions, chopped

1. Place salmon in a shallow ungreased 2 quart microsafe casserole, with the thin ends pointing towards the centre to prevent overcooking. Combine remaining ingredients except green onions and brush on both sides of salmon. Let marinate at room temperature 20 to 30 minutes. Cover with vented microsafe plastic wrap.

2. **MW on HIGH for 8 to 10 minutes.** Rotate the casserole ¼ turn halfway through cooking and turn salmon over, using a wide spatula. Fish should flake when lightly pressed. Let stand covered for 2 to 3 minutes before serving. Garnish with chopped green onions. Serve with steamed rice and Oriental Green Beans Vinaigrette (p. 248).

Yield: 4 servings. Do not freeze.

* Any firm fish fillets or fish steaks can be substituted.
* The juices in the bottom of the casserole will help cook the fish evenly when you turn it over.
* Recipe may be halved, if desired. **Two salmon steaks (about 1 lb.) will take 4 to 4 ½ minutes to cook.** Make full amount of marinade.
* If you remove the bone, the salmon will cook more evenly.

HALIBUT TERIYAKI

Follow directions for Salmon Teriyaki (above), but substitute halibut steaks.

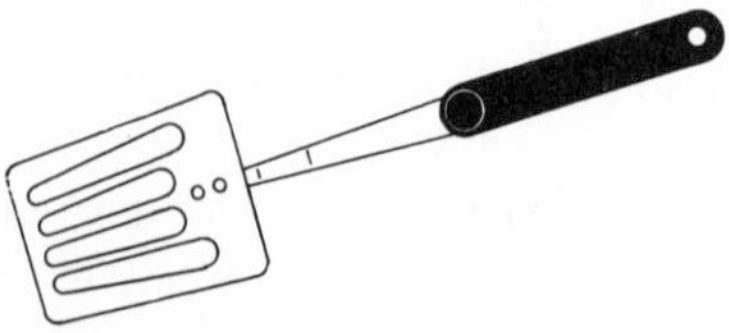

SIMPLE SALMON

4 salmon steaks (about 2 lb.)
salt, pepper & dill
4 tsp. lemon juice, optional
4 tsp. melted butter or margarine, optional

1. Arrange salmon in a single layer in an ungreased microsafe casserole, with the thicker parts towards the outside edge. Sprinkle lightly with seasonings. Drizzle with lemon juice and butter, if desired. Moisten paper towelling under running water. Gently press out excess moisture. Cover top of salmon steaks completely with moist paper towelling.

2. MW on HIGH for 7 to 8 minutes. (Calculate 4 minutes per lb. cooking time.) Use a wide spatula to turn fish over ¾ of the way through cooking. Fish should flake when lightly pressed. Let stand covered for 3 minutes. Garnish with lemon and parsley.

Yield: 4 servings. Do not freeze.

* **One salmon steak (about 8 oz.) will take about 3 minutes to microwave.**
* **Two salmon steaks (about 1 lb.) will take 4 to 4½ minutes to microwave.**
* Salmon fillets, halibut steak or any fish fillets can be substituted for salmon steaks.
* Salmon is also delicious topped with a dab of Garlic Butter (p. 109).
* If you wish, prepare salmon early in the day and serve it chilled with Cucumber Yogourt Sauce (p. 57).

SOPHISTICATED SALMON

Top Simple Salmon (above) with a dollop of sour cream or yogurt. Garnish with a spoonful of black caviar.

GREEN GODDESS SALMON

Prepare Simple Salmon (above) and refrigerate for several hours. Prepare Green Goddess Dip (p. 56) and chill. Coat each salmon steak completely with dip. (Leftover dip can be refrigerated and used as a salad dressing or as a dip for fresh vegetables.)

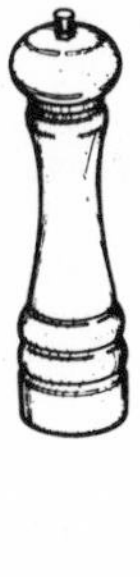

HANNAH'S PICKLED SALMON

Moist, flavorful and scrumptious. You won't have to fish for compliments when you serve this dish!

2 lb. salmon fillets or steaks
1 ½ c. water
1 ½ c. white vinegar
¾ c. sugar
3 tbsp. pickling spices
¾ c. ketchup
¾ tsp. salt
¼ tsp. pepper
1 Spanish onion, sliced

1. Place salmon in an ungreased 9″ x 13″ microsafe casserole. Arrange thicker pieces towards the outer edges of the dish. Cover with vented plastic wrap. **MW covered on HIGH for 7 to 8 minutes,** rotating casserole ½ turn at half time. Salmon should barely flake when lightly pressed. Let stand covered for 5 minutes. Discard skin and bones.

2. Combine water, vinegar, sugar, pickling spices, ketchup and seasonings in a large microsafe bowl. **MW uncovered on HIGH for 10 to 12 minutes,** until liquid is boiling and flavors are blended. Transfer salmon carefully into hot liquid, using a wide spatula. Add onions. Salmon and onions should be completely covered with marinade. Let stand until cool. Cover with plastic wrap and refrigerate for 3 to 4 days to marinate fish. Serve chilled.

Yield: 4 servings as a main course and 8 servings as an appetizer. Do not freeze. Pickled salmon will keep about 1 week in the refrigerator.

> * Halibut or pike can be substituted for salmon.

DILLY BAKED SALMON

4 salmon steaks (about 2 lb.)
salt & pepper
⅓ c. mayonnaise
⅓ c. sour cream or yogurt
2 tbsp. grated Parmesan cheese
2 tbsp. fresh chopped dill
1 tbsp. lemon or lime juice
1 clove garlic, crushed
¼ c. seasoned bread crumbs
paprika to garnish

1. Weigh fish. Calculate 5 to 6 minutes per lb. cooking time for this recipe. Pat dry with paper towels. Arrange fish in an ungreased 10″ ceramic quiche dish, with thickest parts towards the outside edge of the dish. Sprinkle lightly with salt and pepper. Cover with wax paper and **MW on HIGH for half the cooking time, about 5 minutes.** Drain off excess liquid. Discard wax paper.

2. Combine mayonnaise, sour cream, Parmesan, dill, lemon juice and garlic. Add salt & pepper to taste. Spread over fish. Sprinkle with bread crumbs and paprika. **MW uncovered on HIGH 5 minutes longer,** or until fish flakes when lightly pressed. Let stand uncovered for 3 or 4 minutes. Serve with zucchini and Baked Potatoes (p. 270).

Yield: 4 servings. Do not freeze.

* Bake potatoes first. Wrap in a clean dishtowel to keep hot while you cook the fish.
* Zucchini can be sliced in advance and placed in a microsafe serving dish with a dab of butter, salt and pepper. Cover with wax paper. Microwave it during the standing time for the fish. **One lb. of sliced zucchini will cook in about 5 minutes on HIGH.** If fish needs reheating, **MW it uncovered for 1 minute on HIGH.**
* Sole or any firm fish fillets can be used instead of salmon.

CHILLED FILLETS OF SALMON WITH DILL SAUCE

A wonderful summer dish which can be prepared early in the day, leaving you free to relax! Perfect for company. Salmon is cooked in lettuce leaves, which impart a delicate flavor as well as acting as a cover.

2 lb. salmon fillets
Romaine or Iceberg lettuce
½ c. mayonnaise
½ c. sour cream or yogurt
1 tbsp. lemon or lime juice
2 tbsp. fresh dill
salt & pepper

1. Wipe fish dry with paper towels. Wash lettuce leaves and shake off excess water. Place a layer of lettuce in the bottom of an ungreased 7″ x 11″ Pyrex™ casserole. Arrange fish skin-side down on the lettuce, placing thicker parts towards the outside of the dish and overlapping thinner edges. Cover fish completely with another layer of lettuce leaves.

2. MW on HIGH for 8 minutes, rotating dish ¼ turn halfway through cooking. (Check fish after 6 minutes. If it does not appear to be cooking evenly, turn it over carefully with a wide spatula.) Let stand for 3 to 4 minutes after cooking. Fish should flake easily when lightly pressed. Discard lettuce and refrigerate salmon.

3. Combine remaining ingredients and blend well. Place in a pretty serving bowl and refrigerate until serving time. Transfer salmon carefully to a serving platter; decorate platter with parsley, radish roses and thinly sliced lemon. Serve salmon with chilled Dill Sauce. An ideal accompaniment would be Italian Rice Salad (p. 215) or Dill-Icious Potato Salad (p. 278).

Yield: 4 servings. Do not freeze.

* Salmon fillets are also excellent served hot. Top with Lemon Butter or Garlic Butter (p. 109). Salmon trout fillets or salmon steaks can be substituted.

PASTA WITH SALMON PRIMAVERA

The combination of colors and flavors in this dish is wonderful! Use fresh spinach fettucine, if possible.

2 lb. salmon fillets or steaks*
2 cloves garlic
¼ c. parsley
¼ c. dill
1 onion, halved
7 tbsp. butter
3 medium carrots
2 medium zucchini, unpeeled
2 c. broccoli florets
1 lb. fettucine
1 ½ c. whipping cream (35%)
1 c. grated Parmesan cheese
salt, pepper & nutmeg to taste

1. Prepare salmon as directed in recipe for Simple Salmon (p. 121), omitting butter and lemon juice. When cool, discard skin and bones. Flake into large chunks.

2. **Steel Knife:** Mince garlic, parsley and dill. Add onion and chop coarsely, using on/off turns. Combine with 2 tbsp. of the butter in a medium microsafe bowl. **MW uncovered on HIGH for 3 minutes,** until tender-crisp.

3. **Grater:** Grate carrots and zucchini. Add to onion mixture along with broccoli. Cover with vented microsafe plastic wrap. **MW on HIGH for 5 minutes,** or until carrots and broccoli are tender-crisp, stirring at half time. Let stand covered for 2 minutes. Drain excess liquid.

4. Cook pasta conventionally according to package directions. Drain and rinse well. Return pasta to the hot pan and toss with 2 tbsp. butter. Cover to keep hot.

5. Meanwhile, combine remaining 3 tbsp. butter with cream in an 8 cup Pyrex™ measure. **MW uncovered on HIGH for 3 minutes,** until boiling. Stir in Parmesan cheese and seasonings. **MW on HIGH 2 minutes longer,** until thick and smooth.

6. Stir in vegetables and salmon. **(If necessary, MW 1 minute longer on HIGH to heat salmon and vegetables.)** Arrange pasta on dinner plates, top with salmon mixture and serve immediately.

Yield: 6 servings. Do not freeze.

* Canned sockeye salmon can be substituted in Step 1. Drain well; flake into large chunks.

* Salmon, vegetables and sauce can be prepared ahead (Steps 1, 2, 3 & 5), but do not assemble. At serving time, cook pasta conventionally. Meanwhile, **MW sauce with vegetables on HIGH for 4 to 6 minutes,** until piping hot, stirring once or twice. Gently stir in salmon; **MW on HIGH 1 to 2 minutes longer,** until heated through. Drain pasta; arrange on dinner plates and top with salmon mixture.

TUNA OR SALMON CASSEROLE

For variety, try different combinations of vegetables such as cauliflower, peas & carrots, green peppers, onions & mushrooms. If you have a small family, divide casserole in half and freeze one for another day.

12 oz. pkg. rotini (spirals), macaroni or bow ties
10 oz. pkg. frozen French-style green beans
10 oz. pkg. frozen broccoli spears
10 oz. can condensed cream of mushroom or celery soup
½ c. milk
salt & pepper, to taste
¼ tsp. each of basil & thyme
1 c. grated Cheddar or Swiss cheese
2 - 7 oz. cans tuna or 7 ¾ oz. cans salmon, drained & flaked
½ c. bread crumbs mixed with
1 tbsp. melted butter

1. Cook pasta in boiling salted water according to package directions. Drain and rinse well.

2. Meanwhile, place unwrapped package of green beans on a microsafe plate and make several slits in the top of the package with a sharp knife. **MW on HIGH for 6 to 8 minutes,** rotating the plate ¼ turn at half time. The bottom of the plate should feel hot. Repeat with broccoli, but **MW on HIGH for 5 to 6 minutes.**

3. Combine all ingredients except buttered crumbs in a lightly greased 9″ x 13″ Pyrex™ casserole. Mix well; adjust seasonings to taste. Cover with waxed paper. (Can be prepared up to this point and refrigerated until needed.)

4. **MW covered on HIGH for 12 to 15 minutes,** or until hot and bubbly, stirring twice. Top with crumb mixture and **MW uncovered on HIGH 2 minutes longer. (*** For a crusty top, see below.)

Yield: 8 servings. May be frozen. Reheats well.

* It saves time to cook the pasta conventionally while preparing the remainder of the recipe in the microwave.
* Fresh or frozen vegetables must be cooked before adding to the casserole. Canned vegetables can be substituted (peas, green beans, carrots, etc.); just drain and combine with remaining ingredients.
* For a crusty top, **bake uncovered on the CONVECTION CYCLE or in your conventional oven at 400°F for 10 to 15 minutes,** until crisp. No preheating is necessary.
* **CONVECTION/MICROWAVE METHOD:** Follow Steps 1 to 3 as directed above. Preheat oven to 325°F. Place casserole on rack recommended by manufacturer and **bake uncovered on COMBINATION CYCLE suitable for casseroles for 25 to 30 minutes,** or until golden. Temperature will be 160°F on a probe.

MY OVEN'S SETTING ______ MY COOKING TIME______

TUNA OR SALMON & BROCCOLI CASSEROLE

1 c. long grain rice
1 bunch broccoli (about 1 lb.)
¼ c. butter
¼ c. flour
1 tsp. salt
freshly ground pepper
¼ tsp. nutmeg
2 c. milk
1 c. grated Swiss cheese
3 oz. can French Fried onions
2 - 7 oz. cans tuna or
7 ¾ oz. cans salmon,
drained & flaked

1. Cook rice as directed in "How to Cook Rice" (p. 214).

2. Trim broccoli. Cut into 1 ½″ pieces. Rinse under running water and shake off excess. Arrange in a 7″ x 11″ Pyrex™ casserole with the florets in the centre. Cover with vented plastic wrap. **MW on HIGH for 4 to 5 minutes,** until tender-crisp. Let stand covered for 5 minutes.

3. Place butter in a 4 cup Pyrex™ measure. **MW on HIGH for 1 minute,** until melted. Stir in flour and seasonings. Gradually blend in milk. **MW on HIGH for 5 to 6 minutes,** until thick and bubbling, stirring 3 or 4 times during cooking. Add cheese; stir until melted.

4. Reserve half the onions to use as a topping. Add remaining ingredients to broccoli and mix well. Cover casserole with waxed paper. (Can be prepared up to this point and refrigerated until needed.)

5. **MW on HIGH for 10 to 12 minutes,** or until piping hot; rotate casserole ¼ turn halfway through cooking. Top with onion rings and **MW uncovered 2 minutes longer,** until onion rings are hot.

Yield: 6 servings. May be frozen.

* Frozen broccoli can be used, but it must be cooked before adding it to the casserole.
* Four cups of cooked noodles or macaroni can be substituted for cooked rice.
* If desired, divide casserole in half and freeze one for another day. Do not top with onion rings before freezing. They should be added the last 2 minutes of reheating.
* **CONVECTION/MICROWAVE METHOD:** Follow Steps 1 to 4 as directed above, but do not cover. Casserole should be lightly greased to prevent sticking. Preheat oven to 325°F. Place casserole on rack recommended by manufacturer and **bake uncovered on COMBINATION CYCLE suitable for casseroles for 25 to 30 minutes,** or until golden. Temperature will be 160°F on a probe.

MY OVEN'S SETTING ______ MY COOKING TIME ______

CRUSTLESS ZUCCHINI QUICHE

2 c. grated zucchini
2 c. grated Swiss cheese
6 eggs, lightly beaten with ¼ c. milk
½ tsp. salt
⅛ tsp. pepper
dash of nutmeg & basil
2 tbsp. bread or corn flake crumbs

1. Combine all ingredients except crumbs. Mix well. Pour into a lightly greased 10″ ceramic pie plate. Elevate on a microsafe rack or inverted pie plate. **MW on MEDIUM (50%) for 6 minutes.** Break up cooked portions with a fork and move them towards the centre of the dish. Flatten top of mixture.

2. **MW on MEDIUM (50%) 6 minutes longer.** Rotate dish ¼ turn. (Refer below to *** FOIL DONUT.**)

3. **MW on MEDIUM (50%) 3 to 6 minutes longer.** Top should look dry but the centre should jiggle when the dish is shaken gently. When done, a knife inserted near the centre will come out clean, but the centre will still be soft. Sprinkle with reserved crumbs. Let stand directly on the counter for 5 to 10 minutes to complete cooking. Serve with tossed salad and crusty rolls.

Yield: 6 servings. Do not freeze.

- * **One serving will take about 1 minute on MEDIUM (50%) to reheat.**
- * **FOIL DONUT:** If centre of quiche is not cooking evenly, cut a 12″ square of aluminum foil into a 10″ round. Cut a hole in the centre so the foil looks like a donut. Place foil donut over the top of the quiche, leaving the centre uncooked portion exposed. Microwave until done (see Step 3). It won't matter if it takes you a few minutes to cut the "donut" – the quiche will come out fine even if you interrupt the cooking process briefly!
- * Make sure foil is at least 1″ away from the walls of the oven.
- * **CONVECTION METHOD:** Preheat oven to 350°F. Use rack recommended by oven manufacturer for **CONVECTION CYCLE. Bake uncovered at 350°F for 30 to 35 minutes,** until set. If not completely baked, leave in oven for 5 minutes longer with the heat turned off to finish cooking.

QUICK QUICHE

Corn Flake Crumb Crust (p. 327)
1 ½ c. broccoli florets*
1 c. grated Swiss or Cheddar cheese
2 eggs
⅔ c. light cream or milk
salt & pepper, to taste
3 oz. can French Fried onions

1. Prepare crust as directed. Press into the bottom and up the sides of a lightly greased deep 9″ Pyrex™ pie plate or 10″ ceramic quiche dish. **MW uncovered on HIGH for 2 minutes,** rotating dish ¼ turn at half time. Let cool.

2. Rinse broccoli with cold water. Do not drain. Place in a 2 cup Pyrex™ measure and cover with wax paper. **MW on HIGH for 2 to 3 minutes,** until tender-crisp. Drain.

3. Sprinkle cheese on bottom of crust. Top with broccoli. Combine eggs with cream and seasonings. Pour egg mixture over the broccoli. Sprinkle onions over quiche. Place on a microsafe rack or inverted pie plate.

4. **MW uncovered on MEDIUM (50%) for 15 to 18 minutes.** Rotate dish 2 or 3 times during cooking. If centre does not seem to be cooking evenly, cover with a **"Foil Donut"** (p. 127). When done, top of quiche should look dry but the centre should jiggle when the dish is shaken gently. A knife inserted near the centre will come out clean, but the centre will still be soft.

5. Let stand directly on the counter for 5 to 10 minutes to complete cooking. Serve with Brutus Salad (p. 251) and garlic bread.

Yield: 6 servings. Do not freeze.

* One cup of any cooked vegetable or fish can be used instead of broccoli. Some suggestions are: cauliflower florets; sliced zucchini or mushrooms &/or onions.
* Read notes following Crustless Zucchini Quiche (p. 127).

CRÊPES

¾ c. flour
¼ tsp. salt
3 eggs
¼ c. oil
1 c. milk or water

1. Combine all ingredients on the **Steel Knife** of the food processor and blend until smooth, about 15 seconds, scraping down sides of bowl once. Refrigerate batter for at least ½ hour or up to 24 hours.

2. Lightly grease a 6 or 7 inch crêpe pan with a few drops of oil, or spray lightly with non-stick spray. Heat pan over medium heat on stove. Quickly pour about 3 tbsp. batter into pan. Tilt pan in all directions to coat bottom evenly with batter. Pour out excess.

3. Cook crêpe about 1 minute on the first side, until the edges brown. Flip crêpe over with a spatula; cook for 20 seconds on other side. Repeat with remaining batter. Place waxed paper between crêpes to prevent sticking. Fill crêpes as desired.

Yield: 12 to 15 crêpes. Can be made in advance and refrigerated or frozen.

NOTES ON CRÊPES

- The first few crêpes may not be so perfect. This is normal.
- **To freeze:** Place stacks of 4 to 6 crêpes in plastic storage bags. Close tightly and freeze.
- **To thaw:** Remove crêpes from plastic bag; don't bother to remove the waxed paper. **Four crêpes will take 1 minute on HIGH. Six crêpes will take about 1 ½ minutes on HIGH.** Let stand 1 to 2 minutes.
- **To heat:** Fill and roll up. Arrange seam-side down in a single layer in an ungreased microsafe casserole. Cover with waxed paper. **MW covered on HIGH, allowing 20 to 30 seconds per filled crêpe,** until heated through. **One dozen filled crêpes will take 4 to 6 minutes on HIGH.**
- **Suggested fillings:** See Tuna or Salmon & Broccoli Crêpes (below), Triple Cheese Manicotti (p. 224), Ratatouille (p. 260).
- To top filled crêpes with cheese, sprinkle grated cheese on hot crêpes. **MW uncovered on HIGH 1 minute longer,** or just until cheese is barely melted.

TUNA & BROCCOLI CRÊPES

12 crêpes (p. 128)
2 c. Bechamel (p. 85)
1 c. grated Swiss cheese
pinch of nutmeg
10 oz. pkg. frozen chopped broccoli
2 - 7 oz. cans tuna, drained & flaked
salt & pepper, to taste
¼ c. grated Parmesan cheese

1. Prepare crêpes as directed. (Can be made in advance and refrigerated or frozen. Thaw before using.) Prepare a double recipe of Bechamel. Add Swiss cheese and nutmeg to hot mixture; stir until cheese is melted. Set aside.

2. Pierce top of package of broccoli in several places with a sharp knife. Place package on a microsafe plate and **MW on HIGH for 5 to 6 minutes,** until done. Let stand covered for 2 minutes. Drain well.

3. Add 1 cup of sauce to broccoli. Stir in tuna. Season lightly. Divide filling evenly among crêpes. Roll up and place in an oblong microsafe/broilproof casserole (e.g. Corning Ware™). Top with remaining sauce. Sprinkle with Parmesan cheese. Cover with vented plastic wrap. Preheat conventional broiler.

4. **MW on HIGH for 4 to 6 minutes,** until heated through, rotating casserole ½ turn at half time. Uncover and place under broiler. Broil 3 to 4 minutes, until golden brown.

Yield: 4 to 6 servings.

> * **SALMON & BROCCOLI CRÊPES:** Instead of tuna, substitute 2 - 7 ¾ oz. cans sockeye salmon, drained & flaked. Cheddar cheese can be substituted for Swiss cheese; omit Parmesan cheese.

GREAT EGGS-PECTATIONS!

- **Size of eggs** affects cooking time. Times given are for large eggs taken directly from the refrigerator. Extra-large eggs need slightly more time; medium eggs need slightly less time.
- **If your microwave doesn't cook eggs evenly,** microwave them on **MEDIUM (50%) and double the time.** Yolks and whites cook at different rates (yolks cook faster). Scrambled eggs are microwaved uncovered on **HIGH** power. Stir twice during cooking.
- **A tight covering** retains steam and helps eggs cook more evenly. Also, if egg happens to pop (it can happen, even if yolk is pierced), covering prevents a mess in your microwave!
- **Eggs should be undercooked.** They complete their cooking during standing time. Overcooking makes them tough and rubbery.
- **To bring eggs to room temperature quickly,** break them into a microsafe bowl. Don't bother to pierce or cover; they are only in a microwave for a few seconds. **Allow 5 seconds on HIGH for 1 egg, 10 seconds for 2 eggs and 12 to 15 seconds for 3 eggs.**
- **Read Eggs & Egg Dishes (p. 101).**

"HARD-COOKED" EGGS

Never hard-cook eggs in their shell in the microwave! They could burst from an internal build-up of pressure. The following method is quick and easy; no peeling required! Vivian Lapa, one of my students, calls them "No Surprise Eggs" because you can see when they are firm enough!

1. Break eggs into individual custard cups or a microsafe muffin pan. Pierce yolks gently with a fork to make an "x". Cover completely with microsafe plastic wrap. Do not vent. One egg will take **1 ¼ minutes on MEDIUM (50%).** Rotate dish ¼ turn at half time. Let stand covered for 2 minutes. Mash; use in sandwich fillings, etc.

* **3 eggs will take about 3 minutes on MEDIUM (50%).** Remember to rotate dish ¼ turn at half time. Let stand 1 or 2 minutes to complete cooking.

EGG WHITES

1. Mix 2 egg whites lightly in a 10 oz. Pyrex™ custard cup or small microsafe bowl. Cover tightly with microsafe plastic wrap. Do not vent. **MW on MEDIUM (50%) for 1 ¼ to 1 ½ minutes,** just until set. Let stand covered for 1 to 2 minutes.

* Only 15 calories per egg white, and cholesterol-free as well! P.S. No need to grease the dish!

* Egg yolks can be prepared in the same way as egg whites, but the cooking time is shorter. **Two egg yolks will take 50 to 60 seconds on MEDIUM (50%).** Mash; use as a garnish for salads or vegetables.

SUNNY-SIDE UP EGGS

1. Use a separate dish for each egg. Place ½ tsp. butter in each 10 oz. custard cup or a 3 ½″ or 4″ round microsafe bowl. **MW uncovered on HIGH for 30 to 45 seconds,** until melted.

2. Break eggs into separate dishes. Pierce yolk gently with a fork to make an "x". Cover tightly with microsafe plastic wrap. Cook according to cooking times below. **If your microwave doesn't cook eggs evenly, use MEDIUM (50%).** Let stand covered 1 to 2 minutes before serving to complete cooking.

	HIGH	OR	MEDIUM (50%)
1 egg	**30 to 40 seconds**	**OR**	**1 to 1 ¼ minutes**
2 eggs	**1 to 1 ¼ minutes**	**OR**	**2 to 2 ½ minutes**
3 eggs	**1 ½ to 2 minutes**	**OR**	**3 to 3 ½ minutes**
4 eggs	**2 ½ to 3 minutes**	**OR**	**4 to 5 ½ minutes**

"WATERLESS" POACHED EGGS

1. Follow directions for Sunny-Side Up Eggs (above), but omit butter. (Eggs will not stick!) Use a 6 oz. or 10 oz. custard cup for each egg. Cook as directed. Cooking times are the same as for Sunny-Side Up Eggs.

POACHED EGGS

1. Measure ¼ cup water into a 10 oz. microsafe custard cup. **MW on HIGH for 40 seconds.** Break an egg into the boiling water. Pierce yolk gently with a fork. Cover with microsafe plastic wrap. **MW on HIGH for 30 to 40 seconds.** Let stand covered 1 to 2 minutes before serving. The longer the eggs stay in the water, the more they will cook.

* For each egg, use ¼ cup water in a separate custard cup. Break eggs into boiling water. For cooking times, refer to times for Sunny-Side Up Eggs (above), using **HIGH** power.

SCRAMBLED EGGS

1. Use 1 tsp. butter per egg. Heat butter in a glass measuring cup on **HIGH for 30 to 45 seconds,** until melted. Add eggs; blend with 1 tbsp. water or milk per egg plus a pinch of salt and pepper.

2. MW uncovered on HIGH according to times given below, **stirring twice during the last half of cooking.** Let stand for 1 to 2 minutes before serving. Eggs should be slightly moist when you take them out of the microwave. They will continue to cook during standing time.

1 egg	**HIGH**	**30 to 40 seconds**
2 eggs	**HIGH**	**1 to 1¼ minutes**
3 eggs	**HIGH**	**1½ to 2 minutes**
4 eggs	**HIGH**	**2½ to 3 minutes**
6 eggs	**HIGH**	**3½ to 4½ minutes**

* Eggs can be cooked on **MEDIUM (50%).** Double the cooking time.

* **CHEESY SCRAMBLED EGGS:** Add 1 tbsp. grated cheese for each egg and stir into uncooked egg mixture. Cook as directed for Scrambled Eggs, adding a few seconds longer to the cooking time.

MY FAVORITE BREAKFAST

2 frozen sesame seed bagels
2 tsp. butter
4 eggs
2 tbsp. milk
dash salt & pepper
2 tbsp. grated cheese

1. Wrap each bagel in microsafe paper towelling. **MW for 30 seconds on HIGH,** until thawed. Place bagels in toaster oven at 350°F to crisp while you prepare the eggs.

2. Use two 3″ or 4″ round cereal bowls to cook the eggs. Place 1 tsp. butter in each bowl. **MW uncovered on HIGH for 30 seconds,** until melted. To each bowl, add 2 eggs, 1 tbsp. milk, salt, pepper and 1 tbsp. cheese. Beat lightly.

3. MW eggs uncovered on HIGH for 2½ to 3 minutes, stirring every minute. Eggs should still be moist.

4. Split bagels in half. Fill each bagel with eggs; they should fit perfectly. Serve with freshly brewed coffee and a big kiss!

Yield: 2 happy servings.

* We buy our bagel at Montreal's famous Bagel Factory and always have a supply in our freezer. This method of thawing them first in the microwave, then crisping them in the toaster oven, makes them taste like they did when they came out of the wood-burning oven. My sister and brother live in Winnipeg and beg anyone who comes from Montreal to bring them a supply!

MISH MASH OMELET

This delicious concoction is a microwaved version of a brunch speciality served at Beauty's Restaurant in Montreal.

1 onion, chopped
½ green pepper, chopped
1 tbsp. oil or margarine
6 eggs
¼ tsp. salt
dash pepper
6 slices salami, about ¼″ thick
2 hot dogs, sliced diagonally

1. Combine onion, pepper and oil in a 9″ Pyrex™ pie plate. **MW uncovered on HIGH for 4 to 5 minutes,** until tender.

2. Mix eggs with seasonings. Cut salami slices in quarters. Add salami and hot dog slices to vegetables. Pour eggs over mish mash mixture. Cover with wax paper.

3. **MW covered on HIGH for 4 minutes,** until almost set, stirring at half time. Turn cooked portions over and push them towards the centre of the dish; push uncooked portions towards the outer edges. Flatten the top with a spatula and **MW covered on HIGH for 1 to 2 minutes longer,** until almost set. Let stand covered for 2 minutes. Cut in half and place each half on a dinner plate.

Yield: 2 generous servings.

* A Mish Mash is traditionally served with **HOME-FRIED POTATOES.** Potatoes can be microwaved (see Baked Potatoes, p. 270) and stored in the refrigerator for 2 or 3 days. Cut in chunks and fry with onions in hot oil in a skillet on top of the stove until well browned, about 8 to 10 minutes.

FUN IN A BUN

1. Cut a Whole Wheat or Vienna Roll in half. Remove part of the soft bread from the centre to make a hollow to hold the egg. Break egg into hollow in roll. Pierce yolk gently with a fork. Sprinkle with a little grated cheese, if desired. Cover with top of roll.

2. Place on a microsafe paper towel and **MW uncovered on HIGH for 40 to 45 seconds per egg.** No dish to wash!

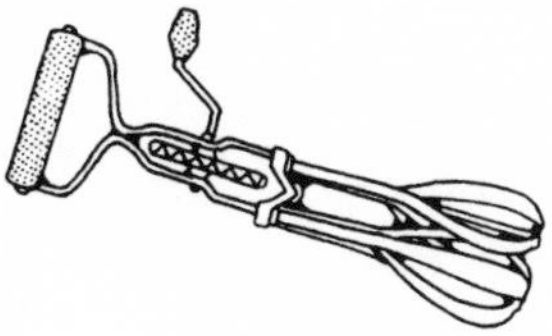

CHEDDAR VEGGIE MELT

Quick and nutritious!

2 slices whole wheat bread
1 c. broccoli florets, cut up
1 medium tomato, sliced
½ c. grated Cheddar cheese
salt & pepper

1. Toast bread conventionally. Meanwhile, prepare remaining ingredients. Rinse broccoli with cold water; shake off excess water. Place in a 2 cup glass measure. Cover with vented plastic wrap. **MW on HIGH for 1 ½ minutes,** until bright green and tender-crisp.

2. Place toast on a microsafe plate lined with a double layer of microsafe paper towels. Top toast with tomato slices and broccoli. Sprinkle with cheese. **MW uncovered on MEDIUM (50%) for 1 ½ to 2 minutes,** rotating plate after 1 minute. When done, cheese should just be melted. Let stand for 1 minute. Sprinkle lightly with salt & pepper. Enjoy without guilt!

Yield: 1 or 2 servings.

* **Calculate 45 to 60 seconds on MEDIUM (50%) for each Veggie Melt.** Lower power levels prevent cheese from becoming tough when microwaving small quantities.
* **6 Veggie Melts will take 2 to 3 minutes on HIGH,** just until cheese is melted. Arrange in a circle 1″ apart. Rotate at half time.
* Use split and toasted English muffins, hamburger buns, dinner rolls or pita bread instead of whole wheat bread.
* Other cooked vegetables can be substituted for broccoli (e.g. cauliflower, asparagus). Leftovers are just fine.

TUNA MELT

1. Prepare as for Cheddar Veggie Melt (above), but omit broccoli. Top each slice of toast with ¼ c. tuna which has been mixed with a little mayonnaise to moisten, finely minced celery plus salt & pepper to taste. Top with tomato slices (optional) and grated cheese.

2. **MW uncovered** on a paper towel-lined microsafe plate **on MEDIUM (50%), allowing 45 to 60 seconds for each Tuna Melt.** Rotate plate at half time.

POULTRY

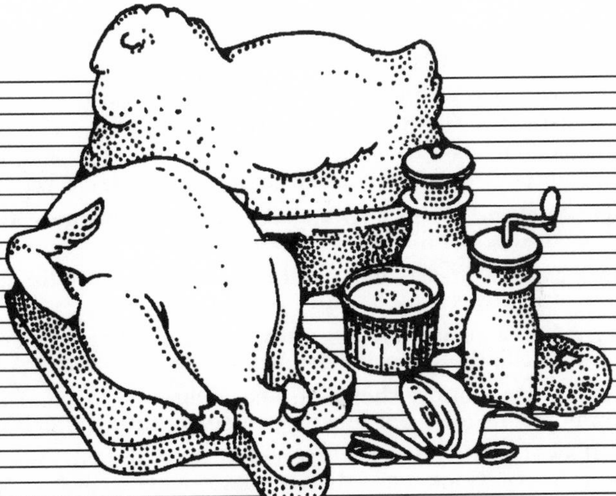

MICRO-WAYS WITH POULTRY

DEFROSTING TECHNIQUES (THE BIG CHILL!)

- **Defrosting chicken** is so easy in the microwave! Remove all wrappings &/or any metal. Place chicken on a microsafe rack or an inverted saucer in a microsafe casserole. **MW on DEFROST (30%), allowing 5 to 7 minutes per lb.** Never defrost poultry at room temperature.
- **To remove chicken easily** if frozen on a styrofoam tray, **MW on HIGH for 30 to 45 seconds.** Tray will come off easily. (There is much concern today that styrofoam is a danger to our environment. Therefore, you may wish to avoid purchasing products which are packaged in styrofoam.)
- **At half time**, turn chicken over and separate the pieces. Shield areas that are getting warm (wings, drumsticks, tail, breastbone) with flat pieces of foil, attaching it with a wooden toothpick.
- **Keep foil at least 1″ away** from the walls of the oven to prevent arcing and sparking.
- **Remove chicken pieces** from the microwave as soon as they are thawed; otherwise they will begin to cook.
- **Larger pieces** such as breasts and thighs take longer to defrost than wings and drumsticks.
- **If pieces start to cook** or get warm on the edges, stop the microwave for a few minutes &/or place chicken under cold running water briefly.
- **A whole chicken (2½ to 3½ lb.) takes 18 to 22 minutes on DEFROST (30%). If cut-up, it will take 14 to 16 minutes.**
- **Boneless chicken breasts only need 4 to 5 minutes per lb. on DEFROST (30%)** or thin edges may begin to cook.
- **Poultry must be completely defrosted** before cooking or some areas may be raw, particularly under the drumstick when cooking a whole chicken.
- **After defrosting**, poultry should still be cold to the touch. The ice crystals in the thicker, meatier portions will dissolve during standing time.
- **Rinse thawed poultry in cold water** and let stand for 5 to 10 minutes before cooking. Cook immediately or refrigerate once it is completely defrosted.
- **Poultry can be stored about 6 months** in the freezer at 0°F if properly wrapped. Do not refreeze raw poultry. Cook it; then you can freeze it again.

STORAGE & PREPARATION

- **Do not store fresh poultry more than a day or two** before cooking it. Keep refrigerated until cooking time.
- **Wash poultry well** inside and out before cooking. Drain well and pat dry with paper towels.
- **Everything that touches raw poultry** should be washed with a sanitizing solution of 1 tbsp. bleach dissolved in 1 gallon of warm (not hot) water. Use this solution to wash down any areas that come in contact with raw poultry. Let air dry — do not rinse. This helps prevent salmonella infection.
- **Discard leftover solution.**

CONVERTING YOUR FAVORITE CHICKEN RECIPES

- **Look for a similar microwave recipe.** Calculate microwave cooking time to be ¼ to ⅓ of conventional cooking time.
- **More food means more time.** In a conventional oven, a single piece of chicken takes about the same length of time to cook as a whole chicken, approximately an hour. In the microwave, **1 lb. of chicken will cook in 6 to 7 minutes, whereas a 3 lb. chicken will take 18 to 21 minutes.**
- **Reduce liquid by at least 25%** because there is less evaporation in microwave cooking. You can always add more liquid if necessary.
- **Oil is usually reduced or eliminated.** As there is no sticking, oil is only needed to provide flavor. Casserole dishes usually don't need greasing, unless you are completing the cooking in a conventional oven.
- **Salt, seasoning salt or garlic salt** should not be sprinkled directly on poultry before cooking; it can cause drying and toughening. You can add salt to a sauce or crumb coating with no problem. Otherwise, season with salt during standing time.
- **Use slightly less herbs** than usual when microwaving. Use more garlic in longer cooking dishes (10 minutes or more); its flavor mellows as it cooks.
- **Marinating chicken** before microwaving will enhance the flavor.
- **I often remove the skin** from chicken before microwaving unless I am cooking it in a sauce or crisping it in the conventional oven after microwaving. Otherwise the skin can be somewhat rubbery. It's also a good way to save on calories!
- **To give color and flavor**, brush the chicken with soya, teriyaki or barbecue sauce. Paprika also adds color.
- **Slashing through skin** and meat at bony end of drumstick allows steam to escape and prevents it from bursting. It also prevents spatters.
- **Chicken may make a popping sound** during cooking. This is steam escaping from under the skin. I once had a small piece of chicken pop right out of the dish because of steam build-up underneath it!
- **The hollow cavity** makes whole poultry ideal for microwaving. Tie legs and wings close to body with string or dental floss (unflavored!) to make a ball shape.
- **Giblets are best cooked conventionally**; when microwaved, the gizzard and heart tend to become tough.
- **Chicken livers** should be cut up if you want to microwave them because they have a membrane covering them.

STUFFING POULTRY (THE RIGHT STUFF!)

- **Never stuff poultry ahead of time.** It should be stuffed just before cooking. Remove any remaining stuffing from poultry before refrigerating leftovers.
- **Stuffing may also be cooked separately** in a casserole dish. It cooks in just minutes because it is very porous.
- **Because stuffing absorbs heat quickly**, it is usually not necessary to increase the total cooking time by more than a minute or two.
- **Test temperature** of stuffing after standing time to be sure that it has reached 165 to 170°F. Otherwise, transfer poultry to a 425°F oven for 15 minutes.
- **As a general guideline**, allow ½ cup stuffing for each pound of turkey or chicken. Stuff loosely because stuffing expands during cooking.
- **To keep stuffing inside poultry** without using skewers, stuff end piece of a loaf of bread into opening or fasten skin closed with wooden toothpicks.

IT'S ALL IN THE ARRANGEMENT!

- **If using chicken pieces**, arrange the meatier portions outwards and thinner, bonier portions inwards (e.g. wings in the centre). Remember, **THIN IS IN!**
- **Drumsticks** should be arranged like the spokes of a wheel, with the meaty portions towards the outside edge of the dish.
- **Place chicken skin-side down** for first half of the cooking time, then turn pieces over and re-arrange so that parts that are more cooked are towards the centre of the dish.
- **Whole birds** should be cooked breast-side-down for the first half of cooking time, then breast-side-up till done.

THE KNACK OF A RACK

- **A microsafe rack** is used when roasting poultry to elevate it out of the pan juices. Otherwise, the parts sitting in the juices will cook faster.
- **Some racks are slotted** and must be placed in a microsafe casserole to catch any juices. Some manufacturers make ridged one-piece racks with a raised edge.
- **Wooden chopsticks** can be laid across the bottom of a casserole to simulate a rack if you don't have one.
- **You can also use an inverted saucer** to elevate poultry, but be sure to remove the saucer from the casserole immediately after cooking is completed. Otherwise, a vacuum forms and it will be difficult to remove.
- **If chicken is cooked in a sauce,** place rack under the cooking dish instead of under the chicken.
- **I often use a rack** for breaded chicken pieces to keep the breading from getting soggy. I usually don't bother for breaded boneless breasts.

PERTINENT POINTERS

- **Poultry should be completely defrosted** before cooking.
- Use **HIGH power** to cook poultry. **Allow 6 to 7 minutes per lb.** If your oven has less than 600 watts, more time will be needed.
- **Drain pan juices** at half time. They can be used to make gravy or sauce, or frozen until needed in ice cube trays. **Allow 30 to 45 seconds on HIGH to melt 1 ice cube.**
- **Turn chicken over**; move pieces that are more cooked towards the centre of the casserole. Add desired sauce and microwave for remaining time. Some recipes call for adding sauce to chicken at beginning of cooking time. No draining is necessary at half time for these recipes.
- **Shield any areas** that have begun to overcook with small pieces of flat aluminum foil (wing tips, drumsticks, breastbone). Attach foil with wooden toothpicks.
- **Allow** ¼ of cooking time as standing time. Chicken finishes cooking during standing time. Covering retains heat.
- **If sauce seems too thin** or you prefer a crispy skin, omit standing time and place chicken in a preheated **425°F oven for 10 to 15 minutes**, or broil briefly. Watch carefully to prevent burning. Make sure that the cooking casserole can be used for broiling.
- **Fifteen minutes in a preheated 425°F oven** after microwaving helps ensure poultry is evenly and thoroughly cooked.

TO COVER OR NOT TO COVER...

- **To retain maximum moisture**, cover with microsafe casserole lid or vented plastic wrap.
- **Waxed paper** makes an excellent cover as it keeps the heat in but allows steam to escape. It also prevents spatters during cooking. If necessary, replace with a fresh piece at half time after re-arranging chicken pieces.
- **Microsafe paper towelling** can be used for breaded chicken, but sometimes it sticks. Uncover at half time if you want a drier coating.
- **Cooking parchment** is excellent for microwaving, as well as for use on the **CONVECTION/MICROWAVE** and/or **CONVECTION** cycles.
- **For easy clean-up**, poultry can also be cooked in oven cooking bags. Follow microwave instructions provided on packaging.
- **Oven cooking bags** are ideal for cooking on the **CONVECTION/MICROWAVE cycle** when your recipe indicates that the chicken should be covered during cooking. Remember to coat the inside of the bag with flour before adding the remaining ingredients. Close end loosely, leaving an opening of about one finger width. Make sure that **inflated cooking bag does NOT touch hot oven walls or rack on the CONVECTION or CONVECTION/MICROWAVE** cycle.
- **A heatproof/microsafe casserole lid** (e.g. Pyrex™) can also be used to cover foods when cooking on the **CONVECTION/MICROWAVE** cycle if covering is needed.
- **If food is cooked covered**, it should remain covered during standing time. If food is cooked uncovered, it is usually left uncovered during standing time, unless heat retention is necessary while preparing other parts of the recipe.

COOKING TIMES

- **All recipes in this book** were tested on a 700 watt microwave oven. Increase cooking time if your oven has a lower wattage and dishes are not cooked in the indicated time. For every 4 or 5 minutes of cooking time, you may have to allow an extra minute or two, depending on your oven's wattage. You will gradually develop your own sense of timing for your particular microwave oven. Practice makes perfect!
- **Allow 6 to 7 minutes per lb. on HIGH for chicken on the bone and 5 minutes per lb. for boneless chicken breasts**. Bite-size pieces take slightly less time. **Chicken wings take about 6 minutes per lb.**
- **Allow 6 to 7 minutes per lb. on HIGH for duck, Cornish hens or goose.** You can also cook on **MEDIUM-HIGH (70%) for 9 to 10 minutes/lb.** (This is the same as cooking on **HIGH** in a 500 watt microwave oven.)
- **For turkey, allow 8 to 9 minutes a lb. on MEDIUM-HIGH (70%).** You can also start the turkey on **HIGH for 10 minutes, then MW on MEDIUM (50%) for 9 to 11 minutes per lb.**
- **Because chicken cooks so quickly**, it's no problem when I need some for a casserole, chicken salad, crêpes or a quick, simple meal. I keep boneless chicken breasts in my freezer. I can thaw, prepare and cook 1 lb. in less than 15 minutes!
- **When you need to cook a large quantity** of chicken and want it to be ready quickly, divide it into 2 batches. Cook the first batch and serve it. While everyone is enjoying first helpings, microwave the second batch. It will be piping hot and ready in minutes and you won't have to worry about keeping the extras hot!

QUICK GUIDE TO COOKING TIMES

Timing is based on using a 700 watt oven. If using **MEDIUM-HIGH (70%), or 500 watts,** cooking time will be about ⅓ longer. Covering retains steam and heat during cooking and/or standing time.

PARTS	POWER	TIME
CHICKEN BREASTS, BONELESS & SKINLESS: *(4 single breasts (2 double breasts) yield 3 c. cooked chicken.)*		
1 single breast (4 to 5 oz.)	**High**	**2½ - 3 mins.**
2 single breasts (8 to 10 oz.)	**High**	**3½ - 4 mins.**
4 single breasts (1 to 1¼ lb.)	**High**	**5 - 7 mins.**
CHICKEN BREASTS, WITH BONE (SKIN OPTIONAL):		
1 single breast (8 to 10 oz.)	**High**	**4 - 5 mins.**
2 single breasts (1 to 1¼ lb.)	**High**	**6 - 8 mins.**
4 single breasts (2 lb.)	**High**	**12 - 14 mins.**
DRUMSTICKS & THIGHS (SKIN OPTIONAL): *Slash through skin and meat at bony end of drumstick.* ***MEDIUM-HIGH*** *prevents bony ends from overcooking when microwaving just one or two pieces. (4 thighs or drumsticks or 2 drumstick/thighs yield 1 c. cooked.)*		
2 drumsticks or 2 thighs or 1 drumstick/thigh (6 to 8 oz.)	**Med. High (70%)**	**4 - 6 mins.**
4 drumsticks or 4 thighs or 2 drumstick/thighs (¾ to 1 lb.)	**High**	**5 - 7 mins.**
CHICKEN WINGS, SPLIT IN TWO, WING TIPS REMOVED: *Brush with sauce before cooking (e.g. BBQ sauce).*		
6 chicken wings (1 lb./12 pieces)	**High**	**6 mins.**
12 chicken wings (2 lb./24 pieces)	**High**	**10 - 12 mins.**

- **A scale** is an excellent investment. Weigh chicken before cooking for best results, or ask your butcher to mark the weight on the packaging.
- **3 - 4 single chicken breasts,** boned & skinned weigh 1 lb.
- **1 whole chicken breast** with bone and skin weighs 1 to 1¼ lb.
- **1 drumstick/thigh combination or 2 drumsticks or 2 thighs weigh just under** ½ lb.
- **6 chicken wings weigh approximately 1 lb.**
- Increase cooking time if your microwave has a lower wattage output and poultry is not cooked in the indicated time. For every 4 or 5 minutes of cooking time, you may have to add a minute or two extra.

STANDING TIME

- **Chicken completes its cooking** during standing time. You can always add more cooking time if necessary.
- **Allow a standing time** of 5 to 10 minutes, covered, for chicken pieces. If cooking just one or two servings, let stand 2 minutes. Allow 10 minutes for whole roast chicken, duck or goose. Allow 20 to 30 minutes for roast turkey.

TESTING FOR DONENESS

- **Poultry is done** when juices run clear when pierced with a fork, particularly under the drumstick, and the drumstick jiggles easily. It should be fork tender. The temperature should register 170 to 175°F on a meat thermometer or microwave probe before standing time. Insert into the meatiest part of the thigh. Temperature will rise about 10 degrees during standing time to 180 to 185°F. For safety's sake, test temperatures in several places, including the underside and the thickest, meatiest parts.

TIPS FOR CALORIE-WATCHERS

- **If you are watching calories or cholesterol,** remove and discard skin from poultry before cooking. The chicken won't stick to the casserole and won't be dry (unless you overcook it)!
- **Sprinkle boneless, skinless chicken breasts** with your favorite herbs and spices for an easy low-calorie meal. Use any of the following: freshly minced garlic or garlic powder (not garlic salt!), pepper, paprika, parsley, tarragon, rosemary, basil &/or oregano. You can also sprinkle chicken with 1 or 2 tbsp. chicken broth, white wine or lemon juice.
- **Microwaving extracts more fat** from poultry than conventional cooking does.
- **Additional oil is not needed** to cook chicken because there is no sticking. A bonus for calorie-watchers!
- **Pierce skin** of poultry on all sides if it is very fat (e.g. duck) so that fat can drain out. Pour off fat several times during cooking.
- **If you refrigerate chicken** after cooking, fat will rise to the surface of the sauce and solidify. Discard fat before reheating.

BROWNING TECHNIQUES

- **If your conventional recipe** calls for browning chicken in oil before cooking, preheat and use a microwave browning dish according to manufacturer's instructions. You can also brown the chicken pieces in a frypan on top of your stove before transferring them to the microwave.
- **Marinating chicken** before cooking in a marinade which contains soya or teriyaki sauce will add color. So will sprinkling chicken with paprika or dry onion soup mix. There are also browning sprays that can be sprayed on the food (e.g. Kitchen Bouquet).
- **Another method** is to prepare chicken as directed in either Combo-Cooked Chicken or Chicken & Your BBQ (directions follow).

COMBO-COOKED CHICKEN — THE DYNAMIC DUO!

- **Combination-cooked chicken** is juicy as well as crispy. **MW uncovered for 5 minutes per lb. on HIGH,** then transfer it to a preheated **425°F oven for 15 minutes.** Baste occasionally.
- **If you wish to use a lower oven temperature,** increase cooking time in the conventional oven by 5 minutes for every 25°F you reduce the cooking temperature (e.g. 400°F takes about 20 minutes, 375°F degrees takes about 25 minutes, 350°F takes about 30 minutes.)
- **Poultry should be cooked** in a casserole which is heatproof as well as microsafe. Grease casserole lightly to prevent sticking.
- **If you have a CONVECTION/MICROWAVE oven,** chicken can be microwaved uncovered for **5 minutes per lb. on HIGH,** then browned on the **CONVECTION CYCLE at 375 to 400°F for 15 to 20 minutes.** (Use lower temperature or cover loosely with foil if overbrowning.) Also see Convection/Micro Ways with Poultry (p. 143).

CHICKEN & YOUR BBQ

(MIKE & BARB — THE PERFECT COUPLE!)

- **Chicken on the BBQ** will cook without scorching and will be very juicy if you precook it first in the microwave. **MW uncovered, allowing 5 minutes per lb. on HIGH. Then transfer it immediately to the preheated BBQ and cook it for 15 minutes** over hot coals, until brown and crispy.
- **If desired,** brush with marinade or barbecue sauce several times during barbecuing. If using marinade, it should be boiled for at least 1 minute before brushing it on poultry.
- **I like to cook tiny new potatoes** in the microwave while the chicken is on the BBQ. I allow about **5 minutes per lb. on HIGH.** Then I put the potatoes on the BBQ, brush them with sauce and get them all crispy. Mmmmm good! Great with salad and garlic toast!

REHEATING POULTRY (SECOND TIME AROUND!)

- **To reheat cooked poultry,** arrange the thicker portions towards the outside. Cover with wax paper if desired to heat more evenly. You may have better results using **MEDIUM-HIGH (70%).**
- **One piece of chicken takes 1 to 2 minutes on HIGH to reheat,** depending on size. **Two pieces take 2 to 3 minutes.**
- **To avoid drying out** the white meat, lay a layer of lettuce leaves over chicken when reheating. This keeps it moist. This technique is excellent for roast chicken. Discard lettuce when serving.
- **A whole chicken will take 7 to 10 minutes on MEDIUM-HIGH to reheat,** depending on size, starting temperature and whether there is a sauce or not. Cover if desired. Turn whole chicken over at half time; pieces should be re-arranged at half time, or if in a sauce, stirred once or twice.
- **If you are heating a plate** containing other foods as well as chicken, arrange so that the vegetables are in the centre and the chicken and potatoes are placed on the outside edge of the dish.
- **Test if chicken is hot enough** by feeling the centre bottom of the dish. It should be hot to the touch. If chicken was stored on a serving plate in the refrigerator, the cold plate may absorb some of the heat from the chicken when you reheat it, so allow an extra 30 seconds.

CONVECTION/MICRO WAYS WITH POULTRY

- **To cook your favorite poultry recipes on the COMBINATION CYCLE, calculate 15 to 18 minutes per lb.** Some ovens are faster and take **10 to 12 minutes per lb.** Other ovens are slower. **See your manufacturer's cookbook** for time guidelines.
- **Cooking time can range** from ½ to ¾ of the time called for in your conventional recipe. You may even find that there is no time difference on certain recipes on the **COMBINATION CYCLE.** However, your chicken will be moist and juicy inside and browned outside when cooked with a combination of microwaves and heat.
- **A three lb. chicken will take from 35 to 60 minutes to cook,** depending on your oven. **Two chickens will take about 1 to 1½ hours.** Look for signs of doneness; chicken will be golden brown and juices will run clear when pierced with a fork. Check temperature to be sure (see below).
- **Use the COMBINATION CYCLE suitable for poultry recommended by your oven manufacturer.** On my oven, I use the automatic setting which has an oven temperature of 375°F and 160 watts of microwave power. Your manufacturer may use or recommend a different setting. This is why I give time variations for my recipes.
- **Preheating is usually not necessary.** Cook uncovered for maximum browning and crisping. Baste occasionally. Casserole lid or cooking parchment can be used if covering is necessary.
- **Use a microsafe/heatproof casserole** (e.g. Pyrex™, porcelain). Greasing casserole lightly will prevent sticking.
- **Elevate poultry during CONVECTION/MICROWAVE cooking** for maximum circulation of hot air around the food or casserole. (Some recipes require putting poultry on a microsafe/heatproof rack or inverted saucer.) Place in a microsafe/ heatproof casserole. Put casserole on rack recommended by your microwave manufacturer for use on the **COMBINATION CYCLE.** Refer to manufacturer's manual &/or cookbook for guidelines for your oven.
- **Metal must not touch the walls** of your oven during the **COMBINATION CYCLE.**
- **Start cooking poultry skin-side down**; whole poultry is started breast-side down. Turn poultry over at half time. Baste poultry several times with pan juices during cooking.
- **If chicken begins to overcook** on wings and ends of drumsticks during cooking, shield with foil "mittens and booties".
- **If your oven has a probe**, you can insert it into poultry (not touching fat, bone or metal) during the second half of cooking cycle. Probe will turn oven off when chicken has reached the required internal temperature.
- **Check temperature in two or three places** to make sure chicken is completely cooked. Chicken should be 175°F on a probe or meat thermometer. It should rise to 185°F during the standing time. Cover with foil during standing time to retain maximum heat. Test temperature in several places.
- **Cut-up potatoes** can be added to chicken during the last 20 minutes of cooking. You may have to increase cooking time slightly to allow for the extra volume of food in the microwave.
- **Read Convection/Micro Ways (p. 28)** and Geri's Combo-Cooked Capon (p. 148).

FREEZING AND THAWING COOKED POULTRY

- **Package foods** in small quantities (1 or 2 servings) for maximum convenience. Two small containers will defrost more evenly than one large one and make a perfect emergency meal!
- **Line a microsafe casserole** with cooking parchment or plastic wrap; arrange chicken pieces in a single layer, with meatier pieces towards the outside edge. Wrap tightly and freeze. When frozen, remove package from casserole and overwrap. Label package with contents of dish, number of servings and date of freezing.
- **To thaw and reheat**, remove wrappings and transfer food back to original casserole. Cover loosely with parchment or wax paper.
- **For one serving** of frozen chicken (8 to 10 oz.), **MW covered for 2 minutes on HIGH,** turn it over and **MW 1 to 2 minutes longer,** until hot.
- **For 2 or 3 servings** (e.g. single chicken breasts with bone), **MW covered on HIGH for 5 minutes.** Turn pieces over. **MW covered on HIGH 2 to 4 minutes longer.**
- **For larger quantities, start covered on HIGH for 5 minutes.** Separate pieces and turn them over. Cover and **MW on MEDIUM (50%) 5 to 15 minutes longer,** or until heated through. If in a sauce, stir every 5 minutes.
- **Another option** is to thaw and reheat in two steps. **MW covered on DEFROST (30%), allowing 6 to 7 minutes per lb., or about 2 minutes per piece.** Let defrosted chicken stand for a few minutes for the temperature to equalize; then **MW covered on HIGH, allowing 1 to 2 minutes per piece,** until hot.
- **Frozen cooked chicken** keeps 1 to 2 months in the freezer. Make sure that it is well wrapped to prevent freezer burn.

RENDERED CHICKEN FAT & CRACKLINGS

(SCHMALTZ & GRIBENES)

Remembered with sighs of ecstasy as a favorite in the olden days B.C. (Before Cholesterol)! No respectable Jewish home was without a jar of "schmaltz" in the fridge (or icebox)! I remember sitting at my grandmother's kitchen table and clutching a folded slice of Chalah and Gribenes in my skinny little fist. Perhaps that's why my fist isn't so skinny today!

1 c. raw chicken fat and skin, cut up
1 large onion, chopped

1. Place fat and skin in a 1 quart heatproof microsafe bowl. **MW uncovered on HIGH for 10 minutes**, until fat is melted and skin begins to get crispy and brown. Stir once or twice. Meanwhile, pat chopped onions dry with paper towels.

2. Add onions to bowl and **MW uncovered on HIGH 2 or 3 minutes longer,** until onions and cracklings are golden brown.

3. Strain, pressing out all fat from the onions and cracklings. Cool fat slightly, then store in a covered jar in the refrigerator. Cracklings can be used to flavor mashed potatoes, chopped liver or sprinkled lightly with salt and served on slices of fresh Chalah or pumpernickel bread!

> * Use tempered microsafe cookware that can withstand high temperatures up to 450°F.

BEA'S "SECRET" HOLIDAY CHICKEN

I was served this yummy chicken at my friend Seline Malament's one Friday night and loved it. She shared the recipe with me, and I decided to adapt it for my book. Afterwards, I found out that her friend Beatrice had given her the recipe with warnings to keep it a secret. Now the secret is out!

⅓ c. oil
2 tbsp. vinegar or lemon juice
1 tsp. garlic powder
¼ tsp. pepper
1 tsp. paprika
2 chickens, about 3 lb. each, cut in 8ths
1 pkg. Kosher onion soup mix
1 c. hot water

1. Combine oil, vinegar and seasonings in a measuring cup and mix well. Place chicken in a lightly greased 9″ x 13″ Pyrex™ casserole. Pour marinade over chicken and rub well on all sides to season. Cover chicken and marinate overnight in the refrigerator, turning it over once or twice.

2. Dissolve onion soup mix in hot water. Arrange chicken skin-side down, with larger, meatier pieces towards the outside of the casserole. Pour soup over chicken.

3. Cover with wax paper and **MW on HIGH for 15 minutes.** Turn chicken pieces over and re-arrange, placing more cooked portions towards the centre of the dish. Baste with juices. Cover and **MW on HIGH 20 minutes longer,** basting twice.

4. Meanwhile, preheat conventional oven to 400°F. Immediately place chicken in preheated oven and **bake uncovered at 400°F for about 20 minutes,** or until golden brown, basting often.

Yield: 6 to 8 servings. Freezes well.

* Potatoes can be peeled, quartered and microwaved in a covered casserole while the chicken is browning in the conventional oven. **Six potatoes (about 2 lb.) will take about 13 to 15 minutes on HIGH.** Test for doneness with a sharp knife. Add potatoes to chicken and baste with gravy. Cook remaining time **(5 to 10 minutes longer) in the conventional oven,** until browned.

* **CONVECTION/MICROWAVE METHOD:** Prepare chicken as directed in Steps 1 and 2. Place casserole on rack recommended by oven manufacturer and **roast uncovered on COMBINATION CYCLE suitable for poultry.** It will take **1 to 1¼ hours,** until golden brown. Time varies with different ovens. Turn chicken over halfway through cooking; baste occasionally. Refer to Convection/Micro Ways with Poultry (p. 143).

MY OVEN'S SETTING______ MY COOKING TIME______

CRISPY ROAST CHICKEN

Roast chicken in half an hour — what could be easier? My students love it! Combination cooking produces the best of both worlds, juicy inside, crispy outside. Chicken can be whole or cut up. If you have your own favorite seasonings, feel free to substitute them.

3 - 3 ½ lb. chicken
2 tbsp. teriyaki or soya sauce
1 or 2 cloves garlic, crushed
paprika

1. Wash chicken and pat dry. Rub with teriyaki or soya sauce, garlic and paprika. If whole, place chicken on a microsafe roasting rack in an oblong Pyrex™ casserole. If chicken is in pieces, arrange skin-side down directly in the casserole. Place thicker, meatier parts towards the outside edge of the dish.

2. MW covered with waxed paper on HIGH for 15 to 18 minutes, allowing 5 minutes per lb. Turn chicken over or rearrange pieces at half time. Shield wing tips and ends of drumsticks with aluminum foil if they are overcooking. Meanwhile, preheat conventional oven to 425°F.

3. Baste chicken with drippings, remove rack and discard foil. Immediately place chicken in preheated oven and **bake uncovered at 425°F for 15 minutes,** until golden and crispy, basting occasionally. Serve with roasted potatoes* or Rice Pilaf (p. 214).

Yield: 3 to 4 servings. Freezes well.

* When roasting a whole chicken, shield wings and ends of drumsticks with foil "mittens and booties" at half time to protect them from overcooking in the microwave. Remove when transferring chicken to the conventional oven.
* You can use a lower oven temperature if you have more time, **350°F for ½ hour.** If oven is not preheated, cooking time will be slightly longer.
* Potatoes can be peeled, quartered and microwaved with 2 tbsp. water in a covered casserole while the chicken is browning in the conventional oven. **Four potatoes (about 1 ½ lb.) will take 9 to 10 minutes on HIGH.** Test for doneness with a sharp knife. Add potatoes to chicken and baste with gravy. **Roast 5 to 10 minutes longer in the conventional oven,** until browned.
* If using Rice Pilaf as a side dish, microwave it while chicken is browning in the conventional oven.
* **CONVECTION/MICROWAVE METHOD:** Prepare chicken as directed in Step 1. Place casserole on rack recommended by oven manufacturer and **roast uncovered on COMBINATION CYCLE suitable for poultry.** It will take **35 to 60 minutes,** until golden brown. Time varies with different ovens. Turn chicken over halfway through cooking; baste occasionally. Refer to Convection/Micro Ways with Poultry (p. 143).

  MY OVEN'S SETTING______ MY COOKING TIME______
* Whole chicken can be stuffed with your favorite stuffing. Cooking time will be about the same. Stuffing must be 165°F on meat thermometer or probe when chicken is done.

HONEY GLAZED CHICKEN

3 - 3 ½ lb. chicken
1 tsp. paprika
¼ tsp. pepper
½ tsp. curry powder
3 tbsp. Dijon mustard
¼ c. honey
2 tbsp. apricot jam

1. Sprinkle chicken with seasonings. Combine mustard, honey and jam. Rub over chicken.

2. Cook as directed for Crispy Roast Chicken (p. 146).

Yield: 4 servings.

HEAVENLY CHICKEN

A family favorite! This recipe usually takes 2 hours to cook conventionally. By using the combination method of cooking, standing time is avoided and the chicken is beautifully browned.

2 broilers, cut up (about 5 lb. total)
¾ c. Italian, French or Catalina salad dressing
¾ c. apricot or peach jam or orange marmalade
1 tbsp. lemon juice
1 pkg. dry onion soup mix

1. Place chicken in a lightly greased 9″ x 13″ Pyrex™ casserole. Combine remaining ingredients and rub over chicken pieces. Arrange the thicker, meatier parts towards the outer edge of the dish; wings and drumsticks should be towards the centre.

2. Cover with waxed paper. **MW on HIGH for 15 minutes.** Turn chicken pieces over and re-arrange, placing more cooked portions towards the centre of the dish. Baste with sauce. Cover and **MW on HIGH 15 minutes longer.**

3. Meanwhile, preheat conventional oven to 400°F. Baste chicken with sauce; immediately transfer to preheated oven. **Cook uncovered at 400°F for 15 to 20 minutes,** until glazed and golden, basting occasionally. Serve over rice.

Yield: 6 to 8 servings. Freezes and/or reheats well.

* Rice can be cooked in the microwave while chicken is browning in the conventional oven.
* **CONVECTION/MICROWAVE METHOD:** Prepare chicken as directed in Step 1. Place casserole on rack recommended by oven manufacturer and **roast uncovered on COMBINATION CYCLE suitable for poultry.** It will take **1 to 1 ¼ hours,** until golden brown. Time varies with different ovens. Turn chicken over halfway through cooking; baste occasionally. Refer to Convection/Micro Ways with Poultry (p. 143).

MY OVEN'S SETTING______ MY COOKING TIME______

GERI'S COMBO-COOKED CAPON

*Geri Kramer is a proficient microwaver. She shared this excellent chicken recipe with me which she cooks on the **CONVECTION/MICROWAVE** cycle of her combination oven. Use your own seasonings if you wish.*

7 - 8 lb. roasting capon
¼ c. soya sauce
¼ - ⅓ c. honey
2 tbsp. lemon juice
2 tsp. dry mustard
freshly ground pepper, to taste
1 onion, peeled
1 apple, peeled

1. Rub chicken inside and out with soya sauce, honey, lemon juice, mustard and pepper. Cut onion and apple in half. Place in cavity of chicken. (This helps keep it moist.) Place chicken breast-side down on a microsafe/heatproof rack. Place rack in a Pyrex™ casserole to catch the drippings.

2. **Roast uncovered on COMBINATION CYCLE recommended by your oven manufacturer for poultry.** (Geri uses **COMBINATION 4** on her oven, which has an automatic setting of 375°F and 160 watts of microwave power. Her total cooking time is about **1 ½ hours.** Times vary with different ovens.) At half time, turn chicken over and baste with pan juices.

3. (If your oven has a probe, insert it into the thickest portion of the thigh, not touching bone or metal. Follow manufacturer's instructions.) Cook remaining time, or until internal temperature of chicken reaches 175°F. Baste occasionally. Chicken should be golden brown and tender when done.

4. Remove from microwave; cover with a tent of aluminum foil. Let stand for 15 minutes. Temperature will rise to 185°F.

Yield: 6 servings. Freezes well.

* Read Convection/Micro Ways with Poultry (p. 143).
* Quartered or small new potatoes can be added the last 20 minutes of cooking. Baste often with pan juices. Adding potatoes can increase total cooking time slightly.
* Capon can be stuffed, if desired. Cooking time will be about the same. Stuff poultry just before cooking. Internal temperature of stuffing should reach 165°F. Remove stuffing from leftovers, or if freezing; wrap and store separately.

MY OVEN'S SETTING______ MY COOKING TIME______

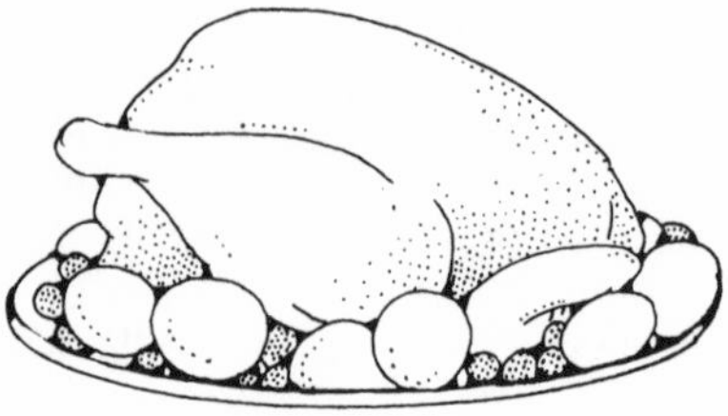

SWEET'N'SASSY BBQ CHICKEN

1 c. Sweet'n'Sassy BBQ Sauce (p. 91) (or bottled BBQ sauce)
3 to 4 lb. chicken pieces

1. Prepare sauce as directed. Refrigerate remaining sauce for another day.

2. Weigh chicken; **calculate 5 minutes per lb.** as your microwave cooking time. Wash chicken; pat dry with paper towelling. Place skin-side down in a single layer in an ungreased 9″ x 13″ Pyrex™ casserole. Arrange the thicker, meatier pieces towards the outer edge of the dish. Cover with wax paper.

3. Start barbecue so it will be hot enough when the chicken is ready to go on the grill.

4. **MW chicken on HIGH** for half the cooking time, **about 8 to 10 minutes.** Drain pan juices and turn chicken pieces over, re-arranging so that more cooked portions are towards the centre of the dish. **MW covered on HIGH for remaining cooking time, 7 to 10 minutes longer,** until almost cooked.

5. Transfer chicken immediately to preheated BBQ. Brush with sauce. **Grill over hot coals** until crisp and golden, **about 15 to 20 minutes,** basting often.

Yield: 4 to 6 servings. Can be frozen.

* Instead of transferring chicken to the BBQ, it can also be completed in a hot oven **(400°F) for 15 minutes,** or until golden brown. Baste occasionally.
* If you have your own favorite sauce or seasoning mix for BBQ chicken, it can be used successfully for this recipe. Do not sprinkle salt on chicken before microwaving.
* Microwave Baked Potatoes (p. 270) while chicken is on the BBQ. Transfer potatoes to the BBQ and brush with BBQ sauce. Grill until skins are crusty, about 10 minutes, turning and basting often. (And please be sure to invite me for dinner!)

CHICKEN IN BROWN BEAN OR HOISIN SAUCE

This scrumptious dish is cooked with a combination of microwaves and conventional heat or the BBQ. Transfer chicken immediately from the microwave directly to the hot grill or oven and cook it to perfection!

2 chickens, (3 lb. each) cut up
6 cloves garlic
ginger the size of a quarter
¼ c. Brown Bean or Hoisin Sauce*
1 tsp. Chili Paste with Garlic*
⅓ c. apricot jam
¼ c. soya sauce
¼ c. honey
½ tsp. Oriental sesame oil*

1. Wash chicken pieces and pat dry. Arrange in a single layer in a lightly greased 9″ x 13″ Pyrex™ casserole. Place chicken skin-side down, with the thicker pieces towards the outside of the dish.

2. **MW covered with waxed paper on HIGH for 15 minutes.** Prepare sauce and preheat BBQ or conventional oven while chicken is cooking.

3. **Steel Knife:** Drop garlic and ginger through feed tube and process until minced. Add remaining ingredients and process a few seconds to blend.

4. Drain juices from chicken. Turn chicken skin-side up and move the more cooked pieces towards the centre of the casserole. Add sauce to chicken and **MW covered on HIGH 15 minutes longer.**

5. Immediately transfer it to the hot BBQ and cook until golden, or else complete the cooking in a **400°F oven. Cooking time on the BBQ or in the oven will be about 15 to 20 minutes.** Baste often with sauce. Serve on a bed of fluffy white rice.

Yield: 8 servings. Freezes well.

* Chinese products are available in Oriental grocery stores.
* **Chili Paste with Garlic Substitute:** To make the equivalent of 1 tsp. as a flavoring for sauces and marinades, combine the following ingredients: 1 tsp. chili powder, 15 drops Tabasco sauce, 1 tsp. vinegar, 1 clove minced garlic and a pinch of sugar.
* Rice can be microwaved while chicken is on the BBQ or in the oven.
* **CONVECTION/MICROWAVE METHOD:** Combine chicken with sauce ingredients in casserole and mix well. Place casserole on rack recommended by oven manufacturer and **roast uncovered on COMBINATION CYCLE suitable for poultry.** It will take **1 to 1¼ hours,** until golden brown. Time varies with different ovens. Turn chicken over halfway through cooking; baste occasionally. Refer to Convection/Micro Ways with Poultry (p. 143).

MY OVEN'S SETTING______ MY COOKING TIME______

FINGER LICKIN' CHINESE CHICKEN

Shared with me by one of my enthusiastic students, Marcy Berger.

3 lb. chicken, cut up
1 tbsp. oil
1/3 c. soya sauce
1/3 c. brown sugar, or honey
1/3 c. water
1/4 c. Mirin (Chinese cooking wine), sherry or apple juice
1 tbsp. ketchup
3/4 tsp. red pepper flakes
2 cloves garlic, crushed
1 green onion, sliced
2 tbsp. cornstarch dissolved in 2 tbsp. cold water
2 tbsp. sesame seeds, optional

1. Arrange chicken skin-side down in a single layer in a lightly greased 9″ x 13″ Pyrex™ casserole. Place the meatier, thicker parts towards the outer edge of the dish. Cover with wax paper and **MW on HIGH for 12 minutes.**

2. Meanwhile, combine remaining ingredients except cornstarch mixture and sesame seeds. Mix well.

3. Drain off cooking juices from chicken. Turn skin-side up and re-arrange so that more cooked pieces are towards the centre of the dish. Pour soya sauce mixture over chicken. **MW covered on HIGH 10 minutes longer.**

4. Stir cornstarch mixture into sauce. Mix well. (No need to remove chicken from casserole.) **MW uncovered on HIGH for 3 to 4 minutes,** until thickened, stirring once or twice. Spoon sauce over chicken pieces to glaze.

5. Let stand covered for 5 to 10 minutes. (If desired, omit standing time, sprinkle with sesame seeds and **bake uncovered in a preheated 400°F oven for 10 to 15 minutes.** Baste once or twice.) Serve over rice or noodles.

Yield: 4 servings. Freezes and/or reheats well.

* To increase the number of servings, **calculate 6 to 7 minutes cooking time for each lb. of chicken.** It is not necessary to increase the quantity of sauce if you double the recipe.
* Beverly Salomon makes a similar recipe using only chicken breasts. In Step 2 substitute 1 pkg. dry onion soup mix and 1 1/4 c. bottled spare rib sauce instead of the remaining ingredients. Cornstarch mixture is optional in Step 4.

SZECHUAN ORANGE CHICKEN

1. Follow recipe for Szechuan Orange Chicken Wings (p. 48), but substitute 3 lb. chicken breasts (about 3 double breasts, cut in half). If you wish to remove the skin, do so before marinating. Arrange chicken in an ungreased 9″ x 13″ Pyrex™ casserole, with the thicker, meatier parts towards the outside of the dish.

2. **MW covered on HIGH for 10 minutes.** Turn chicken over and rearrange. Brush with additional marinade. **MW on HIGH 8 to 10 minutes longer,** until juices run clear. Let stand covered for 5 minutes. Prepare sauce during standing time for chicken. Serve chicken on a bed of fluffy white rice. Top with sauce.

Yield: 4 to 6 servings.

BEV'S ORANGE CHICKEN

Quick to make, even quicker to disappear!

8 single chicken breasts, skinned (about 4 lb.)
1 pkg. onion soup mix
12 oz. can concentrated orange juice, thawed
1 ½ tbsp. cornstarch

1. Place chicken in a lightly greased 3 quart oval or oblong microsafe/heatproof casserole. Combine remaining ingredients and mix well. Pour over chicken. Arrange chicken skin-side down in a single layer, with the thicker, meatier pieces towards the outer edges of the casserole. Cover with wax paper.

2. **MW on HIGH for 12 minutes.** Turn chicken over, re-arranging so that more cooked portions are moved towards the centre of the dish. Baste with sauce. Cover and **MW on HIGH for 12 minutes longer.** Preheat conventional oven to 400°F.

3. Transfer chicken to conventional oven and **cook uncovered at 400°F for 15 to 20 minutes,** until sauce is slightly thickened. Baste occasionally.

Yield: 6 to 8 servings.

* **CONVECTION/MICROWAVE METHOD:** Combine all ingredients in a lightly greased casserole. Place casserole on rack recommended by oven manufacturer and **cook uncovered on COMBINATION CYCLE suitable for poultry.** It will take **1 to 1 ¼ hours,** until nicely browned. Time varies with different ovens. Turn chicken over halfway through cooking; baste occasionally. Refer to Convection/Micro Ways with Poultry (p. 143).

MY OVEN'S SETTING______ MY COOKING TIME______

MIMI'S MARVELOUS CHICKEN CASSEROLE

Everything in one dish Mmm-Marvelous!

3 lb. chicken, cut up
2 or 3 large onions, sliced
4 medium potatoes, peeled & quartered
3 carrots, sliced ½″ thick
1 tsp. salt
½ tsp. pepper
1 to 2 tsp. paprika
1 tsp. garlic powder or 3 cloves garlic, crushed
1 c. BBQ or pizza sauce

1. Remove skin from chicken if you wish. Place chicken and vegetables in a lightly greased 9″ x 13″ Pyrex™ casserole. Add remaining ingredients and mix well. Arrange thicker pieces of chicken towards the outside edge of the casserole. Cover with cooking parchment or waxed paper.

2. **MW on HIGH for 15 minutes.** Uncover carefully to prevent steam burns. Stir; re-arrange so that more cooked portions are towards the centre of the dish. Preheat conventional oven to 400°F.

3. Cover and **MW on HIGH 12 to 15 minutes longer,** until chicken and vegetables are tender. Uncover; transfer chicken to conventional oven **and cook uncovered at 400°F for 15 to 20 minutes.** Baste once or twice. (This will thicken the gravy and brown the chicken.) Adjust seasonings to taste.

Yield: 4 servings. Freezes and/or reheats well.

CHICKEN CACCIATORE

Gremolata elevates this dish from every-day to gourmet fare!

2 cloves garlic, crushed
1 onion, sliced
1 green pepper, sliced
1 c. mushrooms, sliced
1 tbsp. oil
19 oz. can tomatoes
5 ½ oz. can tomato paste
¼ c. red wine or cooking sherry
1 bay leaf
¾ tsp. salt
freshly ground pepper
1 tbsp. sugar
¼ tsp. each basil, oregano and thyme
4 lb. chicken pieces*
Gremolata (recipe follows)

1. Combine garlic, onion, green pepper and mushrooms with oil in an ungreased 9″ x 13″ Pyrex™ casserole. **MW uncovered on HIGH for 5 minutes,** stirring at half time.

2. Add remaining ingredients except chicken and Gremolata. Mix well, breaking up tomatoes. Add chicken pieces, stirring to coat well. Arrange skin-side down, with the meatier, thicker parts towards the outer edge of the dish.

3. Cover with wax paper and **MW on HIGH for 15 minutes.** Turn chicken over and re-arrange, placing the more cooked pieces towards the centre of the dish. Baste chicken with sauce. Recover with fresh wax paper.

4. MW on HIGH 15 to 18 minutes longer, until chicken is tender and juices run clear. Baste once or twice. Let stand covered for 5 to 10 minutes*. Serve over rice or fettucine. Serve over Spaghetti Squash (p. 281) if you are watching your calories. Garnish with Gremolata.

Yield: 4 to 6 servings. Freezes and/or reheats well.

* If you wish, remove skin from chicken before cooking to reduce calories. I use 4 double breasts, split, for this recipe, but you can use a mix of white and dark meat if you prefer.
* If desired, omit standing time and transfer chicken to a **preheated 400°F oven for 10 to 15 minutes.** This will thicken the sauce. Baste occasionally.
* **CONVECTION/MICROWAVE METHOD:** Follow Steps 1 and 2 as directed above. Place casserole on rack recommended by oven manufacturer and **roast uncovered on COMBINATION CYCLE suitable for poultry.** It will take **1 to 1 ¼ hours,** until tender and golden. Time varies with different ovens. Turn chicken over halfway through cooking; baste occasionally. Refer to Convection/Micro Ways with Poultry (p. 143).

MY OVEN'S SETTING________ MY COOKING TIME________

Gremolata

1 tbsp. grated lemon rind
2 tbsp. chopped parsley
2 cloves garlic, crushed

1. Combine all ingredients and mix well.

CHICKEN & RICE CASSEROLE #1

This recipe is so easy. It seems that every time I make it, I go shopping while the casserole completes the last stage of cooking. Whether I get home in an hour or two, it's still piping hot and ready to eat.

1 tbsp. oil
1 onion, chopped
2 cloves garlic, minced
1 green pepper, chopped
1 c. long-grain rice
1 c. tomato sauce
¾ c. hot water or chicken broth
3 lb. chicken, cut up
¾ tsp. salt
¼ tsp. pepper
⅛ tsp. each basil & oregano

1. Combine oil with onion, garlic and green pepper in an ungreased 10″ Corning Ware™ casserole or 2 quart oval or rectangular microsafe casserole. **MW uncovered on HIGH for 3 minutes.**

2. Stir in rice, tomato sauce and water or broth. Arrange chicken skin-side down in a single layer over rice. Place chicken so that the thicker, meatier pieces are towards the outside edge of the dish. Sprinkle with seasonings. Spoon some of the liquid over the chicken. Cover with casserole lid or microsafe plastic wrap, turning back one corner of plastic wrap ⅛″ to vent slightly.

3. **MW on HIGH for 12 minutes.** Uncover carefully; move chicken pieces to one side and stir rice. Turn chicken skin-side up and re-arrange, placing more cooked pieces towards the centre of the casserole. Baste chicken with liquid.

4. **MW covered on MEDIUM (50%) for 35 to 40 minutes,** until liquid is almost completely absorbed and chicken is tender. Let stand covered for 10 to 15 minutes, or up to an hour. Rice will absorb remaining liquid; flavor improves with standing.

Yield: 4 servings. Freezes and/or reheats very well.

* If desired, omit tomato sauce and increase chicken broth to 1 ¾ cups.
* Remove skin from chicken if you wish. I often make this dish with chicken breasts. Do not use boneless breasts or chicken may overcook.
* If using plastic wrap to cover casserole, you may have to replace it at the end of Step 3.

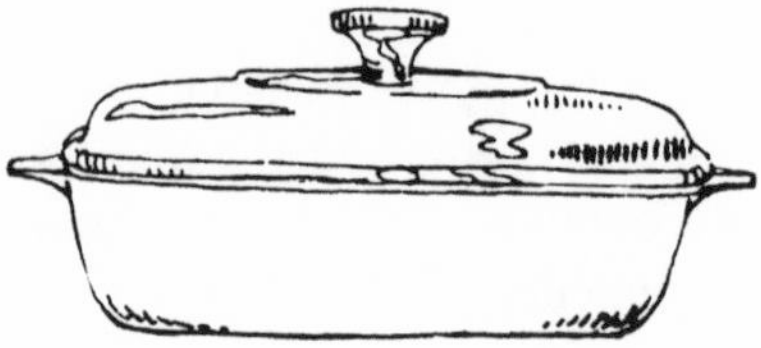

CHICKEN & RICE CASSEROLE #2

When I'm really rushed and don't feel like chopping vegetables, I make this version of the preceding recipe. (Yes, I have days like that too!)

1 c. long grain rice
3 lb. chicken, cut up
1 pkg. dry onion soup mix
⅛ tsp. garlic powder
paprika
1 ¾ c. hot water

1. Place rice in an ungreased 2 quart microsafe casserole. Arrange chicken skin-side down in a single layer on top of rice. Place so that thicker, meatier pieces are towards the outer edge of the dish. Sprinkle chicken and rice with onion soup mix, garlic powder and paprika. Add water to rice in bottom of casserole. Cover with casserole lid or microsafe plastic wrap, turning back one corner of plastic wrap ⅛″ to vent slightly.

2. MW on HIGH for 12 minutes. Uncover carefully; move chicken pieces to one side and stir rice. Turn chicken skin-side up and re-arrange, placing more cooked pieces towards the centre of the casserole. Baste chicken with liquid.

3. MW covered on MEDIUM (50%) for 35 to 40 minutes, until liquid is almost completely absorbed and chicken is tender. Let stand covered for 10 to 15 minutes, or up to an hour. Rice will absorb remaining liquid; flavor improves with standing.

Yield: 4 servings. Freezes and/or reheats well.

BELLA'S CHILI CHICKEN

This dish is chili-icious delicious!

2 onions, chopped
2 green peppers, chopped
3 cloves garlic, minced
2 tbsp. oil
14 oz. can pineapple chunks
¾ c. chili sauce
2 tbsp. brown sugar
1 tbsp. soya sauce
1 tsp. salt
¼ tsp. pepper
3 lb. chicken breasts, skin removed

1. Combine onions, green peppers, garlic and oil in an ungreased 9″ x 13″ Pyrex™ casserole. **MW uncovered on HIGH for 5 minutes,** stirring at half time.

2. Drain pineapple chunks, reserving ¼ cup juice. Combine pineapple juice with chili sauce, brown sugar, soya sauce, salt and pepper. Mix well.

3. Arrange chicken skin-side down in casserole. Place the meatier, thicker parts towards the outer edge of the casserole. Spoon sauce over chicken. Cover with wax paper and **MW on HIGH for 12 minutes.**

4. Turn chicken over and re-arrange, placing the more cooked pieces towards the centre of the dish. Baste with sauce. Cover with fresh wax paper and **MW on HIGH 10 to 12 minutes longer,** or until chicken is tender. Add pineapple chunks. **MW uncovered on HIGH 2 minutes longer,** until pineapple is heated through.

5. Let stand covered for 10 minutes, or omit standing time and place chicken uncovered in a **400°F oven for 12 to 15 minutes,** until sauce is thickened slightly. Serve over rice.

Yield: 4 servings. Freezes and/or reheats well.

MICRO-WAYS WITH BREADED CHICKEN

- **If you wish to bread chicken pieces,** use seasoned crumbs (crackers, cornflake or toasted bread crumbs.) Add paprika for additional color. You can also use packaged coating mixes.
- **Although breaded chicken pieces** will not be as crisp when microwaved, they can be broiled afterwards for 3 to 4 minutes to make them crunchy. (I never bother.)
- **Remove skin before breading chicken** — it doesn't get crispy, so why waste the calories? Rinse chicken under cold running water. Pat dry with paper towelling so breading will stick. Dip chicken pieces first in an egg lightly beaten with 1 tbsp. oil, then in seasoned crumb mixture. The oil helps brown the crumbs.
- **Calorie-watchers** can dip chicken pieces in low calorie salad dressing or diet mayonnaise, then in crumb mixture.
- **Arrange chicken** in a microsafe casserole in a single layer, with pieces not touching each other. It can also be placed on a microsafe rack.
- **Covering chicken loosely** with microsafe paper towelling will prevent spatters and absorb moisture from the chicken, keeping the crumb topping drier.
- **Calculate 6 to 7 minutes per lb. on HIGH for poultry with bone, and 5 minutes per lb. for boneless chicken breasts.**
- **At half time,** re-arrange chicken pieces, placing the more cooked pieces towards the centre of the dish or rack; do not turn them over, except in the case of boneless breasts.
- **Breaded boneless chicken breasts** can be turned over at half time so they will absorb some of the flavor released during cooking (this is optional). The paper towel covering helps absorb excess moisture.
- **CONVECTION/MICROWAVE METHOD:** Preheat oven to 375°F. Place chicken skin-side up in heatproof/microsafe cooking dish; place on rack recommended by oven manufacturer. **Cook on COMBINATION CYCLE suitable for poultry.** Cooking time will be **35 to 60 minutes for 3 lb. of cut-up chicken,** depending on your oven. Re-arrange halfway through cooking. Check for doneness at minimum time. Refer to Convection/Micro Ways with Poultry (p. 143) and Breaded Chicken, Guilt-Free! (p. 157).
- **CONVECTION METHOD** (For maximum crispness): Preheat oven to 375°F. Arrange chicken skin-side up on a lightly greased cookie sheet. Place on oven rack. **Bake on CONVECTION CYCLE at 375°F 35 to 45 minutes,** or until brown and crisp.
- **For fried chicken,** brown in a skillet on the rangetop in hot oil until golden brown on all sides, about 4 to 5 minutes. (A Corning Ware™ 10″ skillet can be used; it is also microsafe.) Drain well. Arrange in a microsafe casserole with the meatiest parts towards the outside of the dish. **MW uncovered on HIGH, calculating 4 to 5 minutes per lb.,** until juices run clear. See recipe for Fried Chicken (p. 158).

BREADED CHICKEN, GUILT-FREE!

This recipe was tested during a big snowstorm when I was housebound and didn't have any chicken breasts in my freezer. My friend Mimi came to the rescue and made this dish with telephone instructions, testing the times for different quantities. She had always felt guilty eating breaded chicken; when she learned that 3 tbsp. of bread crumbs was equivalent to a slice of bread on her diet, she was thrilled!

4 single chicken breasts (2 lb.)
1/4 c. low-calorie Italian salad dressing
3/4 c. seasoned bread crumbs or corn flake crumbs

1. Remove skin from chicken. Do not remove bones. Rinse chicken under cold running water. Pat dry with paper towels. Coat with salad dressing. Sprinkle with crumbs (you will use about 3 tbsp. crumbs for each breast).

2. Arrange chicken skin-side up in a single layer on a large microsafe rack or plate; thicker, meatier parts should be towards the outside edge.

3. Cover with microsafe paper towelling. **MW on HIGH for 12 to 14 minutes,** until juices run clear and chicken is tender. Re-arrange at half time but do not turn pieces over. Let stand covered for 3 or 4 minutes. Serve with a salad or your favorite cooked veggies.

Yield: 4 servings.

* **One single breast** (8 to 10 oz.), bone in, **4 to 5 minutes** to microwave. **Two single breasts** (1 to 1 1/4 lb.) **take 6 to 8 minutes.** For larger quantities, calculate **6 to 7 minutes/lb.**
* You can substitute any low-cal salad dressing you like. Light-style mayonnaise also works well in this recipe.
* **CONVECTION/MICROWAVE METHOD:** Prepare chicken as directed in Steps 1 and 2. Rack or plate should be microsafe and heatproof. Preheat oven to 375°F. Place on rack recommended by manufacturer and **cook uncovered on COMBINATION CYCLE suitable for poultry. Allow 15 to 20 minutes per lb.** Times vary with different ovens. Juices should run clear when chicken is cooked and chicken should be nicely browned. Check at minimum time and add more time if needed. Refer to Convection/Micro Ways with Poultry (p. 143) and Micro-Ways with Breaded Chicken (p. 156).

  MY OVEN'S SETTING________ MY COOKING TIME________
* **CONVECTION METHOD:** See Micro-Ways with Breaded Chicken (p. 156).
* If you have boneless chicken breasts, prepare as directed in recipe for Boneless Chicken Breasts Italiano (p. 160). Omit sauce, if desired.

FRIED CHICKEN

Chicken is browned conventionally to give it a crusty coating, then completed in the microwave oven to make it tender and juicy.

2 - 2 ½ lb. chicken pieces
1 egg
1 tbsp. water
1 c. corn flake or bread crumbs
¾ tsp. salt
¼ tsp. pepper
⅛ tsp. garlic powder
¼ tsp. paprika
¼ tsp. basil
3 tbsp. oil

1. Remove skin from chicken. Blend egg and water in a pie plate. Combine crumbs with seasonings in a plastic bag. Dip chicken in egg, then shake in bag with crumb mixture, coating thoroughly.

2. Preheat oil in a skillet on top of the stove on medium-high heat. Brown chicken in oil on all sides, about 3 to 4 minutes.

3. Place chicken in a single layer in a microsafe casserole with meatiest pieces towards the outside of the dish. **Calculate 4 to 5 minutes per lb. on HIGH.** Cover with microsafe paper towelling.

4. MW covered on HIGH for half the cooking time, about 5 minutes. Rearrange chicken; rotate dish ¼ turn. **MW remaining time, about 3 to 5 minutes longer on HIGH.** Cooking juices should run clear when chicken is done. Let stand for 3 to 4 minutes before serving. Serve with honey.

Yield: 4 servings. Can be frozen.

BONING CHICKEN BREASTS

- **Many butchers** sell chicken breasts already boned. If they are not available in your area or are too expensive, you can prepare them easily yourself.
- **Split breasts in half.** Pull off skin, then turn breast over. With your fingers and a sharp knife, remove breastbone and cartilage. Use your thumbs to loosen meat from rib cage. Pull or scrape meat away from bones. Pull out white tendons.
- **Boning breasts reduces cooking time.** Bones and skin can be frozen; use with leftover wing tips and backbone to make broth.
- **Boneless turkey** cutlets can be substituted in any of the chicken recipes. Some butchers will prepare them for you. Try them instead of veal scallops. Ground chicken or turkey breasts also make an excellent replacement for ground beef or veal. Substitute in your favorite meatball recipe, spaghetti sauce, chili or casseroles. Use your imagination!

BREADED CHICKEN CUTLETS

1 egg
1 tbsp. oil
3/4 c. seasoned bread crumbs
1 1/4 lb. boneless and skinless chicken breasts (about 4 large single breasts)

1. Blend egg with oil in a dish. Place crumbs in a plastic bag. Rinse chicken breasts under cold running water. Pat dry with paper towels. Dip chicken breasts in beaten egg, then coat with crumb mixture. Place in a single layer in a microsafe casserole, with the thicker pieces towards the outer edges of the dish. Cover with microsafe paper towelling.

2. **MW on HIGH for 6 to 8 minutes,** or until tender, turning chicken over at half time. Let stand covered for 2 or 3 minutes.

Yield: 3 to 4 servings. Freezes well.

* Seasoned corn flake or cracker crumbs can be used instead of bread crumbs.
* **To double the recipe,** prepare 8 single breasts as directed above. Arrange in a single layer on a 12″ round microsafe plate. Cooking time will be about **10 to 12 minutes on HIGH (allow 5 minutes per lb.).** Let stand covered for 3 to 4 minutes.
* **For half the recipe, cooking time will be about 4 minutes.**
* Chicken can also be cooked on a rack.

SESAME BREADED CHICKEN CUTLETS

Prepare as for Breaded Chicken Cutlets (above), but substitute sesame seeds for half of the bread crumbs.

BONELESS CHICKEN BREASTS ITALIANO

4 single chicken breasts, skinned & boned (about 1 ¼ lb.)
¼ c. Italian salad dressing
¾ c. bread crumbs
salt & pepper, to taste
dash basil & oregano
¾ c. bottled or home-made spaghetti sauce

1. Rinse chicken breasts under cold running water. Pat dry with paper towels. Dip in salad dressing, then in seasoned crumbs. Arrange in a single layer in a microsafe casserole, with the thicker parts pointing outwards. Cover with microsafe paper towelling.

2. **MW on HIGH for 6 to 8 minutes,** or until tender, turning chicken over at half time. Top each portion with 3 tbsp. sauce and **MW uncovered on HIGH 2 minutes longer,** until sauce is heated through. Serve with noodles.

Yield: 3 to 4 servings.

* **One single boneless breast will cook in 2 ½ to 3 minutes on HIGH. Two single boneless breasts will take about 4 minutes.**

CHICKEN BREASTS À L'ORANGE

An easy and elegant dish for company or perfect for a quicky family meal. For 6 to 8 servings, double all amounts. Any leftover sauce can be kept in the fridge for several days — it reheats perfectly!

Breaded Chicken Cutlets (p. 159)
1 tbsp. cornstarch
⅓ c. sugar
¼ c. lemon juice
¾ c. orange juice

1. Prepare and cook chicken breasts as directed, using 4 single chicken breasts (about 1 to 1 ¼ lb.). Prepare sauce during standing time for chicken.

2. In a 2 cup Pyrex™ measure, combine cornstarch and sugar. Blend in lemon and orange juice. **MW uncovered on HIGH for 2 ½ to 3 minutes,** until thick and bubbling, stirring twice. Place chicken on serving plate. Top with sauce. Perfect with rice and broccoli.

Yield: 4 servings.

* Rice can be cooked in advance and covered tightly. It will keep hot for 20 to 30 minutes, or can be reheated briefly.
* **Timetable for preparation:** While rice is cooking, prepare sauce mixture, chicken and broccoli for microwaving. Microwave sauce; cover it to keep hot. Then cook chicken. Cook broccoli just before serving. (Rice, sauce and chicken all reheat well.)

STUFFED CHICKEN BREASTS WITH VEGETABLES

Dinner on the table all in one dish in just half an hour - what could be better?

Chicken:
4 single chicken breasts, skinned & boned (1 - 1 ¼ lb.)
1 egg, lightly beaten
¾ c. seasoned bread crumbs or corn flake crumbs

Vegetables:
10 oz. pkg. frozen mixed vegetables or peas & carrots

Stuffing:
1 onion, chopped
1 stalk celery, chopped
2 tbsp. oil
½ c. sliced mushrooms
⅔ c. bread crumbs or corn flake crumbs
⅓ c. water or chicken broth
salt & pepper, to taste
⅛ tsp. each thyme & basil

1. **Chicken:** Rinse chicken breasts under cold running water. Pat dry with paper towels. Dip in egg, then in seasoned crumbs. Set aside.

2. **Stuffing:** Combine onion and celery with oil in a 10″ ceramic quiche dish or pie plate. **MW uncovered on HIGH for 3 minutes.** Stir in mushrooms and **MW on HIGH 2 minutes longer,** until tender. Combine with remaining stuffing ingredients and mix well.

3. Pile mixture into four separate mounds around the outside edge of the quiche dish. Leave the centre empty. (It will be filled with the mixed vegetables later.)

4. Top each mound with a breaded chicken breast, placing the thicker part of the chicken towards the outside edge of the dish. Cover with a double layer of microsafe paper towelling. **MW on HIGH for 10 to 12 minutes,** until chicken is done. Rotate dish halfway through cooking, but do not turn chicken over. Let stand covered while you cook the veggies.

5. **Vegetables:** Pierce top of package of frozen vegetables to allow steam to escape. Place on a microsafe plate. **MW on HIGH for 6 minutes,** shaking package after 4 minutes to mix. At end of cooking time, fill the centre of the casserole dish with the vegetables and serve.

Yield: 4 servings.

MOM'S CHICKEN ROLLS

Belle, my mother, is an outstanding cook. She learned to use her microwave by the "hit and miss method" because she is a natural experimenter. We all love this chicken recipe. You will too! Chicken requires browning on top of the stove, then is transferred to the microwave oven to finish cooking quickly.

6 boneless, skinless chicken breasts (about 1 ½ lb.)
Stuffing from Stuffed Chicken Breasts with Vegetables (p. 161)
1 egg, lightly beaten
¾ c. seasoned bread crumbs
2 tbsp. oil

1. Pound chicken breasts to flatten. Prepare stuffing as directed. (You can also substitute your own favorite stuffing recipe.) Cool stuffing slightly. Spread in a thin layer on chicken breasts. Roll up.

2. Dip chicken first in beaten egg, then coat with seasoned crumbs on all sides. Place seam-side down on a plate.

3. Heat oil in a skillet on top of the stove.* Brown chicken in oil on medium-high heat on all sides, about 3 to 4 minutes.

4. Place chicken in a single layer in a microsafe casserole with larger pieces towards the outside of the dish; cover with wax paper. **MW on HIGH for 4 to 5 minutes,** until done, rotating dish ½ turn after 3 minutes. Let stand covered for 2 minutes. Serve with It's Thyme to Cook Carrots (p.256) and a green salad.

Yield: 3 to 4 generous servings. Freezes well.

Timetable for Preparation: Carrots can be microwaved while chicken is browning on the rangetop. Carrots will keep hot for 10 to 15 minutes if tightly covered. Prepare salad earlier in the day and refrigerate. Add salad dressing at serving time.

DOUG'S QUICK CHICKEN DINNER

A complete meal for 1 or 2 in one dish. Recipe doubles easily. My son Doug is an excellent microwaver. He assists me with my microwave classes and my students adore him. Someone always asks him to marry their daughter! Doug loves boneless chicken in any form whatsoever. With his hearty appetite, Doug cooks and eats this whole recipe by himself with absolutely no problem!

1 small onion, chopped
1 or 2 potatoes, peeled & cut in chunks
½ green pepper, sliced
1 carrot, peeled & sliced
½ stalk celery, sliced
2 single boneless, skinless chicken breasts (about ½ lb.)
½ c. tomato sauce or pizza sauce (or BBQ sauce)
salt, pepper, basil & garlic powder, to taste

1. Combine vegetables in a 1 quart microsafe casserole. Cover with casserole lid or vented plastic wrap. **MW covered on HIGH for 5 minutes,** or until potatoes and carrots are almost tender. Stir halfway through and at end of cooking time.

2. Place chicken over vegetables, with the thicker parts towards the outside of the casserole. Combine tomato sauce or broth with seasonings and pour over chicken. (Sauce helps the chicken cook evenly.)

3. **MW covered on HIGH for 4 to 5 minutes,** until chicken is done, rotating the dish ¼ turn at half time. Let stand covered for 2 minutes.

Yield: 1 large or 2 moderate servings.

* You can use any vegetables you like. Be sure to microwave them until almost tender before adding chicken breasts and sauce. This will ensure that the vegetables will be done but the chicken won't be overcooked.
* **To double the recipe:** Double all ingredients, except use just ¾ cup of sauce. Use a 2 quart microsafe casserole. **MW vegetables covered on HIGH for 8 minutes,** stirring at half time. Potatoes and carrots should be almost tender. Add chicken, sauce and seasonings. **MW covered on HIGH 7 to 8 minutes longer,** until chicken is cooked, turning chicken over at half time. Let stand covered for 3 to 4 minutes before serving.
* Chicken broth can be used instead of tomato sauce.

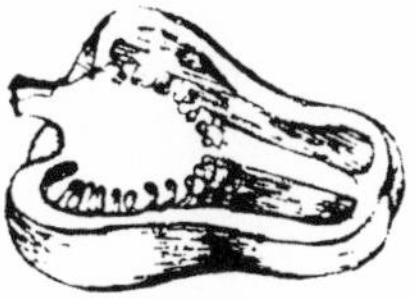

SESAME PINEAPPLE CHICKEN

A wonderful company dish!

Sesame Breaded Chicken Cutlets (p. 159)
Pineapple Sweet & Sour Sauce (p. 93)
2 onions, cut in 1″ chunks
1 c. mushrooms, sliced
1 green pepper, cut in 1″ chunks
1 red pepper, cut in 1″ chunks
1 tbsp. oil

1. Prepare and microwave Sesame Breaded Chicken Cutlets as directed, but cut chicken breasts into 1″ pieces before breading and cooking. Keep cooked chicken covered while preparing rest of recipe.

2. Prepare sauce as directed. Cover to keep hot.

3. Place vegetable in a microsafe bowl with oil. **MW uncovered on HIGH for 4 to 5 minutes,** stirring once. Drain juices. Add vegetables and sauce to chicken; mix well. (Can be prepared in advance up to this point.)

4. **MW uncovered on HIGH for 3 to 4 minutes,** or until chicken is piping hot. Serve with rice.

Yield: 4 servings. Can be frozen.

* **To reheat refrigerated casserole, reheat uncovered on HIGH for 6 to 8 minutes,** until heated through, stirring once or twice.

QUICKY CHICKY WITH FETTUCINE

About 20 minutes from start to finish. So easy, so good — and light in the calorie department! Boil water for pasta while chicken is cooking in the microwave.

1 large onion, in chunks
1 clove garlic, crushed
4 single chicken breasts (about 1 ¼ lb.), boned, skinned & cut in 2″ pieces
1 green pepper, seeded & cut in chunks
8 oz. can pizza sauce
1 lb. fettucine noodles
salt, pepper, basil & oregano

1. Prepare all ingredients. Combine onion, garlic and chicken pieces in a single layer in an ungreased 9″ Pyrex™ pie plate. Cover with waxed paper.

2. **MW covered on HIGH for 5 minutes,** stirring once or twice. Chicken should just be losing its pink color. Drain off liquid. Add green pepper chunks and **MW covered on HIGH 2 minutes longer,** until tender-crisp.

3. Add pizza sauce and mix well. **MW uncovered on HIGH for 2 minutes,** until sauce is hot. Cover with a dinner plate and let stand for 3 minutes.

4. Meanwhile, cook fettucine conventionally. (I use a quick-cooking fresh pasta which takes 1 to 2 minutes to cook.) Drain and rinse well. Top with chicken and vegetables.

Yield: 4 servings.

CHICKEN PRIMAVERA

There is a fair amount of preparation for this dish, but the results are worth it! Use your food processor to help you get the vegetables ready quickly. Vary the vegetables, if you wish. Good enough for company!

4 single chicken breasts, skinned & boned (1 ¼ lb.)
2 tbsp. oil
salt & pepper, to taste
basil & oregano, to taste
2 - 3 cloves garlic, minced
1 medium onion, sliced
½ green pepper, sliced
½ red pepper, sliced
1 c. mushrooms, sliced
1 c. broccoli florets
1 carrot, peeled & sliced
1 c. snow peas, if desired
2 c. Quick Tomato Sauce (p. 89) or bottled vegetarian spaghetti sauce

1. Cut chicken into narrow strips. Place chicken and 1 tbsp. of oil in a 2 quart oval or rectangular microsafe casserole. **MW uncovered on HIGH for 5 to 6 minutes**, stirring every 2 minutes, until chicken is no longer pink. Sprinkle with seasonings. Cover to keep warm while microwaving remaining ingredients.

2. Combine garlic, onion and peppers with 1 tbsp. oil in a 1 quart microsafe bowl. **MW uncovered on HIGH for 3 minutes.** Stir in mushrooms. **MW on HIGH 2 minutes longer,** until tender-crisp. Drain; add to chicken.

3. Place broccoli and carrots in microsafe bowl. Rinse with cold water; drain, but do not dry. Cover with plastic wrap, turning back one corner slightly to vent. **MW on HIGH for 2 to 2 ½ minutes,** until tender-crisp. Drain; add to chicken.

4. Remove tails from snow peas. Rinse and drain, but do not dry. Place in bowl and cover with vented plastic wrap. **MW on HIGH for 1 minute,** until tender-crisp. Add to chicken. Stir in tomato sauce. Season to taste. (Can be prepared in advance up to this point.)

5. **MW uncovered on HIGH for 4 to 6 minutes,** or until heated through, stirring once or twice. (**If refrigerated, increase time to 6 to 8 minutes.**) Serve over fettucine or spaghetti.

Yield: 4 to 6 servings. If frozen, vegetables will not be as crisp.

* Pasta should be cooked conventionally according to package directions, until al dente. It reheats very well in the microwave if you want to cook it in advance.
* **Recipe can be doubled. Increase cooking time by ⅔,** using guidelines given for doneness. Use a 3 quart microsafe casserole to cook chicken.

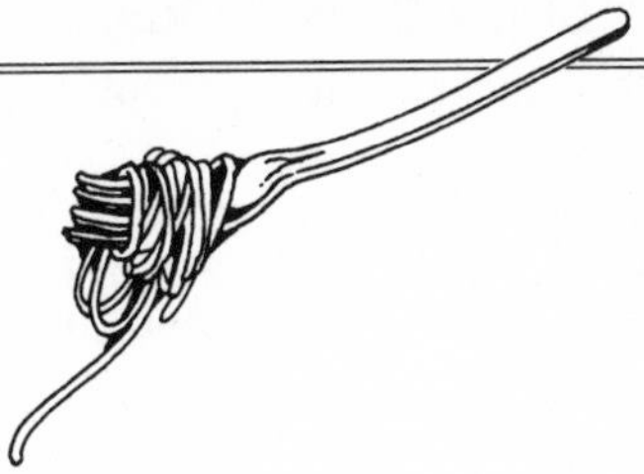

CHINESE CHICKEN WITH BROCCOLI

Marinade:
1 clove garlic
¼ tsp. ground ginger (or 1 slice of fresh ginger the size of a dime)
½ c. water
2 tbsp. dark soya sauce
1 tsp. instant chicken soup mix
1 tbsp. brown sugar

1 ½ lb. boneless, skinless chicken breasts, cut in strips
1 c. sliced carrots
1 medium onion, sliced
2 c. broccoli flowerets
1 tbsp. cornstarch
½ tsp. Oriental sesame oil, if desired

1. Mince garlic and fresh ginger. (Can be prepared in the food processor, using the **Steel Knife.**) Mix with remaining ingredients for marinade. Place chicken strips and marinade in a 2 quart shallow microsafe casserole. (You will need about 4 or 5 large single chicken breasts.) Marinate for 20 to 30 minutes at room temperature or overnight in the refrigerator. Drain marinade into a 1 cup Pyrex™ measure.

2. **MW chicken uncovered on HIGH for 7 to 8 minutes,** until no longer pink, stirring once or twice. Let stand covered while you prepare the veggies.

3. Place all vegetables in a 8 cup Pyrex™ measure. Cover with plastic wrap, turning back one corner slightly to vent. **MW covered on HIGH for 4 to 5 minutes,** or until veggies are tender-crisp, stirring once. (An easy way to stir is to shake the measuring cup so you won't have to remove the plastic wrap.) Let stand covered while you prepare sauce.

4. Blend cornstarch into reserved marinade. Add juices from chicken. Stir to blend. **MW uncovered on HIGH until bubbling and thick, about 1 ½ to 2 minutes,** stirring at half time.

5. Combine marinade with vegetables and chicken. (May be prepared in advance up to this point and completed at serving time.) **MW uncovered on HIGH for 2 minutes,** or until heated through. (**If refrigerated, time will be 5 to 7 minutes.**) Add sesame oil. Serve with rice.

Yield: 4 servings. If frozen, veggies will not be as crisp.

CHINESE CHICKEN WITH BROCCOLI & SNOW PEAS: Remove tail ends from 1 ½ cups pea pods. Omit carrots. Add snow peas to broccoli after it has cooked for 2 minutes. **MW on HIGH 2 minutes longer,** until vegetables are tender-crisp and bright green.

CASHEW CHICKEN WITH BROCCOLI: ½ cup unsalted cashews can be added, if desired. Toast cashews in a 9″ pie plate uncovered on **HIGH for 2 to 3 minutes,** or until toasted, stirring once or twice. Add at serving time.

HOISIN CHICKEN WITH VEGETABLES

Follow recipe for Chinese Chicken with Broccoli (above), but substitute the following marinade:

2 tbsp. Hoisin sauce
2 tbsp. soya sauce
2 tbsp. sherry or wine
2 tbsp. water or orange juice
2 tsp. lemon juice
½ tsp. Chili Paste with Garlic

Recipe also works well with variation using snow peas or cashews.

CHINESE CHICKEN KABOBS #1

This wonderful recipe was adapted from a conventional one given to me by my friend Marilyn Melnick, who has done catering. Mmmmmm-very interesting! Marinade is also excellent on chicken breasts or wings.

4 single boneless, skinless chicken breasts (1 ½ lb.)
2 cloves garlic, minced
½ tsp. grated ginger root
½ tsp. Chinese 5 Spice Powder*
2 tbsp. honey
2 tbsp. dark soya sauce
2 tbsp. sherry (or lemon juice)
1 tbsp. oil
¼ tsp. Oriental sesame oil*

1. Cut each portion of chicken into 12 pieces about 1″ square. Combine remaining ingredients to make a marinade. Marinate chicken at room temperature for 30 minutes or in the fridge up to 24 hours. Stir occasionally.

2. Remove chicken from marinade. Pour marinade into a 2 cup Pyrex™ measure; **MW uncovered on HIGH for 1 minute, until boiling. Boil 1 minute longer.** Thread 6 pieces of chicken on each skewer (you will need 8 long, wooden skewers). Place the smaller pieces in the middle and allow a little space between pieces for even cooking. Arrange skewers in a single layer in a 9″ x 13″ microsafe casserole. Cover with a sheet of wax paper.

3. **MW on HIGH for 6 to 8 minutes,** or until cooked. Brush with marinade once or twice during cooking. Turn skewers over and re-arrange at half time, placing the more cooked ones towards the centre of the dish. Let stand for 1 or 2 minutes. Serve with Fried Rice (p. 214).

Yield: 4 servings.

* Chinese products are available in Oriental grocery stores.
* Prepare rice first; cover tightly to keep hot while you microwave the chicken.

CHINESE CHICKEN KABOBS #2

Follow recipe for Chinese Chicken Kabobs #1 (above), but use the following ingredients to make the marinade:

2 cloves garlic, minced
¼ tsp. ground ginger (or 1 slice fresh ginger the size of a dime, minced)
½ c. chicken broth
2 tbsp. dark soya sauce
1 - 2 tbsp. honey
2 tbsp. Hoisin sauce, if desired

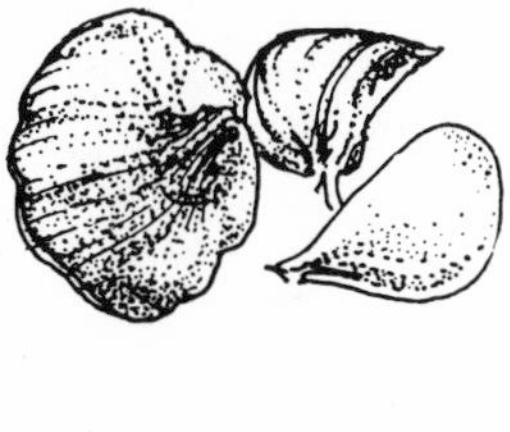

CHICKEN KABOBS WITH MUSHROOMS & PEPPERS

Chinese Chicken Kabobs #1 or #2 (p. 167)
16 small mushrooms (about 1″)
1 green and 1 red pepper, cut into 1″ squares

1. Arrange chicken and vegetables on wooden skewers, placing the vegetables and smaller chicken pieces towards the middle. Brush with marinade.

2. Follow directions for Chicken Kabobs, but **MW on HIGH for 8 to 10 minutes.** Brush chicken and vegetables with marinade once or twice during cooking and turn at half time.

Yield: 4 servings.

SWEET & TANGY LEMON CHICKEN

4 single chicken breasts, skinned & boned (about 1 ½ lb.)
¾ c. chicken broth (reserve part of cooking juices from chicken)
salt & pepper
1 tbsp. cornstarch
¼ c. cold water
2 tbsp. lemon juice
3 tbsp. brown sugar
1 tbsp. soya sauce
¼ tsp. ginger
1 clove garlic, crushed

1. Wash chicken; pat dry with paper towels. Place in a single layer in an ungreased 2 quart shallow microsafe casserole. Arrange so that the thicker parts are towards the outside of the dish. Cover with wax paper.

2. **MW on HIGH for 7 to 8 minutes,** until tender, turning chicken over and re-arranging at half time. Remove chicken from microwave. Pour cooking juices into a Pyrex™ 2 cup measure. Add additional chicken broth to make ¾ cup liquid. Sprinkle chicken lightly with salt & pepper. Cover to keep warm.

3. Dissolve cornstarch in cold water. Stir into chicken broth. Add lemon juice, sugar, soya sauce, ginger and garlic. Mix well. **MW uncovered on HIGH for 2 minutes,** or until mixture is bubbly and thick. Stir once or twice during cooking. Add salt & pepper to taste. Pour over chicken. (**If necessary, reheat uncovered on HIGH for 1 to 2 minutes.**) Serve over fluffy white rice with asparagus or broccoli.

Yield: 3 to 4 servings.

CHICKEN OR TURKEY HAWAIIAN

This is quicker than taking a trip to Hawaii! Use your food processor to slice the vegetables quickly. Microwave rice while preparing the ingredients for the chicken. The rice will stay hot until serving time if tightly covered.

1 onion, sliced
1 carrot, sliced
1 green pepper, sliced
½ red pepper, sliced
½ yellow pepper, sliced
1 stalk celery, sliced
2 cloves garlic, minced
2 tbsp. oil
1 ½ lb. boneless & skinless chicken or turkey breasts, cut in strips
salt & pepper
1 tsp. powdered ginger
14 oz. can pineapple chunks
2 tbsp. honey
1 tbsp. lemon juice
1 tsp. Dijon mustard
1 ½ tbsp. cornstarch
3 c. cooked rice (p. 214)

1. Combine onion, carrot, peppers, celery and garlic with oil in a 3 quart shallow microsafe casserole. **MW uncovered on HIGH 5 minutes,** until tender-crisp, stirring at half time.

2. Season chicken or turkey strips with salt, pepper and ginger. Push vegetables towards the centre of the casserole and arrange chicken around the outside edges. **MW uncovered on HIGH for 7 to 8 minutes,** stirring every 2 minutes. There should be almost no pink left in the chicken. Keep covered while preparing sauce.

3. Combine pineapple juice and chunks with honey, lemon juice, mustard and cornstarch in a 4 cup Pyrex™ measure. Stir well. **MW uncovered on HIGH about 5 minutes,** until sauce is thick and bubbly, stirring twice. Stir into chicken mixture. Push chicken mixture around the edge of the casserole. Fill centre of dish with cooked rice.

Yield: 4 servings. May be frozen, but vegetables will not be as crisp. Reheats well.

CHINESE CHICKEN & PEPPERS

Follow recipe for Chinese Veal & Peppers (p. 204), but substitute boneless chicken breasts.

CHINESE CHICKEN & MUSHROOMS

Follow recipe for Chinese Veal & Mushrooms (p. 204), but substitute boneless chicken breasts.

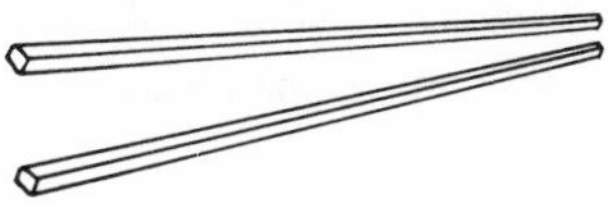

POLYNESIAN CHICKEN BALLS

Chicken Mixture:
1 clove garlic, minced
½ onion, grated
1 lb. raw minced chicken (or ground turkey)
2 eggs
¾ tsp. salt
freshly ground pepper
⅓ c. bread crumbs

Sauce Mixture:
14 oz. can pineapple chunks
⅓ c. ketchup
¼ red wine vinegar
½ c. brown sugar, packed
2 tbsp. cornstarch
1 stalk celery, in ½″ chunks
½ onion, in ½″ chunks
1 green pepper, in ½″ chunks

1. Combine all ingredients for chicken mixture and mix well. Shape into 1″ balls, moistening your hands for easier handling. Arrange in a single layer in a shallow 2 quart casserole. **MW uncovered on HIGH for 6 to 7 minutes,** stirring once. Let stand while you prepare the sauce.

2. Measure ½ cup pineapple juice into a 4 cup Pyrex™ measure. Reserve pineapple chunks. Add remaining sauce ingredients to pineapple juice, including vegetables; mix well. **MW uncovered on HIGH for 6 to 7 minutes,** stirring 2 or 3 times. Vegetables will still be fairly crunchy.

3. Add sauce ingredients and drained pineapple chunks to chicken. Mix well. (Can be prepared in advance up to this point.) **MW covered on HIGH for 5 to 6 minutes,** or until heated through, stirring once or twice. Serve over rice.

Yield: 4 servings. Freezes well.

CHICKEN OR TURKEY GRAVY

4 tbsp. fat from pan juices
4 tbsp. flour
skimmed pan juices plus broth to equal 2 cups
salt & pepper, to taste

1. Measure fat into a 4 cup glass measure. **MW uncovered on HIGH for 45 seconds.** Stir in flour; then gradually blend in liquid.

2. MW uncovered on HIGH for 5 to 7 minutes, until thick and bubbly, whisking 2 or 3 times. Season with salt and pepper.

Yield: 2 cups (8 to 10 servings).

* To remove fat easily from pan juices, pour into a 2 cup glass measure and freeze for 15 minutes. Once fat is removed, broth can be added to pan juices to measure 2 cups of liquid.
* If desired, add 1 or 2 tsp. Worcestershire sauce or ketchup to gravy for color.
* Recipe can be doubled or halved. Increase or decrease cooking time accordingly.
* One cup of refrigerated gravy reheats in about **3 minutes uncovered on HIGH.** Stir at half time. Leftover gravy should boil for 1 minute before serving.
* **BEEF GRAVY:** Use beef broth as the liquid. Season with a pinch of oregano and 2 tbsp. red wine.

LET'S TALK TURKEY!

Defrosting

- **A 10 to 14 lb. turkey takes 1 to 2 hours to defrost in the microwave,** depending on your oven, **plus 1 hour standing time.** (Certainly an improvement on 2 days in the refrigerator!)
- **Automatic defrost programs** often take longer because they are programmed to prevent the food from beginning to cook while thawing. If you do not have automatic defrost, calculate **6 to 7 minutes per lb. on DEFROST.**
- **There should be 2 to 3 inches** between the turkey and the walls and top of your microwave.
- **Discard wrappings and metal clip.** (You can microwave turkey for **1 minute on HIGH** if wrappings are difficult to remove.) Place turkey breast-side down on a microsafe rack. Place rack in a large oblong casserole to catch the juices which are released during defrosting.
- **Turn turkey over 2 or 3 times** during defrosting; drain off any juices which collect in the bottom of the casserole.
- **If wing tips**, drumsticks, tail or breastbone begin to get warm, shield with flat pieces of foil. Fasten with toothpicks.
- **Turkey should still have ice crystals** in the thicker, meatier portions when you remove it from the microwave.
- **Rinse turkey thoroughly** in cold water to dissolve ice. Let stand until completely defrosted, about 1 hour. Rinse and pat dry before seasoning turkey.
- **Uncooked whole turkey** keeps 9 to 12 months in the freezer; it should be tightly wrapped. Cooked turkey can be frozen for 3 to 4 months.

Cooking

- **Cook turkey immediately after thawing,** or cover and store in coldest part of refrigerator.
- **Clean turkey thoroughly**; remove giblets. Weigh giblets and subtract weight from packaged weight of turkey to calculate cooking time. (The giblets from a 10 to 12 lb. turkey will weigh about 1 lb.) Pat turkey dry with paper towelling.
- **If you want to stuff your turkey,** do so just before cooking; you probably won't even have to increase the cooking time. Refer to Stuffing Poultry (The Right Stuff) on p. 137.
- **Leftover turkey** keeps 2 to 3 days tightly wrapped in the fridge. It must be reheated to at least 165°F.
- **Turkey should be cooked on a microsafe rack** or an inverted saucer. (The rack or saucer should also be heatproof if you plan to brown the turkey conventionally afterwards.) Place turkey breast-side down to start. Turn it breast-side up at half time. Baste occasionally.
- **If the turkey is very large**, you may wish to turn it more often for more even cooking. Divide total cooking time into 4 segments. **MW turkey breast-side down for ¼ of the time, then on one side for ¼ of the time, then on the other side for ¼ of the time, then breast-side up for the last ¼ of the time.**
- **Cover turkey with a tent of wax paper** to prevent spattering. Tuck ends of wax paper under rack or turkey.
- **Drain off pan juices** with a bulb baster several times during cooking. The juices are fatty and attract microwave energy.

- **Microwave turkey on MEDIUM-HIGH (70%), allowing 8 to 9 minutes per lb. You could also start turkey on HIGH for 10 minutes, then reduce power to MEDIUM (50%) and MW for 9 to 11 minutes per lb.**
- **Use flat pieces of aluminum foil** to shield any areas that begin to overcook (e.g. breast bone, wing tips, drumsticks). Attach foil to turkey with wooden toothpicks. Shielding is usually needed during the last ½ to ¾ of microwaving. (It may also be needed if cooking turkey on the **CONVECTION/MICROWAVE CYCLE,** particularly if the glaze contains sugar, honey &/or soya sauce.)
- **If cooking with a probe**, insert into meatiest portion of the thigh (not touching bone, fat or metal) during last half of microwaving. Set temperature for 175°F. Double-check temperature at end of cooking by placing probe into other thigh and setting temperature again to 175°F. A few more minutes may be needed. Microwave will shut off when temperature is reached. Temperature will rise 10°F during standing time.
- **For Combo-Cooking, MW turkey** in a microsafe/heatproof casserole **on HIGH for 4 to 5 minutes per lb.** Then transfer turkey to a preheated conventional oven; **roast uncovered for ¾ to 1 hour at 350°F;** baste occasionally. If overbrowning occurs in the conventional oven, cover turkey loosely with a tent of aluminum foil.
- **If microwaving the turkey first**, then browning it on the **CONVECTION CYCLE, MW turkey on HIGH for 4 to 5 minutes per lb.** At the end of the microwave cycle, remove turkey from oven. Place rack recommended by manufacturer for **CONVECTION CYCLE** into oven; preheat oven to 300°F. Meanwhile, baste turkey with pan juices. Place in oven breast-side up and **roast uncovered at 300°F for 45 to 60 minutes.** Baste occasionally. If overbrowning occurs, cover turkey loosely with foil.
- **If you have a CONVECTION/MICROWAVE oven**, turkey can also be cooked completely on the **COMBINATION CYCLE your manufacturer recommends for turkey.** Refer to Convection/Micro Ways with Poultry (p. 143). Place turkey on a microsafe/heatproof rack or inverted saucer. Place in a microsafe/heatproof casserole to catch the drippings. **Time will be 10 to 15 minutes per lb.,** depending on your oven. Refer to a similar recipe in the cookbook which comes with your oven.
- **If you are expecting a large crowd,** buy two 12 lb. turkeys. Start one in the microwave and the other one in the conventional oven, **allowing 4 to 5 minutes per lb. on HIGH.** Then switch places. Both turkeys will be ready to serve in about 2 hours!
- **Turkey should stand for 20 to 30 minutes** after cooking.
- **Use standing time** to make gravy and/or cook vegetables.
- **TURKEY BREAST** (5 to 7 lb.) can be started on **HIGH for 10 minutes, then reduce power to MEDIUM (50%) and MW for 9 to 12 minutes per lb.** Turn turkey over and baste with pan juices at half time. When done, internal temperature should be 170°F on probe or meat thermometer and juices should run clear. Check at minimum time and add more time as needed. After removing from microwave, cover with a tent of foil; let stand 15 minutes. Temperature will rise to 180°F.
- **Uncooked boneless turkey breast** can be thinly sliced into cutlets and substituted for chicken breasts or veal. Ground turkey can be used in recipes calling for minced chicken or hamburger.
- **A variety of turkey parts** are now available, due to the increased popularity of turkey as a nutritious, low-fat food. A 3 oz. serving of turkey breast contains 120 calories. Turkey meat can replace beef or veal in stews, stir-fries, soups, salads and casseroles. Don't overcook. Remove skin to save calories.

COMBO-COOKED ROAST TURKEY

Your turkey will be juicy and tender if you start it in the microwave, then transfer it to your conventional oven until the skin is crisp and golden. A 12 lb. turkey will be on the table in 2 hours! This method also frees the microwave to be used for other tasks.

12 - 14 lb. turkey
4 or 5 cloves garlic, crushed
1 tsp. lemon juice
1 tbsp. paprika
¾ tsp. basil
½ tsp. pepper
¼ c. oil
¼ c. honey

1. Remove giblets from turkey and subtract weight from packaged weight to calculate cooking time. Combine remaining ingredients and mix well. Season turkey inside and out with mixture. Truss turkey, tying legs and wings close to body with unflavored dental floss or string. (Can be done in advance and refrigerated overnight for maximum flavor.)

2. Place turkey breast-side down on a microsafe/heatproof rack or inverted saucer in a large microsafe/heatproof oval or rectangular casserole. Cover with a tent of wax paper. **MW turkey on HIGH, calculating 4 to 5 minutes per lb.** (Total microwave time will be about **45 to 60 minutes**. Set timer for half the cooking time.) Baste several times during cooking. Remove pan juices with a bulb baster as they accumulate. Reserve juices to make gravy.

3. At half time, turn turkey breast-side up. Check wings, legs and breastbone during cooking to prevent them from overcooking; shield with foil, if necessary. (Be sure to keep foil at least 1″ away from the walls of the oven.) Microwave remaining time. Meanwhile, preheat conventional oven to 350°F.

4. Immediately transfer turkey to conventional oven and **roast uncovered at 350°F for 45 to 60 minutes,** until golden brown, basting occasionally. Cover loosely with foil if overbrowning occurs. Cut-up potatoes can be added during the last ½ hour of cooking. The drumstick should wiggle easily when done. Temperature should be 175°F on a meat thermometer.

5. Remove turkey from oven; cover with a tent of aluminum foil (it doesn't matter if it is shiny side up or down!) and let stand for 20 to 30 minutes for easier carving. Temperature will rise to 185°F in the thigh portion. Test temperature in several places, including the underside, in the thickest, meatiest parts.

Yield: 10 to 12 servings. (Allow ¾ to 1 lb. per person.)

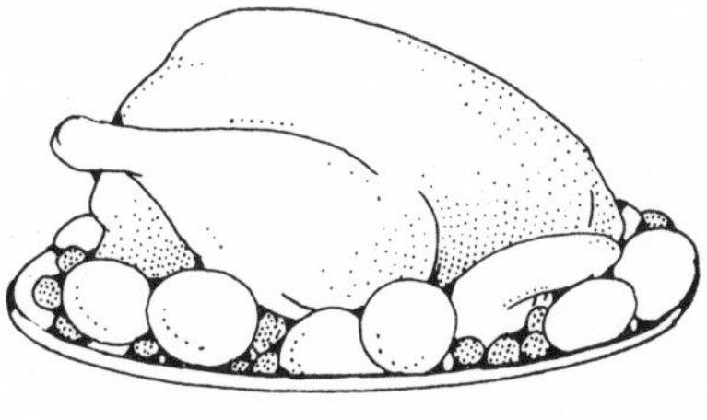

* **Variation:** Turkey can be seasoned with a mixture of ½ c. soya or Teriyaki sauce combined with 4 cloves crushed garlic, 2 tbsp. Dijon mustard and 1 tbsp. paprika.

* You can use your own favorite seasonings for turkey, but omit salt.

* If you wish to stuff turkey, do so just before cooking. **NEVER** stuff turkey in advance. See Stuffing Poultry (The Right Stuff), (p. 137).

* **CONVECTION/MICROWAVE METHOD:** Season turkey; stuff if desired. Place breast-side down on a heatproof/microsafe rack or inverted saucer in a large heatproof/microsafe casserole. Place on rack recommended by oven manufacturer and **cook uncovered on COMBINATION CYCLE suitable for turkey. Allow 10 to 15 minutes per lb. A 12 lb. turkey will take 2 to 3 hours to cook**; times vary with different ovens. Turn breast-side up at half time. Baste occasionally. Shield wings, drumsticks and breast bone with foil if they start to overcook. When done, temperature should be 175°F in the thickest, meatiest part of the thigh. Let stand covered for 20 to 30 minutes before carving. Read Convection/Micro Ways with Poultry (p. 143) and Let's Talk Turkey (p. 171-172).

MY OVEN'S SETTING_______ MY COOKING TIME_______

ROAST TURKEY (MICROWAVE METHOD)

1. To make turkey completely in the microwave, follow preceding recipe for Combo-Cooked Roast Turkey, but **MW on MEDIUM-HIGH (70%), calculating 8 to 9 minutes per lb. (Or MW your turkey on HIGH for 10 minutes, then reduce power to MEDIUM (50%), and MW for 9 to 11 minutes per lb.)** Turkey should not be larger than 10 to 12 lb.

2. Turn turkey 4 times during cooking (breast down, left side, right side, breast up). Baste occasionally with pan drippings. Drain excess fat with bulb baster several times during cooking. Shield wings, drumsticks and breastbone with foil if they start to overcook. When done, turkey should reach an internal temperature of 175°F on a meat thermometer or probe in the thickest, meatiest part of the thigh.

3. For a crispier skin, remove rack (unless it is heatproof) and transfer turkey to a preheated conventional oven **(400°F). Roast uncovered for 25 to 30 minutes;** baste occasionally. If turkey is overbrowning, reduce oven temperature by 25 to 50°F and cover loosely with a tent of aluminum foil. Remove turkey from oven and let stand covered with a tent of foil for 20 minutes. Temperature should rise to 180 to 185°F. Test temperatures in several places, including the underside, in the thickest, meatiest parts.

Yield: 10 to 12 servings.

MEATS

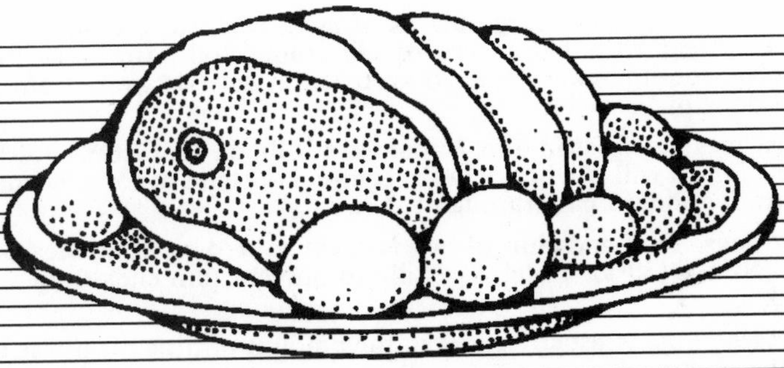

MICRO-WAYS WITH MEATS

DEFROSTING TECHNIQUES (THE BIG CHILL!)

- **Meat should be properly packaged before freezing** for best results when defrosting in the microwave. Ground meat should be shaped in a ring, with an indentation in the centre. Steaks and chops should be individually wrapped, or packaged in a single layer. Wrap in freezerproof wrappings.
- **Remove wrappings.** Place meat on a microsafe rack to keep it elevated out of the juices which are released during defrosting.
- **Place meat with thicker, meatier parts** towards the outside edge of the rack and thinner, bonier parts towards the centre.
- **Cover meat with waxed paper** while defrosting to prevent it from drying out.
- **Turn meat over halfway through defrosting.** Separate any pieces and/or rearrange, placing more thawed pieces towards the centre (e.g. stewing beef).
- **Remove pieces from the microwave** as soon as they are thawed; otherwise they will begin to cook.
- **If edges of roasts or large pieces of meat** begin to get warm or start to cook, shield with flat pieces of aluminum foil. Attach to meat with wooden toothpicks. Be sure to keep foil at least 1″ away from the walls and door of the oven.
- **Most meats defrost in 5 to 7 minutes per lb. on DEFROST (30%).** Large cuts of meat will still be icy in the centre. Let stand to complete defrosting. A skewer should pass through easily.
- **Hot dogs, liver and thin pieces of meat take 4 to 6 minutes per lb. on DEFROST (30%).** Watch carefully to prevent thin ends from starting to cook.
- **Standing time is usually equal** to the amount of time meat was defrosted in the microwave.
- **A quick trick to defrost frozen ground meat:** Unwrap and place meat in a microsafe bowl. **MW on HIGH for 1 minute** at a time. Turn meat over after each minute; scrape off any thawed portions. Break up meat and let stand briefly. **One lb. of meat takes 2 to 3 minutes on HIGH to defrost.** Watch carefully to prevent meat from starting to cook. (It won't matter if you need it for spaghetti sauce!)
- **Defrost meat completely** before cooking for best results.
- **Cook extra steaks and hamburgers on the BBQ** during the summer. First slash fat to prevent edges from curling; undercook slightly. Wrap individually and freeze.
- **To thaw and reheat steak,** place on a microsafe rack. **One 10 to 12 oz. steak will take about 3 to 5 minutes on DEFROST (30%), or 5 to 7 minutes per lb.** Let stand for 2 or 3 minutes to complete thawing. Then **MW on MEDIUM-HIGH (70%) for 2 to 3 minutes**, until hot.
- **One hamburger will take 1 to 2 minutes on DEFROST (30%) to thaw, or 30 to 60 seconds on HIGH to heat,** depending on its size.
- **Most meats can be stored for 6 months** in the freezer at 0°F if properly wrapped. Ground beef or veal will keep 2 to 3 months. Large roasts will keep 9 to 12 months.

- **If meat has thawed,** cook it before you freeze it again. Otherwise its quality and texture will be affected.

ASK THE BUTCHER

- **Make your butcher your friend!** Ask for his help in choosing tender, boneless cuts of meat with a uniform shape for best results. Roasts cook best if tied into a compact roll. Boneless cuts are usually more economical because they yield more servings per lb.
- **Roasts with a smaller diameter** cook more evenly than those with a large diameter. A good size is usually 3 to 4 pounds.
- **Meat that is well marbled** will be more tender than very lean meat. Fat adds flavor. The finished dish can be refrigerated after cooking so that fat solidifies and can be easily removed and discarded.
- **The larger the cut of meat,** the longer it can be kept in the refrigerator before cooking. Ground meat keeps for 1 to 2 days; stewing meat, steaks and roasts can be kept for 2 or 3 days. Refrigerator temperature should be between 35°F and 40°F.
- **One pound of boneless meat** yields 3 average or 2 generous servings.

PERTINENT POINTERS

- **Roasts with a bone or unevenly shaped roasts** require more care to help them cook evenly.
- **Meat around the bone** has a tendency to overcook. This is less of a problem when there is a large proportion of meat to bone.
- **It may be necessary to shield bones &/or fatty areas** with flat pieces of aluminum foil to prevent overcooking. (It doesn't matter if the foil is shiny side in or shiny side out.)
- **Chops and steaks are better if they are thicker** rather than thinner for more even cooking without drying out.
- **If meat requires slicing** before cooking (e.g. for a stir-fried dish), partially freeze it first. It will be much easier to slice. Cut across the grain with a sharp knife; then defrost completely before cooking.
- **Ground beef is usually cooked on HIGH power.** Meatballs can be cooked covered on **MEDIUM (50%)** once the sauce has been added; this helps them absorb the flavor of the sauce. If I am in a hurry, I cook them on **HIGH.** See Notes on Meatballs (p. 45).
- **Spaghetti sauce &/or Chili** can be microwaved completely on **HIGH** because they don't stick to the casserole.
- **Tender roasts** (e.g. roast beef) are started on **HIGH,** then are completed on **MEDIUM (50%).** See Micro-Ways with Roast Beef (p. 209).
- **Tender roasts** are microwaved uncovered. Elevate on a microsafe rack or inverted saucer to raise them out of the cooking juices.
- **Less tender cuts** (e.g. brisket, stews) are cooked covered. They are microwaved on **HIGH for 3 to 4 minutes per lb., then on MEDIUM (50%) or MEDIUM-LOW (30%) for 15 to 20 minutes per lb.,** until tender.
- **A cooking bag, clay baker or tightly covered casserole** are excellent choices for cooking less tender cuts of meat.

CONVERTING YOUR FAVORITE MEAT RECIPES

- **Look for a similar microwave recipe.** Cooking time is about ⅓ to ½ of conventional cooking time, about **6 to 7 minutes per lb. on HIGH power.**
- **Most meat cuts are very dense,** so certain cooking techniques are required to help them cook evenly in the microwave. These Micro-Ways will become easy and automatic after you enjoy the taste of success.
- **Lower power levels, MEDIUM (50%) OR MEDIUM-LOW (30%)** are used for large cuts of meat. This helps them cook evenly, with tender and juicy results. Although cooking time is longer, the results are worthwhile. If meat is microwaved too long or you use too high a power, it can become tough.
- **Oil is usually reduced or eliminated.** Since there is no sticking, oil is only used to provide flavor.
- **Casserole dishes usually don't require greasing,** unless you will be completing the cooking in a conventional oven.
- **Don't sprinkle salt on meats before cooking.** Either dissolve it in the cooking liquid or add after microwaving but before standing time.
- **Arrange the meatier portions** towards the outside of the casserole and the thinner, bonier portions towards the centre. Remember, **THIN IS IN!**
- **Meats should be stirred, turned over or rearranged** halfway through cooking. If you don't have a turntable, rotate casserole dish once or twice during cooking.

SEASONINGS

- **Season meat with** desired herbs and spices. Salt after cooking, or dissolve salt in the cooking liquid. (Garlic salt and onion salt are to be considered as salts.)
- **Koshered meats have been presalted,** which can affect cooking results somewhat. Salting draws the juices to the surface, which can result in the meat steaming instead of roasting, according to microwave "maven" Robert F. Schiffmann, Consultant to the microwave industry.
- **Rinse meat well and pat dry with paper towels** before cooking. (Don't try this with hamburger, or your dinner will go down the drain!)
- **Marinades and sauces enhance taste** and increase tenderness.
- **Marinate meats before cooking** to develop more flavor. Shorter cooking time means flavor may not be as developed in microwaved meats as those which are cooked conventionally. Use lower power levels and increase the cooking time, which gives meats more time to absorb flavor.
- **A plastic bag is ideal for marinating.** Seal well. Instead of turning meat over, just lift the bag and turn the whole thing over. Discard bag after marinating (unless it is a microwavable cooking bag and you are using it to cook the meat).
- **Marinade must be brought to boiling** if you wish to use it as a sauce. Boil for at least 1 minute.

THE KNACK OF A RACK

- **Roasts should be placed fat side down** on a microsafe rack. Standing rib roast is placed bone side down.
- **It is best to use a rack with deep grooves** so that meat is raised out of the cooking juices and will not steam.
- **If you don't have a rack,** use an inverted microsafe saucer as a trivet to elevate meat. Remove saucer immediately after cooking or it will be difficult to remove.
- **Wooden chopsticks** can be placed in the bottom of a microsafe casserole to simulate a rack.
- **Arrange thicker, meatier pieces** towards the outside edge of the rack. Turn over or rearrange once or twice during cooking.

TIMES & POWER LEVELS

- **More food means more time.** Most meats cook in **6 to 7 minutes per lb. on HIGH.** Smaller, thinner pieces cook faster than bigger, thicker pieces or large cuts. A kitchen scale is worthwhile.
- **For larger, less tender cuts** of meat (e.g. brisket), **MW covered on HIGH for 5 to 15 minutes, (about 3 to 4 minutes per lb.)** Then **MW on MEDIUM (50%)** or **MEDIUM-LOW (30%)** until tender, about **15 to 20 minutes per lb.**

  e.g. 4 lb. brisket x 3 minutes per lb. = 12 to 15 minutes on HIGH; then 1 to 1 ¼ hours on MEDIUM (50%)
- **For large, tender cuts** of meat (e.g. roast beef), **MW uncovered on HIGH for half the cooking time,** turn meat over and **MW on MEDIUM (50%) for double the remaining time:**

  e.g. 4 lb. roast x 7 minutes per lb. = 28 minutes on HIGH. CHANGE TO: 14 minutes on HIGH, then 28 minutes on MEDIUM (50%)
- **Microwaves only penetrate meats** to a depth of 1 to 1 ½ inches. The remainder of cooking is a result of heat conduction towards the centre of the meat.
- **Lower power levels** provide slower heat penetration, resulting in tender meat and less shrinkage.
- **Cooking large cuts entirely on HIGH** power can result in overdone, tough exteriors and undercooked interiors.

BBQ BONUS

- **Cook extra steaks, chops or hamburgers on the BBQ** during the summer; undercook slightly. Wrap them well and freeze. Thaw and heat in the microwave for a just-cooked taste in the middle of winter!
- **Thaw frozen barbecued meats on DEFROST (30%),** allowing **5 to 7 minutes per lb.** Elevate meat on a microsafe rack to prevent steaming. Reheat on **MEDIUM-HIGH (70%).** One steak will take 2 to 3 minutes.
- **Meats can be precooked** in the microwave for **4 minutes per lb. on HIGH,** then transferred immediately to a hot BBQ to give that wonderful charcoal flavor. Brush with BBQ sauce during the last few minutes on the BBQ for additional taste. This is excellent for thick steaks.
- **Microwave potatoes while meat is on the BBQ,** undercooking potatoes slightly. Transfer them to the hot BBQ, brush with sauce and cook until nicely browned and crisp, about 10 minutes.

BROWNING TECHNIQUES

- **Soya or teriyaki sauce,** paprika, steak sauce, Kitchen Bouquet, Worcestershire sauce or paprika will give a brown color to meats.
- **Large cuts of meat brown in the microwave** because they are cooked for a long enough period of time. You may prefer to sear smaller cuts (e.g. chops) first, either in a preheated microwave browning dish or in a frypan on top of the stove.
- **A browning dish is a microwave frypan.** Preheat according to time recommended by manufacturer. Instantly place food on hot surface. Use small, flat pieces of meat for best results.
- **Meat can be microwaved first for 4 to 5 minutes per lb. on HIGH (or 4 minutes per lb. for rare roasts).** Immediately **transfer to a preheated conventional oven** and roast uncovered at **425°F for 15 to 20 minutes,** or until nicely browned. Baste occasionally. Meat could also be transferred to a hot BBQ grill. Turn to brown on all sides.

Microwave browning dish

TENDER TIPS

- **Use at least 1 cup of liquid** for less tender cuts to produce steam and help tenderize the meat.
- **Some microwave experts pierce** less tender meats all over with a fork before cooking to allow the cooking liquid to penetrate and tenderize.
- **Tougher cuts of meat** (e.g. pot roasts, stews, brisket) should be tightly covered to hold in steam. If there is too much space between the top of the meat and the casserole lid, place a piece of waxed paper on the surface of the meat to help trap steam.
- **Turn meat over 2 or 3 times** during cooking so that overcooking doesn't occur in the part of the meat sitting in the juices.
- **To prevent large, tender roasts from overcooking** and becoming tough, shield ends with aluminum foil for part of the cooking time. Also shield thin or bony portions with foil. Keep foil at least 1″ away from oven walls.
- **Allow a standing time of 15 to 20 minutes** for large cuts of meat to complete cooking and equalize the temperature throughout. This procedure is exactly the same for conventionally cooked meats. Roasts will slice easier if you allow for standing time.
- **Tougher cuts** (e.g. stews) will develop more flavor when allowed to stand covered after cooking. They taste even better when reheated several hours later or the next day, just like in conventional cooking.

HELPFUL HINTS

- **Thicker, meatier pieces** should be placed towards the outside edge of the casserole. Stir or rearrange meat 2 or 3 times during cooking. Move more cooked portions towards the centre.
- **If your microwave has a probe,** insert it horizontally so that it is in the centre of the meat, not touching bone or fat.
- **Drain cooking juices** as they accumulate and save to make gravy or sauce. For roast beef, I drain juices at the end of cooking time to make beautiful, browned gravy.
- **Waxed paper prevents spatters,** but produces more of a steamed effect. I find it easier to cook tender roasts uncovered, then quickly wipe the microwave clean with a damp cloth afterwards.
- **Foods that contain a large quantity of liquid** (e.g. stews) should be stirred occasionally to equalize cooking.
- **Hot dogs require piercing** or slashing in several places because they are covered with a skin. Because hot dogs are already cooked when you buy them, all that they require is quick heating in the microwave. **One hot dog will take 30 to 60 seconds on HIGH.**
- **Never deep-fry meats in the microwave.**

TESTING FOR DONENESS

- **Smaller pieces of meat** cook faster than large; thin pieces cook faster than thick pieces.
- **A microwavable or instant-read** meat thermometer is a good way to tell if meat is completely cooked. Test internal temperature of meat in 2 or 3 places. The lowest temperature will be in the centre of the meat.
- **If your microwave has a probe,** you can cook meats by temperature instead of time. The probe is attached to the oven and measures the internal temperature of the meat. For roasts, insert into the thickest part, not touching fat or bone. When the probe reaches the desired temperature, the microwave will shut off automatically.
- **The internal temperature of meat** will rise about 10 to 20°F during standing time. If meat was cooked on **MEDIUM-LOW (30%),** the temperature will rise 5 to 10°F.
- **Casseroles are usually cooked** to 160°F. Hot foods should be kept hot (over 145°F) to prevent them from spoiling.
- **Undercook meats slightly.** Standing time completes cooking. Use this time to microwave vegetables. You can always put the meat back in the microwave for a minute or two if it is not done enough after standing time.
- **Smaller pieces of meat** require 2 to 3 minutes of standing time. Roasts need 15 to 20 minutes. Keep meat covered during standing time to retain heat.

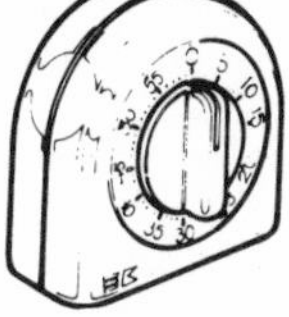

SECOND TIME AROUND

- **Meats don't dry out** if reheated properly in the microwave.
- **If meat cannot be stirred or rearranged** during reheating, particularly if you are reheating a large quantity, use **MEDIUM (50%) or MEDIUM-HIGH (70%).**
- **If possible, arrange meat in a circle** or ring, leaving centre open. For meat casseroles, depress the centre slightly for more even heating.
- **HIGH power is fine for smaller cuts** or individual servings. One generous serving of meat takes **1 to 2 minutes on HIGH. One hamburger takes 30 to 45 seconds on HIGH.** A one quart casserole will take **4 to 6 minutes on HIGH.**
- **To reheat a dinner plate containing meat, vegetables and potatoes:** Place vegetables in the centre; meat and potatoes should be placed around the outside edge of the plate. Spoon gravy or sauce over meat to help it heat more evenly. **One dinner plate of food will take 2 to 3 minutes on MEDIUM-HIGH (70%).**
- **Some microwave ovens come with a shelf.** There is also a rack which you can buy to reheat two plates of food at one time. Switch plates at half time for more even heating.
- **Waxed paper retains heat** but lets steam escape. A glass pie plate inverted over a dinner plate makes a good covering. The pie plate or vented microsafe plastic wrap will retain steam.
- **Breaded chops will not be as crisp** when reheated in the microwave. It helps to elevate them on a microsafe rack; cover chops with microsafe paper towelling.
- **Bottom centre of plate** will feel hot when meat is heated.
- **Refrigerated foods take longer** to reheat than room temperature foods.
- **If food was stored on a plate in the refrigerator,** the cold plate may draw some of the heat out of the meat when you reheat it, causing meat to cool more quickly. Allow an extra 30 seconds of heating time.
- **Roast meat should be covered with sauce or gravy** to prevent it from drying out. Slice thinly for best results; thick pieces don't reheat as evenly. Arrange slices in overlapping layers, with larger, thicker pieces towards the outside of the dish.
- **Lettuce leaves make an excellent covering** when reheating roast beef. Discard lettuce after heating.

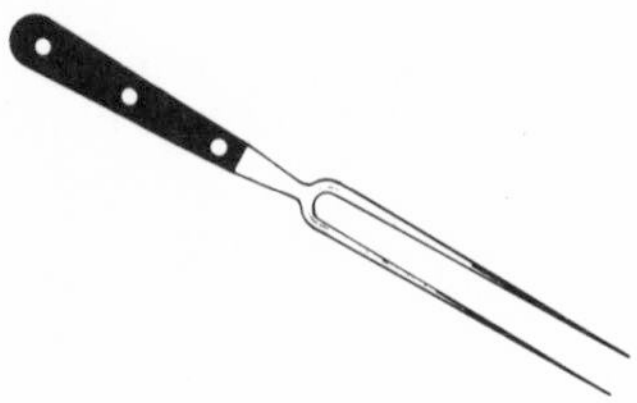

CONVECTION/MICRO WAYS WITH MEATS

- **The COMBINATION CYCLE is ideal** for meats. They will be moist, juicy and beautifully browned.
- **Cooking time will be about ½ the time** of conventional recipes. Times vary with different brands of ovens. Check a similar recipe in the manufacturer's cookbook as a guideline for cooking times and power settings.
- **Use casseroles which are both heatproof and microsafe** (e.g. Pyrex™, Corning Ware™, ceramic, clay bakers).
- **The casserole dish should be placed on the rack** recommended by the oven manufacturer for combination cooking. This allows the heat to circulate during the **CONVECTION** portion of the **COMBINATION CYCLE.**
- **Preheating is usually not necessary.** However, in certain instances, I do recommend preheating to guide you in choosing the oven temperature required on the **COMBINATION CYCLE.**
- **Cook tender cuts uncovered** for maximum browning. Less tender cuts should be covered to help them tenderize.
- **Roasts should be started fat side up** when cooked on the combination setting. Turn roast over halfway through cooking; baste with pan juices. If overcooking occurs, shield with pieces of aluminum foil. Keep foil at least 1″ away from the walls and doors of your oven.
- **Parchment paper can be used** to cover casserole dishes which don't have a lid. Oven cooking bags are excellent for less tender cuts of meat.
- **You can microwave roasts for part of the cooking time, then complete them on the CONVECTION CYCLE.** Remember to elevate the casserole during the **CONVECTION CYCLE** for proper heat circulation.
- **A probe will indicate** if food has reached the required internal temperature. Insert probe into food halfway through the cooking cycle; make sure it is inserted into the centre of the meat, not touching bone or fat. A dual use thermometer could be used; don't use a microwavable or conventional meat thermometer on the **COMBINATION CYCLE.**
- **When cooking large cuts of meat on the CONVECTION CYCLE,** reduce the temperature by 25°F to prevent them from becoming too brown. The combination oven has a smaller cavity than your conventional oven and the food will be much closer to the heat source.
- **Cut-up potatoes can be added** to meat during the last 25 minutes of cooking.
- **Remember to remove meat from the oven** at the end of the **COMBINATION or CONVECTION CYCLE.** The oven takes time to cool down and if you forget to remove the cooked food, it will continue to cook.
- **Read Convection/Micro Ways** (p. 28) and Convection/Micro Ways with Briskets, Pot Roasts and Stews (p. 196).

THE DAILY GRIND

- **Ground beef and veal** are interchangeable in most recipes. Veal will be lighter in color.
- **Ground meat microwaves very well.** You will get great results quickly with meatballs, meatloaf, spaghetti sauce, chili and casseroles. Also read Notes on Meatballs (p. 45).
- **Shape ground meat into a donut or bagel shape** before freezing, making an indentation in the centre. This helps it defrost more evenly.
- BROWNED GROUND: Place ground beef or veal in a microsafe colander. Place colander over a microsafe bowl to catch any drippings. (If you don't have a colander, place meat in a microsafe casserole.) **MW on HIGH, allowing 5 to 6 minutes per lb.** Stir once or twice during cooking to break up meat. If you forget and the meat clumps together into lumps like meatballs, mash it with a potato masher. Discard fatty juices from meat after cooking. Chopped onions, peppers, etc. can be microwaved together with the meat.
- **Microwaved meat loaf** cooks better and faster in a ring shape. Loaf shapes do not cook evenly in the microwave and overcooking can occur on the ends.
- **Microwaving extracts more fat** from ground meat than when it is cooked conventionally. Ask your butcher for lean ground veal or beef (ground chuck is very tasty).
- **Casserole dish does not require greasing** unless you are completing the cooking in a conventional oven or are using the **CONVECTION/ MICROWAVE CYCLE.**
- **If ground beef starts to cook** when you defrost it because you used too high a power or the edges were too thin, don't worry. Just continue to microwave it until it loses its pink color, mashing occasionally; see Browned Ground (above). Use to make In-A-Hurry Spaghetti Sauce (p. 186), Chili with Class (p. 187) or Mistake Casserole (below).
- MISTAKE CASSEROLE: MW 1 chopped onion and 1 green pepper **uncovered on HIGH for 2 minutes.** Mix with 1 lb. "Browned Ground" (above) in a 2 quart microsafe casserole. Add 3 c. cooked rice or noodles, 2 c. tomato sauce, salt & pepper. Add any leftover cooked veggies from your fridge (e.g. peas, corn). Cover and **MW on HIGH for 8 to 10 minutes,** until piping hot. Stir at half time.
- **Frozen Spaghetti Sauce:** Dip container in hot water to loosen. Empty into a microsafe casserole. **For 4 servings, MW** covered with waxed paper **on HIGH for 12 to 15 minutes,** until thawed. Break up sauce 2 or 3 times with a fork. **MW 3 to 5 minutes longer,** until piping hot, stirring occasionally. **One serving of frozen spaghetti sauce will take 3 to 5 minutes on HIGH** to thaw and heat.
- **To reheat refrigerated Spaghetti Sauce: One serving will take 2 to 3 minutes on HIGH; 2 servings will take 5 to 7 minutes. Four servings will take 8 to 10 minutes.** Cover with casserole lid or waxed paper. Stir once or twice during reheating.
- **The largest hamburger on record** was made in Australia in 1975. It was 27 ½ feet in circumference and weighed 2859 pounds. That's a little too large for my microwave oven!

SPAGHETTI SAUCE

If you are watching your cholesterol or calories, make this sauce with ground veal and omit the salami or pepperoni. No oil is needed for this recipe. A food processor makes preparation extra quick.

2 to 3 cloves garlic, minced
2 medium onions, chopped
1 green pepper, chopped
2 lb. lean ground beef or veal
¼ lb. salami or pepperoni, if desired
28 oz. can tomatoes
2 - 5½ oz. cans tomato paste
2 to 3 tbsp. red wine, optional
1 to 2 tsp. salt (to taste)
½ tsp. each pepper, oregano, basil & sugar
1 bay leaf

1. Combine garlic, onions and green pepper in a 3 quart microsafe casserole*. Add ground meat. Finely chop salami or pepperoni. (It gives a wonderful flavor!) Add to casserole.

2. **MW uncovered on HIGH for 10 to 12 minutes,** or until meat is cooked, stirring 2 or 3 times to break up meat. Drain juices from bowl. (If using a colander, transfer meat mixture to bowl.) Add remaining ingredients and mix well; break up tomatoes. Cover with waxed paper.

3. **MW on HIGH for 10 minutes,** or until mixture is bubbling. Stir. **MW on MEDIUM (50%) 25 to 30 minutes longer,** stirring once. Let stand covered for 5 to 10 minutes.

Yield: 8 servings. Freezes well.

* The fat can be drained off easily if you cook ground meat and vegetables in a microsafe plastic colander placed over the cooking casserole.
* Use a food processor to chop vegetables and salami. Follow processor method used for Chili with Class (p. 187).
* If you don't drain the cooking juices, the sauce will be too thin. I add the juices to my dog Tootsie's dinner.
* Waxed paper covering prevents spatters but still allows some of the liquid from the sauce to evaporate.
* If you forgot to stir the sauce and the meat cooks together into lumps like meatballs, just mash it with a potato masher.
* If you like a spicy sauce, add 1 or 2 whole green chilis. Submerge chilis under sauce during cooking. Remove at end of cooking time. **Beware of the seeds - they're fiery hot.**
* **For 4 servings:** Use a 2 quart microsafe casserole. **In Step 2, MW meat and vegetables on HIGH for 5 to 6 minutes. In Step 3, MW sauce covered on HIGH for 15 to 20 minutes.** Stir occasionally.
* If you prefer your own recipe, stick with it; just use my method as a guideline.

IN-A-HURRY SPAGHETTI SAUCE

1 onion, chopped
1 green pepper, chopped
1 lb. lean ground beef
2 cloves garlic, minced
1 tsp. crushed chilis
4 c. bottled spaghetti sauce

1. Place onion, green pepper and meat in a 2 quart microsafe casserole. **MW uncovered on HIGH for 6 to 7 minutes,** breaking meat up with a fork twice during cooking. Meat should lose its pink color. Drain off cooking juices.

2. Add garlic, chilis and sauce to meat. Cover with waxed paper and **MW on HIGH for 10 to 15 minutes*,** until thick and bubbling, stirring once. Adjust seasonings to taste.

Yield: 4 servings. Sauce can be frozen in individual portions.

* Chili Paste with Garlic can be substituted for garlic and crushed chilis. It is available in Chinatown and gives a wonderful flavor to Italian dishes!
* Fresh Tomato Sauce (p. 89) can be substituted for bottled sauce. If refrigerated, cooking time in **Step 2 will be 20 minutes.**

SHIPWRECK

My kids loved this casserole when they were little, but they had trouble pronouncing the name (they thought the "p" was a "t"!) The original recipe took nearly 3 hours to cook. It takes ⅓ of the time to make in the microwave.

2 medium onions, sliced
2 potatoes, peeled & sliced
salt, pepper, garlic powder & paprika, to taste
1 ½ lb. lean ground beef
½ c. rice
2 stalks celery, sliced
3 medium carrots, sliced
2 c. chicken broth

1. Layer sliced onions and potatoes in an ungreased 2 quart round microsafe casserole. Sprinkle lightly with seasonings. Spread meat evenly over potatoes; season lightly. Top with rice. Spread celery and carrots over rice. Season once again. Pour broth over casserole.

2. Cover with casserole lid or vented plastic wrap. **MW on HIGH for 12 minutes.** Rotate casserole ¼ turn. **MW on MEDIUM (50%) 45 minutes longer,** rotating casserole ¼ turn twice during cooking. Let stand covered for 10 to 15 minutes.

Yield: 4 to 6 servings. Reheats well.

CHILI WITH CLASS

My students love my Chili. It's on the table in less than half an hour! Read The Daily Grind (p. 184).

1 - 2 cloves garlic
1 medium onion, quartered
1 green pepper, halved & seeded
1 lb. ground beef or veal
2 oz. salami or pepperoni
19 oz. can tomatoes
5 ½ oz. can tomato paste
19 oz. can red kidney beans, drained
1 tbsp. chili powder
1 tbsp. cocoa, (see Note*)
¼ tsp. ground cumin, optional
few drops Tabasco sauce
1 tsp. salt
freshly ground pepper

1. **Steel Knife:** Drop garlic through feed tube while machine is running. Process until minced. Add onion and green pepper. Process with 3 or 4 quick on/off turns, until coarsely chopped.

2. Place ground beef and vegetables in a 2 quart microsafe bowl. Process salami or pepperoni on **Steel Knife** until finely chopped, about 8 to 10 seconds. Add to hamburger mixture. **MW uncovered on HIGH for 5 to 6 minutes** or until beef is cooked, stirring 2 or 3 times to break up meat. Drain juices from bowl, add remaining ingredients and stir to blend.

3. Cover with waxed paper and **MW on HIGH for 15 to 20 minutes,** stirring occasionally. Let stand covered for 5 minutes. Garnish with chopped onions, if desired. May also be served over spaghetti, rice or toasted hamburger buns.

Yield: 4 to 6 servings. Freezes well.

* Cocoa gives a rich, dark color to this chili. My students always laugh when I tell them if there's an excuse to put chocolate into a dish, I find it!
* Delicious eaten right away, but even better if prepared in advance in order to blend and develop flavors.
* Meat and chopped vegetables can be cooked together in a microsafe plastic colander placed over the casserole.
* **CHICK PEA CHILI:** My friend John Bedrossian substitutes a 19 oz. can of chick peas for the kidney beans. He also uses 1 tsp. Chinese Chili Paste with Garlic instead of chili powder and Tabasco sauce. Omit cumin and cocoa.
* **MACARONI & CHILI CASSEROLE:** Combine Chili with 4 cups of cooked macaroni in an ungreased 9″ x 13″ microsafe casserole; mix well. **MW uncovered on HIGH for 6 to 8 minutes,** until piping hot, stirring once or twice. Makes 6 to 8 servings.

SHEPHERD'S PIE

<u>Meat Mixture:</u>
2 lb. ground beef or veal
2 eggs
1 ½ tsp. salt
¼ tsp. pepper
¼ tsp. basil
2 cloves garlic, crushed
½ c. tomato sauce
½ c. bread crumbs, oatmeal or matzo meal

1. Combine all ingredients for meat mixture in an ungreased 2 quart oblong casserole; mix lightly to blend. Spread in an even layer. **MW uncovered on HIGH for 10 to 12 minutes,** mashing meat with a fork or potato masher once or twice during cooking. When cooked, meat will have lost its pink color. Spread evenly in casserole.

4 to 6 potatoes, peeled and quartered
2 tbsp. water
1 egg
salt & pepper, to taste
½ tsp. baking powder
2 tbsp. margarine
12 oz. can corn niblets, if desired
3 tbsp. bread crumbs
paprika to garnish

2. Place potatoes in a microsafe bowl. You should have about 3 cups. Sprinkle with water and cover with vented plastic wrap. **MW on HIGH for 10 to 12 minutes,** stirring at half time. When done, potatoes will be tender when pierced with a knife. Let stand covered for 2 minutes. Drain off any liquid. Mash well. Add egg, seasonings, baking powder and margarine; mix well.

3. Place drained corn over cooked meat. Carefully spread mashed potatoes over corn. Top with crumbs and sprinkle with paprika. (May be prepared in advance up to this point and refrigerated until serving time.)

4. **MW uncovered on HIGH for 10 minutes,** or until piping hot and potato mixture begins to pull away slightly from the sides of the casserole. Rotate casserole ¼ turn halfway through cooking. (Refrigerated casserole may take slightly longer.) Let stand for 3 minutes.

Yield: 6 to 8 servings. May be frozen.

* **For 3 or 4 servings,** use half the ingredients. Cook the meat mixture in a 1 quart round casserole, mashing meat at half time. Cooking time for meat will be **5 to 6 minutes on HIGH. Three potatoes will take 6 to 7 minutes on HIGH. Assembled casserole will take 7 to 8 minutes on HIGH to cook.**
* **For individual servings,** assemble in separate microsafe casseroles. **Two servings will take 5 to 7 minutes on HIGH to cook.** Rotate each dish ¼ turn halfway through cooking. Freeze extras for another day.
* To save time, potatoes can be cooked conventionally on the stove while you microwave the meat mixture.

SWEET & SOUR MEAT LOAF

1 lb. lean ground beef or veal
1 egg
¼ c. bread crumbs
¾ tsp. salt
⅛ tsp. ground black pepper
1 clove garlic, crushed
⅛ tsp. basil
8 oz. tin tomato sauce, divided in half
¼ c. brown or white sugar
1 tbsp. lemon juice

1. Combine ground beef with egg, crumbs and seasonings. Add ½ cup of the tomato sauce. Mix lightly to blend.

2. Shape into a ring, using a 9″ pie plate as your cooking dish. Place a piece of crumpled microsafe paper towel in the centre of the ring to absorb cooking juices.

3. **MW uncovered on HIGH for 6 to 7 minutes,** rotating the baking dish ¼ turn halfway through cooking. Discard paper towel.

4. Combine remaining sauce with brown sugar and lemon juice. Drizzle sauce over the top of the meat and cook on **HIGH 2 to 3 minutes longer.** Let stand 5 minutes before serving. To serve, fill centre with cooked green peas & carrots. Serve with mashed potatoes.

Yield: 4 servings. Freezes well. Delicious hot or cold.

* For a crispier meat loaf, prepare and microwave as directed in Steps 1 to 4. Then **bake uncovered at 400°F for 15 minutes.** If desired, tomato sauce topping can be omitted.
* **To double the recipe:** Prepare meat loaf as directed in Steps 1 and 2, using a large microsafe platter. **MW uncovered on HIGH for 12 to 15 minutes in Step 3.** Time in Step 4 will be the same.
* **Individual Meat Loaves:** Prepare meat mixture as directed in Step 1. Shape into 4 oval loaves. Arrange individual loaves in a circle on a microsafe plate. Microwave as directed in Steps 3 and 4 (omit paper towel).
* **One serving takes 3 to 4 minutes on HIGH** to cook. Top with a spoonful of sauce (or ketchup) and **MW on HIGH 30 seconds longer.**
* **Timetable for Preparation:** Cook potatoes, then meat loaf, then frozen vegetables. Cover potatoes and meat loaf tightly to retain heat. **If necessary, reheat potatoes uncovered for 1 to 2 minutes on HIGH.**
* Meat loaf can be cooked, sliced into individual servings and frozen on a cookie sheet. Wrap frozen slices with microsafe plastic wrap. To thaw and reheat: unwrap slices and arrange in a circle on a microsafe plate. Cover loosely with waxed paper. **One serving takes 4 to 5 minutes on MEDIUM (50%)** to thaw and heat; **4 servings take 12 to 15 minutes.** Turn slices over at half time.

CABBAGE ROLLS

1 head cabbage (about 3 lb.)
2 tbsp. water
1 lb. ground beef or veal
1 egg
¾ tsp. salt
dash pepper
1 clove garlic, crushed
1 c. cooked rice*
3 tbsp. bread crumbs or oatmeal
19 oz. can tomatoes
5 ½ oz. can tomato paste
⅓ c. brown sugar, packed
2 tbsp. lemon juice

1. Rinse cabbage but do not dry. Place in a deep microsafe bowl with 2 tbsp. water. Cover with vented plastic wrap; **MW on HIGH for 6 to 8 minutes,** until outer leaves are pliable. **(Allow 2 to 3 minutes per lb.)** Let stand covered for 5 minutes. Carefully remove 12 leaves, trimming away tough ribs. If cabbage is not flexible enough when you remove the last few leaves, **MW on HIGH 1 minute longer.**

2. Combine meat, egg, seasonings, rice, crumbs and ⅓ cup juice from canned tomatoes; mix well. Place ¼ cup of meat mixture on each leaf. Roll up, folding in ends. Place seam-side down in an oblong Pyrex™ casserole, placing smaller rolls in the middle.

3. Combine tomatoes, tomato paste, brown sugar and lemon juice; mix well. Pour over cabbage rolls. Cover with waxed paper. **MW on HIGH for 12 minutes,** until bubbling. Turn cabbage rolls over once or twice during cooking to help them cook evenly.

4. **Reduce power to MEDIUM (50%) and MW 25 minutes longer,** or until tender. Let stand covered for 10 to 15 minutes.

Yield: 12 cabbage rolls. Freezes and reheats well.

* Leftover cabbage can be used to make Cabbage Soup (p. 73).
* A handful of raisins and 1 apple, peeled & sliced, can be added with the sauce mixture in Step 3.
* **To make 1 cup of cooked white rice:** Combine ⅔ c. water, a dash of salt and ⅓ c. long-grain rice in a 2 cup glass measure. Cover with vented plastic wrap. **MW on HIGH for 2 minutes, reduce power to MEDIUM (50%) and MW 10 minutes longer.** Let stand covered for 2 to 3 minutes. All the water should be absorbed and the rice will be tender.

STUFFED PEPPERS

The meat and rice are cooked separately, then combined and stuffed into the partially cooked peppers for a brief cooking and blending of flavors.

1 lb. ground beef or veal
1 small onion, chopped
⅓ c. tomato sauce
3 tbsp. bread crumbs or oatmeal
1 c. cooked white rice
¾ tsp. salt
dash pepper
1 clove garlic, crushed
¼ tsp. oregano
4 medium green or red peppers
1 c. additional tomato sauce
1 tbsp. brown sugar
dash of salt, pepper & oregano

1. Combine ground beef and onion in a 1 quart microsafe casserole. **MW uncovered on HIGH for 5 minutes,** until no pink remains, stirring once or twice during cooking. Add ⅓ c. tomato sauce, crumbs, rice and seasonings. Mix well.

2. Cut peppers in half. Remove membranes and seeds. Arrange cut-side up in an oblong Pyrex™ casserole. Cover with waxed paper. **MW on HIGH for 4 to 5 minutes,** until tender-crisp. Drain. Spoon in filling. Combine remaining tomato sauce with brown sugar and seasonings. Spoon over peppers.

3. Cover with waxed paper. (Can be prepared in advance up to this point and refrigerated.) **MW on HIGH for 10 to 12 minutes,** until peppers are tender, rotating the casserole ¼ turn halfway through cooking. Let stand covered for 5 minutes. Serve with a mixed green salad, corn niblets and crusty rolls.

Yield: 4 servings. Can be frozen.

* **Two pepper halves** will take **6 to 7 minutes on MEDIUM (50%)** to microwave. Lower power level is used to help develop the flavor.
* **CONVECTION/MICROWAVE METHOD:** Follow Steps 1 and 2 above. Preheat oven to 375°F. Place casserole on rack used for combination cooking; cook uncovered on the **COMBINATION CYCLE** your manufacturer suggests for casseroles. **Cooking time will be 20 to 30 minutes.** Time varies with different ovens. Baste occasionally. Refer to Convection/Micro Ways with Meats (p. 183).

MY OVEN'S SETTING______ **MY COOKING TIME**______

OLD-FASHIONED HAMBURGERS (KOTLETTEN)

My mother used to make these for me when I was a little girl and I loved them. The hamburgers took at least an hour to steam after they were browned. The microwave steams them perfectly in minutes.

1 lb. ground beef or veal
2 eggs
1 tbsp. water
3/4 tsp. salt
1/8 tsp. pepper
1 clove garlic, minced
1/4 c. matzo meal, oatmeal or 1/2 c. soft bread crumbs*
2 tbsp. oil
1 or 2 onions, sliced

1. Combine ground beef with eggs, water, seasonings and matzo meal. Mix lightly or meat will become tough. Moisten your hands with cold water to facilitate shaping; the mixture will be quite soft. Form meat into 5 or 6 patties.

2. Heat oil in a skillet on top of the stove. **Brown patties in oil on medium-high heat, about 5 to 6 minutes.** Transfer to a covered microsafe casserole. Brown onions quickly in pan drippings. Add to casserole. Cover with casserole lid.

3. **MW on HIGH for 4 to 5 minutes,** until juices run clear. Turn patties over halfway through cooking. Let stand covered for 3 minutes. Serve with mashed potatoes and corn niblets or peas.

Yield: 2 to 3 servings. Freezes well.

* One slice of bread makes 1/2 cup soft bread crumbs.
* **To double the recipe:** Double all ingredients, but use only 2 to 3 tbsp. oil (just enough to prevent burgers from sticking). **In Step 3, MW burgers on HIGH for 7 to 8 minutes.**
* You can use a non-stick skillet, but the oil adds more flavor.

ORIENTAL MEATBALLS

Meat Mixture:
- **1 ½ lb. lean ground beef**
- **1 egg**
- **¾ tsp. salt**
- **¼ tsp. pepper**
- **¼ c. bread crumbs or oatmeal**
- **¼ c. water**
- **⅛ tsp. ground ginger**
- **1 clove garlic, crushed**

Sauce:
- **14 oz. can pineapple chunks**
- **⅓ c. bottled Teriyaki sauce**
- **1 tbsp. soya sauce**
- **⅓ c. honey**
- **2 cloves garlic, crushed**
- **2 tbsp. cornstarch**
- **¼ tsp. ground ginger**
- **1 onion, cut in 1″ chunks**
- **½ green pepper & ½ red pepper, cut in 1″ chunks**

1. Combine all ingredients for meat mixture and mix lightly to blend. Shape into 1″ meatballs. Arrange in a single layer in an ungreased shallow 2 or 3 quart microsafe casserole.

2. **MW uncovered on HIGH for 8 to 9 minutes,** stirring carefully halfway through cooking time. Meatballs should lose their pink color. Let stand while you prepare the sauce.

3. Drain juice from pineapple chunks into a 4 cup glass measure. Add pineapple chunks to cooked meatballs. Add remaining sauce ingredients to juice; stir well. **MW sauce uncovered on HIGH for 4 to 5 minutes,** stirring twice. Mixture will be thick and bubbling and vegetables will be tender-crisp.

4. Add sauce to meatballs. **MW uncovered on HIGH for 3 or 4 minutes,** until heated through. Serve over rice.

Yield: 4 servings as a main course; 6 to 8 servings as an appetizer.

* May be frozen, but vegetables will not be crisp.
* Excellent as an hors d'oeuvre. If you wish, increase meat to 2 lb. Omit onion and peppers. Make tiny meatballs about ¾″ in diameter. Use a 3 quart oval or oblong microsafe casserole. **Cooking time for 2 lb. meatballs in Step 2 will be 10 to 12 minutes on HIGH.** You should have about 60 meatballs (10 to 12 servings). Serve on toothpicks.
* Read Notes on Meatballs (p. 45).

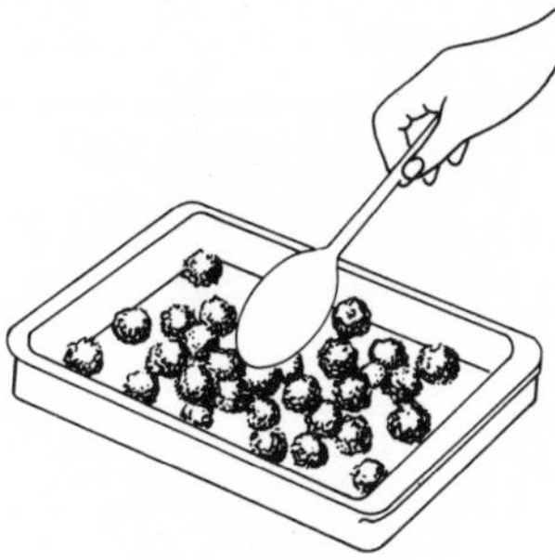

VEAL MEATBALLS WITH PEPPERS

Meat Mixture:
1 lb. ground veal
1 egg
¼ c. oatmeal or bread crumbs
15 oz. can tomato sauce, divided
¾ tsp. salt
freshly ground pepper
1 clove garlic, minced
1 tbsp. Dijon mustard

Sauce & Vegetable Mixture:
¼ tsp. basil
2 cloves garlic, minced
salt & pepper, to taste
2 tsp. sugar
1 green pepper
1 yellow pepper
1 red pepper
2 onions
1 tbsp. oil

1. Meat Mixture: Combine veal with egg, oatmeal, ¼ cup of the tomato sauce, salt, pepper, garlic and mustard. Shape into 1″ meatballs. **MW uncovered on HIGH for 5 to 6 minutes,** stirring carefully at half time.

2. Sauce & Vegetable Mixture: Add remaining tomato sauce and seasonings to meatballs. Mix well. Cover with waxed paper and **MW on HIGH for 5 minutes,** stirring at half time. Let stand covered while you cook the vegetables.

3. Cut peppers and onions into 1″ chunks. Combine with oil in a microsafe bowl. **MW on HIGH uncovered for 6 to 7 minutes,** stirring at half time. Add to meatballs. If not hot enough, **MW on HIGH for 2 minutes.** Serve over rice.

Yield: 3 to 4 servings. Reheats well. Vegetables will become soggy if frozen.

HOT DOGS

When people ask me about my favorite foods, I usually include hot dogs high up on the list — but not just any hot dog! I like them best with a natural casing, so that there is some resistance when I take a bite. My favorite way is with Dijon mustard (no yucky yellow prepared mustard or relish for me!) and lots of fried onions. Whenever I go back home to Winnipeg, my first stop is at Kelekis' Restaurant for the ultimate hot dog!

1. Make 4 or 5 diagonal slashes through the hot dog. Place on a microsafe plate and **MW on HIGH for 30 to 60 seconds,** depending on size. Place in bun, wrap in a napkin and **MW on HIGH 15 seconds longer,** just until bun is warmed. Serve with your favorite condiments.

* **One hot dog takes 45 to 60 seconds on DEFROST (30%) to thaw. One pound takes 4 to 6 minutes;** separate them as soon as possible.
* I usually cook **one hot dog for 1 minute on HIGH,** or **two for 1 ½ minutes,** because I like them kind of crunchy. I also toast the bun.
* Leaner hot dogs are now made from veal, chicken...even tofu for vegetarians!
* Did you know that Americans eat more than 5 billion hot dogs between Memorial Day and Labor Day?

MICRO-WAYS WITH BRISKET

- **Thin edges of brisket** will become tough and dry like shoe leather if you don't follow the following rules: use enough liquid, cover tightly, use a lower power level to slow down the cooking time and tenderize the meat.
- **Start all briskets with 15 minutes on HIGH,** then calculate **18 minutes per lb. on MEDIUM (50%). A 3½ lb. brisket will cook for 15 minutes on HIGH and about 1 hour on MEDIUM (50%).**
- **Use at least 1 cup of liquid** (water, wine, tomato sauce, etc.). This liquid will help cook the meat more evenly as well as create steam for tenderizing.
- **Turning the meat over twice** during cooking helps it cook evenly. Meat should be tender when pierced with a fork.
- **Standing time of 20 minutes** will complete the cooking and make the meat easier to slice. Slice across the grain.
- **Potatoes can be cooked** during the standing time.
- **If meat is not tender enough after slicing, cooking it in the gravy for 20 to 30 minutes on MEDIUM (50%) will soften it.**
- **A clay baker** is an excellent casserole for cooking brisket and other tough cuts of meat in the microwave. Soak the clay baker for 15 minutes in cold water before using. It will release steam during cooking.
- **An oval casserole** with a glass lid also makes an excellent cooking container.
- **Since the cover on clay bakers** and other casseroles is usually domed, place a sheet of waxed paper directly on top of the meat, then put on the casserole cover. This helps to trap the maximum amount of steam for more tenderizing.
- **An oblong microsafe casserole** could be used, with moistened cooking parchment as a covering. Tuck ends of parchment under casserole.
- **Plastic cooking bags (not storage bags!)** are excellent because they are microsafe, hold in the steam and make clean-up easy.
- **Remember to coat the inside** of the bag with 1 tbsp. flour (or potato starch during Passover) according to package directions. Leave an opening the size of a dime when you seal the bag. Don't use metal twist ties. Place cooking bag in a casserole in case juices leak out during cooking.
- **Use oven mitts;** casserole gets hot from the long cooking time.

CONVECTION/MICRO WAYS WITH BRISKETS, POT ROASTS & STEWS

- **Use a microsafe/heatproof container** (e.g. Pyrex™, Corning Ware™, presoaked clay baker or cooking bag).
- **If using a cooking bag,** make sure it doesn't touch the walls of the oven during cooking.
- **If casserole doesn't have a lid,** use cooking parchment.
- **Place casserole on rack recommended by oven manufacturer.** Cook covered on **COMBINATION CYCLE** suitable for pot roasts. **Briskets and pot roasts take about 2 to 2 ½ hours; stews take 1 ½ to 2 hours.** Turn meat (or cooking bag) over halfway through cooking. Baste occasionally. Remember to remove meat from oven at end of cooking time; otherwise it will continue to cook because oven takes time to cool down.
- Read Convection/Micro Ways with Meats (p. 183).

BASIC BRISKET

If you have your own favorite recipe, use it, but follow the microwave method for cooking.

3 onions, sliced
1 c. water (or half red wine and half water)
3 cloves garlic, crushed
1 tsp. paprika
½ tsp. black pepper
1 tsp. basil
1 tsp. dry mustard
3 tbsp. flour
3 tbsp. bottled teriyaki sauce
3 ½ lb. beef brisket

1. Read Micro-Ways with Brisket (p.195). Place onions and liquid in the bottom of a covered microsafe casserole or a microsafe cooking bag. Make a paste of garlic, spices, flour and teriyaki sauce. Rub all over brisket. Place in casserole or bag fat-side down, turning thin ends under to prevent edges from overcooking.

2. **MW covered on HIGH for 15 minutes.** Turn brisket over. **MW on MEDIUM (50%) for 30 minutes;** turn brisket over and baste with sauce. **MW 30 minutes longer,** until tender. Let stand covered for 20 minutes. Slice across the grain. Reheat in the gravy. (If not tender enough, **MW covered for 20 to 30 minutes on MEDIUM (50%),** stirring once or twice.)

Yield: 8 servings. Freezes well. Slice before freezing.

* **CONVECTION/MICROWAVE METHOD:** Follow directions for Convection/Micro Ways with Briskets, Pot Roasts & Stews (above). **Cooking time will be 2 to 2 ½ hours.**

MY OVEN'S SETTING______ MY COOKING TIME______

EASY ROAST BRISKET

3 ½ - 4 lb. beef brisket
1 pkg. dehydrated onion soup mix
1 c. tomato sauce
2 tbsp. brown sugar

1. Read Micro-Ways with Brisket (p. 195). Rub brisket with onion soup mix. Pour sauce into a microsafe casserole; stir in brown sugar. Place brisket fat side down in casserole; baste with sauce. Turn thin ends under. Cover tightly.

2. **MW on HIGH for 15 minutes.** Turn brisket over. **MW on MEDIUM (50%) for 30 minutes;** turn brisket over and baste with sauce. **MW 30 to 45 minutes longer,** until tender. Let stand covered for 20 minutes. Slice across the grain. Reheat in the gravy. (If not tender enough, **MW covered for 20 to 30 minutes on MEDIUM (50%),** stirring once or twice.)

Yield: 8 servings. Freezes well. Slice before freezing.

> * **CONVECTION/MICROWAVE METHOD:** Follow directions on p. 196, Convection/Micro Ways with Briskets, Pot Roasts & Stews. **Cooking time will be 2 to 2 ½ hours.**
>
> MY OVEN'S SETTING______ MY COOKING TIME______

SWEET & SOUR BRISKET

Sliced brisket is returned to the gravy to absorb the delicious flavor and tenderize.

2 medium onions, chopped
3 ½ - 4 lb. brisket
2 tsp. salt
freshly ground pepper
1 tsp. oregano
2 cloves garlic, minced
7 ½ oz. can tomato sauce
½ c. brown sugar, packed
⅓ c. wine vinegar

1. Read Micro-Ways with Brisket (p. 195). Place onions in the bottom of a covered microsafe casserole or a microsafe cooking bag. Rub brisket with seasonings. Place in casserole or bag fat-side down, turning thin ends under to prevent edges from overcooking. Combine remaining ingredients and add to brisket.

2. **MW covered on HIGH for 15 minutes.** Turn brisket over. **MW on MEDIUM (50%) for 30 minutes;** turn brisket over and baste with sauce. **MW on MEDIUM (50%) 30 minutes longer,** until nearly tender. Let stand covered for 20 to 30 minutes. Slice across the grain.

3. Place brisket slices back into the sauce. **Cover and MW on MEDIUM (50%) for 25 to 30 minutes,** until tender. Stir once or twice.

Yield: 8 servings. Freezes well.

> **CONVECTION/MICROWAVE METHOD:** Follow directions on p. 196, Convection/Micro Ways with Briskets, Pot Roasts & Stews. **Cooking time will be 2 to 2 ½ hours.**
>
> MY OVEN'S SETTING______ MY COOKING TIME______

ROAST BRISKET WITH POTATOES

1. Cook desired brisket recipe as directed. Let stand covered for 20 minutes.

2. Meanwhile, peel and quarter 4 large potatoes. Place in a covered casserole with 2 tbsp. water; **MW covered on HIGH for 10 minutes,** until almost tender. Drain well. Add to brisket and baste with gravy. **Cover and MW on MEDIUM (50%) for 20 to 30 minutes,** until tender, basting once or twice.

IN A STEW?

- **To thaw stewing meat:** Remove wrappings and place meat on a microsafe plate. **MW on DEFROST (30%), allowing 5 to 7 minutes per lb.** At half time, turn meat over. Separate pieces and spread out on the plate; pieces that are more frozen should be towards the centre of the dish. Defrost for remaining time. Meat should still be icy. Standing time will be equal to microwave defrosting time. Meat should be completely thawed before cooking.
- **Stewing meat should be cut in 1″ pieces.** Smaller pieces will give more tender results in the microwave. Beef and veal are interchangable, but veal usually takes less time to cook.
- **It is not necessary to brown meat** for stews in hot oil before you combine it with the remaining ingredients.
- **I like to add firm vegetables** (e.g. potatoes, carrots) at the beginning of cooking. Frozen or softer vegetables (e.g. fresh zucchini cut in chunks, frozen mixed vegetables) can be added during the last half hour of cooking.
- **Frozen Cooked Stew (4 servings):** Dip container in hot water to loosen. Empty into a microsafe casserole. **MW covered with waxed paper on DEFROST (30%) for 30 to 35 minutes.** Break up stew 2 or 3 times with a fork. Let stand for a few minutes for temperature to equalize. **Then MW covered on MEDIUM-HIGH for 8 to 10 minutes,** stirring at half time.
- **To reheat refrigerated stew: One serving will take 2 to 3 minutes on HIGH; 2 servings will take 5 to 7 minutes. Four servings will take 8 to 10 minutes.** Cover with casserole lid or waxed paper. Stir once or twice during reheating.

SUPER STEW

Cooking time is less than half of conventional cooking time. Besides, microwaved stew never sticks to the pot!

3 cloves garlic, minced
2 onions, chopped
2 stalks celery, chopped
2 tbsp. oil
2 lb. stewing beef or veal cut in 1″ cubes
4 carrots, peeled, trimmed & cut in 1″ chunks
4 medium potatoes, peeled & cut in 1″ chunks
5 ½ oz. can tomato paste
½ c. red wine
1 c. chicken broth
1 tsp. salt
freshly ground pepper
1 tsp. basil
¼ tsp. thyme

1. Combine garlic, onions and celery with oil in a deep 3 or 4 quart microsafe casserole. **MW uncovered on HIGH for 3 to 4 minutes.** Add meat; **MW uncovered on HIGH for 6 minutes.** Stir, moving less cooked portions towards the outside of the casserole. **MW on HIGH 4 to 6 minutes longer,** until meat is no longer pink.

2. Add remaining ingredients; mix well. Cover with casserole lid. **MW covered on HIGH for 15 minutes,** until bubbling. Mix well.

3. If casserole is very deep, place a sheet of waxed paper on surface of stew to trap the steam. Cover with casserole lid. **Reduce power to MEDIUM (50%) and MW 1 hour and 20 minutes longer,** stirring 2 or 3 times. Meat should be covered by sauce to prevent it from turning dark. Let stand covered for 15 to 30 minutes (or longer if you have the time). Flavor improves with standing.

Yield: 4 to 6 servings. Freezes well, but omit potatoes.

* Read In a Stew? (p. 198).
* After cooking, stew can be chilled. Excess fat will congeal and can be removed easily. Stew tastes even better the next day.
* If desired, omit potatoes. Total cooking time for stew will be about 10 minutes less. Serve stew and its luscious sauce over oodles of cooked noodles. So good!
* **CONVECTION/MICROWAVE METHOD:** Prepare stew as directed in Steps 1 and 2. Then follow cooking directions on p. 196, Convection/Micro Ways with Briskets, Pot Roasts and Stews. **Cooking time will be 1 ½ to 2 hours.** Times vary with different ovens. Stir once or twice during cooking.

MY OVEN'S SETTING________ MY COOKING TIME________

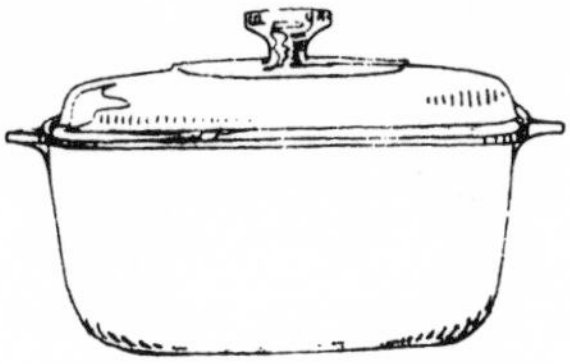

SAUCY FLANKEN (SHORT RIBS)

Use a cooking bag for this recipe to achieve maximum tenderness and minimum mess. The sauce creates steam and also absorbs part of the microwave energy so that the meat cooks more slowly and becomes tender.*

1 tbsp. flour
4 lb. flanken (short ribs)
1 pkg. onion soup mix
1 tsp. dry mustard
1 c. chili sauce or ketchup
¼ c. water
2 tbsp. brown sugar

1. Coat a large microsafe cooking bag with flour as directed in package instructions. Place all ingredients in bag. Mix well. Meatier portions should be towards the outside and bonier portions towards the centre. Close bag, leaving an opening about the size of a dime as a steam vent. Place in an oblong Pyrex™ casserole. Do not let cooking bag touch the walls of the oven.

2. **MW covered on HIGH for 15 minutes.** Turn meat over (or turn the cooking bag over, using oven mitts).

3. **MW on MEDIUM (50%) for 30 minutes.** Turn meat over once again. **MW on MEDIUM (50%) 30 minutes longer,** or until tender. Let stand in cooking bag for 20 to 30 minutes. Empty into casserole. Serve with rice or potatoes. Scrumptious!

Yield: 8 servings. Freezes well.

* Meat could also be cooked in a covered microsafe casserole. However, a cooking bag is much more convenient.
* A clay baker is also an excellent cooking container and produces very tender meat because of the steam released during cooking. First soak clay baker in cold water for 15 minutes. Discard water; add all ingredients. Microwave as directed.
* If using a clay baker or a deep microsafe casserole, place a sheet of waxed paper directly on the meat, then cover with the casserole lid or vented plastic wrap. This traps the maximum amount of steam and tenderizes the meat.
* A good guideline for cooking short ribs (flanken) is to **MW them first for 15 minutes on HIGH, then reduce power to MEDIUM (50%) and allow 15 to 20 minutes per lb.**
* Because short ribs contain a lot of fat, it is best to refrigerate them overnight after cooking so that the fat will solidify. The next day, remove solidified fat and discard it.
* **CONVECTION/MICROWAVE METHOD:** Prepare meat as directed in Steps 1 and 2. Follow cooking directions on p. 196, Convection/Micro Ways with Briskets, Pot Roasts and Stews. **Cooking time will be 2 to 2½ hours.** Times vary with different ovens. Stir once or twice during cooking.

MY OVEN'S SETTING______ MY COOKING TIME______

GLAZED SHORT RIBS

- ½ c. apricot jam
- ¾ c. ketchup
- 3 cloves garlic, minced
- 2 tbsp. lemon juice
- 2 lb. short ribs (flanken)
- 2 onions, sliced

1. Combine jam, ketchup, garlic and lemon juice. Rub over short ribs. Place all ingredients in a microsafe casserole or cooking bag. (If using a cooking bag, coat it with 1 tbsp. flour according to package directions.) Meatier portions should be towards the outside of the bag or casserole and bonier portions should be towards the centre.

2. **MW covered on HIGH for 15 minutes.** Turn short ribs over and rearrange, moving more cooked portions towards the centre of the casserole.

3. **Cover and MW on MEDIUM (50%) for 20 minutes.** Turn meat over and baste with sauce. **MW covered for 15 to 20 minutes longer;** meat should be fairly tender. Let stand covered for 20 to 30 minutes.

Yield: 4 servings. Freezes well.

* Read notes following Saucy Flanken (p. 200).
* This sauce mixture is also excellent for brisket.
* **CONVECTION/MICROWAVE METHOD:** Prepare meat as directed in Steps 1 and 2. Follow cooking directions on p. 196, Convection/Micro Ways with Briskets, Pot Roasts & Stews. Cooking time on **COMBINATION CYCLE will be about 2 hours.**

MY OVEN'S SETTING______ MY COOKING TIME______

SAUCY SHOULDER STEAK

A browning dish is used for this dish. If you don't have one, brown the meat conventionally in a skillet on top of the stove. Then transfer meat to a microsafe serving casserole, add remaining ingredients and complete the cooking in the microwave.

- 1 ½ lb. thinly sliced shoulder steak, cut in 2″ pieces
- ¼ c. flour
- 2 tbsp. oil
- 1 pkg. onion soup mix
- 1 ½ c. tomato sauce
- 2 tbsp. brown sugar
- 1 tbsp. lemon juice
- 1 green pepper, sliced
- ¼ tsp. garlic powder
- pepper, to taste

1. Combine meat and flour in a plastic bag and shake to coat meat. Preheat an empty 10″ square browning dish uncovered **on HIGH for 5 minutes.** Add oil and tip pan carefully to coat bottom. Immediately place meat in a single layer in hot browning dish and **MW uncovered for 2 minutes on HIGH.** Turn meat over and **MW on HIGH 1 minute longer.**

2. Add remaining ingredients, cover and **MW on HIGH for 10 minutes,** until liquid is boiling. Stir. **Reduce power to MEDIUM (50%) and MW 45 minutes longer,** until tender. Stir once or twice during cooking. Let stand covered for 15 minutes. Serve over rice.

Yield: 4 servings.

PEPPER STEAK, ITALIAN STYLE

- 2 cloves garlic
- 2 medium onions, halved
- 1 stalk celery
- 1 green pepper, halved & seeded
- 1 red pepper, halved & seeded
- 2 tbsp. oil
- 1 c. mushrooms
- 2 lb. shoulder steak (about 4 thin slices), cut in 2″ strips
- ¼ c. flour
- 1 tsp. salt
- ¼ tsp. pepper
- 5 ½ oz. can tomato paste
- ½ c. dry red wine
- ½ c. water
- ¼ tsp. basil
- ¼ tsp. oregano

1. **Steel Knife:** Drop garlic through the feed tube while machine is running. Process until minced. Do not empty bowl.

2. **Slicer:** Slice onions, celery and peppers. Transfer to a 10″ square Corning Ware™ or 7″ x 11″ glass casserole. **MW uncovered on HIGH for 3 to 4 minutes,** until almost tender. Meanwhile, slice mushrooms, using light pressure. Add to casserole and **MW on HIGH 2 minutes longer,** until tender.

3. Combine meat with flour, salt & pepper in a plastic bag; shake well. Add meat to casserole along with tomato paste, wine, water and seasonings. Cover with casserole lid or vented plastic wrap.

4. **MW on HIGH for 10 to 12 minutes,** until bubbling. Stir. **MW on MEDIUM (50%) for 40 to 45 minutes,** until tender. Stir once or twice during cooking. Let stand covered for 10 to 15 minutes. Serve on a bed of fluffy hot cooked rice.

Yield: 4 servings. Freezes well.

SWISS STEAK

You'll yodel over this one!

- 2 cloves garlic, minced
- 2 large onions, sliced
- 1 green pepper, sliced
- 2 large stalks celery, sliced
- 2 tbsp. oil
- 1 ½ lbs. shoulder steak, thinly sliced & cut in 2″ x 3″ pieces
- 3 tbsp. flour
- ¾ tsp. salt
- ⅛ tsp. pepper
- ½ tsp. basil
- 1 tsp. paprika
- 1 tomato, diced
- 1 c. tomato sauce
- ½ c. dry white wine
- 1 tbsp. Worcestershire sauce
- ½ tsp. sugar

1. Place garlic, onions, peppers, celery and oil in 10″ square Corning Ware™ or 7″ x 11″ glass casserole. **MW uncovered 5 to 6 minutes on HIGH,** until tender. Stir at half time.

2. Combine meat with flour and seasonings in a plastic bag; shake well. Add meat and remaining ingredients to vegetables in casserole dish. Mix well. Cover with casserole lid or vented plastic wrap.

3. **MW on HIGH for 10 to 12 minutes,** until bubbling. Stir. **MW on MEDIUM (50%) for 40 to 45 minutes,** stirring at half time. Meat should be fork tender. Let stand covered for 10 minutes. Serve over noodles or rice.

Yield: 4 servings. Freezes well.

SARGENT PEPPER'S STEAK

2 cloves garlic, minced
2 onions, sliced
2 tbsp. oil
1 ½ lb. shoulder steak, (about 4 thin slices), cut in 2″ strips
½ tsp. chili paste with garlic*
¼ c. soya sauce
¾ c. chicken broth
1 green pepper, cut in strips
1 red pepper, cut in strips
2 tbsp. cornstarch dissolved in 2 tbsp. cold water

1. Combine garlic and onions with oil in a 10″ square Corning Ware™ or 7″ x 11″ glass casserole. **MW uncovered on HIGH for 3 minutes,** until slightly softened, stirring once.

2. Add meat, chili paste, soya sauce and chicken broth. Mix well. Cover with casserole lid or vented plastic wrap. **MW on HIGH for 10 minutes;** stir. **MW on MEDIUM (50%) for 30 minutes,** until nearly tender.

3. Stir in peppers, cover and **MW on MEDIUM (50%) 10 to 15 minutes longer,** until meat is fork tender.

4. Stir in cornstarch mixture. **MW covered on HIGH for 4 to 5 minutes,** or until mixture is bubbling and thickened, stirring twice. Serve over rice.

Yield: 4 servings. Reheats well.

* Chili paste with garlic is available in Oriental food markets. You can substitute chili powder to taste.
* Peppers will lose their crispness if frozen, but flavor will not be affected.
* **SARGENT PEPPER'S CHICKEN:** Substitute boneless chicken breasts for shoulder steak. **In Step 2, cooking time on MEDIUM (50%) will be 20 minutes.**

BEEF WITH PEA PODS & WATER CHESTNUTS

Follow recipe for Sargent Pepper's Steak (above), but omit peppers and chili paste with garlic. Add a 6 oz. pkg. of frozen pea pods and ½ cup drained sliced water chestnuts to the beef in Step 4. Complete as directed.

CHINESE BEEF WITH BROCCOLI

See recipe for Chinese Chicken with Broccoli (p. 166), but substitute 1 ½ lbs. of thinly sliced boneless steak. Cooking time will be the same.

CHINESE VEAL & PEPPERS

Marinating the veal adds wonderful flavor.

1 or 2 cloves garlic, crushed
2 tbsp. honey
3 tbsp. dark soya sauce
1 tbsp. water
1 lb. thinly sliced veal scallops, (⅛″ thick), cut in 1½″ pieces
2 tbsp. oil
1 onion, cut in chunks
1 green pepper, seeded & cut in chunks
1 red pepper, seeded & cut in chunks
1 tbsp. cornstarch

1. Combine garlic, honey, soya sauce and water in a glass pie plate. Add veal and let marinate for ½ to 1 hour at room temperature or several hours in the refrigerator, stirring once or twice.

2. Place oil, onion and peppers in a shallow 2 quart casserole. **MW uncovered on HIGH for 2 to 3 minutes,** until nearly tender. Remove veal from marinade and drain well, reserving marinade. Push vegetables into centre of casserole and arrange veal around the outside edges.

3. **MW uncovered on HIGH for 5 to 6 minutes,** stirring twice during cooking. There should be almost no pink left in the veal.

4. Dissolve cornstarch in reserved marinade. Stir into veal. **MW uncovered on HIGH until sauce is thick and bubbly, about 2 minutes longer,** stirring once or twice. Serve with white rice (p. 214) and snow peas (p. 245).

Yield: 3 to 4 servings. May be frozen, but vegetables will lose their texture.

* Use Chinese short-grain rice. It can be pressed into a custard cup for a minute or two and will hold its shape when unmolded.

CHINESE VEAL & MUSHROOMS

Substitute 2 cups sliced mushrooms for the peppers. **MW with onions on HIGH for 3 to 4 minutes,** until tender. Set aside. **MW drained veal separately on HIGH for 5 minutes,** or until no longer pink, stirring once. Combine all ingredients and **MW 2 to 3 minutes on HIGH,** until sauce is thickened, stirring once.

VEAL BURGUNDY

This delicious veal dish is an adaptation of a low-fat recipe developed by Jackie Margolese, author of the low cholesterol cookbook "Eat Heart-y". Although the cooking time is almost the same, the microwave method makes a minimum of mess.

2 cloves garlic, minced
1 onion, chopped
1 green pepper, chopped
1 tbsp. oil
2 lb. lean stewing veal, cut in 1″ pieces
¾ tsp. salt
freshly ground pepper
½ tsp. rosemary or tarragon
1 tbsp. chopped parsley
¾ c. chicken broth
⅓ c. Burgundy wine
5 ½ oz. tin tomato paste

1. Combine garlic, onion, green pepper and oil in a 2 quart covered microsafe casserole. **MW uncovered on HIGH for 5 minutes,** until tender.

2. Add remaining ingredients and mix well. Make sure that meat is completely submerged under the liquid. Cover with casserole lid. **MW on HIGH for 10 minutes,** or until bubbling. Stir well.

3. **MW covered on MEDIUM (50%) for 1 hour,** stirring twice. Meat should be fairly tender.

4. Let stand covered for at least 15 minutes. (It is even tastier and more tender if prepared in advance and reheated.) Serve with noodles or rice and green peas.

Yield: 4 to 6 servings. Freezes and/or reheats well.

* Noodles should be cooked conventionally. If serving rice, microwave it during the standing time for the veal. **A 10 oz. pkg. of frozen green peas takes 6 minutes on HIGH to thaw and heat in the microwave,** so "mike" them just before serving time.

EASY VEAL CHOPS

4 veal rib chops, ½″ thick
1 onion, sliced
1 green pepper, sliced
freshly ground pepper
10 oz. can condensed mushroom soup
1 tbsp. brown sugar

1. Arrange veal in a single layer in an ungreased 2 quart Pyrex™ casserole. Place the meaty portions towards the outside edge of the casserole. Top with remaining ingredients; mix well. Cover with casserole lid or vented plastic wrap.

2. **MW on HIGH for 6 to 8 minutes,** until piping hot. **MW on MEDIUM-LOW (30%) for 25 to 30 minutes,** rearranging meat halfway through cooking. Meat should be fork tender. Let stand covered for 10 minutes. Serve on a bed of cooked fettucine or rice.

Yield: 2 to 4 servings.

BRAISED VEAL STEAKS

Veal does not require browning in oil. The flavors blend well in this tasty dish.

2 onions, sliced
1 green pepper, sliced
2 tbsp. oil
2 lb. second cut veal chops, ½″ thick
1 c. tomato sauce
½ tsp. chili powder
1 tbsp. brown sugar
1 tsp. lemon juice
2 tbsp. Hoisin sauce or Teriyaki sauce
½ tsp. minced garlic

1. Combine onions and green pepper with oil in a 2 quart shallow microsafe casserole. **MW uncovered on HIGH for 4 minutes.**

2. Place veal in casserole, arranging so that meatier portions are towards the outside edges of the dish. Combine remaining ingredients and mix well. Add to casserole; mix well. Cover with casserole lid or vented plastic wrap.

3. **MW on HIGH for 10 minutes.** Turn meat over and rearrange. Baste with sauce. **MW on MEDIUM (50%) for 45 to 55 minutes,** until tender. Turn meat over halfway through cooking. Baste occasionally. Let stand covered for 15 minutes. Serve with noodles or Fried Rice (p. 214).

Yield: 4 servings. Freezes well.

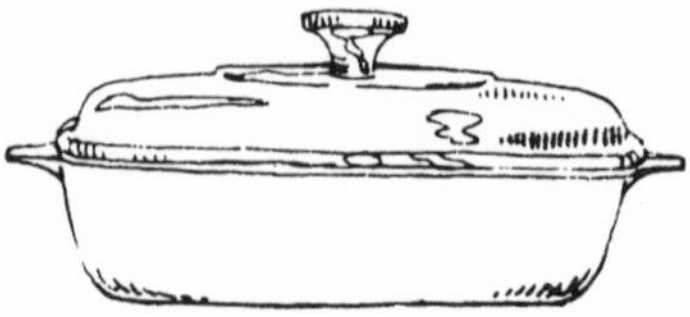

ROLLED VEAL ROAST

Tender & tasty. You'll love it hot or cold. If you have your own favorite seasonings, feel free to substitute them.

1 tbsp. flour
1 tsp. salt
freshly ground pepper
2 tbsp. dry mustard
1 tbsp. paprika
¾ tsp. each basil and thyme
3 cloves garlic, minced
3 tbsp. Teriyaki or soya sauce
3 lb. rolled veal roast
2 onions, sliced
½ c. chicken broth
½ c. Marsala wine (or any good quality dry red wine)

1. Coat a large microsafe cooking bag with flour as directed in package instructions. Combine seasonings, garlic and Teriyaki sauce in a small bowl; mix to make a paste. Brush or rub roast with mixture. Place roast and onions in cooking bag. Combine broth and wine. Add to roast. Seal bag with plastic closure or cotton string, leaving an opening about the size of a dime as a steam vent. Place bag in an oblong Pyrex™ casserole. Do not let cooking bag touch the walls of the oven.

2. Calculate cooking time as directed below. * **For a 3 lb. roast, MW on HIGH for 12 minutes.** Roll cooking bag over so roast will be turned over as well.

3. **MW on MEDIUM (50%) for 45 minutes,** turning roast over at half time. Let stand at least 15 to 30 minutes in cooking bag. Roast should be 170°F on a thermometer. Remove meat from bag and slice. Return meat to gravy in cooking bag or arrange slices in casserole, topping with gravy. Cooked potatoes can be added at this time, if desired.

4. **MW covered on MEDIUM (50%) for 20 minutes,** until tender.

Yield: 6 servings. Freezes well. Slice before freezing.

* To calculate cooking time, **MW veal on HIGH for 4 minutes per lb., then on MEDIUM (50%) for 15 minutes per lb.**
* Use oven mitts when turning over the cooking bag; it will be hot!
* Potatoes can be microwaved during standing time for the meat.
* Meat can be left in the cooking bag until cool, about 1 or 2 hours. It will continue to cook, become tender and absorb the juices. The additional cooking time in Step 4 would not be necessary. Just slice and **reheat on MEDIUM (50%). Allow 1 to 2 minutes per serving.** Overlap slices for more even reheating.
* **CONVECTION/MICROWAVE CYCLE:** Prepare roast as directed in Step 1. Preheat oven to 300°F. Place on rack recommended by oven manufacturer; **cook on COMBINATION CYCLE** suitable for beef or veal roasts. **Cooking time will be about 1½ hours,** until meat is fork tender. Times vary with different brands of ovens. Turn meat over halfway through cooking.

MY OVEN'S SETTING______ **MY COOKING TIME______**

BONELESS LAMB ROAST

4 - 5 lb. rolled boneless lamb
2 tbsp. Dijon mustard
1 tsp. honey
1 tbsp. soya sauce
½ tsp. rosemary
½ tsp. thyme
2 cloves garlic, crushed
freshly ground pepper

1. Combine seasonings and rub well onto all surfaces of roast. Place roast fat side down on a microsafe roasting rack which is inside an oblong Pyrex™ casserole.

2. MW **uncovered on HIGH for 5 minutes per lb., about 20 to 25 minutes.** Turn roast over at half time and drain off juices and fat. Shield any areas that are beginning to overcook with small pieces of aluminum foil (fasten to meat with wooden toothpicks).

3. Meanwhile preheat conventional oven to 425°F. Remove roasting rack and place meat directly in casserole. **Roast uncovered for 15 to 20 minutes longer,** or until roast registers 145°F on a meat thermometer for medium doneness.

4. Remove from oven. Cover roast loosely with aluminum foil. Let stand for 15 to 20 minutes. Carve thinly. Serve with mint sauce. Delicious with Party Rice Casserole (p. 216).

Yield: 8 to 10 servings. Freezes well.

* In Step 3, roast can be browned on the **CONVECTION CYCLE at 400°F for 15 to 20 minutes.** Place casserole on rack recommended by oven manufacturer; no preheating is necessary.
* **CONVECTION/MICROWAVE METHOD:** Cooking time varies with different brands of combination ovens. Use the time and setting for roast lamb in your manufacturer's cookbook as a guideline. If cooking by probe, set temperature to 130°F. Temperature will rise about 15°F during standing time. Insert probe into thick, meaty part of roast, not touching bone or fat.

MY OVEN'S SETTING_______ **MY COOKING TIME_______**

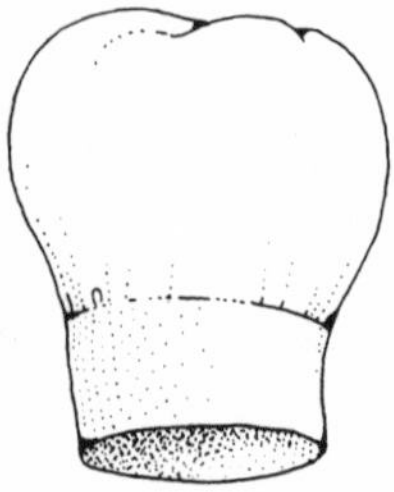

MICRO-WAYS WITH ROAST BEEF

- **Roast beef should be completely defrosted** before cooking. Allow 20 to 30 minutes standing time after defrosting to equalize the temperature. Then season and cook as directed.
- **Place roast beef on a microsafe rack to defrost.** Turn it over 2 or 3 times during defrosting.
- **A roast which is room temperature** cooks more evenly than if refrigerated. Allow slightly longer times for cooking if roast comes directly from the refrigerator (about 45 seconds to 1 minute longer per lb.)
- **Roast should be fairly even in shape.** Shield edges or corners with aluminum foil to reflect the microwave energy during defrosting &/or cooking. Attach pieces of foil with wooden toothpicks. Large roasts may require shielding at either end with foil.
- **Areas next to bone or fat will cook more quickly,** so if you are using a temperature probe, insert it into the centre of the meat, not touching bone or fat. Otherwise the roast will be underdone when the oven turns off.
- **Roast beef should be cooked on a rack** to lift it out of its juices and prevent overcooking in those areas. Place rib roast bone-side down. Let bones act as a natural rack. Turn rib roast onto its side halfway through cooking for most even results. Boneless roasts should be turned over so that the top is on the bottom and vice versa.
- **Do not salt roast prior to cooking.** Other seasonings may be added at the beginning, but salt should only be added to a marinade or at the end of cooking, just before standing time.
- **Waxed paper prevents spatters** but will cause roast to steam. I prefer to cook roast beef uncovered. Any spatters will wipe clean easily with a damp cloth.
- **Allow a standing time of 20 minutes** for roast after cooking. Cover with a tent of aluminum foil to retain the heat. (It doesn't matter if the foil is shiny side out or in!)
- **Temperature of roast will rise about 15 to 20°F** during standing time, juices will settle and the roast will be easier to slice. (The same technique applies to roasts which are cooked conventionally.)
- **Check internal temperature either with a meat thermometer or with the probe** (if your oven has one). Additional time can be added easily, either to the whole roast or to individual slices, so each person can have their roast beef as they like it!
- **During the standing time,** use the microwave to cook potatoes, make gravy and/or prepare vegetables.
- **CONVECTION/MICROWAVE METHOD:** Cooking time varies with different brands of combination ovens. Use the time and setting for roast beef in your manufacturer's cookbook as a guideline. If cooking by probe, set temperature according to chart in recipe for Roast Beef (p. 210). Temperature will rise about 15°F during standing time. Insert probe into thick, meaty part of roast, not touching bone or fat.

ROAST BEEF

Roast will brown in the microwave and be tender and juicy. Read Micro-Ways with Roast Beef (p. 209).

4 lb. standing rib roast
3 tbsp. soya sauce or teriyaki sauce
1 tbsp. Dijon mustard
3 cloves garlic, crushed
paprika, to taste
freshly ground pepper

1. Rub roast with soya or teriyaki sauce, mustard, garlic, paprika and freshly ground pepper; do not add any salt to this mixture. Place roast on a microsafe rack. Place rack in an oblong Pyrex™ casserole.

2. Calculate cooking time according to chart below. **MW for half the time on HIGH.** Turn roast on its side; shield any areas that are beginning to overcook with aluminum foil. **MW on MEDIUM (50%) for double the remaining time.** To cook a 4 lb. roast to medium doneness, **MW for 14 minutes on HIGH and 28 minutes on MEDIUM (50%).**

3. At the end of the cooking time, remove roast from oven. Cover loosely with foil and let stand for 20 minutes. Slice roast across the grain with a sharp carving knife. If any slices are too rare, **MW uncovered on MEDIUM (50%) for 1 to 2 minutes.**

Yield: 6 servings.

Desired Doneness	Cooking Time at HIGH	Temperature before Standing	Temperature after Standing
Rare	6 - mins./lb.	120°F	rises to 140°F
Medium	7 - 8 mins./lb.	130°F	rises to 150°F
Medium-Well	8 mins./lb.	140°F	rises to 160°F
Well	8 - 9 mins./lb.	150°F	rises to 170°F

* Ask your butcher to cut the rib roast off the bone, then retie it. The roast will be much easier to slice.
* An excellent choice for roast beef is Spencer (eye of the rib). It cooks more evenly and requires less attention than a rib roast.
* **COMBO-COOKED ROAST BEEF: MW roast beef for 4 minutes per lb. on HIGH.** Remove rack from casserole if not heatproof. Transfer roast to a preheated conventional oven and **roast uncovered at 400°F for 15 to 20 minutes,** until desired doneness.
* **CONVECTION/MICROWAVE METHOD: MW roast for 4 minutes per lb. on HIGH,** then place casserole on rack recommended by manufacturer for the **CONVECTION CYCLE. Roast uncovered at 400°F for 20 minutes,** until desired doneness. No preheating is necessary. Let stand covered for 20 minutes before carving.

RICE, PASTA & CEREALS

MICRO-WAYS WITH RICE, PASTA & CEREALS

RICE IS NICE!

- **Rice is excellent** in the microwave. You can cook, serve, store leftovers and reheat all in the same casserole, and the rice never sticks to the bottom of the pot!
- **Long-grain (Carolina) or parboiled** (Uncle Ben's converted) rice, short-grain or Oriental (sticky) rice and Basmati rice are all microwaved the same way and take about the same time to cook. Brown rice will take longer.
- **No need to boil the water first.** Just combine rice with hot water or broth and salt in a microsafe casserole. The casserole should be large enough to prevent boil-overs.
- **I use 1 ¾ c. liquid** for every cup of rice. There is no heat to cause evaporation, so less liquid is needed.
- **Don't stir rice during cooking.** If your oven has an uneven cooking pattern, rotate the casserole ¼ turn at half time.
- **Rice should be microwaved** just until liquid is absorbed. Let it stand covered for 5 or 10 minutes to complete cooking.
- **If rice is not completely cooked** or any liquid remains in the bottom of the casserole, return it to the microwave for **2 or 3 minutes on HIGH** to complete cooking.
- **I usually prepare rice first**, then cover it tightly during standing time. It keeps hot for 20 to 30 minutes. Prepare the remainder of your meal during this time.
- **For quick-cooking rice**, actual cooking is not necessary. Rice just needs to be rehydrated. Bring required amount of water to boiling in the serving dish. **It takes 2 ½ to 3 minutes on HIGH to boil 1 cup of water**. Stir in rice and salt; cover and let stand for 5 minutes. Fluff and serve.

PASS THE PASTA!

- **It is not convenient** to cook more than 8 oz. of pasta in the microwave at a time.
- **I usually cook pasta conventionally** while sauce is cooking in the microwave. However, I find the microwave convenient for certain recipes (e.g. Old-Fashioned Macaroni & Cheese, p. 219).
- **Spaghetti and macaroni double when cooked**. Noodles swell slightly. One cup of uncooked noodles (2 ½ oz. in weight) yields 1 ¼ cups cooked, about 1 to 2 servings. One lb. pasta yields 4 to 6 servings. (I love pasta, so who measures!)

SOME LIKE IT HOT!

- **One cup of refrigerated cooked rice, kasha, bulgur or cereal takes 1 minute on HIGH to reheat. Four cups take 3 minutes.** Cover with waxed paper, if desired. Stir once or twice. The bottom of the dish should feel hot when touched in the center.

- **Pasta reheats easily** in the microwave and it can be done right on the serving plate! Sprinkle pasta with a little water, or top with sauce. **MW covered with waxed paper on HIGH, allowing 1 minute for 1 cup, or 3 minutes for 4 cups.** Waxed paper prevents spatters.
- **Do-Ahead Rice or Pasta:** Package in freezer bags in 1 cup portions. Freeze until needed. To defrost and heat in one step, **MW covered on HIGH, allowing 2 minutes per cup.**
- **Reheating Varenikas/Perogies: One takes 25 to 30 seconds uncovered on HIGH to heat; 6 will take 1 ½ to 2 minutes.** Arrange in a circle.
- **To thaw: 1 varenika takes 1 minute uncovered on DEFROST (30%) to thaw. Four will take about 3 minutes.**
- **Knishes take approximately the same time as varenikas** and perogies to thaw or heat. They should be placed on a paper towel or microsafe rack to prevent them from becoming soggy. To crisp the dough, transfer them to the toaster oven for 3 or 4 minutes at 375°F.

GRAINS ARE GOOD FOR YOU!

- **There has been an increased interest** in complex carbohydrates as a good source of nutrition (grains, cereals, pasta, rice, bread, fruits and vegetables). Nutritionists now recommend a diet made up of approximately 50% complex carbohydrates, 20% to 25% protein and 25% to 30% fat (at least 10% polyunsaturated).
- **Carbohydrates contain the same calories as protein**, 4 calories per gram. Fat contains 9 calories per gram, more than twice the calories. The microwave is a wonderful way to prepare care-free, low-fat carbohydrates.
- **Little or no stirring** is required for most grains. Bulgur, couscous, cornmeal and kasha can be prepared right in the serving dish. Make sure it is large enough to prevent boil-overs.
- **A 2 quart microsafe soufflé dish** makes a good cooking container for most grains.
- **Feeling depressed or stressed?** Try a bowlful of kasha, couscous, rice, pasta or cereal!

CHEERY CEREALS

- **Individual servings of cereal** can be prepared right in the serving dish. Don't fill more than ⅓ full to prevent boil-overs.
- **No need to buy expensive**, individually packaged servings of precooked cereal. It's just as easy to prepare the real thing and put some fibre into your life.
- **Instead of using water**, cook oatmeal with apple juice for a delicious flavor. Add a dash of cinnamon, a spoonful of brown sugar and a few slices of peeled apple. **Microwave time will be about 1 minute longer** than usual, just until apple is tender.
- **Oatmeal and oat bran** are believed to help in reducing cholesterol levels. The microwave makes it easy to take care of your health!
- **To reheat refrigerated cereals, allow 1 to 1 ¼ minutes per cup on HIGH, covered.** Stir at half time.

HOW TO COOK RICE

1 c. rice*
¾ tsp. salt
1 ¾ c. tap water or chicken or beef broth

1. Place all ingredients in a round 2 quart microsafe casserole. Cover with casserole cover or vented plastic wrap. **MW on HIGH for 5 to 6 minutes,** or until boiling.

2. **Reduce power to MEDIUM (50%) and MW 10 to 12 minutes longer,** or until liquid is absorbed. Do not uncover; do not stir. Let stand 5 minutes. **(If any liquid remains,** return rice to microwave and **MW covered 2 to 3 minutes longer on HIGH.)** Uncover and fluff with a fork.

Yield: 4 to 6 servings (3 cups cooked rice). May be frozen.

* Use long-grain, short-grain, converted or Basmati rice.
* If you use hot water from the tap or an instant-hot water dispenser, it will take **3 to 4 minutes on HIGH** until mixture boils in Step 1.
* If rice boils over in Step 2, reduce power to **DEFROST (30%).** Rice should simmer. Make sure to use a large enough casserole to prevent boil-overs.
* **To double the recipe,** use a 3 quart microsafe casserole. **MW on HIGH for 7 to 8 minutes,** or until boiling. **Reduce power to MEDIUM (50%) and MW 12 to 14 minutes longer,** until all liquid is absorbed. Let stand covered for 5 minutes.
* **To make 1 cup of cooked white rice,** measure ⅔ c. water into a 2 cup glass measure. Add a dash of salt and ⅓ c. rice. Cover with plastic wrap, turning back one corner slightly to vent. **MW on HIGH for 2 minutes, reduce power to MEDIUM (50%) and MW 10 minutes longer.** Let stand covered for 2 to 3 minutes. All the water should be absorbed and the rice will be tender.

FRIED RICE

1 onion, halved
1 stalk celery, chopped
½ green pepper, chopped
2 tsp. oil
1 c. long-grain rice
1 ¾ c. water or chicken broth
1 to 2 tbsp. soya sauce
⅛ tsp. pepper

1. Place onion, celery, green pepper and oil in a round 2 quart microsafe casserole. **MW uncovered on HIGH for 3 to 4 minutes,** until tender-crisp, stirring once. Add remaining ingredients. Cover with vented plastic wrap or casserole lid. **MW on HIGH for 5 to 6 minutes,** until boiling.

2. **Reduce power to MEDIUM (50%) and MW for 10 to 12 minutes,** or until liquid is absorbed, rotating casserole ¼ turn halfway through cooking. Let stand for 5 minutes. Uncover and fluff with a fork before serving.

Yield: 4 servings. Can be frozen.

RICE PILAF

Prepare as for Fried Rice (above), but omit soya sauce.

SPANISH RICE

- 1 clove garlic
- 1 large onion, quartered
- ½ green pepper, cut in chunks
- 2 tbsp. oil
- 1 c. long-grain rice
- 1 c. hot water
- 7 ½ oz. can tomato sauce
- ¾ tsp. salt
- ¼ tsp. pepper
- ⅛ tsp. basil
- ⅛ tsp. oregano

1. Steel Knife: Drop garlic through feed tube while machine is running. Process until minced. Add onion and green pepper. Process with several quick on/off turns, until coarsely chopped. Combine with oil in a round 2 quart microsafe casserole.

2. MW uncovered on HIGH for 4 minutes, until tender-crisp. Add remaining ingredients, cover with vented plastic wrap or casserole lid. **MW on HIGH for 5 to 6 minutes,** until boiling.

3. Reduce power to MEDIUM (50%) and MW 10 to 12 minutes longer, or until all liquid is absorbed. Do not stir during cooking. Let stand covered for 5 to 10 minutes. Mix well.

Yield: 4 servings. Freezes well.

ITALIAN RICE SALAD

An easy do-ahead salad. Make it for your next barbecue or buffet.

- 1 c. long-grain rice
- 1 ½ c. hot water
- ¼ c. bottled Italian salad dressing
- 1 tsp. salt
- ¼ tsp. each pepper, basil & oregano
- 1 c. frozen peas, thawed
- ¼ c. parsley, minced
- 1 green pepper, chopped
- 1 red pepper, chopped
- 4 green onions, sliced
- 1 jar marinated artichoke hearts (170 ml)

1. Combine rice, hot water, salad dressing and seasonings in a round 2 quart microsafe casserole. Cover with vented plastic wrap or casserole lid. **MW covered on HIGH for 5 minutes,** until boiling. **MW on MEDIUM (50%) for 10 to 12 minutes,** or until all liquid is absorbed. Let stand covered for 5 minutes. Uncover and let cool to room temperature.

2. Add peas, parsley, chopped peppers and onions to rice. Remove artichoke hearts from marinade, reserving marinade. Cut artichoke hearts in 1″ pieces. Add artichokes and reserved marinade to rice; mix well. Adjust seasonings to taste. Chill.

Yield: 6 to 8 servings.

* If desired, add ½ cup of sliced radishes and ½ c. sliced black olives to rice salad.

* **To double recipe**, double all ingredients. Use a 3 quart microsafe casserole to cook rice. **MW rice on HIGH for 7 to 8 minutes,** until boiling. **Reduce power to MEDIUM (50%) and MW 12 to 14 minutes longer,** until liquid is absorbed.

CREAMY ITALIAN RICE SALAD

Follow recipe for Italian Rice Salad (p. 215), but do not add marinade from artichokes to rice. Add ¼ c. mayonnaise, ¼ c. sour cream and 1 or 2 tbsp. grated Parmesan cheese. Mix well.

PARTY RICE CASSEROLE

Bea Kreisman, one of my students, gave me this fantastic recipe which I have adapted for the microwave.

- **½ c. butter***
- **4 c. chopped onions**
- **2 c. long-grain rice**
- **½ c. pine nuts**
- **3 ¾ c. boiling chicken stock***
- **½ c. raisins or currants**
- **½ tsp. salt**
- **freshly ground pepper**
- **2 tomatoes, peeled, seeded & chopped**
- **¼ c. chopped parsley**
- **½ c. peeled pistachio nuts**

1. Place butter in a round 3 quart microsafe casserole. **MW uncovered on HIGH for 1 to 1 ¼ minutes,** until melted. Add onions; **MW uncovered on HIGH for 7 to 8 minutes,** until tender, stirring at half time.

2. Stir in rice and pine nuts. **MW uncovered on HIGH for 4 minutes,** stirring at half time. Add chicken stock, raisins and seasonings. Cover with casserole lid or vented plastic wrap.

3. MW covered on HIGH for 8 to 9 minutes, or until boiling. **Reduce power to MEDIUM (50%) and MW 12 to 15 minutes longer,** until all liquid is absorbed. Stir in tomatoes and parsley. Let stand covered for 10 minutes. Uncover and stir in pistachio nuts. Adjust seasonings to taste.

Yield: 10 to 12 servings. Reheats well, but add pistachio nuts just before serving.

> * If you observe the Jewish dietary laws, substitute pareve margarine for butter. Instead of chicken stock, substitute 3 ¾ cups boiling water plus 4 tsp. pareve instant chicken soup mix.
>
> * **Reheat covered on HIGH for 6 to 8 minutes,** stirring twice. Bottom of casserole dish should feel hot when touched in the centre.

WILD RICE

Wild rice is not actually rice, but a grass which grows in Minnesota, North-Western Ontario, Manitoba and Saskatchewan. It is expensive but very nutritious. You may wish to combine it with white or brown rice, nuts and vegetables to make it more economical.

- **1 c. wild rice**
- **2 ¼ c. water**
- **salt & pepper, to taste**
- **1 tbsp. butter or margarine**

1. Rinse wild rice; drain well. Combine wild rice and water in a 2 quart round microsafe casserole. Cover with casserole lid and **MW on HIGH for 6 to 7 minutes,** until boiling.

2. Reduce power to MEDIUM (50%) and MW for 25 to 30 minutes, or until most of grains have burst. Let stand covered for 10 minutes. Drain any excess liquid; add salt, pepper and butter.

Yield: 4 servings.

RICE ITALIAN STYLE (RISOTTO)

Risotto is made with Arborio rice, which is short-grain and pearly in color. This recipe can also be made successfully with long-grain converted rice.

2 cloves garlic, minced
1 large onion, chopped
2 tbsp. butter or margarine
1 tbsp. oil
1 c. Arborio or long-grain converted rice (Uncle Ben's)
2 c. chicken broth*
¼ tsp. salt
freshly ground pepper
¼ tsp. dried basil
¼ c. grated Parmesan cheese, if desired*

1. Place garlic, onion, butter and oil in a round quart microsafe casserole. **MW uncovered on HIGH for 4 minutes,** until onion is tender. Stir in rice. Mix well. Add remaining ingredients except Parmesan cheese. Cover with vented plastic wrap or casserole lid.

2. **MW on HIGH for 5 to 6 minutes,** or until boiling. **Reduce power to MEDIUM (50%) and MW 10 to 12 minutes longer,** until liquid is absorbed. Uncover and stir in Parmesan cheese.

Yield: Serves 4. May be frozen.

> * If you observe the Jewish dietary laws, use 2 tsp. pareve chicken flavored soup mix dissolved in 2 c. water instead of chicken stock and use pareve margarine instead of butter.

BROWN RICE

2 ½ c. boiling water
¾ tsp. salt
1 c. brown rice

1. Combine all ingredients in a round 2 quart microsafe casserole. Cover with casserole cover or vented plastic wrap. **MW covered on HIGH for 5 to 6 minutes,** or until boiling.

2. **MW on MEDIUM (50%) for 25 to 30 minutes,** until liquid is absorbed. Let stand covered for 10 minutes before serving.

Yield: 3 cups rice (4 servings). May be frozen.

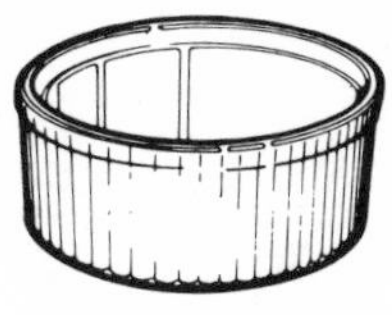

BROWN RICE PILAF

1 onion, chopped
1 stalk celery, chopped
2 tbsp. oil
1 c. brown rice
2 ½ c. boiling water plus 2 tsp. instant chicken soup mix
½ tsp. salt
freshly ground pepper

1. Combine onion and celery with oil in a round 2 quart microsafe casserole. **MW uncovered on HIGH for 4 to 5 minutes,** until tender.

2. Add remaining ingredients and cover with vented plastic wrap or casserole lid. **MW on HIGH for 5 to 6 minutes,** until boiling. Then **MW on MEDIUM (50%) 25 to 30 minutes longer,** until liquid is absorbed. Let stand covered for 10 minutes before serving.

Yield: 4 servings. May be frozen.

* Substitute home-made or canned chicken stock for the water and instant soup mix, if you wish.

MICROWAVED PASTA

It is not practical to cook more than 8 oz. (250 g) of pasta in the microwave. Cooking time is about the same as on the stove.

1. Place 8 oz. spaghetti or lasagna noodles* in a 7″ x 11″ glass casserole. Pour 4 or 5 cups boiling water over spaghetti; it should be covered with water. Add 1 tsp. salt and 1 tsp. oil. Cover with plastic wrap, turning back one corner to vent.

2. **MW on HIGH for 8 to 10 minutes**. At half time, stir pasta through the vented opening with a wooden chopstick or the handle of a wooden spoon. Let stand covered for 3 to 5 minutes. It should be "al dente". Drain and rinse well.

Yield: 3 to 4 servings.

* For macaroni, bow ties and medium noodles, cook in a round 2 quart microsafe casserole for **10 to 12 minutes**. Refer to Old-Fashioned Macaroni & Cheese (p. 219). Fine noodles will take **8 to 10 minutes** to microwave.

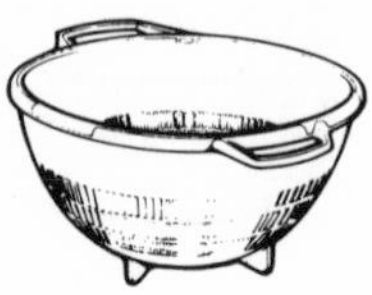

OLD-FASHIONED MACARONI & CHEESE

4 c. hot water
1 tsp. salt
2 c. elbow macaroni
2 cups Cheese Sauce (p. 85)
salt & pepper to taste
⅓ c. toasted bread crumbs

1. Place hot water and salt in a round 2 quart microsafe casserole. **MW uncovered on HIGH for 7 to 8 minutes, until boiling.**

2. Add macaroni; cover with vented plastic wrap or casserole lid. **MW on HIGH for 10 to 12 minutes,** until tender, stirring once. Let stand covered 2 or 3 minutes. Drain and rinse well. Return macaroni to casserole.

3. Prepare sauce as directed. Stir hot sauce into macaroni. Season to taste. Top with crumbs. **MW uncovered on HIGH 3 to 4 minutes,** until heated through, rotating casserole ¼ turn at half time.

Yield: 4 servings. May be frozen.

* Grease top edge of casserole with a little oil to help prevent boil-overs.
* **Variation:** Omit Cheese Sauce in Step 3. Add 1 cup grated cheddar cheese, 2 tbsp. butter and ⅓ cup milk to macaroni. Stir well. Add 1 cup drained chopped tomatoes, if desired. Top with crumbs; **MW uncovered on HIGH for 3 to 4 minutes.**
* My kids (even though they're grown up!) love macaroni and cheese best when I add a 7 oz. can of drained, flaked tuna. **Microwave time in Step 3 will be about 1 minute longer.**
* Casserole can be topped with crushed potato chips or canned French fried onions instead of crumbs. Kids love it!
* **If refrigerated, allow 1 ½ minutes per serving uncovered on HIGH to reheat. Four servings will take about 5 minutes on HIGH.** Rotate casserole twice during heating.
* **For a crusty top, bake uncovered at 400°F for 10 to 15 minutes,** until golden brown. No preheating of oven is necessary. If using the **CONVECTION CYCLE** of a combination oven, place casserole on rack recommended by manufacturer.

BOW TIES & COTTAGE CHEESE

4 c. hot water
1 tsp. salt
2 c. bow ties or elbow macaroni
salt & pepper
1 c. creamed cottage cheese
1 tsp. butter or margarine

1. Place hot water and salt in a 2 quart microsafe measure or bowl. **MW uncovered on HIGH for 7 to 8 minutes,** until boiling. Add pasta; cover with vented plastic wrap or casserole lid. **MW on HIGH for 10 to 12 minutes,** until tender, stirring once or twice through the vented opening with a wooden chopstick. Let stand covered 2 or 3 minutes. Drain and rinse well.

2. Combine with remaining ingredients and mix well. If necessary, **reheat on MEDIUM (50%) for 1 minute.**

Yield: 2 servings.

PASTA PRIMAVERA

This recipe is a quick and easy stand-by for me when I have company on a busy day. While the pasta is cooking conventionally, I prepare my sauce and veggies in the microwave. If I make a Caesar salad, I have an easy gourmet meal!

1 lb. rotini (spiral pasta)*
1 onion, cut in 1″ chunks
1 green & 1 red pepper, seeded & cut in 1″ chunks
2 c. broccoli florets
1 c. sliced carrots
1 c. snow peas, tails removed
2 tbsp. butter
additional vegetables, if desired*
double recipe Alfredo Sauce (p. 86)*
1 tsp. basil, minced, or 2 tbsp. Pesto (p. 90)

1. Cook pasta conventionally according to package directions. Drain well and rinse with cold water to prevent sticking.

2. Meanwhile, combine onion, peppers, broccoli, carrots and butter in a 2 quart microsafe bowl. **MW uncovered on HIGH for 4 minutes.** Stir in snow peas. (*If adding mushrooms and zucchini, also add them at this time.) **MW on HIGH 3 to 4 minutes longer,** until tender-crisp, stirring at half time.

3. Prepare Alfredo Sauce. (A double recipe of sauce will take about 1 ½ times as long to microwave.) Combine all ingredients in a 3 quart oval or rectangular microsafe casserole and mix well. (Can be prepared in advance up to this point, covered and refrigerated until serving time.)

4. **MW covered on HIGH for 5 to 8 minutes,** or until piping hot, stirring once or twice. (Reheating time will depend on whether pasta has just been prepared and is still quite warm, or if it was prepared in advance and refrigerated.) Test for doneness; the centre bottom of the casserole will be hot to the touch.

Yield: 6 servings. Can be frozen.

* Other pasta can be substituted, but you will probably use only a single recipe of sauce. Rotini requires more sauce because there is more surface to cover. Any leftover sauce can be refrigerated for 2 or 3 days; delicious over fish or vegetables.
* 1 cup sliced mushrooms &/or zucchini can be added with the snow peas; adding them at half time prevents the more tender vegetables from overcooking.
* Cauliflower florets, yellow peppers or asparagus tips can be substituted or used as part of the vegetables for this dish. It all depends on what I have in my fridge! The idea is to have lots of color and variety.
* **A single serving will take 2 to 3 minutes on MEDIUM-HIGH (70%) to reheat.** Stir at half time.

TORTELLINI PRIMAVERA

Follow recipe for Pasta Primavera (p. 220), but substitute 1 lb. of cheese tortellini and use a single recipe of Alfredo Sauce. I keep them in my freezer and cook them conventionally from the frozen state in about 15 minutes. Use half spinach tortellini and half regular tortellini for added color and flavor.

To make your own Cheese Tortellini, use won ton wrappers. Cut in 1″ rounds with a cookie cutter and moisten edges of dough with water or lightly beaten egg. Fill with the cheese and spinach mixture for Stuffed Mushrooms Florentine (p. 54). Fold in half and press to seal well. Freeze in a single layer on a cookie sheet. When frozen, wrap well. When needed, drop frozen tortellini into boiling salted water and cook for 15 to 20 minutes, until done.

PASTA PEPPERONATA

1 lb. spaghetti or fettucine
2 onions, cut in 1″ chunks
2 green peppers, seeded & cut in 1″ chunks
1 red pepper, seeded & cut in 1″ chunks
2 tbsp. oil
4 c. Fresh Tomato Sauce* (p. 89) or Quick Tomato Sauce (p. 89)

1. Cook pasta conventionally according to package directions. Drain well and rinse with cold water to prevent sticking.

2. Meanwhile, combine onions, peppers and oil in a 2 quart microsafe bowl. **MW uncovered on HIGH for 4 to 5 minutes,** until tender-crisp.

3. To reheat sauce, cover loosely with waxed paper and **MW on HIGH for 5 to 6 minutes,** until steaming hot, stirring once. To reheat pasta, **MW covered with waxed paper on HIGH for 2 or 3 minutes,** stirring once.

4. Arrange pasta on individual serving plates. Top with sauce and garnish with vegetables. Serve with salad and garlic bread.

Yield: 4 to 6 servings.

* Four cups of good quality bottled vegetarian spaghetti sauce may be substituted.
* If desired, sprinkle vegetables and sauce with grated Parmesan cheese at serving time.

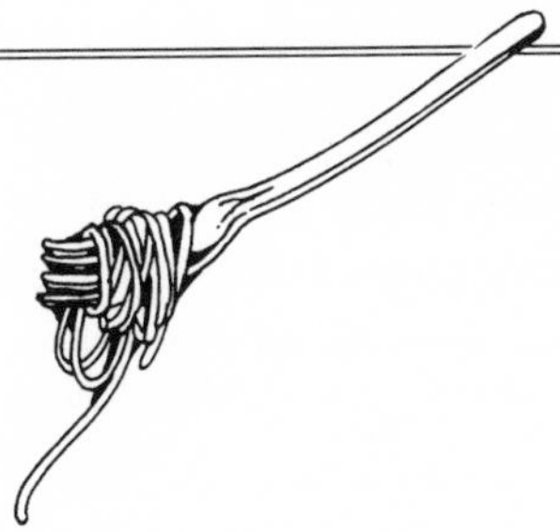

LASAGNA FLORENTINE

The noodles require no precooking for this lasagna. A lower power level and lots of sauce are necessary to tenderize the noodles. Easy and delicious!

4 c. Quick Tomato Sauce (p. 89)
Parmesan Sauce (p. 85)
10 oz. pkg. frozen spinach
1 lb. Mozzerella cheese, chilled
9 uncooked Lasagna noodles

1. Prepare sauces as directed. Cool slightly. (May be prepared in advance and refrigerated until needed.)

2. Place unwrapped package of spinach on a microsafe plate; slash top of package in several places with a sharp knife. **MW on HIGH for 5 to 6 minutes,** until cooked, rotating ¼ turn at half time. Let cool; unwrap and squeeze dry.

3. **Grater:** Keep Mozzerella refrigerated until needed. Grate, using medium pressure. You should have about 4 cups.

4. Arrange in layers in an ungreased 7″ x 11″ Pyrex™ casserole:

⅓ of Tomato Sauce
3 uncooked Lasagna noodles
½ of Parmesan Sauce
½ of spinach
⅓ of Mozzerella cheese

Repeat layers once again. Top with remaining noodles and Tomato Sauce. Do not add remaining Mozzerella at this time or it will overcook and become tough. Cover casserole with waxed paper, then with microsafe plastic wrap, turning back one corner ⅛″ to vent.

5. Elevate lasagna on a microsafe rack or inverted pie plate. **MW covered on HIGH for 10 to 12 minutes,** until bubbling hot. (Time will be slightly longer if lasagna was refrigerated.) Rotate casserole ½ turn. **MW on MEDIUM (50%) 20 to 25 minutes longer,** rotating casserole ½ turn at half time. Noodles should be tender when you pierce the centre of the lasagna with a knife.

6. Top with reserved cheese; cover and let stand 10 minutes longer, until cheese is melted. Serve with Caesar Salad and garlic bread.

Yield: 6 servings. Freezes well.

* **To reheat:** Cover with waxed paper and **MW on HIGH for 5 minutes, then on MEDIUM (50%) for 8 to 10 minutes. One serving will take 2 to 3 minutes on MEDIUM (50%).** Centre of dish should be hot when touched underneath.
* **Don't reheat small quantities on HIGH;** cheese may get rubbery.
* If you don't observe the Jewish dietary laws, recipe can be made using 4 ½ cups of meat sauce instead of Tomato Sauce.

VEGETARIAN LASAGNA

4 c. Quick Tomato Sauce (p. 89)*
9 lasagna noodles (regular or spinach lasagna)
1 lb. Mozzerella cheese, chilled
3 c. Ricotta cheese
1 egg
⅔ c. grated Parmesan cheese

1. Prepare sauce as directed. (May be prepared in advance and refrigerated.) Cook lasagna noodles according to package directions; drain well. Lay flat on a clean towel; pat dry.

2. **Grater:** Keep Mozzerella refrigerated until needed. Grate, using medium pressure. You should have about 4 cups. Mix Ricotta cheese with egg.

3. Arrange in layers in a lightly greased 9″ x 13″ Pyrex™ casserole:

1 ⅓ cups sauce
3 cooked Lasagna noodles
½ of the Ricotta/egg mixture
⅓ c. Parmesan cheese
⅓ of Mozzerella cheese

Repeat with sauce, noodles and cheeses. Top with noodles, then with remaining sauce. Cover with waxed paper, then with microsafe plastic wrap, turning back one corner slightly to vent. Reserve remaining Mozzerella cheese. (Can be prepared in advance and refrigerated for several hours or overnight.)

4. Elevate on a microsafe rack or inverted pie plate. **MW covered on MEDIUM-HIGH (70%) for 15 to 18 minutes,** until bubbling hot, rotating casserole ½ turn at half time. Bottom centre of casserole dish should be hot.

5. Uncover and sprinkle with reserved Mozzerella. **MW uncovered on HIGH for 2 to 3 minutes,** until cheese is melted. Let stand for 10 to 15 minutes. (Standing time makes it easier to cut.)

Yield: 8 servings. May be frozen.

* Bottled vegetarian spaghetti sauce or cooked Ratatouille (p. 260) can be used instead of Quick Tomato Sauce. Coarsely chop Ratatouille on the **Steel Knife** of the food processor, using quick on/off turns.

* After sprinkling lasagna with Mozzerella in Step 5, you could **bake it uncovered at 400°F for 10 to 15 minutes,** until golden. (This will make lasagna firmer.) No preheating of oven is necessary. If using **CONVECTION CYCLE** of a combination oven, place casserole on rack recommended by oven manufacturer.

TRIPLE CHEESE MANICOTTI

3 c. Quick Tomato Sauce (p. 89) or vegetarian spaghetti sauce
½ lb. manicotti or 15 crêpes (p. 128)
2 c. grated Mozzerella cheese

Filling:
2 c. grated Mozzerella cheese*
1 c. Ricotta or dry cottage cheese
½ c. grated Parmesan cheese
2 eggs
dash salt
freshly ground pepper
½ tsp. dried parsley
½ tsp. dried basil

1. If using Quick Tomato Sauce, cook as directed; let cool. Cook pasta according to package directions, undercooking slightly. Drain well. (If using crêpes, prepare as directed.) Reserve Mozzerella cheese.

2. Filling: Combine filling ingredients; mix well. Stuff manicotti or fill crêpes with cheese mixture.

3. Spoon 1 cup tomato sauce into an ungreased 2 quart oblong microsafe casserole. Arrange manicotti in a single layer over the sauce. (If using crêpes, place seam-side down.) Top with 2 cups sauce. Any leftover sauce may be refrigerated or frozen. Cover with waxed paper, then with microsafe plastic wrap, turning back one corner ⅛″ to vent. (Can be prepared in advance and refrigerated.)

4. Place on a microsafe rack or inverted pie plate. **MW covered on MEDIUM (50%) for 10 to 12 minutes**. Rotate casserole ½ turn. **MW on MEDIUM (50%) 10 to 12 minutes longer,** until bubbling hot. Centre bottom of casserole should be hot to the touch.

5. Uncover and sprinkle with reserved Mozzerella cheese. Cover and let stand for 10 minutes, until cheese is melted. Serve with buttered broccoli and garlic bread.

Yield: 6 servings.

* **Alternate Filling:** Omit Mozzerella from filling; increase Ricotta cheese to 2 cups. If desired, add 2 tbsp. fresh dill, minced.
* Manicotti can be filled with cheese mixture by using a pastry bag fitted with a plain large round tube.
* Reheating should be done on **MEDIUM (50%)** to prevent cheese from toughening. It is preferable to prepare Manicotti up to the end of Step 3, then complete cooking ½ hour before serving time.
* **To reheat 1 serving:** Cover loosely with waxed paper. **MW on MEDIUM (50%) for 2 to 3 minutes,** until bottom of dish is hot. Rotate plate ¼ turn at half time.

STUFFED PASTA SHELLS

Follow recipe for Triple Cheese Manicotti (above) or Spinach & Ricotta Manicotti (p. 225), but substitute 20 cooked jumbo pasta shells for the manicotti or crêpes.

SPINACH & RICOTTA MANICOTTI

2 c. Quick Tomato Sauce (p. 89) or vegetarian spaghetti sauce
1 c. Bechamel (p. 85)
½ lb. manicotti or 15 crêpes (p. 128)
2 c. grated Mozzerella cheese

Filling:
10 oz. pkg. frozen spinach, cooked (p. 245)
⅓ c. grated Parmesan cheese
1 egg
1 lb. Ricotta or cream cheese (or dry cottage cheese)
1 tsp. salt
¼ tsp. pepper
¼ tsp. basil

Prepare sauces. Assemble as for Triple Cheese Manicotti (p. 224), but in Step 3, pour Bechamel over Manicotti, then top with remaining cup of tomato sauce. Microwave cooking times are the same.

Yield: 6 servings.

YANKEE DOODLE DANDY

An American adaptation of old-fashioned Jewish noodle pudding. This recipe will be a feather in YOUR cap!

Noodle Mixture:
½ lb. medium noodles or spinach fettucine, cooked
10 oz. pkg. frozen spinach, cooked & squeezed dry (p. 245)
6 tbsp. grated Parmesan cheese
1 c. plain yogourt
2 eggs
1 tsp. salt
¼ tsp. pepper
¼ tsp. basil

Topping:
1 tbsp. butter
¼ c. seasoned bread crumbs
1 tbsp. grated Parmesan cheese
dash each of salt, pepper & basil

1. Combine all ingredients for noodle mixture in a large mixing bowl. Mix well. Lightly grease a 10″ ceramic quiche dish (or use non-stick cooking spray). Spread noodle mixture evenly in dish, depressing the centre slightly. Cover with waxed paper, then with microsafe plastic wrap, turning back one corner slightly to vent.

2. Place on a microsafe rack or inverted pie plate. **MW on MEDIUM (50%) for 16 to 18 minutes;** rotate dish ¼ turn at half time. Edges should be set and a knife inserted in the centre will come out clean. Let stand covered while you prepare the topping.

3. **Topping: MW butter uncovered on HIGH for 30 seconds**. Stir in crumbs, Parmesan cheese and seasonings. **MW uncovered on HIGH for 45 to 60 seconds,** until toasted, stirring once. Sprinkle evenly over top of noodle pudding. Cut in wedges to serve.

Yield: 6 servings as a side dish. Delicious with fish. Freezes well.

NOODLE KUGEL (NOODLE PUDDING)

Kugel will not brown in the microwave oven, but will cook in ¼ the time. It will not have a crisp crust but is lighter and puffier in texture; I like it better! Kugel is also delicious served in chicken soup.

12 oz. pkg. medium egg noodles
6 eggs
1 c. chicken broth
¼ c. oil
1 ½ tsp. salt
¼ tsp. pepper
2 tsp. oil to grease casserole
4 tbsp. cornflake crumbs or bread crumbs
paprika

1. Cook noodles conventionally according to package directions. Drain, rinse with cold water and drain once again.

2. Combine cooked noodles with eggs, chicken broth, ¼ c. oil, salt & pepper in a large bowl; mix well.

3. Grease a 7″ x 11″ Pyrex™ casserole or 10″ square Corning Ware™ casserole with 2 tsp. oil; coat with 3 tbsp. of the crumbs. Spread noodle mixture in pan, pushing mixture well into the corners; make a slight depression in the centre. Sprinkle with remaining crumbs and paprika. Cover with waxed paper, then with microsafe plastic wrap, turning back one corner slightly to vent.

4. Elevate casserole on a microsafe rack or inverted pie plate. **MW on HIGH for 12 to 14 minutes (or 10 to 12 minutes for Crispy Kugel*);** rotate casserole ¼ turn at half time. When done, top of kugel will be dry to the touch. A knife inserted into the centre should come out almost clean.

5. Let stand covered on a flat surface for 10 minutes. Kugel will complete its cooking during standing time.

Yield: 8 to 10 servings. Freezes well.

* **CRISPY KUGEL:** In Step 4, **MW kugel on HIGH for 10 to 12 minutes,** or until the edges are beginning to set but the centre is still slightly moist. **Bake uncovered at 400°F about 15 minutes,** or until golden. If using the **CONVECTION CYCLE** of a combination oven, place kugel on rack recommended by oven manufacturer. No preheating of oven is necessary.

* **One serving of kugel will take approximately 30 to 45 seconds on HIGH to reheat**. If frozen, thaw before heating.

NOODLE RAISIN KUGEL

Make Noodle Kugel (above) as directed, but omit salt and pepper from noodle mixture. Stir in ½ cup raisins, ¼ c. sugar and 1 tsp. cinnamon. Sprinkle top of kugel with crumbs and cinnamon instead of paprika. Cook as directed.

MOM'S DAIRY NOODLE KUGEL

My mother made this scrumptious kugel when she came to visit from Winnipeg. At the time, I was testing recipes on the CONVECTION/ MICROWAVE CYCLE and this one passed the test. It was moist, tender and yummy.

12 oz. pkg. medium egg noodles
1 c. milk
3 tbsp. butter (or oil)
4 eggs, lightly beaten
2 tbsp. sugar (or to taste)
dash of salt
1 c. sour cream or plain yogurt

1. Cook noodles conventionally according to package directions. Drain well; rinse with cold water and drain once again. Place in a large mixing bowl.

2. MW milk uncovered on HIGH for 1½ to 2 minutes, until steaming hot. Place butter in a 7″ x 11″ Pyrex™ casserole. **MW on HIGH for 45 seconds,** until melted. Add butter and milk to noodles; stir in remaining ingredients and mix well. Pour back into lightly greased casserole. Bake kugel by any of the methods described below. Serve hot with sour cream or yogurt. Top with fresh strawberries or blueberries.

CONVECTION/MICROWAVE METHOD: Push noodle mixture towards the corners and leave a slight depression in the centre of the kugel. Preheat oven to 350°F. Place casserole on rack recommended by manufacturer and **bake uncovered on COMBINATION CYCLE suitable for casseroles.** Cooking time will be about **40 to 45 minutes,** until kugel is set and lightly browned.

CONVECTION METHOD: Spread mixture evenly in casserole. Place rack recommended by manufacturer in oven. Preheat oven to 350°F. **Bake uncovered for 35 to 40 minutes at 350°F,** until set and lightly browned. Check for doneness at minimum time. (**Kugel takes 50 to 60 minutes at 350°F in a preheated conventional oven.**)

MICROWAVE METHOD: Use the recipe for Noodle Kugel (p. 226) as a guideline. If adding cottage cheese (* see **Noodle Cheese Kugel** below), use **MEDIUM (50%) power and MW covered for approximately double the time.** Begin checking 5 minutes before end of cooking time for doneness.

Yield: 8 to 10 servings. Freezes well.

* **NOODLE CHEESE KUGEL:** Add 1 c. creamed cottage cheese to kugel mixture in step 2. For a sweet kugel, add ½ cup raisins and 1 tsp. cinnamon. Increase sugar to ¼ cup.
* **CRUMB-TOPPED KUGEL: MW 2 tbsp. butter on HIGH until melted, about 30 seconds.** Mix together with ½ c. cornflake or bread crumbs. Add ½ tsp. cinnamon, if desired. Sprinkle over kugel before baking by **CONVECTION/ MICROWAVE or CONVECTION METHOD,** or after cooking by **MICROWAVE METHOD.**
* **One serving will take about 1 minute on MEDIUM (50%) to reheat.**

CHINESE NOODLE SALAD WITH PEANUT BUTTER SAUCE

This unusual Oriental recipe for cold noodle salad was given to me by my friend Jeff Kushner, who is a very creative cook.

250 gram pkg. bean threads* or 12 oz. pkg. fine noodles
4 c. hot water
4 green onions, with tops
1 stalk celery
8 oz. can sliced water chestnuts

Sauce:
1 small slice fresh ginger (the size of a dime)
½ c. peanut butter
½ c. sugar
½ c. rice wine (Mirin)* or red wine vinegar
½ tsp. salt
2 tbsp. soya sauce
2 tsp. Chinese Hot Chili Sauce* or 6 drops Tabasco sauce
½ tsp. sesame oil, if desired

1. Combine bean threads with hot water in a large microsafe bowl. **MW uncovered on HIGH for 3 to 4 minutes,** until water is almost boiling. Let stand 10 minutes to soften. (If using fine or medium noodles, cook them in boiling salted water according to package directions.) Meanwhile, prepare vegetables and sauce.

2. Steel Knife: Cut green onions and celery in chunks. Process with 3 or 4 quick on/offs, until coarsely chopped. Transfer to a small bowl. Place water chestnuts in a strainer and rinse under cold running water. Drain well.

3. Sauce: Drop fresh ginger through feed tube while machine is running. Process until minced. Add remaining sauce ingredients and process until blended, about 10 seconds.

4. Drain noodles well. Return to bowl. Combine with remaining ingredients and mix well. Refrigerate at least 1 hour to blend flavors.

Yield: 4 servings. Do not freeze.

* Bean threads look like stiff white nylon fishing line. They are a noodle made from mung beans and water. Most people are familiar with them in Chinese cooking as transparent noodles. They "explode" into a large crisp mass when dropped into hot oil in their dry state. (This is **NOT** to be done in the microwave!)

* Bean threads, rice wine vinegar and hot chili sauce are available in Oriental markets.

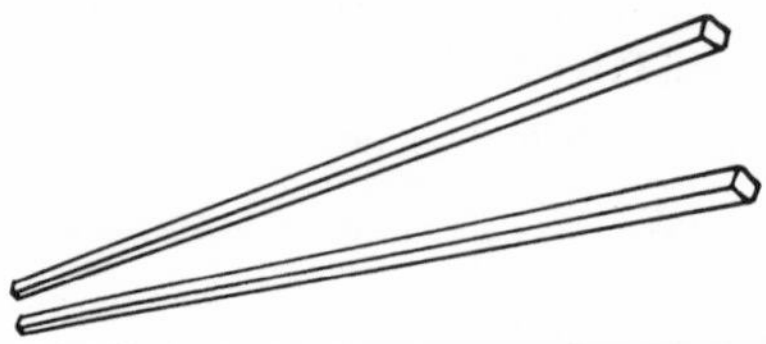

COUSCOUS

I never made couscous before I had a microwave oven because my recipe required a special steamer. It also called for rubbing the grains together to keep them separate and fluffy. The microwave makes perfect couscous with no fuss, no muss.

1 c. couscous
2 c. chicken broth or water
1 onion, chopped
2 cloves garlic, minced
2 tbsp. margarine or oil
½ tsp. salt
¼ tsp. pepper

1. Combine couscous and chicken broth in a 2 quart microsafe casserole. Let stand while you prepare the vegetables.

2. Combine onion, garlic and margarine in a 2 cup Pyrex™ measure. **MW uncovered on HIGH for 3 to 4 minutes,** until tender-crisp. Add to couscous/broth mixture. Stir in seasonings.

3. Cover with casserole lid or vented plastic wrap. **MW covered on HIGH for 7 to 8 minutes,** until all liquid is absorbed. Let stand covered for 2 minutes. Fluff with a fork. If too dry, add a little water. If too moist, return to the microwave for a minute or two. Season to taste. Serve with meat, chicken, fish and/or cooked vegetables.

Yield: 4 servings. Freezes and/or reheats well.

* **To double recipe, MW onions and garlic on HIGH for 5 minutes.** Add to couscous, cover and **MW on HIGH for 12 to 14 minutes,** or until all liquid is absorbed. Let stand covered for 2 or 3 minutes.
* Couscous will keep hot for 20 to 30 minutes if tightly covered.

COUSCOUS & MUSHROOM CASSEROLE

2 c. couscous
2 c. tomato sauce
2 c. chicken broth
2 onions, chopped
2 tbsp. oil
2 c. mushrooms, sliced
salt & pepper, to taste

1. Place couscous in a 3 quart oval microsafe casserole. Add tomato sauce and chicken broth; let stand while you prepare the vegetables.

2. Combine onions and oil in a 1 quart microsafe bowl. **MW uncovered on HIGH for 4 minutes.** Stir in mushrooms; **MW on HIGH 3 minutes longer.** Set aside.

3. Cover couscous mixture with vented plastic wrap. **MW on HIGH for 10 minutes,** until liquid is almost absorbed. Uncover and stir in onions and mushrooms. **MW uncovered on HIGH 2 minutes longer.** Season to taste.

Yield: 8 servings. Freezes and/or reheats well.

MEDITERRANEAN BULGUR PILAF

Bulgur is a favorite in Middle Eastern cuisine, where it is known as Burghul. The microwave makes preparation easy.

½ c. dried apricots, chopped
½ c. raisins
½ c. water
1 onion, chopped
1 stalk celery, chopped
½ green pepper, diced
2 tbsp. oil
1 c. bulgur (cracked wheat)
10 oz. can chicken stock
1 c. water
salt & pepper, to taste
¼ tsp. allspice
1 tbsp. chopped parsley
½ c. pistachio nuts, coarsely chopped

1. Combine apricots and raisins in a 2 cup glass measure. Add water. **MW uncovered on HIGH for 1 ½ to 2 minutes,** until steaming hot. Let stand uncovered while you prepare the remaining ingredients.

2. Combine onion, celery, green pepper and oil in a 2 quart microsafe casserole or soufflé dish. **MW uncovered on HIGH for 3 minutes,** until tender. Stir in bulgur. Add chicken stock, water and seasonings. Cover with casserole lid or vented plastic wrap.

3. MW on HIGH for 12 to 14 minutes, rotating casserole ¼ turn at half time. Liquid should be absorbed. Let stand covered for 5 minutes. Fluff with a fork; stir in apricots and raisins. Season to taste. Garnish with parsley and pistachios.

Yield: 4 servings. Reheats well, but add pistachios just before serving.

Variation: Dates can be substituted for apricots, currants for raisins and pine nuts for pistachios.

TRUE GRITS

These grits stick to your ribs, not to the pot!

1 c. hominy grits (not instant)
3 ¾ c. water or broth
½ tsp. salt

1. Combine grits, water and salt in a 3 quart microsafe bowl. Cover with vented plastic wrap. **MW on HIGH for 5 minutes.** Stir well. (A wooden chopstick through the vented opening works well.) **MW on HIGH 5 to 7 minutes longer,** until all liquid is absorbed. Let stand covered for 2 or 3 minutes. Stir and serve.

Yield: 4 to 6 servings.

* Southerners serve grits for breakfast as a cereal with a pat of butter, maple syrup or sugar and a splash of milk or cream.
* Serve grits instead of potatoes as a side dish with chicken or pot roast; top with gravy. Use chicken or beef broth instead of water as the cooking liquid.
* **For 1 serving:** Combine ¼ c. grits, 1 c. water and a pinch of salt in a 4 cup glass measure. Cover with vented plastic wrap. **MW on HIGH for 4 minutes,** stirring at half time.

OLD-FASHIONED FARFEL

Old-Fashioned or Haimishe Farfel is a Jewish specialty which can be used as an alternative to noodles or rice. It is usually found in the Kosher section of supermarkets. My non-Jewish students love this dish!

2 onions, chopped
2 tbsp. oil or margarine
7 oz. pkg. old-fashioned farfel
2 c. chicken broth
salt & pepper, to taste

1. Place onions and oil in a 2 quart round microsafe casserole. **MW uncovered on HIGH for 5 minutes,** until tender, stirring at half time.

2. Add farfel, chicken broth and seasonings. Cover with vented plastic wrap or casserole lid. **MW on HIGH for 12 to 14 minutes,** until liquid is absorbed. Let stand covered for 3 or 4 minutes. Mix well and serve. Delicious in soup or as a side dish with meat or poultry. Top with gravy, if desired.

Yield: 4 servings. Can be frozen.

* **One cup of farfel takes 1 minute on HIGH to reheat.** Covering is optional.
* **One cup of frozen farfel takes 2 minutes on HIGH to thaw and reheat.** Cover with waxed paper.
* Cooking time will be about 2 minutes shorter if the chicken broth is boiling before adding it to the other ingredients.
* Add a dash of garlic powder and basil, if desired.

QUICK FARFEL CASSEROLE

The vegetables and farfel are cooked together in one step in this quick and easy dish! Use the processor to chop the vegetables.

1 stalk celery, chopped
1 medium onion, chopped
½ green pepper, chopped
7 oz. pkg. old-fashioned farfel
½ pkg. onion soup mix
2 c. boiling water
2 tbsp. margarine
10 oz. can sliced mushrooms, if desired

1. Combine all ingredients in an ungreased 2 quart round microsafe casserole. Cover with vented plastic wrap or casserole lid. **MW on HIGH for 10 to 12 minutes,** until liquid is absorbed. Let stand covered for 3 or 4 minutes. Stir well. Serve with meat or poultry. Top with gravy, if desired.

Yield: 4 servings. Can be frozen.

* Do not add salt. Onion soup mix is salty.

EGG BARLEY PILAF

Egg barley is not actually barley, but small, round grains of pasta. It is often served in soup, but this recipe will be enjoyed by those who like pasta in any form.

2 medium onions, chopped
1 stalk celery, chopped
2 tbsp. oil
340 gram pkg. egg barley (1 ¾ cups)
2 ½ c. boiling water
2 tsp. instant chicken soup mix
salt, pepper & basil, to taste

1. Place onions, celery and oil in a round 2 quart microsafe casserole. **MW uncovered on HIGH for 3 to 4 minutes,** until tender-crisp.

2. Add remaining ingredients; cover with vented plastic wrap or casserole lid. **MW on HIGH for 12 to 14 minutes,** stirring at half time. Water should be completely absorbed. Let stand covered for 3 or 4 minutes. Fluff with a fork. Delicious topped with gravy and served with roast brisket, veal or chicken. If barley seems sticky, add about 2 tbsp. additional water and mix well.

Yield: 4 to 6 servings. May be frozen.

QUICK EGG BARLEY CASSEROLE

340 gram pkg. egg barley (1 ¾ cups)
2 ½ c. boiling water
½ pkg. onion soup mix
1 tbsp. margarine

1. Combine egg barley, boiling water and soup mix in a round 2 quart microsafe casserole. Cover with vented plastic wrap or casserole lid. **MW on HIGH for 12 to 14 minutes,** stirring at half time. Liquid should be completely absorbed.

2. Let stand covered for 3 or 4 minutes. Add margarine and fluff with a fork. Delicious topped with gravy and served with roast brisket, veal or chicken. If farfel seems sticky, add about 2 tbsp. additional water and mix well.

Yield: 4 to 6 servings. May be frozen.

* Drain a 10 oz. can of sliced mushrooms and add to casserole. Cook as directed above.

BARLEY CASSEROLE

1 medium onion, chopped
1 c. mushrooms, sliced
2 tbsp. oil
1 carrot, grated
1 c. pearl barley
2 c. boiling water
2 tsp. instant chicken soup mix
1 tsp. salt
¼ tsp. pepper
1 tsp. dried parsley flakes
¾ tsp. paprika
½ tsp. garlic powder

1. Combine onion, mushrooms and oil in a round 2 quart microsafe casserole. **MW uncovered on HIGH for 3 to 4 minutes,** until tender.

2. Add remaining ingredients to casserole and mix well. Cover with casserole lid or vented plastic wrap. **MW on HIGH for 3 to 4 minutes,** until boiling. **Reduce power to MEDIUM (50%) and simmer covered for 35 to 40 minutes,** until tender, stirring once. Let stand covered for 10 minutes.

Yield: 4 servings. Can be frozen.

DIDDLE DIDDLE DUMPLINGS

3 tbsp. fresh parsley or dill
1 ½ c. flour
2 tsp. baking powder
¾ tsp. salt
dash pepper
3 tbsp. margarine
½ c. chicken broth
1 egg

1. **Steel Knife:** Process parsley with flour, baking powder, seasonings and margarine until blended, about 8 to 10 seconds. Add broth and egg and process with several quick on/off turns, just until mixed.

2. Drop by heaping tablespoons onto hot stew (or cook in broth as directed below*). Cover with casserole lid or vented plastic wrap and **MW on HIGH for 8 to 9 minutes,** until set. Let stand covered for 5 minutes. A cake tester inserted in the centre will come out clean.

Yield: 12 dumplings.

* **Variation:** Bring 2 ½ cups of water or chicken broth to boiling in an 8 cup glass measure, **about 6 to 7 minutes on HIGH**. Drop dumplings by heaping spoonfuls into broth. Cover with vented plastic wrap. **MW on HIGH for 7 to 8 minutes,** rotating casserole ¼ turn at half time. Let stand covered for 5 minutes. Remove from liquid with a slotted spoon. Delicious topped with gravy or tomato sauce.

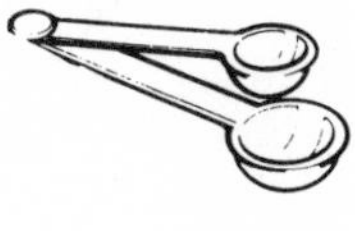

BOW TIES & KASHA

Quick, easy and clean. Nothing sticks to the pot, and you don't have to watch out for the burst of steam which occurs when you cook kasha conventionally! Make and serve in the same dish.

2 onions, sliced
2 tbsp. oil
1 c. fine or medium grain kasha (buckwheat groats)
1 egg, lightly beaten
1 ¾ c. hot chicken broth or water
1 tsp. salt
¼ tsp. pepper
8 oz. pkg. bow tie noodles

1. Place onions and oil in a 2 quart oblong or round microsafe casserole. **MW uncovered on HIGH for 5 minutes,** until tender.

2. Add kasha and egg to onions. Mix well. **MW uncovered on HIGH for 1 minute.** Break up grains with a fork to separate them. **MW 1 minute longer** and break up grains once again. Kasha should be dry.

3. Add hot broth and seasonings, cover with waxed paper and **MW on HIGH for 5 minutes.** Stir at half time. Liquid should be absorbed and kasha should be tender. Let stand covered for 2 minutes.

4. Meanwhile, cook pasta in boiling salted water conventionally, according to package directions. Drain and rinse well. Combine all ingredients and mix well. Season to taste. If necessary, **MW for 1 or 2 minutes to reheat.**

Yield: 4 to 6 servings. Freezes well.

* **To reheat** if made in advance and refrigerated, **MW covered for 5 minutes on HIGH,** stirring once or twice. **On cup takes 1 minute on HIGH.**
* **Frozen Kasha:** It is not necessary to defrost before heating. **Allow 2 minutes per cup on HIGH, covered.**
* For a light and fluffy texture, try adding ½ cup bulgur (cracked wheat) to the kasha/egg mixture. Increase chicken broth to 2 ¼ cups. Cooking time will take about 5 to 6 minutes for the liquid to be fully absorbed.
* Whole grain kasha takes twice as long to cook as medium or fine grain and the results are more satisfactory when cooked conventionally.
* If you like a very toasted flavor, brown kasha and egg mixture conventionally on the stove in a Corning Ware™ casserole, then transfer casserole to the microwave to finish cooking.

OH MY, MAMALIGA!

Not for calorie-counters!

Mamaliga or Polenta (p. 236), but omit butter
3 tbsp. butter or margarine
2 onions, sliced
sour cream or yogurt

1. Cook Mamaliga as directed, but do not add butter. Spread in a single layer in a lightly greased loaf or square pan. Cover and refrigerate until chilled. It will thicken into a solid mass. Slice in ½″ thick slices.

2. Melt butter in a skillet over medium heat on top of the stove. Add onions and sauté until golden. Push to one side. Add Mamaliga slices; fry on both sides until golden. Serve with sour cream or yogourt.

Yield: 2 or 3 generous servings as a main dish, 4 to 6 servings as a side dish.

* **Variation:** Omit onions. Top fried slices with sour cream and strawberry or blueberry jam. Fresh berries are also delicious.

POLENTA, ITALIAN STYLE

An excellent and inexpensive vegetarian meal.

Mamaliga or Polenta (p. 236), but omit butter
3 tbsp. olive oil
1 ½ c. vegetarian spaghetti sauce
1 ½ c. grated Mozzerella cheese

1. Prepare Polenta as directed, but do not add butter. Spread in a single layer in a lightly greased loaf or square pan. Cover and refrigerate until chilled. It will thicken into a solid mass. Slice in ½″ thick slices.

2. Heat oil in a large skillet over medium heat on top of the stove. Add cornmeal slices; fry on both sides until golden. Meanwhile, **MW spaghetti sauce uncovered on HIGH for 2 minutes,** stirring at half time.

3. Arrange browned cornmeal slices in a single layer in an ungreased 2 quart oblong casserole. Top with sauce. Sprinkle with cheese. **MW uncovered on HIGH for 2 minutes,** just until cheese is melted. Serve with a mixed green salad and crusty rolls.

Yield: 4 servings as a main dish.

MAMALIGA OR POLENTA

(CORNMEAL MUSH)

No matter what you call it, it still tastes good! Roumanian Jews love Mamaliga. In spite of its humble beginnings, today it is considered a delicacy!

¾ c. yellow cornmeal
3 c. water
¾ tsp. salt
2 tbsp. butter or margarine, optional

1. Combine cornmeal, water and salt in an 8 cup microsafe measure. Cover with vented plastic wrap. **MW on HIGH for 10 minutes,** stirring at half time. (Use a wooden chopstick to stir through the vented opening.) Let stand covered for 3 or 4 minutes. Stir in butter or margarine. Eat hot or cold. (See hints below for serving suggestions.)

Yield: 4 to 6 servings as a side dish.

* White corn meal can be used.
* Top with lots of fried onions and/or mushrooms. Also delicious with gravy from roasted brisket or stew.
* Serve hot topped with butter and cottage cheese.
* Stir fried onions and grated Cheddar cheese into hot cornmeal mixture.
* For a thicker version, cook ⅓ cup cornmeal with 1 cup water and a dash of salt in a 4 cup glass measure. **MW covered on HIGH for 5 minutes,** stirring at half time. Eat as a cereal with milk or cream and sugar to taste. Serves 1 or 2.
* When chilled, cornmeal mixture can be sliced. Roumanians used to slice Mamaliga with a strong piece of thread or string.
* Top slices with grated Mozzerella cheese and broil briefly.

CREAM OF WHEAT

1. For one serving, use ¼ c. cream of wheat and 1 cup tap water or apple juice. Combine in a microsafe bowl which holds at least twice the volume. **MW uncovered on HIGH for 2½ to 3 minutes,** stirring twice. Let stand for 1 minute. Stir in ⅓ c. milk; sweeten to taste.

* Delicious sweetened with honey, maple syrup or brown sugar. Try it with apple sauce, raisins, dried apricots or any dried fruit. What about sliced fresh fruit, chopped nuts or granola?
* As a change, serve cream of wheat with fruit-flavored yogourt instead of milk.

QUICK COOKING OATMEAL

Make sure to use a large enough cooking container as cereal boils over very easily. No sticking, no scorching — what a pleasure!

¼ c. quick-cooking oatmeal
½ c. water or apple juice
pinch of salt
⅓ c. milk (skim or regular)
2 tsp. brown sugar
1 tsp. butter or margarine, if desired

1. Combine oatmeal, water and salt in a 16 oz. microsafe bowl. **MW uncovered on HIGH for 1 ½ minutes,** until bubbling, stirring once. (**Or MW uncovered on HIGH for 1 minute, then on MEDIUM-LOW/DEFROST (30%) for 1 minute.** Less chance of boil-over!) Let stand for 1 minute.

2. Add milk, brown sugar and butter. (Calorie counters can add artificial sweetener and omit the butter!) If desired, **MW uncovered on HIGH 20 seconds longer.** (I like my porridge hot!)

Yield: 1 serving.

* If desired, add 2 tbsp. raisins, chopped dates or apricots and a sprinkling of cinnamon at the beginning of Step 2.
* **For 4 servings:** Use 1 c. oatmeal + 2 c. water or apple juice. Use a 2 quart casserole. **MW uncovered on HIGH for 4 to 5 minutes,** until thick, stirring halfway through cooking time. Stir and let stand for 2 to 3 minutes. Meanwhile, **MW 1 ⅓ c. milk uncovered on HIGH for 2 minutes,** until hot. Add ⅓ cup of hot milk to each serving of cereal. Sweeten to taste.

OLD-FASHIONED OATMEAL

3 c. hot water
½ tsp. salt
1 ⅓ c. oatmeal

1. Combine hot water, salt and oatmeal in a 3 quart microsafe casserole. **MW uncovered on HIGH for 8 to 9 minutes,** stirring at half time. Stir and let stand for 3 minutes.

Yield: 4 servings. Reheats well.

OAT BRAN CEREAL

1. For 1 serving, measure ¼ cup oat bran cereal into a microsafe bowl (about 20 oz. capacity). Add ¾ cup tap water. **MW uncovered on HIGH for 1 minute, then on MEDIUM-LOW/DEFROST (30%) for 2 minutes.** Stir in ⅓ c. milk; sweeten to taste.

GREAT GRANOLA

Easy to make and healthier for you than the commercial brands.

¼ c. oil
¾ c. honey
¼ c. brown sugar, firmly packed
3 c. quick cooking oats or oat bran, or a combination of both
½ c. shredded coconut, optional
2 tbsp. wheat germ, optional
½ c. sesame seeds
¾ c. chopped nuts (pecans, filberts, walnuts or almonds)
1 tsp. cinnamon
1 tsp. vanilla
½ c. raisins

1. Combine oil, honey and brown sugar in an 8 cup glass measuring cup or a large heat resistant plastic bowl.* **MW uncovered on HIGH for 2 to 3 minutes,** until boiling, stirring every minute.

2. Add remaining ingredients except raisins to bowl and mix well. Spread mixture in a 9″ x 13″ x 2″ baking pan or casserole. Place on rack recommended by oven manufacturer and **bake uncovered on the CONVECTION CYCLE at 275°F for 30 to 35 minutes,** or until toasted, stirring occasionally. (No preheating of oven is necessary.) See hints below for ***Conventional Oven Method.**

3. Stir in raisins. Let cool, stirring with a fork occasionally to break up mixture. Store in an airtight container in a cool, dry place.

Yield: about 6 cups. Can also be frozen.

* To prepare this recipe totally in the microwave, see Passover Granola (p. 378).
* Use plastic cookware specially designed to use in both conventional and microwave ovens and which can withstand temperatures up to 400°F.
* **PLEASE NOTE:** Although there are many microwave recipes for Granola which are cooked entirely in the microwave, the manufacturers of glass and glass-ceramic cookware (e.g. Pyrex™, Corning Ware™) do not recommend carmelizing sugar or microwaving sugar mixtures beyond 250°F (hard-ball stage) in their products. Doing so can cause chipping or breakage of any glass or glass-ceramic vessel. (When tested completely in the microwave, Great Granola reached temperatures varying from 270 to 290°F.)
* **CONVENTIONAL OVEN METHOD:** If you do not have a **CONVECTION/MICROWAVE** oven, you can complete the toasting process in Step 2 in your conventional oven. **Preheat oven to 300°F. Time will be about 30 to 35 minutes.**
* Walls and door of combination oven are hot during **CONVECTION CYCLE.** Use oven mitts!

VEGETABLES

MICRO-WAYS WITH VEGETABLES

- **Frozen packaged vegetables** are usually precooked and just require thawing and heating. Many can be cooked right in the cardboard package! Remove wrapper and pierce the package in several places with a sharp knife in order to allow steam to escape.
- **Printed paper wrappers** on frozen food packages should be removed before microwaving. The ink could stain the floor of the oven, or be absorbed by the food. If wrapper is not removeable, transfer vegetables to a microsafe cooking dish.
- **General Rule:** Most frozen vegetables cook in **5 to 6 minutes on HIGH for a 10 oz. (300 gram) package,** or about 1 ½ cups. **Two packages will take about 8 to 10 minutes.** Add more time if necessary. Time depends on density, moisture content and size of vegetable.
- **A 10 oz. pkg. of frozen vegetables will take 6 to 7 minutes on DEFROST (30%) to thaw;** turn package over, or break up with a fork at half time. When thawed, a knife will pass through the centre, but vegetables will still be icy.
- **It is not necessary to add water** to frozen vegetables. The ice crystals in the package are sufficient to create steam when melted and heated.
- **Check for doneness at minimum time.** The bottom of the package or casserole will be hot in the centre and a knife should pass through the centre of the package or vegetables easily. When you touch the knife, it should feel hot.
- **Boil-in-the-bag pouches** can be used in the microwave. Just cut an "X" in the top of the package. Place on a serving plate and **MW** according to the time given on the package, **usually 5 to 7 minutes on HIGH for a 10 oz. bag.** Flex pouch halfway through cooking. When done, let stand briefly, then invert package over serving dish and empty.
- **Fresh or frozen vegetables** should stand covered for 2 to 4 minutes after microwaving to complete their cooking, usually just enough time to get them to the table. They should be cooked last when preparing a meal.
- **A trick I often use** is to undercook veggies slightly, then let them stand covered a little longer. This way, they are ready when I am!
- **If vegetables seem to be overcooking, uncover immediately.** If necessary, place under cold running water immediately to stop the cooking process. When cold, they can be microwaved again briefly just until heated through.
- **Most vegetables will require little,** if any, salt. Their flavor will be superior because so little liquid is used to cook them.
- **Sprinkling salt** directly on vegetables before cooking will toughen them. Sprinkle with salt after cooking. However, if liquid is added to cook the veggies, salt can be dissolved in the cooking liquid at the beginning of cooking.
- **Most vegetables don't require the addition of much water.** I usually rinse them well in cold water, shake off the excess and microwave them covered with just the water clinging to them.
- **Sometimes I add 1 to 2 tbsp. of water** if veggies are not too fresh. Because additional liquid increases the cooking time, use the minimum amount possible.

- **Hard, dense vegetables** such as carrots and green beans require the addition of liquid. One pound of carrots usually needs ¼ cup of liquid. I add ½ cup liquid to one pound of green beans to help tenderize them.
- **The fresher the vegetable,** the faster it cooks. Microwaved vegetables are so full of flavor, you'll wonder how you ever ate them any other way!
- **Weighing vegetables** is the most accurate method of cooking. Weigh after trimming. Cut in uniform pieces for more uniform cooking. Larger pieces take longer to cook than small pieces. Cooking time increases if quantity increases.
- **When cooking vegetables of different sizes,** place larger pieces towards the outside of the casserole. Broccoli florets and asparagus tips should be towards the centre.
- **Make a 1″ cut** in the base of broccoli stems if they are very thick for more even cooking. Make an "X" in the base of brussel sprouts.
- **If cooking a platter** of assorted veggies, arrange vegetables which have a longer cooking time towards the outside of the plate (e.g. broccoli, cauliflower). Place more tender veggies towards the centre (e.g. mushrooms, snow peas). Cover with a damp paper towel. A dinner plate of assorted vegetables will take **5 to 7 minutes on HIGH.**
- **Fresh vegetables** are usually cooked on **HIGH** power. Most vegetables cook in **5 to 7 minutes per lb.** If they are tougher (e.g. green beans) they may take a little longer. If they are softer (e.g. tomatoes, spinach), they will take less time.
- **If cooking half the amount, cooking time will be ⅔.** Half a pound of most veggies takes about **3 to 4 minutes.** If cooking double the amount, cooking time will be 1 ½ times longer. Check at minimum time and add more time if needed.
- **Doneness depends on individual taste.** Some people like their veggies crisp, others prefer them soft. Add more time after standing time if they aren't tender enough for your liking.
- **A quick guide is 1 to 2 minutes per cup of vegetables.**
- **A quick snack for dieters:** Place broccoli spears, cauliflower or asparagus like a bouquet of flowers in a 2 cup glass measure, stems downward. Rinse under cold running water and drain. Cover with moistened parchment paper or vented plastic wrap. **MW on HIGH for 1 to 2 minutes,** until crisp-tender and bright green. Let stand briefly, then munch away!
- **A pound of vegetables** yields different quantities: Potatoes - 2 cups; Carrots - 3 cups; Green Beans - 4 cups; Cabbage - 5 cups.
- **If vegetables are cooked** with a little oil or butter (e.g. when sautéeing onions, peppers, celery), I usually microwave them uncovered.
- **Stir vegetables or rearrange** at half time for more even cooking. Some vegetables should be turned over (e.g. potatoes, squash, eggplant).
- **Make sure to set your timer correctly.** One cook thought she set her timer for 4 minutes but accidentally punched in 40 minutes. Her potato caught on fire!
- **A quick way to "stir" veggies** is to shake the cardboard package or casserole dish (with the cover on, of course). Don't try this if there is a lot of liquid in the casserole!
- **Coverings:** If vegetables are cooked covered, use the casserole lid or vented plastic wrap to retain maximum steam and heat. Cooking parchment, waxed paper or a damp paper towel also make good coverings. Plastic wrap should not touch surface of food.

- **Wrap vegetables entirely in moistened parchment paper,** twisting ends to seal. No cooking dish to wash!
- **Vegetables can also be covered** with a double layer of microsafe paper towelling which has been placed under water, then squeezed gently to remove excess liquid. They are steamed when done this way and are so good!
- **Remove cover away from you** to prevent steam burns.
- **Vegetables with a skin** must be pierced before cooking (e.g. potatoes, squash, tomatoes, eggplant, etc.). Prick with a fork in several places to allow steam to escape during cooking. Cook on a microsafe rack. This prevents condensation from forming and making them soggy (e.g. potatoes).
- **If you like your potatoes to be crispy,** put them in the toaster or conventional oven at 400°F for 5 to 10 minutes after microwaving them. They are also excellent on the BBQ.
- **Don't wrap potatoes in foil** after microwaving them. They will get soggy. Wrap them in a clean dishtowel. They will stay hot for 20 to 30 minutes and the skins will be nice and dry.
- **To reheat leftover vegetables,** arrange thicker or larger pieces towards the outside of the dish. **MW on HIGH for 1 to 1½ minutes per cup.** (If refrigerated, reheating takes longer than if food is at room temperature.) Cover with waxed paper if you wish. Bottom centre of plate should feel hot.
- **Canned vegetables are already cooked.** All that is required is reheating. Drain off most of liquid and place in a microsafe serving bowl. Covering is optional. **Allow 1 to 1½ minutes per cup of vegetables on HIGH.** Stir at half time.
- **Canning is not recommended in the microwave. However,** there is a new microwave canner available which is used to can small quantities. Since I never do canning, I have not used this product, but several people I know have used it and like it.

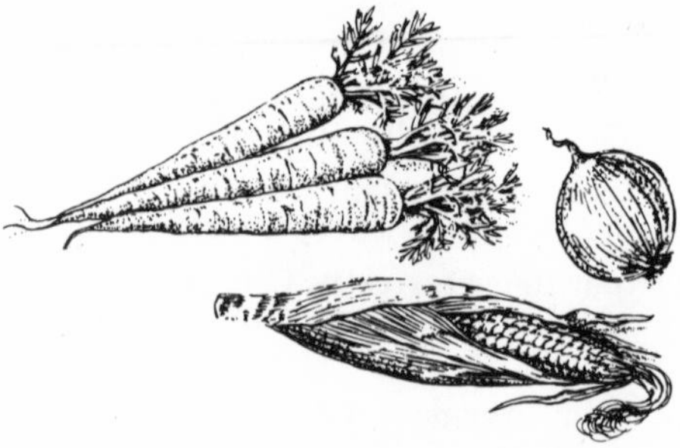

HOW TO PREPARE VEGETABLES FOR FREEZING

- **Vegetables can be blanched** in the microwave, but you will have to work with small quantities at a time. The general guideline is to microwave them covered for **¼ to ½ of their usual microwave cooking time.** When blanched, they should be bright in color, but crisp. The temperature on a probe or thermometer should be 190°F.
- **Immerse them immediately in ice cold water** to stop the cooking process. When cold, drain and dry well; freeze as quickly as possible.
- Use **ultra fresh veggies** for best results. **One quart of most vegetables will take about 3 to 5 minutes on HIGH to blanch** (broccoli, carrots, cauliflower, zucchini). Quicker cooking vegetables take less time **(spinach takes 1 ½ minutes). Green beans take longer, about 5 to 6 minutes.** Check at minimum time. Use a probe or thermometer to check temperature (190°F).
- **Pack in freezer containers** and seal tightly. Label and date each package. Frozen vegetables will keep for 9 to 12 months at 0°F.
- **For large quantities,** you may prefer to blanch vegetables conventionally.

FROZEN VEGETABLES

1. Place a 10 oz. package of frozen vegetables (about 1 ½ cups) on a double sheet of microsafe paper towelling. Pierce package in 2 or 3 places to vent. (Or empty into a 1 quart microsafe covered casserole.)

2. **MW on HIGH** for time indicated on Vegetable Cooking Chart (p. 244-245), **usually 5 to 7 minutes.** Shake package or rotate casserole halfway through the cooking time. Let stand 3 minutes.

Yield: 3 to 4 small servings.

* Don't thaw vegetables before cooking.
* Vegetables are ready when the package or the bottom of the cooking dish feels hot in the centre. A knife will pass through the package easily.
* **For 2 packages, allow about 8 to 10 minutes on HIGH power** (about 1 ½ times longer than for 1 package.) Test for doneness; add more time if necessary.
* If vegetables are in a plastic cooking bag, cut an "X" in the top of the package before cooking. Place on a microsafe serving plate. Flex pouch halfway through cooking. Microwave cooking times are the same.

VEGETABLE COOKING CHART

Sprinkle fresh vegetables with water and place in a microsafe casserole; **cover to retain steam, unless otherwise directed.** *Do not add water to frozen vegetables. They can be microwaved right in the package! Pierce package; shake to mix at half time. Stir or turn over fresh veggies at half time. Vegetables with a skin should be pierced and cooked uncovered on a microsafe rack or paper towelling; do not add water. Standing time completes cooking. Read Micro-Ways with Vegetables (p. 240-243).*

QUANTITY	TIME (HIGH)	STANDING TIME
ARTICHOKES, Fresh *(Sprinkle with water.)*		
1 (6 to 8 oz.)	6 to 7 mins.	3 mins.
2	6 to 9 mins.	
3	9 to 12 mins.	
4	13 to 15 mins.	
ARTICHOKE HEARTS, Frozen		
10 oz. pkg.	6 to 7 mins.	3 mins.
ASPARAGUS *(Tips inward for fresh asparagus; sprinkle with water.)*		
1 lb. fresh	5 to 6 mins.	2 mins.
10 oz. pkg. frozen	5 to 7 mins.	3 mins.
BEANS, Green or Wax *(Add 1/2 c. water to fresh beans.)*		
1 lb. fresh	7 to 8 mins.	3 mins.
10 oz. pkg. frozen	7 to 9 mins.	3 mins.
BEETS, Fresh *(Unpeeled; leave on 1″ of stems to prevent bleeding of color. Add ½ c. water. Peel after standing time.)*		
2″ diameter	15 to 18 mins.	5 mins.
BROCCOLI *(Stems outward; sprinkle with water.)*		
1 lb. fresh, spears or florets	6 to 7 mins.	2 to 3 mins.
10 oz. pkg. frozen	6 to 7 mins.	3 mins.
BRUSSEL SPROUTS *(For fresh, cut an x in the base of each one; add 2 tbsp. water.)*		
1 lb. fresh	5 to 7 mins.	3 mins.
10 oz. pkg. frozen	6 to 7 mins.	3 mins.
CABBAGE *(½ medium cabbage is about 2 lb., or 5 c. shredded after coring and trimming. Wedges take 1½ times as long to cook. Add ¼ c. water.)*		
5 c. shredded	6 to 8 mins.	3 mins.
CARROTS *(Add ¼ c. water to fresh carrots.)*		
1 lb. fresh, sliced	7 to 8 mins.	3 mins.
1 lb. fresh, grated	6 to 7 mins.	3 mins.
10 oz. pkg. frozen	6 to 7 mins.	3 mins.
CAULIFLOWER *(Trim; remove core. Leave whole or break into florets. Sprinkle with water.)*		
1 lb.	6 to 7 mins.	2 to 3 mins.
10 oz. pkg. frozen	6 to 7 mins.	3 mins.
CORN, Fresh *(Can also be cooked in husks; sprinkle with water.)*		
1 ear	2 to 3 mins.	1 min.
2 ears	4 to 5 mins.	2 mins.
4 ears	8 to 9 mins.	3 mins.
6 ears	12 to 14 mins.	5 mins.
10 oz. pkg. whole kernel, frozen	5 to 6 mins.	3 mins.
EGGPLANT *(Cook whole; pierce skin. Do not cover. Cook on microsafe rack.)*		
1 to 1¼ lb.	5 to 7 mins.	5 mins.

QUANTITY	TIME (HIGH)	STANDING TIME
MINIATURE VEGETABLES *(Keep whole. Serve with butter and herbs.)*		
6 to 8 oz.	2 to 3 mins.	1 to 2 mins.
1 lb.	5 to 7 mins.	2 to 3 mins.
MUSHROOMS *(Wipe clean; MW uncovered with 1 tbsp. butter or oil. Drain after cooking.)*		
1 lb. sliced	4 to 6 mins.	1 min.
ONIONS *(Peel. Slice or chop; add butter or oil for flavor. Do not cover unless cooking whole.)*		
1 medium	2 to 3 mins.	—
1 lb. whole small (add ¼ c. water)	6 to 8 mins.	3 mins.
PARSNIPS *(Peel; slice. Add ¼ c. water.)*		
1 lb.	6 to 8 mins.	3 mins.
PEAS, GREEN *(2 lb. in pod yields 2 cups; add 2 tbsp. water. Serve with butter, salt and mint.)*		
2 c. shelled	4 to 6 mins.	3 mins.
PEAS, PEAS & CARROTS, Frozen		
10 oz. pkg.	5 to 6 mins.	3 mins.
PEAS, SNOW (Pea Pods)		
1 lb. fresh	3 to 4 mins.	2 mins.
6 oz. pkg. frozen	4 to 5 mins.	2 mins.
PEPPERS, GREEN OR RED *(Core and seed. Chop or slice; add butter or oil for flavor. Do not cover.)*		
1 medium	2 to 3 mins.	—
1 lb. (3 peppers)	6 to 7 mins.	3 mins.
POTATOES, Baked *(Pierce skins; place 1" apart on microsafe rack or paper towels. Do not cover. One medium potato weighs 7 oz.)*		
1 lb.	6 to 7 mins.	3 to 5 mins.
1 medium	3½ to 4 mins.	2 mins.
2 medium	5 to 7 mins.	3 to 5 mins.
4 medium	10 to 12 mins.	3 to 5 mins.
8 to 10 small new	6 to 8 mins.	3 to 5 mins.
POTATOES, Boiled *(Peel; slice or cut up. Sprinkle with 2 tbsp. water.)*		
2 c. (1 lb.)	5 to 6 mins.	3 mins.
4 medium	8 to 10 mins.	3 mins.
6 medium	10 to 12 mins.	3 mins.
POTATOES, SWEET *(See Baked Potatoes for times and preparation.)*		
SPINACH *(MW fresh spinach with water clinging to the leaves.)*		
10 oz. fresh leaf	3 to 4 mins.	3 mins.
10 oz. frozen	5 to 6 mins.	3 mins.
SQUASH: ACORN, BUTTERNUT, SPAGHETTI *(Pierce skin. Place on microsafe rack or paper towels. Do not cover.)*		
1 lb.	5 to 7 mins.	5 mins.
10 oz. pkg. frozen	5 to 7 mins.	3 mins.
TOMATOES *(Cut off tops. Slice, if desired. Do not cover.)*		
1 lb. (4 medium)	3 to 4 mins.	2 mins.
TURNIPS *(Peel; chop or slice. Add ¼ cup water.)*		
1 lb.	6 to 8 mins.	3 to 5 mins.
VEGETABLES, MIXED *(Drain off all but 2 tbsp. liquid from canned vegetables. Covering is optional for canned vegetables.)*		
10 oz. pkg. frozen	5 to 7 mins.	3 mins.
14 to 16 oz. can	2 to 4 mins.	—
ZUCCHINI *(Do not peel. Slice; do not add water.)*		
1 lb. (3 c. sliced)	4 to 6 mins.	2 mins.

ARTICHOKES WITH LEMON BUTTER

4 medium artichokes
1 lemon, cut in half
¼ c. water
¼ c. butter or margarine
1 clove garlic, crushed

1. Remove 1″ from tops; trim sharp points. Trim bottoms so artichokes will sit flat. Rinse under cold running water; shake off excess. If desired, remove choke*. Rub cut surfaces with lemon to prevent discoloration. Measure 2 tbsp. lemon juice and set aside. Arrange artichokes in a circle 1″ apart in a covered microsafe casserole; add ¼ c. water to bottom of dish.

2. **MW on HIGH for 13 to 15 minutes,** rotating dish ¼ turn twice during cooking. Let stand covered for 3 minutes. When done, a centre leaf will pull out easily and you can pierce the bottom of the artichoke with a sharp knife. (If undercooked, return to the microwave for another minute or two.)

3. Place butter, 2 tbsp. lemon juice and garlic in a small microsafe serving dish. **MW uncovered on HIGH for 1 minute,** until butter is melted.

4. Artichokes should be eaten with your fingers. Pull off outer leaves one at a time. Dip fleshy part in lemon butter. Pull leaf through your teeth and strip off the fleshy portion. Have a large empty plate available for the discarded leaves. When you get to the heart, spoon or scrape out the fuzzy choke and discard*. Cut the heart into small pieces and enjoy!

Yield: 4 servings. Serve hot or chilled.

* Remove the choke before cooking for a more elegant presentation. Hold trimmed artichoke under running water until leaves open. Pull out pink-tipped prickly centre leaves. Scrape out the hairy choke with a small spoon. Sprinkle with lemon juice and press the leaves closed once again.
* If cooking 1 or 2 artichokes, wrap individually in moistened parchment paper and omit ¼ c. water.
* Hot or chilled artichokes are also delicious dipped in Mayonnaise (p. 88) or Hollandaise Sauce (p. 87). If you have removed the choke before cooking, you can place a spoonful of dipping sauce in the centre of each artichoke at serving time.

ASPARAGUS

Pencil-thin asparagus is best! Delicious hot or cold.

1. Break woody portion from asparagus stems and discard. Rinse asparagus under cold running water. Do not dry. Arrange in an oblong microsafe casserole with stalks towards the outside of the casserole and tips meeting in the centre. Cover with vented plastic wrap.

2. **MW on HIGH for 5 to 6 minutes per lb.** Let stand covered for 2 minutes. Season with butter or margarine, a few drops of lemon juice and salt & pepper.

Yield: 1 lb. serves 2 to 3.

* **½ lb. asparagus (1 to 2 servings) will take 3 to 4 minutes on HIGH. 1½ lb. takes 6 to 8 minutes and serves 4.**

* If I want to cook just a few stalks of asparagus for myself, I rinse them with cold water, then stand them with the tips pointing upwards in a 1 cup glass measure. I cover the asparagus and measuring cup with parchment or a damp paper towel and **MW them on HIGH for 1 to 2 minutes,** until bright green. Let stand covered for 1 minute.

* **ASPARAGUS HOLLANDAISE: Microwave 1½ lb.** asparagus as directed, about **6 to 8 minutes on HIGH.** During standing time, prepare Hollandaise Sauce (p. 87). Drizzle over asparagus. If desired, garnish with sieved hard-cooked egg white (p. 130).

* **ASPARAGUS VINAIGRETTE:** Prepare asparagus as directed above, but only **MW for 4 to 5 minutes per lb. on HIGH.** It should be tender-crisp. Arrange on a serving plate. Combine ½ c. olive oil, 3 tbsp. wine vinegar, 1 tsp. Dijon mustard, 1 clove crushed garlic, salt & pepper. Drizzle over asparagus. Garnish with alternating bands of sieved hard-cooked egg yolk and egg white. Chill before serving.

* **ORIENTAL ASPARAGUS:** Drizzle cooked asparagus with 1 to 2 tbsp. soya or Teriyaki sauce and a few drops of Oriental sesame oil. Sprinkle lightly with sesame seeds.

GREEN BEANS AMANDINE

2 tbsp. butter or margarine
½ c. slivered almonds
1 lb. green beans, washed, trimmed & cut in 1″ pieces
½ c. water
salt & pepper, to taste
¼ tsp. rosemary, crushed

1. Place butter and almonds in a 9″ microsafe pie plate. **MW uncovered on HIGH for 3 minutes,** until golden, stirring every minute. Let stand while you prepare the green beans. Almonds will continue to brown.

2. Place beans and water in a 1 quart microsafe casserole. Cover with casserole lid or vented plastic wrap. **MW on HIGH for 7 to 8 minutes,** stirring at half time. Let stand covered for 3 minutes. Drain.

3. Stir in almonds and butter. Season to taste. Serve immediately.

Yield: 4 servings.

* **For 2 servings: ½ lb. green beans plus ¼ cup water takes 4 to 5 minutes covered on HIGH to microwave;** stir at half time. Use a 1 quart covered round microsafe casserole. Let stand covered for 3 minutes to complete cooking.

* **¼ cup almonds plus 1 tbsp. butter will take 2 to 3 minutes uncovered on HIGH.** Stir every minute.

* Two 10 oz. pkgs. frozen green beans can be substituted for 1 lb. fresh green beans. Do not add water. **MW covered for 11 to 13 minutes on HIGH,** stirring at half time. **(One 10 oz. pkg. takes 7 to 9 minutes.)** Let stand covered for 3 minutes. Add toasted almonds, butter and seasonings.

ORIENTAL GREEN BEANS VINAIGRETTE

Excellent! My students love the wonderful flavor. The sauce is delicious over cooked asparagus or broccoli.

1 lb. green beans (about 4 cups)
½ c. water plus ½ tsp. salt
1 clove garlic, minced
½ tsp. fresh ginger, minced (or ¼ tsp. dried ginger)
3 tbsp. lemon juice
½ c. peanut or corn oil
1 tbsp. soya sauce
¼ tsp. sesame oil
½ tsp. dry mustard
salt & pepper, to taste
¼ c. chopped red pepper, to garnish

1. Wash and trim beans. Place in a 1 ½ quart round casserole with salted water. Cover with vented plastic wrap or casserole lid. **MW on HIGH for 7 to 8 minutes,** stirring at half time. Let stand covered for 2 to 3 minutes. Test for doneness; beans should be crisp and bright green. Rinse with cold water to stop cooking process; otherwise beans will shrivel. Drain thoroughly.

2. Steel Knife: Drop garlic and ginger through feed tube while machine is running. Process until minced. Add remaining ingredients except beans and red pepper. Process a few seconds to blend. Pour over beans and toss well to mix. Sprinkle with chopped red pepper. Refrigerate 1 to 2 hours for maximum flavor. Serve chilled.

Yield: 4 servings. Do not freeze. Beans will keep for 2 or 3 days in the refrigerator.

* If desired, garnish marinated beans at serving time with toasted almonds. Place ¼ cup sliced or slivered almonds in a 9″ microsafe pie plate. **MW uncovered on HIGH for 3 to 4 minutes,** or until golden, stirring twice during cooking.
* Wax beans may be substituted for half or all of the green beans.
* **Two 10 oz. packages of frozen beans** can be substituted for fresh beans. Pierce each package in several places with a sharp knife and place in a microsafe casserole. (Beans could also be emptied into a microsafe casserole and cooked covered.) **MW on HIGH for 11 to 13 minutes.** Turn over and switch packages at half time, or stir. When cooked, let stand covered for 2 to 3 minutes. Drain under cold running water and continue as directed above in Step 2.

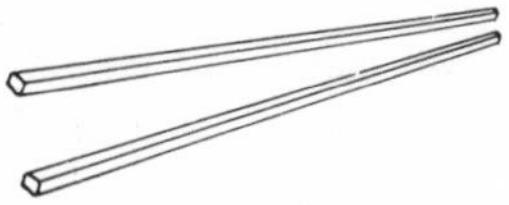

BEST BEAN SALAD

This is a great do-ahead recipe. Even though it may seem long, it is very easy to prepare. Try it, you'll love it!

2 c. fresh green beans*
2 c. fresh wax beans*
½ c. water
10 oz. pkg. frozen baby lima beans
19 oz. can chick peas, drained
½ c. canned red kidney beans, drained
½ Bermuda onion, chopped
½ red pepper, seeded & chopped
½ green pepper, seeded & chopped
2 or 3 cloves garlic, crushed

Dressing:

1 c. red wine vinegar
½ c. sugar
½ c. oil
1 tsp. dry mustard
1 tsp. salt
freshly ground pepper

1. Wash and trim green beans and wax beans. Cut in 1″ pieces. Combine with water in a 1 ½ quart round microsafe casserole. Cover with casserole lid or vented plastic wrap. **MW on HIGH for 6 to 7 minutes,** stirring halfway through cooking. Beans should be tender-crisp. Let stand covered for 2 to 3 minutes. Rinse well with cold water to stop cooking process. Drain well.

2. Pierce top of package of lima beans in several places with a sharp knife. Place on a microsafe plate. **MW on HIGH for 5 to 7 minutes,** shaking box halfway through cooking to mix lima beans. Let stand covered for 2 minutes. Remove from package and rinse with cold water to stop cooking process. Drain well.

3. Combine all ingredients except dressing in a large bowl. Mix well.

4. Combine all ingredients for dressing in an 8 cup Pyrex™ measure. **MW uncovered on HIGH for 3 minutes,** stirring at half time, until steaming hot. Pour hot dressing over vegetables and mix well. Refrigerate.

Yield: 12 servings. Keeps about a week to 10 days in the refrigerator.

* A 10 oz. pkg. of frozen green beans and a 10 oz. pkg. of frozen wax beans can be used instead of fresh beans in Step 1. Pierce top of each package. Stack one on top of the other in a microsafe dish. **MW on HIGH for 10 to 12 minutes,** switching the packages around halfway through cooking. Let stand for 3 minutes. Rinse under cold water to stop the cooking. Drain well; continue as directed in Step 2.

GREEN BEAN CASSEROLE

1 lb. green beans, washed & trimmed
½ c. water
10 oz. can cream of mushroom soup
1 tbsp. soya sauce
dash of salt & pepper
8 oz. can bamboo shoots or water chestnuts, drained
3 oz. can French fried onions

1. Combine green beans and water in a 1 quart round microsafe casserole. **MW covered on HIGH for 7 to 8 minutes,** until crisp-tender, stirring once. Drain. Rinse under cold water to set the color and prevent the beans from overcooking. Drain well.

2. Add remaining ingredients except French fried onions and mix well. (Can be prepared in advance up to this point.)

3. **MW covered for 5 to 6 minutes on HIGH,** until heated through, stirring once or twice. Top with onions and **MW uncovered on HIGH 1 to 2 minutes longer,** until piping hot.

Yield: 4 servings.

* **Two 10 oz. packages of frozen green beans** can be used. They will **cook in 11 to 13 minutes on HIGH.** Do not add water. Rinse with cold water to set the color. Drain well. Continue as directed from Step 2.
* 2 cups of chow mein noodles can be substituted for French fried onions.

STEAMED BEAN SPROUTS

Steamed bean sprouts are low in calories — just 28 calories per cup.

1 lb. fresh bean sprouts
2 cloves garlic, crushed
2 tbsp. soya sauce
freshly ground pepper, to taste

1. Place bean sprouts in a 2 quart covered casserole. Cover with cold water and soak for 1 minute. Drain well, but do not dry. Stir in garlic.

2. Cover with vented plastic wrap and **MW on HIGH for 3 minutes. Stir. MW 1 to 2 minutes longer,** until tender-crisp. Let stand covered for 3 minutes. Drain excess liquid. Season with soya sauce and pepper.

Yield: about 3 cups cooked.

* Cooked bean sprouts can be combined with cooked noodles or rice. Add sautéed onions, celery, green peppers and mushrooms. Season with soya sauce, freshly ground pepper and a dash of sesame oil.

HARVARD BEETS

Canned beets make this recipe a breeze to prepare.

3 tbsp. sugar
2 tsp. cornstarch
¼ tsp. salt
freshly ground pepper
19 oz. can sliced beets, drained (reserve ⅓ c. liquid)
¼ c. vinegar
2 tbsp. butter or margarine

1. Combine sugar, cornstarch and seasonings in a 1 quart microsafe casserole. Stir in beet liquid and vinegar. Blend until smooth. **MW uncovered on HIGH for 1 to 1½ minutes,** until boiling and thickened, stirring once.

2. Stir in beets; cover and **MW on HIGH for 2 to 3 minutes,** until heated through, stirring at half time. Stir in butter. Let stand covered for 3 minutes.

Yield: 4 servings.

* **Variation:** Substitute ¼ c. orange juice for vinegar; reduce sugar to 2 tbsp. If desired, add ¼ tsp. cinnamon to seasonings.

BRUTUS SALAD

Similar to Caesar, but without the anchovies or egg. The microwave acts as a helper to prepare some of the ingredients.

juice of 1 lemon
2 cloves garlic
½ c. olive oil
1 tsp. Dijon mustard
⅓ c. grated Parmesan cheese
1 tsp. HP or steak sauce
salt & pepper, to taste
1 large head Romaine lettuce
1 c. Croutons (p. 312)

1. **MW lemon on HIGH for 20 seconds** to release more juice.

2. **Steel Knife:** Drop garlic through feed tube while machine is running. Process until minced. Remove any bits of peel. Add remaining ingredients except lettuce and croutons; process for 6 to 8 seconds to blend. Refrigerate until serving time.

3. Lettuce can be washed and dried in advance. Store in the refrigerator in a plastic bag with some paper towelling to absorb any moisture. Prepare croutons as directed and let cool.

4. At serving time, combine Romaine with dressing and croutons; mix well. Serve immediately. If desired, serve with additional Parmesan cheese.

Yield: 4 servings.

SUPER COLESLAW

This coleslaw will keep for about 1 month in the refrigerator! Heating the dressing keeps the coleslaw crisp. The recipe was given to me several years ago by my Aunt Adele of Winnipeg, who was a super cook. You will be too, if you make her recipe!

1 head cabbage (about 3 lb.)
1 green pepper, cut in long, narrow strips
3 carrots, peeled & trimmed
2 cloves garlic, peeled
3 green onions, in 2″ pieces

Dressing:
1 c. white vinegar
½ c. sugar
¾ c. oil
1 tsp. salt
¼ tsp. pepper

1. **Slicer:** Cut cabbage into wedges to fit feed tube. Discard core. Slice, using very light pressure. (If too thick, you can chop it briefly in batches on the **Steel Knife,** using quick on/off turns.) Empty into a large mixing bowl. Stack pepper strips vertically in feed tube. Slice, using medium pressure.

2. **Grater:** Grate carrots, using firm pressure. Add to cabbage.

3. **Steel Knife:** Drop garlic and green onions through feed tube while machine is running. Process until minced. Add to cabbage.

4. Combine all ingredients for dressing in an 8 cup Pyrex™ measure. **MW uncovered on HIGH for 3 minutes,** stirring at half time, until steaming hot. Pour hot dressing over vegetables and mix well. Refrigerate.

Yield: 12 to 16 servings.

* Artificial sweetener may be used instead of sugar, but coleslaw will not keep as well.
* Hot dressing can be poured over any combination of vegetables for a delicious marinated salad.
* If you don't have a food processor, slice cabbage very thin with a sharp knife. Coarsely chop green pepper; grate carrots; crush garlic; mince green onions.

CRUMB-TOPPED BROCCOLI (CRUMMY BROCCLE-TREES)

Our young friend Alexi, age 5, loves to eat broccoli because "they look like trees!"

1 ½ lb. broccoli
1 tbsp. lemon juice
2 tbsp. butter or margarine
½ c. seasoned bread crumbs

1. Trim broccoli, removing tough ends of stems. If desired, peel stems (I usually don't bother). Weigh after trimming. Cut broccoli into spears. Soak in cold water for 3 or 4 minutes. Drain well, but do not dry.

2. Place broccoli in a 2 quart oblong casserole or on a 12″ round microsafe platter; the heads should point inwards. Sprinkle with lemon juice. Cover completely with waxed paper or a damp paper towel.

3. **MW for 6 to 7 minutes a lb.,** rotating dish ¼ turn at half time. Check for doneness at minimum time; broccoli should be tender-crisp and can be pierced with a fork. Let stand covered for 3 minutes. Drain.

4. Combine butter or margarine with bread crumbs. **MW uncovered on HIGH for 1 to 1½ minutes,** until toasted, stirring once or twice. Sprinkle over broccoli.

Yield: 4 to 6 servings.

* Stems and florets can be cut-up, if desired. Arrange florets around outside edge of casserole. Slice stems ¼″ thick and place towards the centre. **1 lb. cut-up broccoli takes 5 to 7 minutes to MW on HIGH, covered. One cup of broccoli florets takes about 2 minutes. Four cups will take about 8 to 10 minutes.**
* If desired, top broccoli with Cheese Sauce (p. 85); sprinkle with a 3 oz. can of French fried onions instead of butter/crumb mixture.
* **CRUMB-TOPPED CAULIFLOWER:** Substitute cauliflower for broccoli. My friend Seline adds 1 hard-cooked egg, finely chopped, to crumb mixture.

BROCCOLI & CAULIFLOWER A LA SUISSE

A delicious vegetable dish to serve with fish. The vegetables are partly cooked in the microwave, then the assembled dish is cooked conventionally to a beautiful golden color. Nice enough to serve to company.

¾ lb. broccoli
½ medium cauliflower
1 to 2 tbsp. water
3 eggs
1 ½ c. whipping cream (35%)
salt & pepper
dash of nutmeg
½ c. grated Swiss cheese
2 tbsp. grated Parmesan cheese

1. Trim broccoli and cauliflower. Cut up into florets; reserve broccoli stems for another use. Arrange broccoli and cauliflower in alternating circles in a lightly greased 10″ ceramic quiche dish, with the larger florets towards the outside of the dish. Sprinkle with water. Cover with waxed paper or a damp paper towel.

2. **MW on HIGH for 6 to 7 minutes,** until tender-crisp, rotating dish ¼ turn halfway through cooking. Let stand covered for 2 minutes. Drain excess liquid. Uncover.

3. Beat eggs. Blend in cream and seasonings. Pour mixture over broccoli and cauliflower. Sprinkle with cheeses. (May be prepared in advance up to this point and refrigerated for 6 to 8 hours, if desired.) Preheat conventional oven to 400°F or combination oven to 375°F.

4. **Bake conventionally or on the CONVECTION CYCLE for 20 to 25 minutes,** until mixture is set and nicely browned.

Yield: 6 to 8 servings.

* **Variation:** Substitute a 10 oz. pkg. frozen spinach or 1 lb. sliced zucchini. No extra water should be added. In Step 2, **MW covered for 4 to 5 minutes,** until tender-crisp. Continue as directed in Step 3.

WHOLE CAULIFLOWER AU GRATIN

So easy. Cook the cauliflower whole for a pretty presentation.

1 medium to large cauliflower
Cheese Sauce (p. 85)
paprika to garnish

2 c. cooked broccoli florets or 10 oz. pkg. frozen mixed vegetables (p. 243), if desired*

1. Leave cauliflower whole. Trim away leaves and hollow out centre core slightly. This helps the cauliflower cook evenly in the centre. Weigh after trimming. Rinse with cold water but do not dry. Place on a microsafe serving plate and wrap in cooking parchment or waxed paper.

2. MW on HIGH, allowing 6 to 7 minutes per lb. for cooking time. **A medium cauliflower will take about 8 to 10 minutes to cook; a large cauliflower will take 10 to 12 minutes.** Rotate the plate ¼ turn halfway through the cooking time. Let stand covered for 4 to 5 minutes while you prepare the sauce.

3. Drain any liquid from cauliflower. Top with sauce. Sprinkle lightly with paprika. If desired, surround with a border of cooked mixed vegetables or broccoli florets*.

Yield: 4 servings.

* **Two cups of broccoli florets, covered, will take about 3 minutes on HIGH.** Rinse with cold water; do not drain. Use a 4 cup microsafe bowl or casserole and cover with vented plastic wrap or casserole lid.
* A 10 oz. pkg. of frozen mixed vegetables also makes a pretty border. It will take **6 minutes on HIGH.** It can be cooked during the standing time for the cauliflower. Undercook cauliflower slightly and let it stand covered while you prepare the mixed vegetables. They will both be hot at serving time.
* Cheese sauce can be prepared first. If tightly covered after cooking, it will still be hot when the vegetables have completed their standing time. If necessary, you can always microwave it for a minute or two to reheat.
* Cauliflower can also be broken up into flowerets. Place larger pieces towards the outside of the cooking dish. Cooking time will be slightly faster.

CAULIFLOWER POLONAISE

Prepare Cauliflower au Gratin as directed above. During standing time, **MW 1 tbsp. butter on HIGH for 30 seconds,** until melted. Stir in ⅓ c. seasoned bread crumbs. **MW on HIGH for 30 to 45 seconds,** until hot. Sprinkle over sauce-topped cauliflower.

IT'S THYME TO COOK CARROTS!

1 lb. carrots, scraped & trimmed
¼ c. water
½ tsp. salt
⅛ tsp. pepper
¼ tsp. thyme*
½ tsp. lemon juice
1 tbsp. butter or margarine

1. **Grater:** Place carrots crosswise in feed tube. Grate, using medium pressure. Place in a 1 quart round microsafe casserole. Add remaining ingredients except butter and mix well. Place butter in the centre. (This will help the carrots cook evenly.) Cover with casserole lid or vented plastic wrap.

2. **MW covered on HIGH for 6 to 7 minutes,** until tender. Stir halfway through cooking. Let stand covered for 3 or 4 minutes.

Yield: 4 to 6 servings.

* If you don't like thyme, this recipe is equally delicious if you substitute ½ tsp. dried dill weed or 1 tsp. minced fresh dill.
* If carrots are sliced instead of grated, cooking time will be increased to **7 to 8 minutes per lb.**
* 1 lb. yields 3 cups of sliced or grated carrots.
* **2 cups grated or sliced carrots (3 to 4 servings) will cook in about 5 minutes.**

QUICK & CREAMY CARROTS

This recipe was given to me at a wedding dinner by the young lady sitting next to me. Pat Smith was a new microwaver, but she was already experimenting at adapting old favorites. The bride, Chantal Briggs, makes her version of this recipe with tarragon.

4 tbsp. butter
1 tsp. sugar
3 c. sliced carrots
¼ c. water
3 tbsp. sour cream
½ tsp. dried dill or tarragon
salt & pepper
1 tbsp. chopped parsley

1. Combine 1 tbsp. of the butter with sugar, carrots and water in a 1 quart round microsafe casserole. Mix well. Cover with vented plastic wrap or casserole lid and **MW on HIGH for 7 minutes,** until tender, stirring at half time. Let stand covered for 3 minutes. Drain.

2. Add remaining butter, sour cream and seasonings. Stir well. **MW uncovered on MEDIUM (50%) for 45 to 60 seconds,** just until heated through. Do not boil or sour cream will separate. Sprinkle with parsley.

Yield: 4 servings.

GLAZED CARROTS

1 lb. carrots, peeled & grated
¼ c. water
salt & pepper
¼ c. brown sugar, lightly packed
½ tsp. cinnamon
1 tsp. Dijon mustard
2 tsp. butter or margarine
1 tbsp. cornstarch dissolved in 2 tbsp. cold water

1. Place carrots in a 1 quart round microsafe casserole. You should have about 3 cups. Add water, salt, pepper, brown sugar, cinnamon and mustard and mix well. Cover and **MW on HIGH for 7 minutes,** until tender, stirring once during cooking.

2. Add butter and cornstarch mixture. Mix well. **MW uncovered on HIGH 2 minutes longer,** until thickened, stirring once.

Yield: 4 servings. Can be frozen.

* **To double the recipe, cook carrots for 12 to 14 minutes in Step 1.** Use a 2 quart casserole. Cooking time in Step 2 will not change.

PINEAPPLE GLAZED CARROTS

14 oz. can pineapple chunks, packed in its own juice
2 lb. carrots, peeled, trimmed & sliced
½ tsp. salt
¼ tsp. pepper
½ c. honey
2 tbsp. cornstarch
1 tbsp. butter, margarine or oil

1. Drain pineapple, reserving ¾ cup juice. Combine ½ cup of the juice with sliced carrots, salt, pepper and honey in a 2 ½ quart microsafe casserole. Mix well. Cover with casserole lid or vented plastic wrap.

2. **MW on HIGH for 16 to 18 minutes,** stirring once or twice. Carrots should be almost tender.

3. Blend cornstarch with remaining ¼ cup pineapple juice. Stir into carrots along with drained pineapple chunks and butter. (May be prepared in advance up to this point and refrigerated until serving time.)

4. Cover and **MW on HIGH for 4 to 6 minutes,** until heated through and thickened, stirring once or twice. (Time is slightly longer if carrots were refrigerated.) Let stand covered for 5 minutes.

Yield: 8 servings. May be frozen.

SWEET & SPICY CARROTS

- 1 lb. carrots, peeled & trimmed
- ½ c. ketchup
- ¼ c. honey
- ¼ c. orange marmalade
- ¼ tsp. each salt, pepper & garlic powder
- ¼ tsp. Worcestershire sauce
- ¼ tsp. chili powder
- 6 to 8 drops Tabasco sauce
- 2 tbsp. oil or margarine
- 3 tbsp. brown sugar

1. Grater: Cut carrots to fit crosswise in feed tube. Grate, using medium pressure. (You should have about 3 cups.) Combine with remaining ingredients in a round 1 ½ quart microsafe casserole. Mix well. Cover with casserole lid or vented plastic wrap.

2. MW on HIGH for 10 minutes, or until tender, stirring at half time. Let stand covered for 3 or 4 minutes. Stir and serve.

Yield: 4 servings. Freezes well.

CHAYOTE

Chayote (also known as mirliton or vegetable pear) is marvelous in the microwave because it gets too waterlogged when boiled in water conventionally. It is a member of the squash family.

Cooking Method #1

1. Pierce skin of chayote in several places with the point of a sharp knife. Wrap in waxed paper or parchment paper, twisting ends to seal. **MW on HIGH for 6 minutes,** turning it over at half time. Let stand covered for 2 minutes. Unwrap, cut in half and remove centre seed and white pith. Scoop out pulp. Mash pulp well; add butter, salt & pepper to taste.

Yield: 1 or 2 servings.

Cooking Method #2

Peel 3 chayotes; cut in half and remove seed and white pith. Cut chayotes in slices or cubes. Place in a 1 quart microsafe casserole (you should have about 2 cups). Sprinkle lightly with water; cover with casserole lid or vented plastic wrap. **MW on HIGH for 6 to 8 minutes,** until barely tender. Let stand covered for 2 minutes. Drain. Serve with butter, salt & pepper.

Yield: 4 servings.

* The seed is edible; it can be eaten either raw or cooked. Raw chayote is delicious when peeled, thinly sliced and mixed with 2 tbsp. oil, 2 tsp. lemon juice, 1 minced green onion, salt and pepper.
* The correct pronunciation is "cha-yo-tay". In the Caribbean, chayote is known as cho-cho.

CHAYOTE RATATOUILLE

This is a wonderful way to serve Chayote. The food processor makes quick work of preparing the veggies.

2 to 3 cloves garlic, crushed
2 medium onions, chopped
1 green pepper, chopped
1 red pepper, chopped
2 tbsp. oil
2 chayotes, peeled & cut in 8ths
1 medium zucchini, ends trimmed
3 or 4 tomatoes, chopped
1 c. tomato sauce
1 tsp. salt
freshly ground pepper
½ tsp. basil
¼ tsp. oregano
½ tsp. sugar

1. Combine garlic, onions, peppers and oil in a 3 or 4 quart microsafe casserole or bowl. **MW uncovered on HIGH for 5 minutes.**

2. Remove centre seed and white pith from chayotes. Slice chayotes and zucchini. (Zucchini does not require peeling.) Add to casserole and cover with casserole lid or vented plastic wrap. **MW for 5 to 7 minutes on HIGH,** or until tender, stirring at half time.

3. Stir in tomatoes, tomato sauce and seasonings. **MW covered on HIGH 12 to 15 minutes longer,** or until vegetables are tender, stirring at half time. Let stand covered for 5 minutes. Adjust seasonings to taste. Serve hot or cold.

Yield: 8 to 10 servings. Freezes well.

* A 19 oz. can tomatoes can be used instead of fresh tomatoes and tomato sauce, if desired.
* For a thicker version, add a 5 ½ oz. can of tomato paste along with the tomatoes.
* Also delicious with sliced yellow crookneck squash. Add to casserole along with zucchini and chayotes. Cooking time in Step 2 will be **8 to 10 minutes.**
* This makes an excellent vegetarian sauce to serve over noodles or spaghetti. Try it over cooked spaghetti squash for a delicious diet dinner!

RATATOUILLE

If you have a food processor, use it to speed up preparation of the vegetables. Ratatouille makes an excellent vegetarian sauce to serve over noodles, rice, spaghetti or spaghetti squash.

3 to 4 cloves garlic, crushed
1 large onion, chopped
2 tbsp. oil
1 medium eggplant, peeled
1 green pepper, chopped
1 red pepper, chopped
2 medium zucchini, sliced
19 oz. can tomatoes, drained*
2 c. tomato sauce*
1 tsp. salt (or to taste)
freshly ground pepper
1 tbsp. fresh basil or 1 tsp. dried basil
¼ tsp. oregano
1 to 2 tsp. sugar (to taste)

1. Place garlic, onions and oil in a 5 quart Corning Ware™ casserole. **MW uncovered on HIGH for 4 minutes,** until tender.

2. Cut eggplant in long, narrow strips. Cut crosswise into 1″ chunks. Add eggplant, peppers and zucchini to casserole. **Cover and MW for 10 minutes on HIGH,** stirring once or twice. Mixture will almost fill casserole before cooking, but will reduce in volume.

3. Add remaining ingredients. **MW covered on HIGH 10 to 15 minutes longer,** or until vegetables are desired tenderness. Stir once or twice. Adjust seasonings to taste. Serve hot or cold.

Yield: 10 to 12 servings. Freezes well. Can be kept in the refrigerator up to 1 week.

* Four large, fresh tomatoes may be substituted for canned tomatoes, if desired.
* For a thicker version, substitute a 5 ½ oz. can of tomato paste for the tomato sauce. Add a little water or red wine if mixture is too thick for your liking.
* Use Ratatouille instead of tomato sauce when making lasagna. Also delicious as a filling for Crêpes (p. 128).
* Ethel Cherry of Toronto adds ½ c. each of sliced celery and mushrooms to the garlic and onions. She adds a 19 oz. can of drained chick peas or kidney beans in Step 3 (be sure to push chick peas or kidney beans under the cooking liquid).
* **TOFU & RATATOUILLE:** Evita Smordin of Winnipeg adds tofu, cut in ½″ chunks, to Ratatouille for an excellent vegetarian variation. **MW on HIGH for 1 to 2 minutes,** just until tofu is heated through. Allow ¾ c. tofu per person.
* **RATATOUILLE AU GRATIN: MW 1 cup Ratatouille in a microsafe casserole on HIGH uncovered for 2 minutes,** until hot. Stir. Top with 2 oz. sliced or grated Mozzerella cheese. **MW 1 minute longer on HIGH** to melt cheese. Enjoy! Great for dieters!
* **MEATBALL RATATOUILLE:** Dona Stefanatos adds cooked meatballs to leftover Ratatouille. **MW covered on MEDIUM (50%) for 12 to 15 minutes,** stirring occasionally. Drained canned chick peas, a dash of cumin and chili powder make this a tasty dish.

CORN ON THE COB

There are several methods of cooking corn in the microwave. All methods work well. Use a microsafe dinner plate or oblong microsafe casserole. Cooking time can vary, depending on size of corn and freshness.

Method 1: Leave the husks on to act as a natural cover for the corn. I usually remove the silk (my mother doesn't)! Rinse corn under cold water and shake off excess moisture. Recover with husks. Arrange on plate or in casserole. (Cooking time is a few seconds longer because the husks absorb some of the microwave energy.)

Method 2: Remove husks and silk. Rinse corn under cold water and shake off excess moisture. Arrange on plate or in casserole and use waxed paper or moistened cooking parchment as the covering.

Method 3: Remove husks and silk. Rinse corn under cold water and shake off excess moisture. Use waxed paper, plastic wrap, cooking parchment or a double layer of microwave paper towelling to wrap each individual cob. Twist ends like a firecracker to seal. (If using paper towelling, fold ends under; hold under running water to moisten; gently press out excess water.) Arrange corn on plate or in casserole.

To Cook: MW on HIGH, allowing 2 to 3 minutes per ear of corn. Re-arrange corn at half time. (I allow 2 to 2½ minutes if cooking one ear of corn (depending on size) and 2 minutes per ear if cooking 4 or more.) Let stand covered 2 to 3 minutes to complete cooking. Unwrap, brush with butter and sprinkle with salt and pepper.

* A neat way to butter the corn is to butter slices of bread, wrap bread around corn and rotate corn to coat with butter.
* Frozen corn on the cob does not need defrosting before microwaving. Place frozen corn in a microsafe casserole, cover with vented plastic wrap and cook on **HIGH for 3 to 4 minutes per cob.**
* **BBQ Corn:** MW corn on **HIGH for 2 minutes per ear,** then unwrap carefully and and transfer immediately to the hot BBQ. Grill for several minutes, turning often, to acquire that just-roasted flavor.

EGGPLANT & ASPARAGUS CASSEROLE

Louise Azzizi served this luscious eggplant casserole at a Mother's Day lunch for the family. She got the recipe from her friend Eva Marks, and I adapted it for the microwave because I liked it so much.

2 lb. eggplant, peeled & thinly sliced
1 medium onion, chopped
2 tbsp. oil
2 c. sliced mushrooms
10 oz. can cream of mushroom soup
¾ c. mayonnaise
½ c. milk
½ tsp. Tabasco sauce
¼ tsp. each salt & pepper
14 oz. can asparagus spears, drained
1 c. grated Swiss cheese
¼ c. toasted bread crumbs

1. Arrange eggplant slices in an ungreased 3 quart oval or rectangular microsafe casserole, with the larger slices towards the outside of the dish. Cover with waxed paper and **MW on HIGH for 6 minutes.** Turn eggplant over and re-arrange, placing more cooked slices towards the centre. Cover and **MW 4 to 6 minutes longer,** or until tender. Let stand covered for 5 minutes. Drain excess liquid.

2. Combine onion and oil in an 1 quart microsafe bowl. **MW uncovered on HIGH for 3 minutes.** Stir in mushrooms. **MW on HIGH 3 minutes longer,** until tender. Cool slightly.

3. Combine mushroom soup, mayonnaise, milk, Tabasco sauce and seasonings in a large mixing bowl. Mix well with a whisk, until smooth.

4. Remove eggplant from casserole. Spread half of sauce mixture to cover the bottom of the casserole. Arrange eggplant in a layer over sauce. Top with asparagus, onions and mushrooms. Add remaining sauce and spread evenly. Cover with a piece of cooking parchment directly on the surface. Can be prepared up to this point and refrigerated until serving time.

5. MW covered on MEDIUM-HIGH (70%) for 18 to 20 minutes, rotating casserole ½ turn halfway through cooking. (If refrigerated, cooking time will be 20 to 25 minutes.) When done, sauce should be bubbling and bottom of casserole dish should be hot in the centre. Uncover; sprinkle with cheese and crumbs. **MW uncovered on HIGH 2 to 3 minutes longer,** just until cheese melts. Let stand 5 minutes before serving.

Yield: 8 to 10 servings. Do not freeze.

* Casserole can be prepared a day or two ahead and refrigerated. To reheat, cover with waxed paper and **MW on HIGH for 5 minutes.** Rotate casserole ¼ turn. **MW covered on MEDIUM (50%) for 15 to 18 minutes,** or until bottom of casserole dish is hot in the centre, rotating casserole ¼ turn halfway through cooking.

EGGPLANT PARMESAN

1 large eggplant (1 ½ lb.)
2 c. tomato sauce
salt, pepper, basil, oregano & garlic powder
⅔ c. grated Parmesan cheese
½ lb. Mozzerella cheese, grated

1. Cut eggplant in half lengthwise. Slice crosswise into ¼″ slices.* Spoon about ⅓ of the tomato sauce in bottom of 7″ x 11″ microsafe casserole. Arrange half of eggplant over sauce. Sprinkle lightly with seasonings. Sprinkle with half the Parmesan cheese. Repeat once again with sauce, remaining eggplant, seasonings and Parmesan cheese. Top with remaining sauce. Cover with waxed paper, then with microsafe plastic wrap, turning back one corner slightly to vent.

2. MW covered on HIGH for 10 to 12 minutes, rotating casserole ¼ turn halfway through cooking. Eggplant should be tender when pierced in the centre of the casserole with the point of a knife.

3. Uncover eggplant and sprinkle with cheese. **MW uncovered on HIGH for 2 to 3 minutes longer,** just until cheese is melted. Let stand uncovered 3 to 4 minutes. Serve with a Caesar Salad and crusty rolls.

Yield: 6 servings.

* If you have the time, eggplant slices can be sprinkled lightly with salt, placed on a baking sheet and weighed down with another baking sheet. This removes any excess liquid and bitter juices. Let stand for 15 to 20 minutes. Rinse well and pat dry before continuing with recipe.

BRAISED FENNEL

If you like licorice, you'll love fennel!

1 large or 2 medium heads fennel (about 1 ¼ lb.)
1 onion, chopped
2 tbsp. margarine
¼ c. chopped parsley
¼ c. chicken broth
salt & pepper

1. Trim stems from fennel; peel the tough bottoms and cut away any dry or discolored stalks. Chop the fronds and reserve. Cut fennel into thin slices.

2. Combine onion with margarine in a 1 ½ quart microsafe casserole. **MW uncovered on HIGH for 2 minutes,** until tender-crisp. Add fennel, parsley and chicken broth. Cover with casserole lid or vented plastic wrap.

3. MW on HIGH for 6 to 8 minutes, just until tender, stirring at half time. Let stand covered for 1 or 2 minutes. Season with salt & pepper. Garnish with reserved fronds.

Yield: 4 servings.

DO-AHEAD GARLIC

1. Separate 2 or 3 heads of garlic into cloves. Place on a cutting board and smash with the flat side of a chef's knife. Discard peel. Process garlic on the **Steel Knife** of your food processor until finely minced, scraping down sides of bowl as necessary. Transfer to a small glass jar, cover completely with a layer of vegetable oil and refrigerate. Keeps about a month in the fridge.

THE GREAT GARLIC TRICK

When you need a large quantity of garlic for recipes where it will be cooked with the other ingredients, this technique is wonderful. Don't use it in recipes where the garlic is not cooked (e.g. in salad dressings), because it loses some of its pungency.

1. Cut the top off 1 head of garlic with a sharp knife, exposing the cut cloves. Place 1 tsp. water in a small microsafe dish. Place garlic cut-side up in dish. **MW uncovered on HIGH for 30 seconds.** Turn garlic over and **MW on HIGH 30 seconds longer.** Let stand for 1 minute. Separate into cloves. Hold clove from the uncut end and squeeze gently; the garlic will pop out!

* To remove the smell of garlic from your hands, rub them with lemon juice and salt.
* To freshen your breath after eating garlic, eat a sprig or two of fresh parsley. (The other alternative is to only eat with people who enjoy garlic as much as you do!)

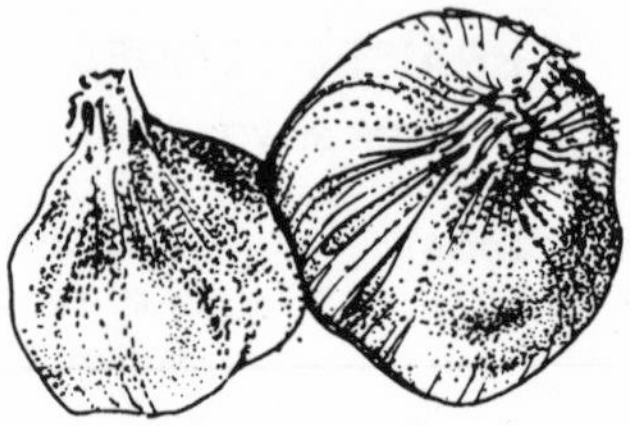

DO-AHEAD GINGER

1. Peel ginger root with a vegetable parer. Cut in 1″ chunks. Process on the **Steel Knife** of the food processor until finely minced, scraping down sides of bowl as necessary. Transfer to a small glass jar, cover completely with a layer of cooking sherry and refrigerate. Keeps about 2 months in the fridge, as long as it is completely covered by the sherry. The sherry can be used in cooking. Just add more sherry to the ginger to replace what you have used.

HERBS

Many people dry herbs in their microwave oven. However, this is no longer recommended because there have been many cases where the herbs have caught on fire. I use the following method to freeze basil from my garden which was developed by cookbook author Paula Wolfert for coriander. It's great!

3 c. fresh herbs (basil, mint, coriander)
2 c. water

1. Wash herbs very well. Drain; cut off any tough stems. Process herbs with water on the **Steel Knife** until finely minced, about 30 to 45 seconds. Mixture will look like thick slush. Spoon into ice cube trays. Freeze until solid. Transfer to freezer containers, cover tightly and label.

* **To thaw: 1 "herb cube" takes 25 to 30 seconds on HIGH.** Each cube equals 2 tbsp. fresh or 2 tsp. dried herbs.
* Lucinda Halbrook cleans fresh tarragon or basil, then puts it in a jar covered with oil. (She likes to use cold-pressed olive oil, but any vegetable oil will do.) It will keep for several months in the refrigerator. Drain herbs before using. The herb-flavored oil is excellent for salad dressings.
* Use 1 tbsp. fresh herbs for 1 tsp. dried.

SWEET & SOUR LENTILS

1 c. lentils
2 cloves garlic, minced
1 large onion, chopped
1 green pepper, seeded & chopped
2 tbsp. oil
2 c. water
½ c. chili sauce
½ tsp. salt
freshly ground pepper
3 tbsp. brown sugar

1. Soak lentils according to method for Quick Soaking of Dried Peas, Beans & Lentils (p. 70). Rinse and drain well in a colander.

2. Combine garlic, onions and peppers with oil in an 8 cup microsafe bowl. **MW uncovered on HIGH for 4 minutes,** until tender. Add remaining ingredients; cover with vented plastic wrap.

3. **MW on HIGH for 15 minutes. Stir. Reduce power to MEDIUM (50%) and simmer for 45 minutes,** or until lentils are fairly tender, stirring occasionally. (Use a chopstick to stir the lentils through the vented opening.) Let stand covered until cool. Refrigerate. Lentils will be tastier and more tender the next day.

Yield: 6 servings.

To reheat: MW covered on MEDIUM-HIGH (70%) for 8 to 10 minutes, or until bubbling hot, stirring once or twice.

MIXED VEGETABLE PLATTER

No stirring or rearranging of vegetables is necessary if you arrange the longer cooking vegetables towards the outside of the platter and the quicker cooking ones towards the centre. So pretty!

2 c. cauliflower florets
2 c. broccoli florets
2 c. sliced carrots
2 c. sliced zucchini
1 c. medium mushrooms
2 tbsp. water
3 tbsp. butter or margarine
1 tbsp. minced fresh parsley
1 tbsp. minced fresh dill
1 tbsp. lemon juice
salt & pepper, to taste

1. Arrange cauliflower florets in a ring around the outside edge of a 12″ round microsafe serving platter. Repeat with broccoli florets, then with carrot slices, then with zucchini; fill centre of platter with the mushrooms. Sprinkle vegetables with water.

2. Cover with microsafe plastic wrap, turning back one corner slightly to vent. **MW on HIGH for 7 to 9 minutes,** until tender-crisp, rotating the dish ¼ turn halfway through cooking. Let stand covered while you prepare the butter mixture.

3. Place butter in a 1 cup glass measure. **MW uncovered on HIGH for 30 to 40 seconds,** until melted. Stir in parsley, dill and lemon juice.

4. Carefully drain water from the vegetable platter. Uncover vegetables and drizzle with butter mixture. Sprinkle with salt and pepper. Serve immediately.

Yield: 6 to 8 servings.

* **For 4 servings:** A dinner-sized plate of vegetables will take **5 to 7 minutes on HIGH** to microwave. An ideal cover is an inverted glass pie plate. Let stand covered for 1 or 2 minutes before serving.
* Vegetables can be varied according to what is in season. Just remember to arrange the longer cooking vegetables towards the outer edge of the dish.
* **Variation:** Arrange tomato wedges around outer edge of platter in Step 4; **MW uncovered on HIGH 2 minutes longer,** just until heated through. Drizzle with butter mixture, salt & pepper; serve immediately.
* If you are watching your calories, omit butter; drizzle vegetables with lemon juice and herbs.
* Soya sauce or teriyaki sauce can be used to moisten vegetables instead of water. Season with minced garlic, ginger and a dash of dry mustard.
* If you aren't watching your calories, vegetables can be topped with Hollandaise (p. 87) or Cheese Sauce (p. 85)!

COOKIE'S VEGETABLE MEDLEY

My sister Cookie (whose real name is Rhonda) shared her recipe for this easy, colorful vegetarian dish. The vegetables can vary. Cookie's comment is "Use the most of the ones you like the most."

½ tsp. minced garlic
1 tbsp. margarine
1 onion, cut in chunks
2 carrots, thinly sliced
1 c. cauliflower florets
1 green pepper, cut in chunks
1 red pepper, cut in chunks
2 zucchini, thinly sliced (do not peel)
1 c. small whole mushrooms
2 c. chow mein noodles
2 tomatoes, cut in wedges
freshly ground black pepper
¼ c. grated Parmesan cheese

1. Combine garlic, margarine and onion in a 2 quart round microsafe casserole. **MW uncovered on HIGH for 2 minutes,** until onion is tender-crisp.

2. Stir in carrots and cauliflower; cover with casserole lid or a microsafe plate. **MW covered on HIGH for 3 minutes,** until tender-crisp. Shake casserole back and forth with a tossing motion to mix vegetables. (Hold firmly onto lid so it doesn't fall off!)

3. Uncover and add peppers, zucchini and mushrooms. **MW covered on HIGH 4 minutes longer,** stir-shaking vegetables at half time.

4. Stir in noodles. Add tomatoes and black pepper; mix gently. Sprinkle with Parmesan cheese. **MW covered on HIGH 2 minutes longer,** until heated through. Serve immediately.

Yield: 4 to 6 servings.

* Cheese topping can be browned under the broiler for 3 or 4 minutes in Step 4, but use a microwavable and broilerproof dish to cook the vegetables.
* **TOFU VEGETABLE MEDLEY:** Omit Parmesan cheese. Add 2 c. tofu, cut in 1″ squares, and ¼ c. soya sauce along with chow mein noodles and pepper in Step 4. **MW covered on HIGH for 2 minutes,** until heated through.
* Cooked pasta or rice can be used instead of chow mein noodles.

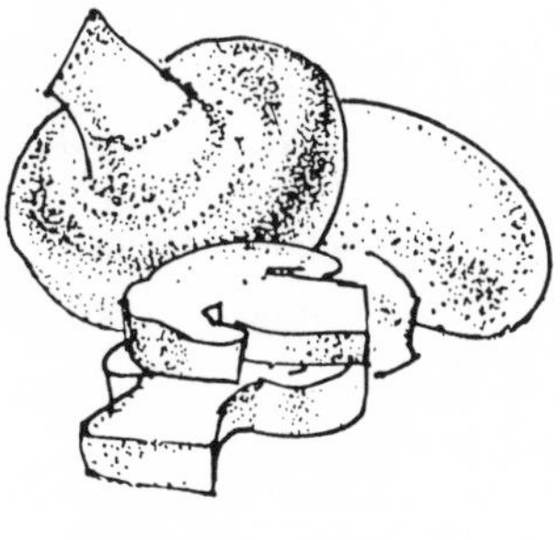

BEV'S VEGGIES FOR A CROWD

This easy vegetable casserole comes from Bev Binder of Winnipeg. If we lived in the same city, we would probably spend half the day concocting recipes and the other half eating them! Bev is most generous with her recipes and cooking tips and is a wonderful cook, baker and very special friend.

2 - 10 oz. pkgs. frozen cauliflower
1 - 10 oz. pkg. frozen broccoli
17 oz. can creamed corn
16 oz. can corn niblets
½ lb. Swiss cheese, grated
10 oz. can cream of celery soup
¼ lb. sliced mushrooms
4 slices rye bread
2 tbsp. butter or margarine

1. Slash top of packages of cauliflower and broccoli. Stack cauliflower packages one on top of the other on a microsafe plate. **MW on HIGH for 5 minutes.** Switch places, moving the package on the top to the bottom and vice versa. Rotate plate ¼ turn. **MW on HIGH 3 to 5 minutes longer,** until a knife can pass easily through the centre of the packages. Let stand covered for 3 minutes.

2. **MW broccoli on HIGH for 5 to 6 minutes,** turning package ¼ turn halfway through cooking. Let stand covered for 3 minutes. Cut into chunks.

3. In a very large mixing bowl, combine vegetables, cheese, soup and mushrooms. Mix gently but thoroughly. Spread evenly in a lightly greased 9″ x 13″ microsafe casserole. Cover with waxed paper.

4. **MW on MEDIUM-HIGH (70%) for 15 to 18 minutes,** until bubbling; the centre bottom of the casserole dish should be hot to the touch. Meanwhile, prepare crumb topping. Tear bread into chunks. Process on the **Steel Knife** for 30 seconds. Add butter and process 15 to 20 seconds longer, or until coarse crumbs are formed. You should have about 2 cups.

5. Sprinkle casserole with crumb mixture. Bake in conventional oven or on **CONVECTION CYCLE at 400°F for 10 to 15 minutes,** until topping is golden and crisp. (No preheating is necessary.) Let stand 10 minutes before serving.

Yield: 12 servings.

* Can be prepared ahead and refrigerated, but microwave time in Step 4 will be slightly longer, about **18 to 20 minutes.**
* Casserole can be microwaved ahead of time and reheated at serving time, but topping will not be as crisp. To reheat refrigerated cooked casserole, **MW uncovered on HIGH for 5 minutes.** Rotate casserole ½ turn. **MW on MEDIUM (50%) for 8 to 10 minutes,** until bottom centre of casserole is hot to the touch. If desired, place in a **400°F oven for 10 minutes** to crisp the top.
* Fresh cauliflower and broccoli can be used instead of frozen.

MICRO-WAYS WITH POTATOES

- **Potatoes should not be stored in the refrigerator,** or the starch will convert to sugar. Store in a cool, dark place, with good ventilation (no plastic bag, please). Don't store potatoes next to onions.
- **Cut away any green portions** before cooking; they are extremely bitter.
- **An average potato** weighs about 7 oz. (almost ½ lb.) and **takes about 4 minutes on HIGH to cook. Four potatoes weigh 1 ½ to 1 ¾ lb. and take 10 to 12 minutes (calculate 6 to 7 minutes per lb.)** A scale will help you choose the correct timing.
- **Potatoes must be pierced** all over with a fork so steam can escape. Dry very well.
- **Try to choose potatoes** that are similar in size and shape for even cooking. A fat round potato takes longer to cook than a long, narrow one. Place smaller potatoes in the centre.
- **A microsafe rack** prevents potatoes from becoming soggy. If your microwave has a shelf, it can be used instead.
- **Test for Doneness:** Potato will be almost tender, but the centre will offer a bit of resistance when pierced with a knife.
- **Smaller potatoes cook more quickly,** so remove them from the microwave first.
- **Do not overcook.** If you microwave them until they are soft, the skins will be wrinkled after standing time.
- **If some potatoes are not soft** after standing time, **MW on HIGH 30 to 60 seconds per potato.**
- **A clean dishtowel** is perfect for keeping baked potatoes hot. It also keeps the skins dry. Don't wrap baked potatoes in tinfoil or skins will steam and become soggy.
- **Potatoes will stay hot for ½ hour** if wrapped in a towel; use this time to microwave the remainder of your meal. If necessary, reheat potatoes briefly.
- **For crusty skins, bake potatoes for 10 minutes in a 400°F oven** or toaster oven. (They're also great on the BBQ!)
- **If you have more than 8 potatoes,** bake them conventionally.
- **Idaho potatoes** are excellent for baking and stuffing.
- **POTATO TOPPERS:** Cooked broccoli, cauliflower, sautéed onions &/or mushrooms, tuna, etc., make tasty toppings. If desired, drizzle hot Cheese Sauce (p. 85) over potatoes. So good!

SWEET POTATOES/YAMS

- **The variety of sweet potato** known as the yam in North America has a deep orange flesh, reddish brown skin and is actually a sweeter sweet potato. The variety called sweet potato has a paler skin and its flesh is golden yellow.
- **Follow the same guidelines** for preparation as for potatoes. However, when done, sweet potatoes should be tender and offer no resistance when pierced with a knife.
- **Overcooking may occur** on the pointed ends. Just cut away and discard any hard, overcooked portions.
- **Mash pulp** and mix with butter, orange juice, brown sugar and a dash of cinnamon. A splash of rum can't hurt!

BAKED POTATOES

4 medium baking potatoes (about 1 ½ lb.)

1. Read Micro-Ways with Potatoes (p. 269). Scrub potatoes; pierce skin in several places with a fork. Dry well. Arrange in a circle 1″ apart on a microsafe rack, with the narrow ends pointing inwards.

2. **MW uncovered on HIGH for 6 minutes.** Turn potatoes over and rearrange. **MW on HIGH 4 to 6 minutes longer,** until almost tender when pierced with a sharp knife.

3. Remove potatoes from microwave and wrap in a towel. Let stand covered for 5 minutes. They will finish cooking during standing time.

Yield: 4 servings.

STUFFED BAKED POTATOES (STUFFED SPUDS)

This recipe is dedicated to Marty Putz (Yes folks, that's his real name), a very funny young comedian from Toronto. His favorite food is potatoes, so I promised to dedicate a recipe in my book to him. He gets rave reviews wherever he performs, and if you make this recipe, you will too!

4 Baked Potatoes (above)
¼ c. butter or margarine
⅓ c. sour cream, milk or yogourt
1 tsp. salt
⅛ tsp. pepper
½ c. grated Cheddar or Swiss cheese
2 tbsp. Parmesan cheese, if desired
4 green onions, minced
paprika to garnish

1. Prepare potatoes as directed. When cool enough to handle, cut potatoes in half lengthwise. Scoop out pulp, leaving a shell ¼″ thick.

2. Mash potato pulp. Combine with remaining ingredients and mix well. Restuff potato skins, using a pastry bag if you have one. Sprinkle with paprika. Line a microsafe serving platter with paper towels. Arrange potatoes in a circle 1″ apart. (May be prepared in advance up to this point.)

3. **MW uncovered on HIGH for 3 to 4 minutes (or 30 to 45 seconds per potato half),** until piping hot; rotate plate ¼ turn at half time. Serve immediately.

Yield: 4 to 6 servings. These freeze well.

* If potatoes are large, cooking time will be longer, about **12 to 14 minutes.**
* If the potato skins break when scooping out the pulp, no problem! Once they are stuffed, no one will know the difference.
* Stuffed Spuds can be browned briefly under a hot broiler, if desired.
* To freeze, arrange in a single layer and wrap well.
* **FROZEN STUFFED SPUDS:** No need to thaw; just heat and eat! Cover with waxed paper and **MW on HIGH, allowing 6 to 7 minutes per lb.** (4 to 6 stuffed potato halves weigh 1 lb.) Rearrange at half time. When done, the bottom of the plate will feel hot and a knife will pass through the centre of potatoes easily. If potatoes are hot, the knife should feel hot.

PIZZA POTATO SKINS

4 Baked Potatoes (p. 270)*
¾ c. pizza or tomato sauce
¼ c. chopped green pepper
¼ c. chopped mushrooms
1 c. grated Mozzerella cheese

1. Cut baked potatoes in half crosswise. Scoop out cooked potato and reserve for another use. Line a microsafe serving plate with paper towels. Arrange potato skins cut-side up in a circle. Brush each potato skin with 1 or 2 tbsp. pizza sauce. Sprinkle with chopped green pepper and mushrooms; top each one with 2 tbsp. grated Mozzerella cheese.

2. MW uncovered on HIGH for 2½ to 3 minutes (or 30 to 45 seconds per potato skin), just until cheese is melted. Rotate plate ¼ turn halfway through cooking.

Yield: 8 portions (2 to 4 servings, depending on who's eating!)

* If making half the recipe, 2 potatoes will take **6 to 7 minutes on HIGH** to bake.

* Cooked potato from skins can be used to make Dill-Icious Potato Salad (p.278).

* For a crispy skin on potatoes, they require baking in a conventional oven **(or on the CONVECTION CYCLE) at 400°F for 12 to 15 minutes.**

PIZZA POTATO ROUNDS

So easy, yet so good! This will become a family favorite.

2 medium potatoes, unpeeled
¼ c. pizza sauce
¾ c. grated Mozzerella cheese
2 tbsp. grated Parmesan cheese

1. Wash potatoes; dry well. Slice ⅜″ thick. Arrange in a single layer in a large microsafe serving casserole, placing the smaller slices in the centre of the dish. Cover with plastic wrap, turning back one corner slightly to vent.

2. MW on HIGH for 5 to 7 minutes, until tender, rotating platter ¼ turn halfway through cooking. Uncover carefully with the steam vent away from you. Brush each potato slice with pizza sauce. Top with Mozzerella cheese. Sprinkle lightly with Parmesan cheese.

3. MW uncovered on HIGH for 1 to 2 minutes, just until cheese melts.

Yield: 2 servings.

* **NACHO POTATO ROUNDS:** Use salsa or taco sauce instead of pizza sauce. Use Monterey Jack &/or Cheddar cheese instead of Mozzerella and Parmesan cheeses.

YUM-YUM POTATO WEDGIES

Crusty outside, fluffy inside, the best of both worlds with a combination of microwave and conventional cooking!

4 med. baking potatoes (about 1 ¾ lb.)
1 to 2 tbsp. oil
salt, pepper, paprika & garlic powder

1. Do not peel potatoes, but scrub well. Cut each potato lengthwise into 4 wedges. Rinse, but do not dry. Rub oil and seasonings on all surfaces. Arrange in a single layer in a lightly greased oblong Pyrex™ casserole. Preheat conventional oven to 400°F.

2. **MW potatoes uncovered on HIGH for 10 minutes,** until crisp-tender, stirring at half time.

3. **Bake uncovered at 400°F for 15 to 20 minutes,** turning occasionally, until brown and crispy. (Potatoes can also be browned in a combination oven on the **CONVECTION CYCLE at 400°F for 15 to 20 minutes.** No preheating is necessary. Place casserole on rack recommended by oven manufacturer.)

Yield: 4 servings.

* Potatoes can be cut in rounds instead of wedges, if desired. Microwave cooking time will be slightly faster.

PARMESAN POTATO SLICES

4 med. baking potatoes (1 ¾ lb.)
2 tbsp. butter
salt, pepper, paprika & garlic powder
⅓ c. grated Parmesan cheese

1. Do not peel potatoes, but scrub well. Cut each potato into thick slices. Rinse, but do not dry. Arrange in a single layer in a lightly greased oblong Pyrex™ casserole. Cover with plastic wrap, turning back one corner slightly to vent.

2. **MW covered on HIGH for 10 to 12 minutes,** until tender, shaking casserole back and forth at half time to mix potatoes. Uncover carefully. Mix potatoes with butter, seasonings and Parmesan cheese. **MW uncovered 2 minutes longer**, stirring once, until piping hot.

Yield: 2 to 4 servings, depending on who's eating!

"BOILED" POTATOES

One of my students, a brand new microwaver, was sure that the cookbook which came with her oven must have accidentally omitted the water in its recipe for boiled potatoes, so she added enough water to cover them completely. Needless to say, they took forever to cook! This method is much quicker.

5 to 6 medium potatoes, peeled & cut in chunks
2 tbsp. water

1. Weigh potatoes after peeling; allow 5 minutes per lb. as your cooking time. (You should have about 1 ¾ to 2 lb., about 4 cups.) Place in a 1 quart round microsafe casserole. Sprinkle lightly with water.

2. Cover with casserole lid. **MW on HIGH for 5 minutes.** Shake casserole back and forth with a tossing motion to mix potatoes. (Hold firmly onto lid so it doesn't fall off!) **MW on HIGH 4 to 5 minutes longer.** Potatoes should be tender when pierced with a knife. Let stand covered 5 minutes. Uncover and drain off any excess liquid.

Yield: 4 to 6 servings.

* Three or four potatoes, cut in chunks, take **6 to 8 minutes on HIGH** to microwave. If you are cooking for 1 or 2, store any extras in the refrigerator. Leftovers are delicious pan-fried in hot oil in a skillet on your rangetop.

MASHED POTATOES

Boiled Potatoes (above)
½ c. sour cream, milk or yogurt
2 to 3 tbsp. butter or margarine
salt & pepper, to taste

1. Cook potatoes as directed. Mash with a potato masher or put through a ricer. Potatoes should be smooth and lump-free. Add sour cream, butter and seasonings; beat well.

Yield: 4 to 6 servings.

* The late Bert Greene, author of one of my favorite cookbooks, "Greene on Greens", recommends using low-starch or waxy new varieties for mashed potatoes. Baking potatoes tend to remain lumpy and old, and high-starch potatoes turn gluey and thick.
* For a light texture, I sometimes add ½ tsp. baking powder to mashed potatoes.

CHEESY SCALLOPED POTATOES

This recipe takes 1 hour and 15 minutes in the conventional oven! Sauce and potatoes are cooked in the same casserole, saving on clean-up.

3 tbsp. butter or margarine
3 tbsp. flour
1 ½ c. milk
¾ tsp. salt
¼ tsp. pepper
½ tsp. dry mustard
1 c. Cheddar cheese, grated
4 to 5 large potatoes, peeled (4 c. sliced)
1 onion, sliced (optional)
paprika to garnish

1. Place butter and flour in a 2 quart round microsafe casserole or soufflé dish. **MW uncovered on HIGH for 1 minute,** until butter is melted. Slowly blend in milk and seasonings. **MW uncovered on HIGH about 3 to 4 minutes,** stirring twice, until bubbling and thick. Stir in cheese.

2. Add ½ of potatoes to casserole. Stir to coat with sauce. Add onion and remaining potatoes. Mix again. Build up sides and depress centre of potatoes slightly with the back of a spoon for more even cooking. Sprinkle with paprika.

3. Cover with casserole lid or vented plastic wrap. **MW on HIGH for 18 to 22 minutes,** rotating the casserole ¼ turn halfway through cooking. A knife inserted through the centre of the potatoes will find almost no resistance. Let stand covered for 5 minutes.

Yield: 4 to 6 servings. Do not freeze.

* **SWISS SCALLOPED POTATOES:** Substitute Swiss cheese instead of Cheddar cheese. Omit dry mustard; substitute ¼ tsp. nutmeg.
* **GOLDEN SCALLOPED POTATOES:** Substitute chicken stock for milk and dried dill for dry mustard. Omit cheese. If you observe the Jewish dietary laws, use pareve margarine.
* Leftover scalloped potatoes reheat well. **MW on HIGH, allowing 1 ½ minutes per cup** of refrigerated potatoes.
* Cooking time depends on quantity of potatoes used. Weigh potatoes after peeling. **1 ½ lb. potatoes will cook in about 16 to 18 minutes, 2 lb. will take 20 to 22 minutes.** Potatoes will continue to cook during standing time. Cooking time will be slightly longer if you add onion.
* To keep cooked potatoes hot while you are preparing the rest of your dinner, do not uncover. They will stay hot for at least 20 minutes. If you have used plastic wrap as a cover, place a dinner plate on top. Voila, plate will be warmed for your dinner!

SID'S SCALLOPED SPUDS

It used to take my friend Sid Bagel 1 ½ hours to cook this recipe conventionally. I showed him how to make it in the microwave in 25 minutes!

3 tbsp. butter
10 oz. can condensed cream of mushroom soup
⅓ c. milk
8 medium potatoes, peeled & sliced
salt & pepper, to taste
paprika to garnish

1. Place butter in a large microsafe bowl. **MW uncovered on HIGH for 45 seconds,** until melted. Blend in mushroom soup and milk. Add sliced potatoes. Sprinkle with salt and pepper; mix well. Spread mixture in an ungreased oblong Pyrex™ casserole. Push potato mixture slightly higher into the corners and depress the centre slightly. Sprinkle with paprika.
2. Cover with waxed paper, then with microsafe plastic wrap, turning back one corner slightly to vent. **MW on HIGH for 12 minutes.** Rotate casserole ½ turn. **MW on HIGH 12 to 14 minutes longer.** Test for doneness by piercing centre of potato mixture with a knife. It should pass through easily. If not, patch the plastic wrap with a fresh piece and **MW the casserole 2 or 3 minutes longer on HIGH.**
3. Let stand covered for 10 minutes. (If desired, omit standing time and bake the casserole in a conventional oven or on the **CONVECTION CYCLE** on rack recommended by oven manufacturer. **Bake uncovered at 400°F for 10 to 15 minutes,** until golden. No preheating is necessary.)

Yield: 8 servings.

QUICK POTATO & CARROT SCALLOP

Colorful, delicious and easy! It's worth every calorie.

6 oz. Swiss cheese
6 medium potatoes (about 2 lb.)
4 large carrots (2 c. sliced)
1 onion, halved
1 tsp. salt
freshly ground pepper
1 c. whipping cream (35%)
paprika to garnish

1. **Grater:** Grate cheese. Set aside. You should have 1 ½ cups.
2. **Slicer:** Slice potatoes, carrots and onion. Empty into a lightly greased 7″ x 11″ Pyrex™ casserole. Mix with seasonings. Spread fairly evenly, building up the corners slightly for more even cooking. Sprinkle cheese evenly over the top. Drizzle cream over cheese. Sprinkle with paprika. Cover with waxed paper, then with plastic wrap, turning back one corner slightly to vent.
3. **MW covered on HIGH for 18 to 20 minutes,** rotating casserole ½ turn halfway through cooking. Let stand covered for 5 minutes. A knife should pass easily through the centre of the casserole.

Yield: 4 to 6 servings.

* This dish reheats very well. **Allow 1 ½ minutes per cup on HIGH** if refrigerated. The complete casserole will reheat in about **5 to 7 minutes on MEDIUM-HIGH (70%).**
* Can be prepared up to ½ hour in advance and kept hot if tightly covered. If necessary, reheat briefly.
* **QUICK POTATO SCALLOP:** Follow recipe for Quick Potato & Carrot Scallop (above), but omit carrots and use 6 cups sliced potatoes. Also delicious if you substitute 1 thinly sliced leek for the onion.

POTATO PUDDING (KUGEL)

The microwave oven cooks the potato mixture quickly and makes a creamy-textured kugel; the conventional oven produces the crispy top.

6 medium potatoes, peeled
1 medium onion, halved
3 eggs
1 ¼ tsp. salt
¼ tsp. pepper
¼ c. oil
3 tbsp. flour or potato starch
2 tsp. oil to grease casserole
2 tbsp. cornflake or bread crumbs

1. Grater: Grate potatoes, using medium pressure. Measure 4 cups.

2. Steel Knife: Process onion until finely ground, about 6 to 8 seconds. Add grated potatoes, eggs, seasoning, oil and flour; process with 3 or 4 on/off turns, just until mixed. Do not overprocess or mixture will be too fine. Grease a 10″ ceramic quiche dish with oil; coat with crumbs. Spread potato mixture in dish, depressing the centre slightly. Cover with parchment paper or waxed paper, tucking ends under dish.

3. Elevate kugel on an inverted pie plate. **MW on HIGH for 15 minutes,** rotating dish ¼ turn twice during cooking. The kugel will be set and the edges will just begin to pull away from the sides of the dish.

4. Uncover and brush top of kugel lightly with oil. Bake uncovered in a preheated conventional oven or on the **CONVECTION CYCLE (not preheated) at 400°F for 12 to 15 minutes,** or until top is golden and crisp. If using **CONVECTION CYCLE,** place casserole on rack recommended by oven manufacturer.

Yield: 6 to 8 servings. May be frozen.

* For Passover, use ground soup nuts (mandlen) instead of cornflake crumbs to coat the quiche dish.
* If you use an oblong casserole dish, the kugel could overcook on the corners. If necessary, shield corners with flat pieces of aluminum foil for the last 5 minutes of cooking time in the microwave. Be sure to keep foil at least 1″ away from the walls of the oven.

POTATO ZUCCHINI KUGEL

The Italian Jewish Connection! This recipe was one of many shared with me by my friend Rhoda Gorin. She even gave me the zucchini to make it!

3 medium zucchini, unpeeled
2 large potatoes, peeled
3 eggs
1 tsp. salt
¼ tsp. pepper
⅛ tsp. each basil & oregano
⅓ c. matzo meal or bread crumbs
3 oz. can French fried onions
paprika to garnish

1. **Grater:** Grate zucchini and potatoes, using medium pressure. You should have about 4 cups in total.

2. **Steel Knife:** Combine all ingredients except French fried onions and paprika in processor bowl. Process with several on/off turns, just until mixed.

3. Lightly grease a deep 9″ Pyrex™ pie plate or 10″ ceramic quiche dish. Spread half the French fried onions in the bottom of the pie plate. Spread potato mixture, depressing the centre slightly. (This helps the kugel cook more evenly.) Top with remaining onions; sprinkle with paprika. Cover with a sheet of microsafe paper towelling.

4. Elevate on an inverted pie plate or microsafe rack. **MW covered on HIGH for 10 to 12 minutes,** rotating plate ¼ turn at half time. When done, edges will be set and top will be dry when touched lightly with your fingertips.

5. Discard paper towel. Bake kugel in a preheated conventional oven or on the **CONVECTION CYCLE (not preheated) at 400°F for 12 to 15 minutes,** or until crisp and golden. If using **CONVECTION CYCLE,** place on rack recommended by oven manufacturer.

Yield: 6 to 8 servings. May be frozen.

* If desired, omit onion rings.
* **POTATO ZUCCHINI KUGEL AU GRATIN:** In Step 5, sprinkle kugel with 1 c. grated Mozzerella or Cheddar cheese. **MW uncovered on HIGH 2 minutes longer,** just until cheese melts. Completing the kugel in the conventional oven is not necessary.

DILL-ICIOUS POTATO SALAD

- 4 medium potatoes (about 1 ½ lb.), peeled & cut into chunks
- 2 tbsp. water
- 3 eggs
- ¼ c. parsley, minced
- ¼ c. fresh dill, minced or 1 tbsp. dried dill weed
- 4 green onions, chopped
- 2 stalks celery, chopped
- ⅓ c. mayonnaise*
- ⅓ c. sour cream or yogurt*
- ½ tsp. dry mustard
- 2 tsp. lemon juice
- salt & pepper, to taste
- paprika, to garnish

1. Place potatoes in a microsafe casserole, sprinkle with water and cover with casserole lid or vented plastic wrap. **MW on HIGH for 8 to 10 minutes,** stirring at half time. Potatoes should be tender when pierced with a knife. Let stand covered 3 minutes. Uncover and let cool.

2. Crack eggs into ungreased Pyrex™ custard cups or a microsafe muffin pan. Pierce yolks with a fork. Cover tightly with plastic wrap. Do not vent. **MW on MEDIUM (50%) for 3 to 3 ½ minutes,** rotating cooking dish halfway through cooking. Eggs should be firm. Let stand covered for 3 minutes. Cool completely. Cut into chunks.

3. Combine all ingredients together and mix well. Chill before serving.

Yield: 6 to 8 servings. Do not freeze.

* **Variation:** Increase mayonnaise to ⅔ cup and eliminate sour cream. Mustard and lemon juice are optional.

* Baked Potatoes (p.270) can be used. Cool, peel and cut into chunks. Continue from Step 2.

PUMPKIN PURÉE

1. Wash pumpkin and cut in half or quarters. **(MW pumpkin on HIGH for 2 or 3 minutes so you can cut it more easily.)** Remove seeds and stringy portion. Place in a large microsafe casserole. Cover with waxed paper.

2. **MW on HIGH, allowing about 5 minutes per lb.** Pumpkin flesh should be tender. Scoop out cooked pulp and process on the **Steel Knife** of the food processor until puréed. Place in a sieve to allow excess liquid to drain off. Can be frozen.

Yield: 2 to 3 cups, depending on size.

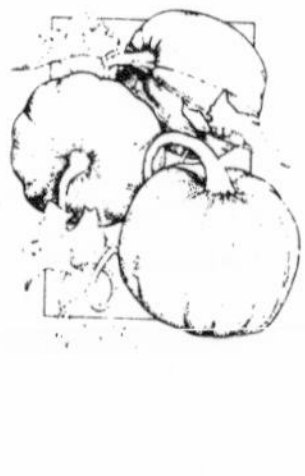

PUMPKIN SEEDS

1 c. pumpkin seeds
1 tbsp. butter or margarine, if desired
salt to taste

1. Wash pumpkin seeds very well; pat dry. Place a double layer of microsafe paper towels in a 7″ x 11″ oblong microsafe casserole. (Paper towels MUST NOT be made from recycled paper because they could ignite.) Sprinkle seeds evenly on top of paper. **MW uncovered on HIGH for 6 minutes.** Remove paper towels from casserole, letting seeds slide back into bottom of dish.

2. **MW seeds on HIGH 4 to 6 minutes longer,** stirring halfway through cooking. Seeds should be dry but still white in color. Let stand for 5 minutes to continue drying.

3. Place butter in a small microsafe dish. **MW uncovered on HIGH for 30 seconds,** until melted. Add to seeds. Sprinkle with salt and mix well. Store uncovered.

ROSY RADISHES

One day when we were testing recipes, there was an abundance of radishes left over from a cooking class on garnishing. This recipe was the delicious result.

2 green onions, sliced
1 c. radishes, sliced
2 tsp. butter or margarine
½ tsp. lemon juice
salt & pepper, to taste
dash each of basil & dill weed
1 tsp. sugar

1. Combine green onions, radishes and butter in a small microsafe bowl. **MW uncovered on HIGH for 2 to 3 minutes,** until tender-crisp, stirring once. Add remaining ingredients. Serve immediately.

Yield: 2 to 3 servings.

ORIENTAL SNOW PEAS

1 lb. snow peas
½ tsp. minced garlic
½ tsp. minced ginger
1 tbsp. soya sauce
14 oz. can baby corn cobs, drained
½ c. sliced water chestnuts, drained
2 green onions, finely chopped
½ red pepper, finely chopped

1. Remove tail ends from snow peas. Rinse well with cold water. Shake off excess. Place snow peas in a 1 ½ quart microsafe casserole with garlic, ginger and soya sauce. Cover with casserole lid or vented plastic wrap. **MW on HIGH for 2 minutes.**

2. Stir in remaining ingredients; **MW covered on HIGH 2 minutes longer,** until heated through. Serve immediately.

Yield: 4 servings.

SNOW PEAS WITH PINE NUTS

My friend Roz Brown makes this quick vegetable dish for company.

½ lb. snow peas
2 tsp. butter or margarine
½ c. pine nuts (pignola)
lemon pepper, to taste

1. Remove tail ends from snow peas. Rinse well with cold water; shake off excess water. Place in a 1 quart microsafe casserole. Cover and **MW on HIGH for 2 minutes.** Let stand for a few seconds. Drain well. Add remaining ingredients and mix well. Serve immediately.

Yield: 2 to 3 servings.

* **For 4 to 6 servings:** Double all ingredients. **1 lb. snow peas will take 3 minutes on HIGH.** Stir at half time.
* If your casserole doesn't have a lid, place a double layer of microsafe paper towelling under running water. Gently squeeze out excess water. Use to cover snow peas during microwaving.

SNOW PEA & MANDARIN SALAD

A favorite in my entertainment cooking classes. Colorful and wonderful!

1 lb. snow peas
2 - 10 oz. cans mandarin oranges, well drained
1 green pepper, halved & seeded
1 red pepper, halved & seeded
½ Bermuda onion, peeled
½ c. white vinegar
1 c. oil
salt & pepper, to taste
½ tsp. tarragon
2 tbsp. sugar

1. Remove tail ends from snow peas. Rinse under cold running water. Drain but do not dry. Place in a 2 quart round microsafe bowl; cover with vented plastic wrap.

2. MW on HIGH for 2 minutes. Snow peas will be bright green. Let stand covered for 1 minute. Uncover and rinse under cold water to stop cooking process; otherwise they will overcook.

3. Pat mandarin oranges dry with paper towelling. Thinly slice peppers and onion. Combine all ingredients and mix well. Transfer to a pretty serving bowl, cover and chill until serving time.

Yield: 6 to 8 servings.

* This salad can be made up to several hours in advance and refrigerated. However, the brilliant green color of the snow peas will fade after 1 or 2 days.

SPAGHETTI SQUASH

1. Weigh squash. Wash and dry well. Pierce all over with the point of a sharp knife. Place on a microsafe rack and **MW on HIGH, allowing 5 to 6 minutes per lb.** (An average spaghetti squash will cook in 15 to 20 minutes.) Turn squash over halfway through cooking. When squash is done, it will still be firm to the touch.

2. Wrap in a clean dishtowel and let stand for 5 to 10 minutes. Test for doneness with a knife. It should pass through the squash easily.

3. Cut in half crosswise, remove seeds and pull gently with a fork to separate into spaghetti-like strands.

4. Season with salt, pepper and a little butter or margarine. Also delicious when topped with Spaghetti Sauce (p. 185) or Quick Tomato Sauce (p. 89).

Yield: 3 lb. will yield 4 to 6 servings.

SPAGHETTI SQUASH WITH RATATOUILLE

1. Prepare Ratatouille or any of the variations given as directed on p. 259-260. (Can be prepared in advance and reheated.) Cook and prepare spaghetti squash as directed above, up to the end of Step 3. Arrange a bed of squash on each serving plate. Top each serving with 1 cup of hot Ratatouille. Garnish with fresh basil or parsley.

* **One cup of Ratatouille will take 1 ½ to 2 minutes** to reheat. Stir at half time.

ACORN SQUASH

1. Weigh squash. Wash and dry well. Pierce all over with the point of a sharp knife. Place on a microsafe rack and **MW on HIGH, allowing 6 minutes per lb.** Turn squash over halfway through cooking. When squash is done, it will still be firm to the touch.

2. Wrap in a clean dishtowel and let stand for 5 to 10 minutes. Test for doneness with a knife. It will pass through the squash easily.

3. Cut in half, remove seeds and season with salt, pepper and a little butter. Also delicious when topped with 2 tsp. brown sugar, maple syrup or honey and ½ tsp. grated orange or lemon rind. Freshly grated nutmeg also tastes great.

Yield: 2 servings.

* Squash can be filled with buttered green peas &/or carrots for a colorful company dish. Cut a small slice from the bottom of each squash half so that they will not tip over when served!
* For an interesting variation, fill squash halves with Chayote Ratatouille (p. 259).
* If you have a recipe that calls for cutting a raw squash in half (e.g. if you plan to stuff it), you'll find your job much easier if you microwave it first for **2 to 3 minutes on HIGH.**
* Make sure the squash has no soft spots when you buy it and that you pierce it well. I had the experience of having a wedge blow out of a squash during a cooking class. Thank goodness microwave ovens are a snap to wipe clean!

TOMATOES AU GRATIN

4 firm tomatoes (about 1 ¼ lb.)
salt, pepper, basil & oregano
¼ c. seasoned bread crumbs
¼ c. grated cheese, optional

1. Cut tops from tomatoes. Place tomatoes cut side up on a serving plate. Sprinkle with seasonings. Mound crumbs on top of tomatoes. **MW uncovered on HIGH for 2 minutes.** Rotate plate ¼ turn. If adding cheese, sprinkle it on top of crumb mixture at this time.

2. MW on HIGH 2 minutes longer, until tomatoes are hot and cheese is melted.

Yield: 4 servings.

* If overcooked, tomatoes will collapse and turn to mush!
* Different cheeses can be used; try Swiss, Parmesan, Mozzerella or Cheddar.
* Other nice toppings for tomatoes are crushed canned French fried onions, potato chips or corn chips.

SAUCY LEMON ZUCCHINI

2 tbsp. butter or margarine
1 lb. zucchini, ends trimmed
1 onion, quartered
1 clove garlic, crushed
½ tsp. salt
⅛ tsp. pepper
¼ tsp. basil
1 tbsp. sugar
1 ½ tbsp. lemon juice
2 tsp. cornstarch dissolved in 2 tbsp. cold water

1. Place butter in a 1 ½ quart casserole. **MW uncovered on HIGH for 45 seconds,** until melted.

2. Slicer: Slice zucchini and onions. Add to casserole. Add remaining ingredients except cornstarch mixture and mix well. Cover and **MW on HIGH for 5 to 6 minutes,** stirring at half time. Zucchini should be almost translucent.

3. Stir in cornstarch mixture and **MW uncovered on HIGH 2 minutes longer,** until sauce is thickened and zucchini is piping hot. Stir and serve immediately.

Yield: 3 to 4 servings.

EASY ZUCCHINI

1 lb. zucchini (about 3 medium), sliced ¼″ thick
2 tbsp. bottled or home-made Italian salad dressing

1. Place zucchini slices in a 1 ½ quart microsafe casserole. Sprinkle with salad dressing. Cover with casserole lid or vented plastic wrap.

2. MW on HIGH for 5 minutes, until tender-crisp, stirring at half time.

Yield: 4 servings.

CAKES, MUFFINS & BREADS

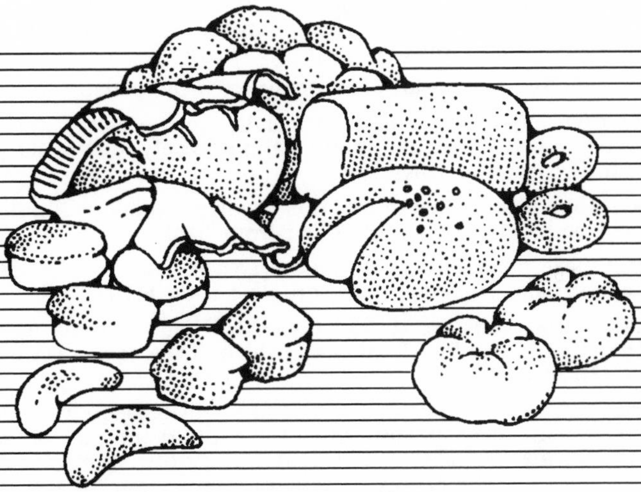

MICRO-WAYS WITH CAKES, MUFFINS & BREADS

YOU TAKE THE CAKE!

- **I find the taste and texture** of microwaved cakes different from conventionally baked cakes (which I prefer). However, the recipes I developed for this book are all delicious, quick and easy. I'm sure you will enjoy them too.
- **Microwaved cakes will be higher,** more spongy in texture and will not brown (except for chocolate cakes)! The lack of browning can be disguised with a glaze or icing.
- **Measure accurately.** Use measuring cups with a lip to measure liquids. Use nested measuring cups for dry ingredients.
- **To convert recipes for the microwave,** I usually reduce liquid by 25% (¼) because there is little evaporation due to the lack of heat in microwave cooking. Reduce leavening by about half.
- **After pouring batter into pan,** let it stand for 5 to 10 minutes before microwaving to give leavening a chance to work.
- **Raisins, nuts &/or chocolate chips** may sink to the bottom of microwaved cakes unless batter is thick. Let rest 10 minutes, sprinkle nuts over batter, stir in gently and microwave.
- **Elevate cake on a microsafe rack** or inverted pie plate.
- **If your oven has a turntable,** it is usually not necessary to rotate cakes during baking. If your cake is not baking evenly, rotate the pan 3 or 4 times during microwaving.
- **If baked cake has an uneven top,** don't worry; no one will notice because cake will be inverted when removed from pan!
- **You may have more success** if you start your cake on **MEDIUM (50%)** for the first half of baking, then complete it on **HIGH.**
- **If a cake recipe calls for 10 minutes on HIGH, you could MW the cake on MEDIUM (50%) for 10 minutes (which is the equivalent of 5 minutes on HIGH), then MW it 5 minutes on HIGH.**
- **For fruit cakes,** you may find your cake will bake more evenly if you wrap a 2″ wide strip of aluminum foil around the outside edge of the pan and elevate the cake on a microsafe rack during microwaving. This allows the microwave energy to penetrate only from the top and bottom of the pan (A suggestion from Australian microwave consultant Joan McDermott.)
- **Opening and closing the door** of your oven won't cause the cake to fall!
- **When done, cake will be moist on top.** Scratch the slightly moist surface with a wooden toothpick. Cake should be cooked underneath. If not, **MW on HIGH 30 seconds at a time,** until done.
- **If you have problems** and your cake doesn't turn out, just cut it up to make a Trifle (p. 324) or Rum Balls (p. 351).
- **If you are a nibbler** and eat half the batter before you microwave the cake, remember to reduce your cooking time! Less food takes less time.
- **Because there is no crust** on microwaved cakes, wrap them well to prevent them from drying out.
- **P.S. You never have to "preheat"** the microwave oven!

- **Sponge, chiffon and angel cakes** don't do well in the microwave; they should be baked conventionally. There are some recipes and cake mixes that have been formulated specially for the microwave.

Microwave Baking Pans

- **A Bundt shaped microwavable clear plastic pan** gives excellent results. It is ring shaped, which gives the most even results in microwaving. Also, if the pan is clear, it's easy to check if the bottom of the cake is completely baked, or if there are any raw areas. I use a 3 litre (12 cup) clear 10″ Bundt pan made by Micro Mac Products Ltd. of Calgary, Alberta, which is available throughout Canada and the USA.
- **For layer cakes,** use a deep 9″ round layer pan of heatproof glass or specially tempered plastic. The pan should have higher sides because microwaved cakes rise higher than those baked conventionally. Microwave one layer at a time.
- **It's easy to make your own ring-shaped pan.** Place a heatproof drinking glass (open end up) in the centre of a large heatproof glass mixing bowl (e.g. the bowl from your electric mixer).
- **If you use square or rectangular pans,** the corners of your cake will be overdone. Microwaves adore corners! Shielding corners with foil for part of the cooking time will be necessary.
- **Preparing Baking Pans:** Although many microwave experts don't grease microwave cake pans, the following method gives me the best results:- Grease cake pan lightly with butter or shortening, then add 3 tbsp. graham wafer crumbs (or chocolate wafer crumbs for chocolate cakes). Rotate pan so that crumbs coat the surface. Pour out any excess crumbs.
- **Instead of butter, spray pan** with non-stick spray, then coat with crumbs (a tip from microwave expert Rita Polansky).
- **The crumb coating gives a brown color** to the exterior of your cake, making it appear more like a conventionally baked cake. It also keeps the cake from sticking to the pan. Without the crumb coating, white cakes are so pale they look like they've been through a bleach cycle in your washing machine!
- **Line a round cake pan with two circles of waxed paper** for easy removal. Lightly grease bottom of dish so waxed paper will stay in place when batter is spread in pan.
- **Don't fill cake pans more than** ⅓ to ½ full. Use excess batter to make cupcakes (perfect nibbles for hungry kids).
- **Spread batter slightly lower around the centre** of the cake and slightly higher around outside edge for more even cooking.
- **After pouring cake batter into the baking pan,** let it stand for 5 to 10 minutes before baking. This gives the leavening time to work, since baking times are so short for microwaved cakes.
- **Use the waiting period** to clean up the dishes, put ingredients away and microwave any cupcakes. (I don't bother with the waiting time for cupcakes since the amount of batter is so small.)
- **CUPCAKES:** If you make cupcakes from excess cake batter, use two paper liners in each microsafe muffin compartment. This will absorb any excess moisture. One cup of cake batter yields 6 cupcakes (use 2 tbsp. for each cupcake); **MW on HIGH for 2 to 2½ minutes.** The batter for one layer cake makes 14 to 16 cupcakes. Paper liners should not be more than ½ full. Read Micro-Ways with Muffins (p. 301).

BAKING TIMES

- **Since every microwave oven is different,** watch carefully the first few times you bake to find the best time for your oven. My recipes were tested on a 700 watt oven, so if your oven has a lower wattage or isn't on a separate circuit, you may have to increase the cooking time slightly. It's always better to check 1 or 2 minutes before time is up; add more time if necessary.
- **If you have a 500 to 600 watt oven, allow an extra 1 to 2 minutes on HIGH (100%) for a Bundt pan recipe, or 30 to 60 seconds more for each layer pan.**
- **Layer cakes will take 5 to 6 minutes per layer on HIGH; Bundt cakes will take 8 to 12 minutes.** A major time saving!
- **Cakes cook about 20% faster** in microsafe plastic pans than in glass pans **(usually 1 minute less for every 5 minutes on HIGH).**
- **Microwave time will be 2 to 2½ minutes on HIGH for 6 cupcakes,** just like muffins. Rotate ¼ turn at half time.

Up and Around She Goes!

- **Elevate cakes on a microsafe rack,** inverted Pyrex™ pie plate or dinner plate for more even baking.
- **Rotate cake ¼ turn every 3 or 4 minutes during baking.** Don't bother if your oven has a turntable.
- **As I am always in a hurry when I use my microwave,** I tend to use **HIGH** power as much as possible. **If your cake rises** in humps and bumps during baking, **reduce power level from HIGH to MEDIUM (50%) and double the remaining baking time left** on your timer.

Test for Doneness

- **Top of cake will spring back** when lightly touched. Top will be slightly damp to the touch, but will dry during standing time because heat within the cake rises to the surface and cooks any moist patches.
- **Test by touching the wet spot** with a piece of paper towel or napkin, or by scratching the area with a wooden toothpick. If the cake is baked underneath, it is done.
- **A wooden skewer inserted halfway between the outer and inner edges** of a cake baked in a Bundt pan will come out clean.

Underbaked Cakes

- **Don't worry about wet spots** on the surface of the cake. If you microwave it until the top is completely dry, the whole cake will be dry and overbaked. Small wet spots cook during standing time.
- **Cake is underbaked** if there are large areas of wet batter on the surface.
- **Add an additional 30 seconds on HIGH** for each tablespoon of unbaked batter.

When the Cake is Done....

- **Cool cake directly on the countertop** for 15 minutes (not on a rack). Cake will finish baking during standing time.
- **The top of a microwaved cake** might still be be sticky after standing time. To dry the top, sprinkle it with 1 tbsp. graham wafer crumbs after baking, or blot surface with a paper towel.

To Remove Cake From Pan

- **Loosen inside and outside edges of cake** from pan as well as the bottom, using a flexible narrow metal spatula.
- **Flex pan to allow air to get between** the pan and the cake.
- **Place serving plate upside down** on top of cake pan and invert.
- **Flex pan and shake gently.**
- **Cool cake before glazing or frosting.**

Frostings & Glazes

- **Texture of microwaved cakes** is fragile, so make frostings slightly thinner than usual. Apply a light layer of frosting, let it set, then frost with the remainder.
- **Use a glaze for Bundt-type cakes.** Thin your regular frosting recipe with a little additional liquid and drizzle over cake.
- **Refrigerated frostings can be brought to room temperature** quickly. **MW uncovered on HIGH for 15 to 20 seconds** at a time. Do not overheat or frosting will melt.

CAKE MIXES PLUS PUDDING

19 oz. pkg. of your favorite cake mix
1 pkg. (4 serving size) instant pudding mix your favorite flavor)
½ c. vegetable or corn oil
¾ c. water, milk, sour cream or orange juice
4 eggs

1. **Steel Knife:** Place dry ingredients in processor bowl. Add remaining ingredients through the feed tube while the machine is running. Process 1 minute, until smooth. Pour batter into a 10″ microsafe Bundt pan which has been greased and sprinkled with cookie crumbs. Let stand for 10 minutes.

2. Elevate on a microsafe rack or inverted pie plate. **MW uncovered on HIGH for 8 to 10 minutes,** rotating pan ¼ turn every 3 minutes. Test for doneness (p. 286). Let stand directly on the counter for 10 to 15 minutes. Remove from pan. Glaze when cool, if desired.

Variations

* Yellow Cake Mix, Vanilla Instant Pudding, Orange Juice.
* Devil's Food Cake Mix plus 1 tsp. instant coffee, Chocolate Instant Pudding, Milk or Sour Cream.
* White or Yellow Cake Mix, Caramel Instant Pudding, Sour Cream.
* Spice Cake Mix, Butterscotch Instant Pudding, Sour Cream.

ICE CREAM CONECAKES

Fill flat-bottom ice cream cones half-full with batter. Arrange in a circle on a microsafe plate. Bake as for cupcakes. **MW on HIGH, allowing about 30 seconds per cone, or 2 to 2½ minutes for 6 Conecakes.** When cool, frost with your favorite frosting.

RITA'S APPLE SPICE CAKE

My friend Rita Polansky teaches microwave cooking classes in Montreal and shares my love of good food. This wonderfully moist apple and walnut cake is a winner!

3 tbsp. graham wafer crumbs (to coat pan)
4 eggs
¾ c. granulated sugar
¾ c. brown sugar, packed
1 c. oil
1 ½ c. flour
1 ½ tsp. baking powder
1 tsp. baking soda
1 tsp. cinnamon
¼ tsp. nutmeg
⅛ tsp. allspice
3 medium apples, peeled, cored & grated (about 2 cups)
½ c. walnuts, chopped
Glaze, if desired (recipe follows)

1. Grease a 12 cup microsafe Bundt pan and coat surface with a thin layer of graham wafer crumbs.

2. Beat eggs and sugar until light. Add oil and beat well. Sift together dry ingredients. Add to egg mixture; mix until smooth. Fold in grated apples and walnuts. Pour batter into prepared pan. Push batter slightly higher towards outside edges of pan. Let stand 10 minutes.

3. Elevate pan on a microsafe rack or inverted pie plate. **MW uncovered on MEDIUM-HIGH (70%) for 11 to 13 minutes,** rotating cake ¼ turn every 4 minutes. Test for doneness (p. 286). There will be small moist areas on top of the cake, but these will dry during standing time. If there are large wet patches, **MW on HIGH 1 to 2 minutes longer.**

4. Place cake directly on the counter and let stand 15 minutes. Any moist spots will evaporate during standing time. Loosen edges with a flexible spatula, flex pan and invert onto a serving plate. If desired, top with Glaze (recipe follows). Kids like it sprinkled with icing sugar.

Yield: 12 servings. Can be frozen, but do not glaze.

Glaze

3 tbsp. margarine
½ c. brown sugar, packed
2 tbsp. brandy or cognac
2 tbsp. apple juice or water
¼ c. chopped walnuts

1. Place margarine in a 2 cup glass measure. **MW uncovered on HIGH for 30 seconds,** until melted. Stir in brown sugar, brandy and apple juice. **MW uncovered on HIGH for 2 minutes,** stirring at half time. **MW on HIGH 30 seconds longer.**

2. Pierce cake all over with a long skewer. Slowly pour most of glaze over warm cake. Mix remaining glaze with nuts. Garnish top of cake with glazed nuts.

BLUEBERRY LEMON CAKE

3 tbsp. graham wafer crumbs to coat cake pan
1 ½ c. blueberries (fresh or frozen)
2 tbsp. flour
2 eggs
¼ lb. butter or margarine, cut in chunks
1 c. sugar
1 tsp. baking soda
¾ c. plain yogurt
1 tbsp. lemon juice
2 tsp. grated lemon rind
2 c. flour
1 tsp. baking powder

1. Butter a 10″ microsafe Bundt pan and coat surface with graham wafer crumbs.

2. If berries are frozen, **DEFROST (30%) for 2 minutes** in a 2 cup Pyrex™ measure. Berries will still be slightly frozen. Toss with 2 tbsp. flour.

3. **Steel Knife:** Process eggs, butter and sugar for 2 minutes. Do not insert pusher in feed tube. Dissolve baking soda in yogourt in a 2 cup measure. Let stand for 1 minute. Add to processor along with lemon juice; process for 5 seconds. Add rind, flour and baking powder. Process with 3 or 4 quick on/off turns. Carefully stir in blueberries. Spoon batter into prepared pan. Spread batter evenly and carefully; push batter slightly higher towards outside edges of pan. Let stand 10 minutes.

4. Elevate pan on a microsafe rack or inverted pie plate. **MW uncovered on HIGH for 9 to 12 minutes,** rotating cake ¼ turn every 3 minutes. Test for doneness (p. 286). If tested with a wooden skewer, no batter should cling to it. Some blueberry may adhere, but that's okay!

5. Place cake directly on the counter and let stand 15 minutes. Any moist spots will evaporate during standing time. Loosen edges with a flexible spatula, flex pan and invert onto a serving plate. Glaze with Cream Cheese Glaze (below), using lemon juice and rind as flavoring.

Yield: 10 to 12 servings. Cake freezes well.

* If you heat the lemon for **20 seconds on HIGH** it will release more juice.
* If cake begins to overcook around the edges but the centre is not done, make a Foil Donut (p. 127) and place over top of cake during the last few minutes of microwaving.

CREAM CHEESE GLAZE

2 tbsp. butter or margarine
¼ c. cream cheese
1 tsp. lemon or orange rind
1 tbsp. lemon or orange juice
1 - 2 tbsp. water
1 c. icing sugar

1. **Steel Knife:** Process all ingredients for 15 seconds until smooth. Drizzle over inverted cooled cake, letting glaze run over the top and sides of cake in an attractive design.

Yield: for a 10″ Bundt cake.

CARROT CAKE

Carrots are good for your eyes, so they say. Make this yummy cake and see how quickly it disappears!

2 or 3 medium carrots, scraped & trimmed
2 eggs
¾ c. brown sugar, firmly packed
½ c. oil
¼ c. orange juice
1 tsp. orange rind
1 c. flour
1 tsp. baking powder
¼ tsp. baking soda
⅛ tsp. salt
1 ½ tsp. cinnamon
½ c. chopped pecans or chocolate chips

1. **Grater:** Grate carrots, using medium pressure. Measure 1 cup, firmly packed. Set aside.

2. **Steel Knife:** Process eggs, brown sugar and oil for 1 minute, until well blended. Do not insert pusher in feed tube. Add carrots, orange juice and rind; process for 10 seconds. Add flour, baking powder, baking soda, salt and cinnamon. Process with 3 or 4 on/off turns, just until flour disappears. Sprinkle nuts or chocolate chips over batter. Give 1 or 2 more quick on/off turns, just until mixed.

3. Lightly grease the bottom of a deep 9″ microsafe cake dish. Line with a double circle of waxed paper. Spread batter evenly in pan, depressing centre slightly. Let stand for 5 minutes.

4. Elevate on a microsafe rack or inverted pie plate. **MW uncovered on MEDIUM (50%) for 8 minutes,** rotating dish ¼ turn halfway through cooking. **MW for 2 to 4 minutes on HIGH.** Test for doneness (p. 286). Let stand directly on the counter for 10 minutes. Invert onto serving plate. Peel off waxed paper. Cool completely. Split into 2 layers. Fill and frost with Cream Cheese Frosting (below).

Yield: 8 servings. Freezes well.

* If desired, press 1 cup finely chopped pecans into the sides and top of iced cake. Garnish top of cake with rosettes of icing. Top each rosette with a pecan half.

CREAM CHEESE FROSTING

¼ c. butter or margarine
½ c. cream cheese
2 c. icing sugar
1 tbsp. orange juice
1 tsp. grated orange rind

1. Remove wrappings from butter and cream cheese. Place in a microsafe dish (or your processor bowl, if microsafe). **MW uncovered on MEDIUM (50%) for 1 minute,** until softened.

2. Combine all ingredients and process until smooth and blended, about 10 to 12 seconds.

Yield: To fill and frost a 9″ cake.

QUICK COFFEE CAKE

My son Doug tested many of the recipes in The Microwave Bible *for me. When he made this cake, he was surprised to learn that there was no coffee in the ingredients. I never knew that he had refused to eat coffee cake for years because he hates coffee! Doug prepared the cake with ease, ate it with gusto and declared the recipe a success.*

Topping:

1 c. pecans or walnuts
½ c. brown sugar, packed
2 tsp. cinnamon
2 tbsp. cocoa, if desired

1. **Steel Knife:** Process nuts, brown sugar, cinnamon and cocoa for 10 to 12 seconds, until finely chopped. Empty bowl. Butter a 10″ microsafe Bundt pan. Sprinkle ⅓ of filling in bottom of pan. Rotate pan so nut mixture will coat sides.

¼ lb. butter or margarine, cut in chunks
2 eggs
1 c. sugar
1 tsp. vanilla
1 c. sour cream or yogourt
1 tsp. baking soda
1 tsp. baking powder
2 c. flour

2. **Steel Knife:** Process butter, eggs, sugar and vanilla for 2 minutes. Do not insert pusher in feed tube. Add sour cream; process for 5 seconds. Add dry ingredients and process with quick on/off turns, just until blended.

3. Spread ½ of the batter in pan. Sprinkle with filling. Repeat once more, ending with filling. Let stand for 5 to 10 minutes. (Use this time to clean up the kitchen!)

4. Elevate pan on a microsafe rack or inverted pie plate. **MW uncovered on MEDIUM (50%) for 10 minutes,** rotating cake ¼ turn every 3 or 4 minutes. **MW on HIGH 2 to 4 minutes longer.** Test for doneness (p. 286).

5. Let cake stand directly on the counter for 15 minutes. Any moist spots will evaporate during standing time. Loosen edges with a flexible spatula; invert cake onto a serving plate. Let cool.

Yield: 10 servings. Freezes well.

* When cool, wrap cake well to retain maximum freshness. Cake is delicious warm, but cover any remaining cake with foil or plastic wrap to prevent cut surfaces from becoming dry.
* Toast any dry (or fresh!) slices in the toaster oven for a few minutes. It makes a wonderful treat for breakfast or as a snack.

CINN-FULLY GOOD COFFEE CAKE

I wanted to include one special cake recipe to show how to convert a conventional cake recipe for the CONVECTION CYCLE. I know you'll love it. I have included conventional baking instructions as well.

Filling

2 c. pecans
¾ c. brown sugar, packed
1 tbsp. cinnamon
2 tbsp. cocoa
1 c. chocolate chips

Batter:

¾ c. butter or margarine, cut in chunks
1 ½ c. sugar
3 eggs
2 tsp. vanilla
3 c. flour
1 ½ c. sour cream
1 ½ tsp. baking soda
1 ½ tsp. baking powder

1. Insert rack recommended by oven manufacturer; preheat on **CONVECTION CYCLE** to 325°F. (Preheat conventional oven to 350°F.)

2. Steel Knife: Process pecans, sugar, cocoa and cinnamon until nuts are coarsely chopped, about 10 seconds. Transfer to another bowl. Reserve chocolate chips.

3. Steel Knife: Process butter, sugar, eggs and vanilla for 2 minutes. Do not insert pusher in feed tube. Add half of flour and sour cream; process with 3 or 4 on/off turns, until nearly blended. Add remaining ingredients for batter. Process with several quick on/off turns, just until blended.

4. Spread ⅓ of batter in a greased and floured 10″ metal Bundt or tube pan. Sprinkle with ⅓ of nut mixture and ½ of the chocolate chips. Repeat once again. Top with remaining batter; sprinkle with remaining nut mixture.

5. Bake on CONVECTION CYCLE at 325°F for 55 to 60 minutes. A cake tester should come out clean. If not, let cake remain in oven for 5 minutes with the heat off and test once again. **(In a conventional oven, bake for 55 to 60 minutes.)** Let cake cool on counter for 15 minutes before removing from pan.

Yield: 12 servings. Freezes well.

* **CONVECTION TIPS:** Preheating of oven is necessary for cakes. If using light-colored pans, batter may not bake all the way through, although top of cake may be quite brown. Cover loosely with foil or leave cake in oven at end of cooking time for 5 or 10 minutes with heat off to finish baking if not quite done.
* **OLD-FASHIONED COFFEE CAKE:** For filling, omit cocoa and chocolate chips; use white sugar instead of brown.

EASY PAREVE CHOCOLATE CAKE

This is NOT exactly the same recipe as in my book The Pleasures of your Processor, but it is quick and delicious. I tried a dozen different ways to adapt the original recipe, and this is the result.

3 tbsp. chocolate wafer crumbs (to coat pan)
3 eggs
1 ¾ c. sugar
1 tsp. vanilla or Kahlua
1 c. oil
¾ c. cold coffee, orange juice or water
1 ½ c. flour
¾ c. cocoa
¾ tsp. baking powder
½ tsp. baking soda

1. Grease a 10″ microsafe Bundt pan and coat surface with crumbs.

2. **Steel Knife:** Process eggs, sugar and vanilla for 1 minute. Do not insert pusher in feed tube. Add oil and process for 30 seconds. Add coffee through feed tube and process a few seconds longer. Add remaining ingredients and blend in with on/off turns, just until flour disappears. Pour into prepared pan and spread batter evenly; push batter slightly higher towards the outside edges of pan. Let stand 10 minutes.

3. Elevate pan on a microsafe rack or inverted pie plate. **MW uncovered on HIGH for 7 ½ to 9 ½ minutes,** rotating cake ¼ turn every 3 minutes*. Test for doneness (p. 286).

4. Let stand directly on the counter for 15 minutes. Any moist spots will evaporate during standing time. Loosen edges with a flexible spatula; invert cake onto a serving plate. Cool completely before glazing with Pareve Chocolate Glaze (see page 294).

Yield: 10 servings. Freezes well.

* If your oven has a turntable or it cooks evenly, it is not necessary to rotate the cake during microwaving.
* Leftover cake can be used to make Blow your Diet Chocolate Trifle (p. 324).
* This recipe makes delicious chocolate cupcakes. **Six cupcakes take 2 to 2 ½ minutes on HIGH to microwave.** Rotate pan ¼ turn halfway through cooking.

CHOCOLATE GLAZE

⅓ c. whipping cream (35%)
½ c. semi-sweet chocolate chips
1 tsp. vanilla or 2 tsp. Kahlua or Amaretto

1. Place cream in a 2 cup Pyrex™ measuring cup. **MW uncovered on HIGH for 1 minute,** until bubbly.

2. Add chocolate chips and flavoring; stir until melted. Cool. Drizzle over your favorite chocolate cake.

Yield: for a 10″ Bundt cake.

PAREVE CHOCOLATE GLAZE

1 square unsweetened chocolate
1 ½ c. icing sugar
2 tbsp. water or coffee
½ tsp. vanilla

1. Place chocolate in a small microsafe bowl. **MW uncovered on HIGH for 1 to 1 ½ minutes,** until almost completely melted, stirring at half time. Stir to complete melting.

2. Combine with remaining ingredients and blend until smooth. Drizzle over your favorite chocolate cake.

CHOCOLATE TRUFFLE GLAZE (GANACHE)

This makes the most wonderful topping for Brownies! It's also great on chocolate cake.

¾ c. whipping cream (35%)
8 oz. semi-sweet or bittersweet chocolate, cut in chunks
2 tsp. Kahlua, Cognac, Amaretto or Grand Marnier

1. **MW cream uncovered on HIGH for 1 ½ minutes,** or until almost boiling.

2. **Steel Knife:** Process chocolate with several on/off turns to start, then let processor run until chocolate is fine, about 30 seconds. Pour hot cream through feed tube while machine is running. Process until smooth. Blend in liqueur.

3. Refrigerate mixture for 20 to 30 minutes, until cooled and slightly thickened. Pour over Brownies or drizzle over your favorite chocolate cake. Glaze will be dark and shiny. Refrigerate.

Yield: for a 10″ Bundt cake or 1 recipe of Brownies (p. 347). Freezes well.

WHIPPED CHOCOLATE GANACHE

1. Prepare Chocolate Truffle Glaze (above) as directed, but increase cream to 1 cup. **Heating time for cream will be 1 ¾ to 2 minutes on HIGH.** Chill glaze until slightly thickened.

2. **Steel Knife:** Process mixture until light and thick, about 45 seconds, scraping down sides of bowl as necessary. Mixture will become light in color and thick like frosting. (Can also be whipped on your electric mixer for 1 to 1 ½ minutes.) Use immediately to frost your favorite cake or Brownies. Refrigerate.

Yield: for an 8″ or 9″ cake or 1 recipe of Brownies (p. 347 and 349). Freezes well.

STEEL KNIFE

CHOCOLATE FROSTING

1 oz. unsweetened chocolate
¼ c. butter
1 ½ c. icing sugar
2 tbsp. milk
½ tsp. vanilla or mint flavoring

1. Place chocolate and butter in a small microsafe bowl (or the bowl from your processor if microsafe). **MW uncovered on HIGH for 1 ½ to 2 minutes,** just until melted, stirring once or twice.

2. Steel Knife: Process all ingredients until smooth and blended, about 10 seconds, scraping down sides of bowl as necessary. Add a few drops of milk if icing seems too thick.

Yield: For an 8″ or 9″ cake or 1 recipe of Brownies (p. 347). Freezes well.

> * For a large cake, double all ingredients. **Two squares of chocolate will take 2 minutes on HIGH to melt.** Stir after 1 minute.

MICRO-WAYS WITH CHEESECAKES

- **Cheesecakes are excellent in the microwave** because they don't crack. As it is difficult to find a microsafe springform pan, I make my cheesecakes in a white ceramic quiche dish. Even though the edges are fluted, the cheesecake cooks evenly. Cook and serve from the same dish.
- **If you use a 9″ pie plate for your cheesecakes**, choose one that is fairly deep with straight sides for best results. If sides of pie plate flare out too much, cheesecake will overcook on the edges.
- **To substitute cottage cheese for cream cheese** in cheesecakes, add 1 tbsp. flour for every ½ lb. cottage cheese to adjust for its higher moisture content. Cheesecake can also be made using half cottage cheese and half cream cheese with no addition of flour necessary.
- **To soften cream cheese,** remove wrappings and place cheese in a microsafe bowl. **MW uncovered on MEDIUM (50%). Do not use High power** as cheese could melt and/or curdle.

¼ lb. takes 30 to 45 seconds.
½ to 1 lb. takes 1 to 1 ½ minutes.
1 ½ lb. takes 1 ½ to 2 minutes.

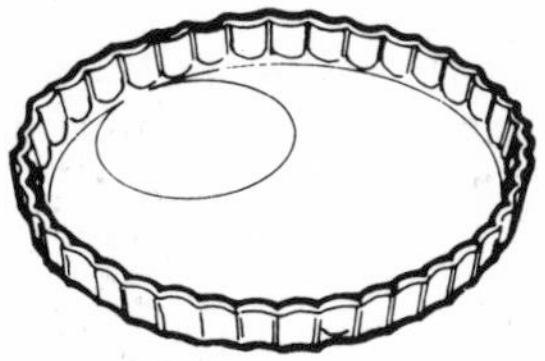

MARBLED HAZELNUT OR ALMOND CHEESECAKE

Absolutely scrumptious! This recipe takes about 20 minutes from start to finish using the food processor and microwave. The bonus is that microwaved cheesecake never cracks!

Crust:
1 c. filberts (hazelnuts) or almonds
1 c. chocolate wafer crumbs
2 tbsp. white or brown sugar
¼ c. melted butter or margarine
½ tsp. cinnamon

Filling:
1 ½ lb. cream cheese, in chunks
1 c. sugar
3 eggs
1 tbsp. Franjelica, Amaretto, Kahlua, Triple Sec or vanilla
⅓ c. chocolate chips

1. **Steel Knife:** Process nuts until finely ground, about 30 seconds. Empty bowl. Combine remaining crust ingredients with ¼ cup of the ground nuts and process just until mixed. (Reserve remaining nuts to garnish cheesecake.) Press crust mixture evenly into the bottom and up the sides of a lightly greased 10″ ceramic quiche dish. **MW uncovered on HIGH for 2 minutes, until set.**

2. Unwrap cream cheese and place in a 2 quart microsafe bowl. **MW uncovered on MEDIUM (50%) for 1 ½ to 2 minutes,** until softened. Do not wash bowl.

3. **Steel Knife:** Combine cheese, sugar, eggs and liqueur; process with several on/off turns to start, then let machine run until mixture is smooth, about 30 seconds. Do not insert pusher in feed tube. Pour mixture into the 2 quart bowl. **MW uncovered on HIGH for 5 to 6 minutes,** stirring twice. Mixture will be hot and thick like pudding.

4. Pour about 1 cup of hot mixture into a measuring cup. Pour most of remaining mixture into baked crust, leaving about 1 cup in the bowl. Add chocolate chips to bowl and stir until melted. Drizzle chocolate mixture over white mixture in quiche dish. Top with reserved white mixture. Cut through batter gently with a knife to marble.

5. Elevate on a microsafe rack or inverted dish. **MW uncovered on MEDIUM for 5 to 6 minutes,** rotating dish ¼ turn at half time. When done, the center 2″ will jiggle slightly like cellulite when you shake the dish, but won't stick when touched with your finger. Top with reserved nuts. Place directly on the counter to cool for ½ hour. Cheesecake will firm up as it stands. Chill 3 to 4 hours or overnight before serving.

Yield: 8 to 10 servings. Keeps 3 to 4 days in the fridge.

* **Defrost frozen cheesecake uncovered on LOW (10%). One slice takes 1 to 2 minutes. Whole cheesecake takes 10 minutes.** Let stand for 10 minutes. Crust softens slightly if frozen.

SOUR CREAM CHEESECAKE

Graham Wafer Crust (p. 327)
1 ½ lb. cream cheese, cut in chunks (half cottage cheese may be used)
1 c. sugar
3 eggs
2 tbsp. lemon juice

Topping:
1 c. sour cream
2 tbsp. sugar
1 tbsp. lemon juice

1. Prepare and microwave crust as directed. Unwrap cream cheese and place in a 2 quart microsafe bowl. **MW uncovered on MEDIUM (50%) for 1 ½ to 2 minutes,** until softened. Do not wash bowl.

2. **Steel Knife:** Combine cheese, sugar, eggs and lemon juice; process with several on/off turns to start, then let machine run until mixture is smooth, about 30 seconds. Do not insert pusher in feed tube. Pour mixture into the 2 quart bowl. **MW uncovered on HIGH for 5 to 6 minutes,** stirring twice. Mixture will be hot and thick like pudding. Pour into crust.

3. Elevate on a microsafe rack or inverted dish. **MW uncovered on MEDIUM (50%) for 5 to 6 minutes,** rotating dish ¼ turn at half time. When done, the centre 2″ will jiggle slightly like cellulite when you shake the dish, but won't stick when touched with your finger. Cheesecake will firm up as it stands.

4. Combine ingredients for topping and spread over cheesecake. Let stand directly on countertop for ½ hour to cool. Chill 3 to 4 hours or overnight before serving.

Yield: 8 to 10 servings. Keeps 3 to 4 days in the fridge. To freeze, omit sour cream topping. Crust softens slightly when frozen.

CHOCOLATE CHEESECAKE

Follow recipe for Sour Cream Cheesecake (above) but use a Chocolate Wafer Crust (p. 327) and omit sour cream topping. Blend 3 squares of melted semi-sweet chocolate into cheesecake batter in Step 2. Garnish chilled cheesecake with swirls of sweetened whipped cream and grated chocolate.

* **Three squares of chocolate will take 1 ½ to 2 minutes on HIGH to melt.** Stir every minute.

GRAND MANDARIN CHEESECAKE #1

Follow recipe for Sour Cream Cheesecake (above), but use Grand Marnier instead of lemon juice in batter and topping. When cool, garnish with a border of sweetened whipped cream and drained canned mandarin oranges. This is delicious with a Chocolate Wafer Crust (p. 327).

GRAND MANDARIN CHEESECAKE #2

Follow recipe for Sour Cream Cheesecake (p. 297), but use Grand Marnier instead of lemon juice in the batter; omit sour cream topping. If desired, substitute ¼ cup ground almonds for ¼ cup of the crumbs in crust. Cool cheesecake completely. Prepare the following topping:

3 - 10 oz. cans mandarin oranges
½ c. apricot preserves
1 tbsp. Grand Marnier

Drain mandarin oranges; pat dry. Combine apricot preserves with liqueur in a microsafe bowl. **MW uncovered on HIGH for 45 seconds,** until melted. Strain. Brush a thin layer of glaze over cheesecake. Arrange mandarin oranges in an attractive design. Brush oranges with remaining preserves. Chill 3 to 4 hours or overnight.

RASPBERRY OR STRAWBERRY CHEESECAKE

Prepare as for Grand Mandarin Cheesecake #2 (above), but substitute 2 pints raspberries or hulled and halved strawberries for the mandarin oranges. Use either apricot preserves, red currant or strawberry jelly to glaze fruit.

PUMPKIN CHEESECAKE

Gingersnap Crust (p. 327)
1 lb. cream cheese
1 c. canned pumpkin
3 eggs
1 c. brown sugar, packed
2 tbsp. flour
1 tsp. cinnamon
¼ tsp. ground ginger
¼ tsp. nutmeg
1 tsp. vanilla or Grand Marnier
Sweetened whipped cream, to garnish

1. Prepare and microwave crust as directed. Unwrap cream cheese and place in a 2 quart microsafe bowl. **MW uncovered on MEDIUM (50%) for 1 minute,** until softened. Do not wash bowl.

2. **Steel Knife:** Combine all ingredients except whipped cream. Process with several on/off turns to start, then let machine run until mixture is smooth, about 30 seconds. Do not insert pusher in feed tube. Pour mixture into the 2 quart bowl. **MW uncovered on HIGH for 5 to 6 minutes,** stirring twice. Mixture will be hot and thick like pudding. Pour into crust.

3. Elevate on a microsafe rack or inverted dish. **MW uncovered on MEDIUM (50%) for 9 to 12 minutes,** rotating dish ¼ turn at half time. When done, the centre 2″ will jiggle slightly like cellulite when you shake the dish, but won't stick when touched with your finger. Cheesecake will firm up as it stands.

4. Let stand directly on countertop for ½ hour to cool. Chill 3 to 4 hours or overnight before serving. Garnish with swirls of whipped cream.

Yield: 8 to 10 servings. Keeps 3 to 4 days in the fridge. Crust softens slightly when frozen.

* Leftover canned pumpkin can be used to make Chinese Plum Sauce (p. 93) or Cream of Pumpkin Soup (p. 81).

JUST A LITTLE CHEESECAKE

This idea was given to me by Pam Collacott, who writes the microwave column for the Ottawa Citizen. It's perfect for small families!

Crust:
1/3 c. graham wafer crumbs
1 tbsp. brown sugar
2 tbsp. butter or margarine
1/8 tsp. cinnamon

Filling:
1/2 lb. cream cheese, at room temperature
1/3 c. sugar
1 egg
1 tsp. lemon juice or vanilla extract
your favorite jam (raspberry, blueberry, strawberry)

1. **Crust:** Measure crumbs into a 2 cup glass measure. Stir in sugar. Add butter and **MW uncovered on HIGH for 30 seconds; stir. MW 30 seconds longer.** Cool slightly. Divide crumb mixture into four 6 oz. glass custard cups and pat down.

2. **Filling:** (If cream cheese is not at room temperature, unwrap it and place in a microsafe mixing bowl or the bowl from your food processor. **MW uncovered on MEDIUM (50%) for 1 minute.)** Blend cream cheese with sugar. Beat in egg and lemon juice; blend until smooth. Divide evenly over crumb mixture. Tap the bottom of the cups on the counter to level cheese mixture.

3. Place cups in a circle on a microsafe rack or inverted dish. **MW uncovered on MEDIUM (50%) for 4 to 5 minutes**, until barely set. Mixture will jiggle slightly, but will firm up as it cools. Place directly on the countertop and let cool. Top with a spoonful of your favorite jam. Refrigerate.

Yield: 4 mini cheesecakes. Can be frozen. **One mini cheesecake takes 1 to 2 minutes on LOW (10%) to thaw. Four will take 4 to 6 minutes.**

* Mixture can also be made in 6 microsafe muffin cups. Line each compartment with 2 paper cupcake liners. Cheesecake mixture will come almost to the top, but since they are cooked on **MEDIUM** power, cheesecakes do not overflow.
* To substitute dry cottage cheese for cream cheese, add 2 tsp. flour to the filling.

MINI PECAN CHEESECAKES

Follow recipe for Just a Little Cheesecake (above), but substitute 1/3 c. firmly packed brown sugar for the granulated sugar in the filling and flavor with vanilla. Instead of topping cheesecakes with jam, sprinkle each one with a spoonful of finely chopped pecans while still warm.

CRUSTLESS TROPICAL CHEESECAKE

Pretty as a picture!

1 ½ lb. cream cheese or dry cottage cheese
3 eggs
1 c. sugar
2 tbsp. lemon juice
¼ c. sour cream or yogurt
2 tbsp. flour

Topping:
1 pint strawberries, hulled & halved lengthwise
2 kiwi fruit, peeled & sliced
10 oz. can mandarin oranges, drained
½ c. apricot preserves, red currant or strawberry jelly

1. **Steel Knife:** Combine cheese, eggs, sugar and lemon juice and process with several on/off turns to start, then let machine run until mixture is smooth, about 30 seconds. Do not insert pusher in feed tube. Add sour cream (or yogurt) and flour and process about 10 seconds more, until blended. Pour into an ungreased 10″ ceramic quiche dish. Spread evenly.

2. Elevate on a microsafe rack or inverted pie plate. **MW uncovered on MEDIUM (50%) for 18 to 20 minutes,** rotating dish ¼ turn halfway through cooking. Edges will begin to pull away from the sides of the pan, but the centre will still jiggle slightly when you shake the dish. Batter may stick slightly to your fingertips when lightly touched, but will dry during standing time.

3. Place directly on the counter and let cool for 30 to 45 minutes. Cheesecake will firm up as it stands.

4. Arrange a border of strawberry halves around the outside edge of the cheesecake, with the pointed ends towards the centre. Make an inner circle of overlapping kiwi slices, then fill the centre with a circle of mandarin oranges.

5. **MW preserves or jelly uncovered on HIGH for 45 seconds,** until melted. Carefully glaze fruit, using a pastry brush. Refrigerate 4 to 6 hours before serving.

Yield: 8 servings. May be frozen, but fruit topping must be added after thawing.

* Thaw frozen cheesecake in refrigerator overnight or **MW uncovered on LOW (10%) for 10 minutes.** Let stand 10 minutes to complete thawing. **One slice takes 1 to 2 minutes on LOW (10%) to defrost.**
* Fresh blueberries, seedless grapes, banana slices (dipped in lemon juice), drained canned apricots and/or peaches are alternative toppings.

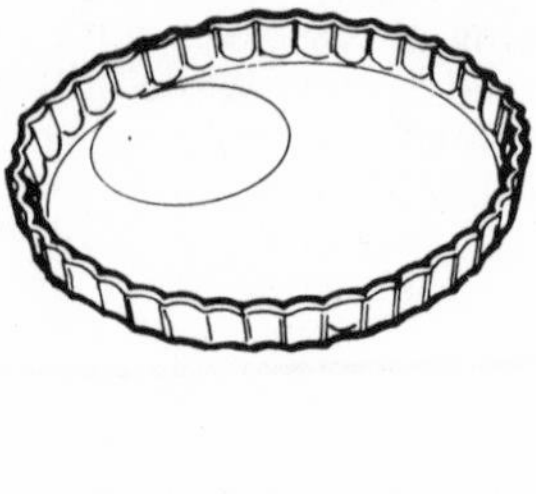

MICRO-WAYS WITH MUFFINS

- **Small ramekins and glass custard cups** make excellent cooking containers for microwaved muffins.
- **Large glass custard cups** (10 oz.) are ideal to make jumbo microwaved muffins. **One jumbo muffin will take 50 to 60 seconds on HIGH to cook.**
- **Line each muffin cup** with two paper cupcake liners to absorb the excess moisture released.
- **It may be necessary to turn** the individual cups if muffins are baking unevenly.
- **Muffins will be slightly moist on top when done;** the extra moisture will evaporate during standing time.
- **Microwaved muffins will have flat tops** and be fairly light in color. However, they cook in moments in the microwave and there is no need to wait for the oven to preheat! For a browner color, sprinkle unbaked muffins with a topping (p. 306).
- **Wrap muffins in a napkin** or microsafe paper towel to reheat.
- **One micro-cooked muffin will be warmed in 10 seconds or defrosted in 15 to 20 seconds on HIGH.** Conventionally baked muffins are slightly larger, so they will take a few seconds longer to warm or thaw.
- **A frozen jumbo muffin from a specialty shop takes about 30 to 40 seconds on HIGH to thaw and warm.**
- **Because muffins and bread products are very porous,** thawing and warming can be done in one step, using HIGH power.
- **If you like crusty, rounded tops** on your muffins, bake them conventionally and freeze the leftovers. Use your microwave to defrost and warm.
- **I sometimes bake one batch** of muffins conventionally and bake the leftover batter in my microwave oven instead of waiting 20 minutes for the pan to be free again. That way I have a muffin to munch on while cleaning up!
- **Microwaved muffins are usually smaller** than conventional ones because of the size of the compartments in the muffin pan. Therefore, you will get more microwaved muffins when converting your conventional recipe for microwave cooking.

MUFFIN COOKING TIMES at HIGH POWER

1 muffin	**35 - 45 seconds**	**3 - 4 muffins**	**1 ¼ - 1 ¾ minutes**
2 muffins	**45 - 55 seconds**	**5 - 6 muffins**	**2 - 2 ½ minutes**

REHEATING TIMES FOR ROLLS, BAGEL, MUFFINS & DANISH

Micro-cooked muffins are smaller, so reduce time. 2 slices of bread is equal to 1 roll.

Quantity	From Room Temperature	Power	From Frozen
1	10 - 15 seconds	HIGH	20 - 25 seconds
2	20 - 25 seconds	HIGH	35 - 40 seconds
3	25 - 30 seconds	HIGH	45 - 50 seconds
4	30 - 45 seconds	HIGH	50 - 60 seconds
1 loaf bread (16 oz.)	35 - 45 seconds	HIGH	1 - 1 ¼ minutes

EVER-READY BRAN MUFFINS

Leftover batter can be stored in the refrigerator up to 6 weeks in an airtight container. Increase cooking time slightly when using refrigerated batter. In a conventional oven, these muffins take 20 minutes at 400°F to bake!

1 c. water
3 c. bran cereal
½ c. corn or vegetable oil
1 ½ c. brown sugar, firmly packed
2 tbsp. vinegar or lemon juice plus milk to make 2 cups
2 eggs
2 ½ tsp. baking soda
½ tsp. salt
1 tbsp. cocoa
2 ½ c. flour
¾ c. raisins

1. **MW water uncovered on HIGH until boiling, 2 ½ to 3 minutes.** Measure cereal into a large mixing bowl; pour boiling water over and stir to mix. Cool slightly. Stir in oil, brown sugar, milk mixture and eggs. Add remaining ingredients and mix until blended.

2. Line 6 microsafe muffin cups or 6 glass custard cups with double paper cupcake liners. Do not grease. Fill half full (use about 2 tbsp. batter for each muffin).

3. **MW uncovered on HIGH for 2 to 2 ½ minutes,** rotating ¼ turn halfway through cooking. Tops should not stick when touched with your fingers and a toothpick inserted in muffins will come out dry. There may be some surface moisture, but it will evaporate during standing time. Let stand 1 minute. Remove from pan and repeat with remaining batter. Store leftover batter tightly covered in refrigerator for another day.

Yield: approximately 3 dozen muffins. Muffins freeze well.

* **CONVECTION CYCLE:** Insert rack recommended by oven manufacturer. Preheat oven to 375°F. Prepare muffins as directed, using an aluminum muffin pan lined with paper liners. Fill ⅔ full. **Bake at 375°F for 18 to 20 minutes,** until done.

BRAN MUFFINS

- 6 tbsp. butter or margarine, cut in chunks
- ½ c. brown sugar, packed
- ¼ c. honey or molasses
- 2 eggs
- 1 c. milk
- 1 ½ c. All Bran or natural bran cereal
- 1 c. flour
- 1 ½ tsp. baking powder
- ½ tsp. baking soda
- ¼ tsp. salt
- ½ c. apricots, cut up (or Sultana raisins or chocolate chips)
- 1 tsp. grated orange zest

1. **Steel Knife:** Process butter, brown sugar, molasses and eggs for 1 minute. Do not insert pusher in feed tube. Add milk and process 2 or 3 seconds to blend. Add remaining ingredients except for apricots. Process with 3 or 4 quick on/off turns. Blend in apricots with 2 quick on/off turns. Let mixture stand for 5 minutes.

2. Line 6 microsafe muffin cups or 6 glass custard cups with double paper cupcake liners. Do not grease. Fill half full (use about 2 tbsp. batter for each muffin).

3. **MW uncovered on HIGH for 2 to 2 ½ minutes,** rotating ¼ turn halfway through cooking. Tops should not stick when touched with your fingers and a toothpick inserted in muffins will come out dry. There may be some surface moisture, but it will evaporate during standing time. Let stand 1 minute. Remove from pan and repeat with remaining batter.

Yield: 20 medium muffins. These freeze well.

* **CONVECTION CYCLE:** Insert rack recommended by oven manufacturer. Preheat oven to 375°F. Prepare muffins as directed, using an aluminum muffin pan lined with paper liners. Fill ⅔ full. **Bake at 375°F for 18 to 20 minutes,** until done. **Yield:** 12 to 14 muffins.

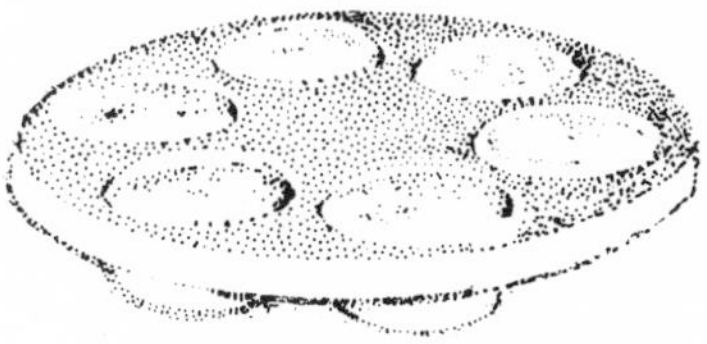

OAT BRAN MUF-FITS (MUFFINS)

This healthy muffin is high in fibre and pectin, as well as low in cholesterol. Current medical research has shown that oat bran is an excellent way to help reduce cholesterol levels.

Cinnamon Nut Topping (p. 306), optional
2 ¼ c. oat bran cereal
1 ½ tsp. cinnamon
1 tbsp. baking powder
1 apple, peeled & cored*
¼ c. oil
¼ c. honey
1 ¼ c. apple juice or skim milk
2 egg whites (or 1 egg)
½ c. raisins or chopped nuts

1. Prepare topping; set aside. Process oat bran cereal on the **Steel Knife** of the food processor for 1 minute. (This makes a muffin with a finer texture.) Blend in cinnamon and baking powder. Empty into a mixing bowl. Process apple until finely minced. Add to oat bran mixture. Add remaining ingredients except topping. Mix just until blended. Do not overmix or muffins will be tough.

2. Line a microsafe muffin pan with two paper liners in each compartment. Fill each one half full (about 2 tbsp. of batter). Sprinkle muffins with topping.

3. **MW 6 muffins at a time uncovered on HIGH for 2 to 2 ½ minutes,** rotating pan ¼ turn halfway through cooking. When done, muffins will be almost dry on top. Do not overcook. Any moist patches will dry during standing time. Let stand for 2 minutes. Remove from pan. Repeat with remaining batter.

Yield: 14 to 16 microwaved muffins.

* **CONVECTION CYCLE:** Insert rack recommended by oven manufacturer. Preheat oven to 375°F. Prepare muffins as directed in Steps 1 and 2. Spoon batter into aluminum muffin pans lined with paper liners. Fill ¾ full. Topping is optional. **Bake at 375°F for 18 minutes.** When done, a toothpick will come out almost dry. Don't overbake. (**In a conventional oven, bake at 400°F for 18 minutes.**) Makes 10 to 12 medium muffins.
* Two medium carrots, grated, may be used instead of the apple.
* **One muffin will take about 30 seconds on HIGH** to cook in the microwave.
* Place extra muffins in an airtight container and freeze.

ZUCCHINI/CARROT MUFFINS

This recipe is one of my favorites! I prefer to bake this moist and scrumptious muffin recipe conventionally because I prefer the way the flavor develops with oven heat. The microwave thaws or reheats leftovers in moments.

1 medium zucchini
2 medium carrots
1 c. brown sugar, lightly packed
2 eggs
½ c. oil
1 tsp. orange zest
1 tbsp. Kahlua or Grand Marnier*
1 ½ c. flour
½ tsp. baking powder
½ tsp. baking soda
1 tsp. cinnamon
¾ c. raisins

1. **Grater:** Trim ends off zucchini, but do not peel. Trim and peel carrots. Grate, using medium pressure. Measure 2 cups in total, loosely packed.

2. **Steel Knife:** Process brown sugar, eggs, oil, orange zest and liqueur for 1 minute, scraping down sides of bowl once or twice. Do not insert pusher in feed tube. Add zucchini and carrots; process 10 seconds longer. Add flour, baking powder, baking soda and cinnamon. Blend in with on/off turns, just until flour disappears. Stir raisins into batter.

3. Fill paper-lined muffin tins ¾ full. **Bake in a preheated 350°F oven for 20 to 25 minutes,** until done. (Can also be baked on the **CONVECTION CYCLE** on rack recommended by oven manufacturer. Check at minimum time for doneness.)

Yield: 16 muffins.

* One tsp. vanilla can be used instead of liqueur.
* **ZUCCHINI PECAN CHIP MUFFINS:** Omit carrots and raisins. Use 2 c. grated zucchini. Increase cinnamon to 1 ½ tsp. Stir ½ c. chopped pecans and ¾ c. chocolate chips into muffin batter. Bake as directed. (Be prepared to make these often!)
* These taste even better the next day and also freeze well (providing you bake them when no one is around and hide them quickly)!
* **MINI MUFFINS:** Because these are addictive and I can really binge on them, I sometimes bake them in miniature muffin tins so I don't feel so guilty when I go back for second and third helpings! **Miniatures take 15 to 18 minutes at 350°F to bake conventionally (or 12 to 15 minutes on the CONVECTION CYCLE).** Recipe makes about 4 dozen miniatures. Three mini muffins are the equivalent of 1 regular muffin.
* **One mini muffin will take 5 to 7 seconds on HIGH to thaw and warm. Three will take 12 to 15 seconds.**

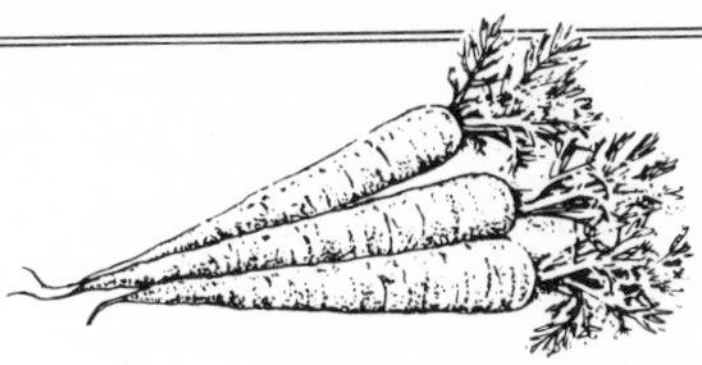

TOPPINGS FOR MUFFINS

CINNAMON SUGAR

Combine ½ c. white or brown sugar with 1 tsp. cinnamon. Sprinkle on unbaked muffins.

CINNAMON NUT TOPPING

Combine ¼ c. packed brown sugar, ¼ c. finely chopped nuts and ½ tsp. cinnamon. Sprinkle on unbaked muffins.

STREUSEL CRUMBLE

¾ c. flour
½ c. sugar
¼ c. butter or margarine
½ tsp. cinnamon, optional

1. **Steel Knife:** Process all ingredients until crumbly, about 10 seconds. Sprinkle on unbaked muffins (about 1 tbsp. per muffin.) Remainder may be stored in a container in the fridge or freezer.

STREUSEL NUT TOPPING

½ c. nuts
⅓ c. brown sugar, packed
¼ c. flour
3 tbsp. butter or margarine
1 tsp. cinnamon

1. **Steel Knife:** Process all ingredients until crumbly, about 12 to 15 seconds. Sprinkle on unbaked muffins (about 1 tbsp. per muffin). Remainder may be stored in a container in the fridge or freezer.

ARE YOU WELL-BREAD?

- **Do your rolls become rocks?** Is your bread tough stuff? You're overheating them in the microwave! Microwave just until warm, NEVER until hot! See Reheating Times on p. 301.
- **Do you suffer from soggy bottoms** when reheating bread or rolls? If you've been putting them on a plate to reheat, this is the problem. When microwaved, the bread becomes warm, the plate stays cool and condensation occurs.
- **Wrap bread or rolls in microsafe paper towelling to reheat.** A microsafe rack can also be used. No more soggy rolls!
- **Breads, rolls and muffins** can be reheated in a wicker basket, providing there are no metal staples. Line basket with a cloth napkin or microsafe paper towelling. Reheat briefly, just until warm to the touch.
- **Because bread products are so porous,** they can be defrosted and warmed in just one step. **One large roll or bagel takes 20 to 25 seconds on HIGH to thaw and heat. It takes 15 seconds to thaw 1 large roll or bagel on HIGH. One frozen dinner roll or 2 slices of bread take 10 to 15 seconds on HIGH.**
- **Refresh day-old bread by sprinkling** with a few drops of water. Wrap in microsafe paper towels and microwave briefly, just until warm. It will be so fresh you may have to slap it!
- **If overheated, bread products become hard and chewy.** This is usually most evident after standing time. **To salvage them, just microwave them a little longer, about 45 seconds per slice.** They will become dry and crisp. (Watch carefully; bread can burn in the microwave if overdried!) Break into chunks and process on the **Steel Knife** of the processor to make bread crumbs.
- **Taco shells reheat quickly** in the microwave. Wrap in paper towelling; **MW on HIGH about 8 to 10 seconds each.**
- **Tortillas will stay soft** if you wrap them in a damp paper towel and place on a microsafe plate. Cover with an inverted plate. **MW on HIGH; allow 8 to 10 seconds for each tortilla.**
- **For crusty bagels, pop them into the toaster oven at 350°F for 3 or 4 minutes** after thawing them in the microwave. They'll taste just-baked!
- **Sweet fillings and toppings** such as raisins, jelly, jam and icing get much hotter than the dough in products such as cinnamon buns and donuts when microwaved. Let stand for a minute to equalize the heat so you won't burn yourself!
- **If heating sandwiches** in the microwave, place on a paper towel, napkin or microsafe rack to prevent them from getting soggy. Using frozen bread, rolls or toasted bread also helps. Otherwise, heat fillings and bread separately. Then assemble.
- **For easy "grilled cheese" sandwiches,** toast batches of bread conventionally and store in the freezer. Place sliced cheese between 2 slices of toast, wrap in paper towelling and **MW on HIGH for 25 to 30 seconds for 1 sandwich.** Toast will defrost and cheese will melt. (Careful — cheese will be hot, so let stand for 30 seconds or so to let the cheese cool down.)
- **If you are lucky enough to have a microwave oven at the office,** assemble your "grilled cheese" sandwich at home and heat it at work wrapped in a napkin or microsafe paper towel. Add a bowl of soup for a quick and nutritious lunch!

YEAST BREADS IN THE MICROWAVE

- **I love to rise yeast doughs in the microwave,** but prefer to bake them conventionally for best results.
- **Your oven** MUST HAVE a power level of **WARM or LOW (10%), no more than 60 to 75 watts.** Otherwise, do not attempt to rise yeast doughs in your microwave, or parts of the dough may start to cook and form a crust before rising is complete.
- **Both methods for rising yeast doughs** in the microwave work well; the choice is yours.
- **If you wish to rise dough a second time** after it has been punched down, it will take 25 to 30 minutes. Leave it in the warm microwave oven without turning it on.
- **If you don't have a larger microsafe bowl** for the water bath, you can use a 2 quart oblong casserole. Fill with 3 to 4 cups of water so that water level comes up as high as possible around the bowl containing the yeast dough.
- **To test if yeast dough has doubled in bulk,** make an indentation in the dough with your finger. If the indentation remains, the dough has doubled. If not, let it rise a little longer.
- **Use dark or dull finished pans** for maximum browning when baking yeast doughs on the CONVECTION CYCLE of a combination oven. Otherwise, crust will not brown properly.
- **If breads are not browned on the bottom** after baking, remove from pan and bake upside down on a baking sheet 5 minutes longer.

RISING METHOD #1 - BOILING WATER METHOD

1. Place yeast dough in a greased 2 quart microsafe bowl. Cover with vented plastic wrap. Place in a larger microsafe bowl. Carefully pour 3 cups of boiling water into the larger bowl. (**Three cups of water will take about 8 minutes on HIGH to boil.**) This forms a water bath around the bowl containing the yeast dough. **MW on WARM or LOW (10%) for 5 minutes.** Let stand in microwave for 15 minutes.

2. **MW on WARM or LOW (10%) for an additional 5 minutes.** Let stand in microwave until dough has doubled in bulk. Punch down and shape as desired.

RISING METHOD #2 — TEPID WATER METHOD

1. Place yeast dough in a greased 2 quart microsafe bowl. Cover bowl with vented plastic wrap. Place in a larger microsafe bowl. Carefully pour 3 cups of tap water into the larger bowl. This forms a water bath around the bowl containing the yeast dough. **MW on WARM or LOW (10%) for 20 minutes.**

2. Check if dough seems too warm. If so, let stand in microwave until double in bulk, about 10 to 15 minutes longer. If not, **MW 5 to 10 minutes longer on WARM or LOW (10%).** Punch down and shape as desired.

TIPS & TRICKS

- **To scald milk, MW uncovered on HIGH until steaming, 170 degrees on your probe. One cup of milk takes 1 ½ to 1 ¾ minutes on HIGH.** Stir; let cool to lukewarm before adding to yeast dough.
- **I usually prefer** to warm the milk rather than scald it. **I heat it to 130°F on the probe, about 1 ¼ minutes on HIGH.** Stir; cool slightly.
- **Yeast doughs made with milk** are more tender than those made with water.
- **For a low cholesterol yeast dough,** use corn or safflower oil instead of butter. Substitute 2 egg whites for each egg. Skim milk or water can be used instead of whole or 2% milk.
- **Raisins can be plumped easily** in the microwave. If they are just slightly dry, place in a microsafe dish, sprinkle with a few drops of water and **MW uncovered on HIGH for 30 to 60 seconds,** until softened.
- **If raisins are dry and hard,** add ½ c. water to 1 c. raisins and **MW uncovered for 2 to 3 minutes on HIGH** until hot. Let stand 3 or 4 minutes to plump. Drain off liquid.

DEFROSTING FROZEN BREAD DOUGH

2 c. hot water

1 loaf frozen bread dough

1. Pour hot water into a 7″ x 11″ microsafe casserole. **MW uncovered on HIGH for 4 to 5 minutes,** until boiling hot. Remove dough from package and place in a greased microsafe loaf pan. Cover dough with waxed paper. Place loaf pan into casserole of hot water.

2. **MW on WARM or LOW 10% (65 to 75 watts) for 4 to 5 minutes, or DEFROST (30%) for 3 to 4 minutes.** Turn dough over and repeat once more. Let stand in microwave oven with the door closed for 10 minutes, until thawed. Use as desired in your favorite recipe.

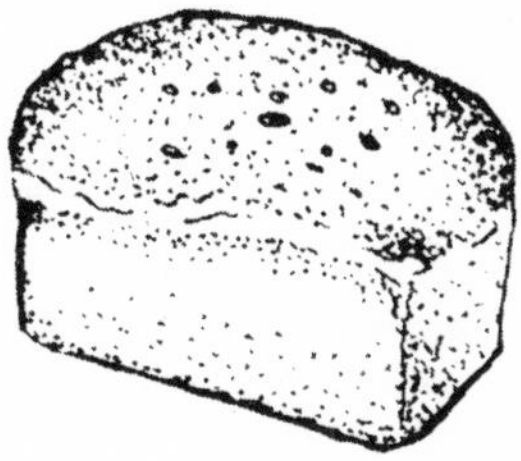

QUICK TRICKS WITH BREAD DOUGH

Thaw frozen bread dough in the microwave, then use to make these yummy yeast treats. You can also make Zippit-Zappit Yeast Dough (p. 311). You'll have a smaller yield when you use frozen dough, so baking time will be shorter for some recipes.

PIZZA: Roll out dough thinly. Place on a 12″ greased pizza pan; brush with 1 tsp. oil. **Bake crust at 400°F (or 375°F on the CONVECTION CYCLE) for 12 to 15 minutes,** until lightly browned. Top with your favorite toppings (pizza sauce, sliced mushrooms, red &/or green peppers, onions, grated Cheddar, Mozzerella &/or Parmesan cheeses). **Bake at 400°F (or 375°F on the CONVECTION CYCLE) 12 to 15 minutes longer,** until nicely browned.

CINNAMON BUNS: Roll dough into a rectangle. Spread with butter, brown sugar, cinnamon, raisins and/or nuts. Roll up and cut in 1″ slices. Place cut-side down on a greased cookie sheet. When double in bulk, brush with Egg Glaze*. **Bake in conventional oven at 375°F (or 350°F on the CONVECTION CYCLE) for 15 to 20 minutes,** until golden.

CHEDDAR CHEESE BREAD: Roll dough into a rectangle. Spread with ¾ to 1 c. grated Cheddar cheese. Roll up and shape into a loaf. Place on a lightly greased aluminum baking sheet. When double in bulk, brush with Egg Glaze*. **Bake in conventional oven at 375°F (or 325°F on the CONVECTION CYCLE) for 25 to 35 minutes,** until golden. When done, bread will sound hollow when lightly tapped.

ITALIAN BUBBLE BREAD: Shape dough into 3 dozen 1″ balls. **Melt ½ cup garlic butter for 1 minute on HIGH.** Roll balls in melted butter. Arrange half the balls in a single layer in a greased 10″ metal Bundt pan. Measure ½ cup grated Parmesan cheese. Sprinkle half of the cheese over dough in pan. Repeat with remaining dough, garlic butter and cheese. When double in bulk, **bake in conventional oven at 375°F (or 325°F on the CONVECTION CYCLE) for 25 to 35 minutes,** until nicely browned. It will sound hollow when tapped with your fingertips. Let stand 15 minutes. Loosen edges with a spatula, invert and remove from pan.

CINNAMON BUBBLE BREAD: Prepare and bake exactly as for Italian Bubble Bread, but roll balls of dough in ½ cup melted butter, then in Cinnamon Sugar (p. 306); (you'll need about 1 cup). If desired, sprinkle chopped nuts over dough. (Cover with aluminum foil for the last few minutes of baking to prevent overbrowning.)

* **Egg Glaze:** Blend 1 egg yolk with 1 tbsp. water.
* Preheat oven for best results. On the **CONVECTION CYCLE,** temperatures should be 25 to 50°F lower (larger items overbrown easily). Bake on rack recommended by oven manufacturer.
* If overbrowning occurs, reduce temperature by 25°F, or cover loosely with aluminum foil.

ZIPPIT-ZAPPIT YEAST DOUGH

This dough is like your basic black dress or suit; it will take you anywhere!

½ c. water
1 tsp. sugar
1 envelope yeast (1 tbsp.)
3 c. flour (approximately)
1 to 3 tbsp. sugar*
1 tsp. salt
2 to 4 tbsp. oil*
¾ c. lukewarm water (or milk)

1. Measure ½ cup water into a 1 cup glass measure. **MW on HIGH for 20 seconds.** It should be 105 to 115°F. Add 1 tsp. sugar; mix well. Sprinkle yeast over and let stand for 8 to 10 minutes, until foamy. Stir to dissolve.

2. **Steel Knife:** Place flour, yeast mixture, sugar, salt and oil in processor bowl. Process 6 to 8 seconds. Add water or milk through the feed tube while the machine is running. Process until dough gathers together and forms a mass around the blades. (It's better if dough is stickier rather than drier.) Let machine knead dough for 30 to 45 seconds. If machine slows down, add 2 to 4 tbsp. flour through the feed tube.

3. Turn out dough onto a lightly oiled counter. Knead for 1 to 2 minutes, until smooth and elastic. Place in a lightly greased 8 cup glass measure. Follow Rising Method #1 or #2 (p. 308). Punch down. If desired, rise dough a second time. (I usually don't bother.)

4. Shape dough into bread, rolls, cinnamon buns or whatever you like. (See Quick Tricks with Bread Dough on p. 310.) Let rise until double in bulk, about 1 hour at room temperature. (For pizza, dough does not have to double; you will have enough dough to make two 12″ pizzas.) Bake as directed.

* Use maximum amounts of sugar and oil if dough will be used for cinnamon buns or sweet breads. Use minimum amounts to make bread, dinner rolls or pizza. Milk makes a more tender dough.

* **CHALAH:** Break 2 eggs into a measuring cup. Add enough lukewarm water to make ¾ cup. (Use this to replace the ¾ cup of lukewarm water.) In Step 4, divide dough into 3 long ropes. Braid; tuck ends under. When double, brush with egg glaze and sprinkle with sesame seeds. **Bake at 375°F for 30 to 35 minutes (or 325° on the CONVECTION CYCLE),** until golden. Bread will sound hollow when tapped with your fingertips.

* **WHOLE WHEAT BREAD:** Substitute whole wheat flour for half the flour. In Step 4, roll dough into a rectangle. Roll up. Seal ends by pressing down with the edge of your hand. When double, **bake at 375°F for 30 to 35 minutes (or 325°F on the CONVECTION CYCLE).**

* When larger foods (e.g. bread) are baked on the **CONVECTION CYCLE,** oven temperature is reduced by 50°F so bread will cook through completely without overbrowning on the surface. For smaller items such as rolls, reducing temperature by 25°F is sufficient.

CROUTONS

1. Cut white or French bread into ½″ squares. Measure 4 cups. Place in a large microsafe bowl and **MW uncovered on HIGH for 5 minutes,** stirring 2 or 3 times. Bread will be dry and crisp. Let cool. Store in an airtight container. Use in salads or to top casseroles.

ITALIAN STYLE CROUTONS

1 tbsp. butter or margarine
1 tbsp. grated Parmesan cheese
1 tsp. dried parsley flakes
¼ tsp. each salt, garlic powder, basil & oregano
8 slices white or French bread

1. Melt butter or margarine on HIGH for 30 to 40 seconds in a large microsafe bowl. Add Parmesan cheese and seasonings.

2. Cut white or French bread into ½″ squares. Measure 4 cups. Toss bread cubes in seasoned butter mixture. **MW uncovered on HIGH for 5 minutes,** stirring 2 or 3 times. Bread will be dry and crisp. Let cool. Store in an airtight container. Use in salads or to top casseroles.

BREAD CRUMBS

1. Prepare Croutons (regular or Italian Style) as directed above. When cool, process on the **Steel Knife** of the processor until finely crushed.

PUDDINGS, PIES & DESSERTS

MICRO-WAYS WITH PUDDINGS, PIES & DESSERTS

- **Puddings are cooked uncovered on HIGH** power for easy stirring and maximum evaporation of liquid.
- **Stir during cooking** because cornstarch (and potato starch even more so) settles to the bottom of the bowl. Insufficient stirring results in lumpy pudding.
- **Watch carefully** as pudding has a tendency to boil over. Open the microwave oven door and boil-over will stop immediately.
- **To prevent a skin** from forming on top of puddings or pie fillings, place wax paper directly on the surface immediately upon removing it from the microwave.
- **The recipes for home-made pie fillings** in this section are less sweet, less expensive and more flavorful than packaged fillings. They contain no additives and are quick to make, using ingredients you have in your pantry.
- **For a quick and easy** elegant dessert, alternate layers of cooled pudding and whipped cream in parfait glasses. Sprinkle with chopped nuts or grated chocolate.
- **An easy way** to fill parfait glasses is to use a wide mouth canning funnel.
- **CHOCOLATE CREAM PIE:** Cooked pudding can be poured into a baked Cookie Crumb Pie Crust (p. 327) for a quick company dessert. Garnish with swirls of sweetened whipped cream.
- **BANANA CREAM PIE:** Slice 2 bananas and sprinkle with lemon juice. Place in a baked Cookie Crumb Pie Crust. Top with vanilla pudding and garnish with whipped cream.
- **To soften ice cream, MW on DEFROST (30%) for 30 seconds for 1 pint, 45 seconds for 1 quart or litre, or 1 minute for ½ gallon (2 litres).**
- **When you need a cookie crust** for a recipe that calls for a metal springform pan (e.g. refrigerator desserts), mix the ingredients for the crust in a microsafe bowl and **MW uncovered on HIGH for 2 minutes**, stirring at half time. Empty into a lightly greased springform pan and press down firmly with a flat bottomed glass. Crust will set as it cools.
- **For hints on pie crusts**, refer to Easy as Pie (p. 325) and That's the Way the Cookie Crumbles (p. 327).
- **Meringues must be microwaved on MEDIUM (50%). Allow about 1 minute for each egg white in the meringue. A 3 egg meringue will be set in 3 minutes**. It will not brown. Place it under a hot broiler for a minute or two if you wish to brown it.
- **Crisps** are easy and delicious. They are ready to serve within 20 minutes and make a quick dessert for unexpected company.
- **Empty a 10 oz.** pkg. of frozen unsweetened or sweetened fruit (e.g. strawberries, raspberries) into a microsafe bowl. **MW uncovered on DEFROST (30%) for 3 to 4 minutes**, stirring once or twice. **A 16 oz. pkg. takes 4 to 5 minutes**. Let stand 5 to 10 minutes to complete defrosting. Stir once or twice.
- **Baked apples** are a nutritious dessert and make a perfect after-school snack for hungry kids or midnight sweet-seekers. **One apple (just 60 calories) takes 2 to 3 minutes to microwave**. A tablespoon of raisins adds 26 calories. Cook and serve apple in the same dish. What could be easier?

HOME-MADE CHOCOLATE PUDDING

Puddings are a pleasure to microwave! When I was a young bride, I used to burn my chocolate pudding, no matter how carefully or how often I stirred. I finally got a special aluminum pot that helped the problem, but the pudding still stuck to the pot. The microwave oven provided the perfect solution. It also left less in the pot for me to scrape out and snack on! Oh well, sometimes solutions create other problems.

½ c. sugar
¼ c. cocoa*
3 tbsp. cornstarch or potato starch
dash salt
2 ¼ c. milk (regular or skim)
1 tsp. vanilla or 1 tbsp. Kahlua

1. Blend dry ingredients in an 8 cup microsafe measuring cup or bowl. Gradually whisk in milk. **MW uncovered on HIGH 6 to 7 minutes**, stirring every 2 minutes, until mixture is boiling and thickened. Blend in flavoring.

2. Pour into individual serving dishes or a baked pie shell. Chill thoroughly. If desired, top with whipped cream and grated chocolate.

Yield: 4 servings.

* If you wish to use artificial sweetener, add to pudding once it has cooked in order to avoid a bitter flavor.
* No cocoa in the cupboard? No problem. Decrease sugar to ⅓ cup. Cook mixture until boiling and thickened. Add 1 cup semi-sweet chocolate chips and stir until melted.

KOKO-MOKO PUDDING

Follow directions for Home-Made Chocolate Pudding (above), but add 2 tsp. instant coffee to the dry ingredients.

VANILLA PUDDING

1. Follow directions for Home-Made Chocolate Pudding (above), but omit cocoa and decrease sugar to ⅓ cup. Use vanilla or Grand Marnier as the flavoring.

2. Pour into individual serving dishes or a baked pie shell. Chill thoroughly. If desired, top with sweetened whipped cream flavored with a little Grand Marnier. Garnish with mandarin oranges.

BUTTERSCOTCH PUDDING

½ c. dark brown sugar, lightly packed
3 tbsp. cornstarch or potato starch
dash salt
2 ¼ c. milk
1 tsp. butterscotch or vanilla extract

1. Blend first 3 ingredients in an 8 cup microsafe measuring cup or bowl. Gradually whisk in milk. **MW uncovered on HIGH for 6 to 7 minutes,** stirring every 2 minutes, until boiling and thickened. Blend in flavoring.

2. Pour into individual serving dishes. Chill thoroughly. If desired, top with whipped cream and chopped pecans.

Yield: 4 servings. Mixture can also be poured into a baked Cookie Crumb Pie Crust (p. 327) made with gingersnap cookies for a quick company dessert.

PACKAGED PUDDING MIX

1. Combine pudding mix with milk in an 8 cup microsafe measuring cup or bowl as directed on the package. **MW uncovered on HIGH for 6 to 7 minutes for a 4 serving package and 8 to 10 minutes for a 6 serving package,** until boiling and thickened. Stir every 2 to 3 minutes. Pour into individual serving dishes or a baked pie crust and chill.

CHOCOLATE PUDDING JUST FOR ME!

So quick!

2 tsp. cornstarch
½ c. milk
dash salt
¼ c. semi-sweet chocolate chips

1. Combine all ingredients in a 2 cup Pyrex™ measure and mix well. **MW uncovered on HIGH for 1 minute**. Stir well. **MW 30 to 45 seconds longer,** until thick and bubbling. Stir again. Chill.

Yield: 1 serving.

BUTTERSCOTCH PUDDING JUST FOR YOU

I prefer chocolate!

Prepare Chocolate Pudding Just For Me (above) as directed, but substitute butterscotch chips for the chocolate chips.

DIETER'S CHOCOLATE PUDDING

2 tsp. cornstarch
1 tbsp. cocoa
pinch of salt
½ c. skim milk
artificial sweetener to equal 2 tbsp. sugar

1. Combine cornstarch, cocoa, salt and skim milk in a 2 cup Pyrex™ measure. Blend well.

2. **MW uncovered on HIGH for 1 minute.** Stir well. **MW on HIGH 30 to 45 seconds longer**, until thick and bubbling. Stir in artificial sweetener. Chill.

Yield: 1 serving. About 92 calories per serving.

FROZEN PUDDING ON A STICK

1. Prepare your favorite flavor of home-made or packaged pudding mix as directed. If desired, stir in ½ cup marshmallow fluff. Pour hot pudding into 4 paper drinking cups. Cut a small slit in center of 4 circles of waxed paper. Place waxed paper directly on surface of pudding. Insert wooden sticks. Freeze. Peel away paper cup at serving time.

Yield: 4 servings.

CREAMY RICE PUDDING

No need to cook the rice separately for this delicious recipe. Although the cooking time is fairly long, the rice pudding requires little attention during cooking. Short grain rice gives a creamy texture.

½ c. short grain rice
⅓ c. sugar
dash salt
3 ½ c. milk
1 tsp. vanilla
⅓ c. raisins
cinnamon

1. Combine rice, sugar, salt and milk in a 3 quart microsafe bowl. Cover with vented plastic wrap. **MW on HIGH for 9 to 10 minutes**, until mixture comes to a boil. Remove plastic wrap and stir.

2. **Reduce power to MEDIUM (50%) and MW uncovered 40 to 45 minutes longer**, until milk is almost completely absorbed and mixture is thick and creamy. Stir occasionally. Stir in vanilla, raisins and a dash of cinnamon. Let stand for 10 minutes while rice absorbs additional liquid. (If mixture gets too thick, just add a little milk.)

3. Spoon into dessert dishes and sprinkle lightly with cinnamon. Serve hot or cold. If refrigerating, cover with plastic wrap.

Yield: 6 servings. Do not freeze.

STEAMED PUDDING

This recipe takes 6 hours of steaming when cooked conventionally. The microwave cooks it to perfection in less than 20 minutes!

2 c. fresh breadcrumbs
½ c. coarsely chopped nuts (almonds, walnuts or pecans)
1 apple, peeled, cored & grated
1 c. mixed candied peel (fruit cake mix)
1 c. Sultana raisins
½ c. flour
¾ c. brown sugar, packed
1 tsp. cinnamon
¼ tsp. nutmeg
pinch of cloves
2 eggs
½ c. orange juice
1 tbsp. lemon juice
⅓ c. oil

1. To make crumbs, process 4 or 5 slices of rye, pumpernickle or raisin bread until fine on the food processor, using the **Steel Knife**. Transfer to a large mixing bowl. Add remaining ingredients in order given. Mix well.

2. Spread evenly in a lightly greased 6 cup microsafe ring mold (or 2 quart glass casserole with a glass placed open end up in the centre). Cover with plastic wrap, turning back one corner ⅛″ to vent.

3. **MW on MEDIUM (50%) for 14 to 16 minutes**, rotating pan ¼ turn every 5 minutes. When done, a toothpick inserted in the centre will come out clean, although top of pudding may appear somewhat moist. Let stand covered on counter 15 minutes. Loosen edges with a spatula and unmold onto a serving platter. Serve warm with Brandy Hard Sauce (see below).

Yield: 6 to 8 servings. Can be frozen.

* Can be prepared up to 2 weeks in advance. Wrap cooled pudding well with foil and refrigerate. (May also be wrapped in cheesecloth that has been well moistened with brandy, then overwrapped tightly with foil.)
* To reheat, remove wrappings. Place on serving plate. **MW covered with waxed paper on MEDIUM (50%) for 5 to 6 minutes,** until warm.
* To flame the pudding, warm 2 tbsp. brandy in a 1 cup Pyrex™ measure for **15 seconds on HIGH.** Pour over warmed pudding and ignite. (Turn off all the lights for maximum effect!)

BRANDY HARD SAUCE

1 tbsp. grated orange rind
1½ c. icing sugar
½ c. soft butter
3 tbsp. brandy
1 tsp. vanilla

Combine all ingredients and beat until smooth. (This takes about 15 to 20 seconds on the food processor.) Pour over Steamed Pudding.

BAKED CUSTARD

1 ⅓ c. milk
3 eggs
¼ c. sugar
dash of salt
1 tsp. vanilla
dash of nutmeg or cinnamon

1. **MW milk uncovered in a 2 cup Pyrex™ measure on HIGH about 3 minutes**, or until steaming. Mix eggs, sugar, salt and vanilla just until blended. Slowly blend in milk. Divide into four 6 oz. Pyrex™ custard cups or ceramic ramekins. Sprinkle with nutmeg or cinnamon.
2. **MW uncovered at MEDIUM-HIGH (70%) for 5 to 6 minutes**, rotating custard cups twice during cooking. Centres will shake like partially-set jello when done, but will set when cooled. Let cool; refrigerate.

Yield: 4 servings.

* If overcooked, custard will "wrinkle" during standing time!
* If your oven has an uneven cooking pattern, some custards may cook more quickly than others. Just remove them when done.
* **COFFEE CUSTARD:** Dissolve 2 tsp. instant coffee in the hot milk.

CRÈME PÂTISSIÈRE (PASTRY CREAM)

So easy with a food processor and microwave! You'll be an instant gourmet cook. Use to fill flans, fruit tartlets, cream puffs or milles feuilles.

1 c. milk
3 egg yolks
¼ c. sugar
¼ c. flour
1 tbsp. butter
1 tbsp. Grand Marnier or your favorite liqueur

1. **MW milk uncovered in a 4 cup Pyrex™ measure on HIGH for 2 minutes**, until steaming hot.
2. **Steel Knife:** Process egg yolks with sugar and flour about 15 to 20 seconds, until mixed. Add hot milk through feed tube while machine is running and process until smooth. Pour mixture back into measuring cup.
3. **MW uncovered on HIGH 2 minutes**, until very thick, whisking every 30 seconds to prevent lumping. Whisk in butter and flavoring. Cover surface of mixture with plastic wrap to prevent a skin from forming. (May be prepared 3 to 4 days in advance and refrigerated until needed.)

Yield: About 1 ¼ cups, enough to fill an 11″ flan.

* For a delicious variation, whip 1 cup whipping cream until stiff. Fold into cooled pastry cream and serve in individual parfait dishes. Also may be poured into a baked pie shell as a light and creamy filling for cream pie, or alternated with layers of sponge cake and fruit to make a quick trifle.
* **CHOCOLATE PASTRY CREAM:** Add ½ cup chocolate chips to hot Crème Pâtissière and stir to blend. Use a chocolate flavored liqueur such as Kahlua or Tia Maria. Also delicious with Franjelica.

HOME-MADE CHOCOLATE ICE CREAM

Ice cream in the microwave? Absolutely, and so easy too! There is no scorching of the cream or milk when you make the custard, and if you have a probe, it's even easier! If you are calorie-conscious, you can make this recipe with 3 cups of milk and omit the cream. It won't be as creamy, but it is still delicious.

1 ½ c. whipping cream or light cream
1 ½ c. milk
¾ c. sugar
4 egg yolks, lightly beaten
1 tsp. vanilla or 2 tbsp. liqueur
3 oz. semi-sweet chocolate

1. Combine cream and milk with sugar in an 8 cup microsafe measuring cup or bowl. **MW uncovered on HIGH for 7 to 9 minutes**, until almost boiling.

2. Remove from microwave and whisk about 1 cup of the hot mixture gradually into the yolks. Whisk egg yolk mixture back into milk mixture.

3. MW uncovered on HIGH for 1 to 2 minutes longer, until mixture reaches 170°F on the microwave probe or a thermometer. (If you don't have a thermometer, dip a spoon into the mixture and draw your finger across the mixture clinging to the back of the spoon. It should leave a path. If overcooked, you will get scrambled eggs!) Stir in flavoring. Let stand while you prepare the chocolate.

4. MW the chocolate uncovered in a dry microsafe bowl **on HIGH for 2 minutes**, stirring at half time. Chocolate should be almost melted; stir to complete melting. Let cool for 5 minutes. Slowly whisk chocolate into the the hot cream mixture; mix until smooth. Let cool to room temperature. Chill thoroughly.

5. Freeze in ice cream machine according to manufacturer's instructions. (If you don't have an ice cream machine, read We All Scream for Ice Cream, p. 321.) When set, serve immediately (it will be somewhat soft) or transfer to a storage container, cover tightly and freeze it from 2 to 24 hours (if you can wait!) to allow flavor to develop. Home-made ice cream can be stored in your freezer for 2 weeks.

Yield: about 1 quart (1 to 8 servings!)

* **Microwave the leftover whites** and use them as a garnish for asparagus — then you can eat the ice cream without guilt! **Four egg whites will take about 1 minute covered on HIGH.**

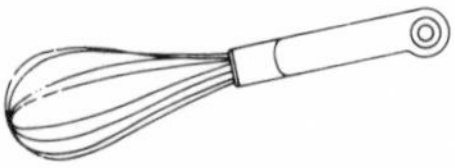

WE ALL SCREAM FOR ICE CREAM!

- **Using liqueur** instead of vanilla extract results in a slightly softer ice cream. Use any of the following: Kahlua, Amaretto, Grand Marnier, Vandermint or Sabra.
- **If you don't have an ice cream machine**, pour mixture into ice cube trays, cover and freeze in the coldest part of your freezer. Process "ice cream cubes" one cup at a time on the **Steel Knife** of the processor until smooth and creamy. If you don't have a processor, mix ice cream several times during the freezing process to break up the ice crystals.
- **If using an ice cream machine**, fill cannister ¾ full. This prevents too much air from being beaten into your ice cream, giving you a better quality product.
- **If you wish to add chunks of cookies or brownies** to your ice cream, add them just before it is completely frozen, about 2 or 3 minutes from the end. Otherwise they get soggy and also will not be evenly mixed throughout the ice cream.

All the variations below are based on the recipe for Home-Made Chocolate Ice Cream (p. 320).

CHOCOLATE BROWNIE ICE CREAM: Use 1 tsp. vanilla or 2 tbsp. Kahlua to flavor ice cream. Stir 1 cup coarsely chopped Brownies into nearly-set ice cream mixture.

CHOCOLATE COOKIE ICE CREAM: Use 1 tsp. vanilla to flavor ice cream. Stir 1 cup of coarsely broken Oreo or chocolate chip cookies into nearly-set ice cream mixture.

CHOCOLATE CHUNK ICE CREAM: Use 1 tsp. vanilla or 2 tbsp. Kahlua or Vandermint liqueur to flavor ice cream. Stir 2 oz. semi-sweet chocolate, or ¾ cup after-dinner mints, coarsely chopped, into the nearly-set ice cream mixture.

CHOCOLATE ALMOND CHIP ICE CREAM: Use ¼ tsp. almond extract or 2 tbsp. Amaretto to flavor ice cream. Stir ½ cup of chopped toasted almonds and 2 oz. semi-sweet chocolate, coarsely chopped, into the nearly-set ice cream mixture.

FRENCH VANILLA ICE CREAM: For those of you who don't share my love affair with chocolate, make Home-Made Chocolate Ice Cream as directed, but omit flavoring and semi-sweet chocolate. Split 1 vanilla bean in half lengthwise and **MW on HIGH** together with the cream, milk and sugar for **7 to 9 minutes,** until simmering. Let stand for ½ hour to extract the flavor. Remove vanilla bean; Microwave milk mixture once again until almost boiling. Continue as directed from Step 2.

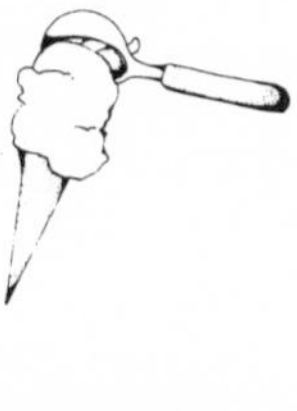

WHITE CHOCOLATE MOUSSE

Guaranteed to bring raves from your guests!

½ c. whipping cream (35%)
½ c. unsalted butter
8 oz. white chocolate, in chunks
4 egg yolks
2 tbsp. Amaretto liqueur
4 egg whites
1 tbsp. sugar

1. Combine cream and butter in a 2 cup Pyrex™ measure. **MW uncovered on HIGH for 1½ to 2 minutes**, until cream is boiling and butter is melted. Meanwhile, process white chocolate on **Steel Knife** of food processor until finely chopped, about 30 seconds. Pour hot cream mixture through feed tube while machine is running. Process until smooth and blended.

2. **MW egg yolks uncovered on HIGH for 10 to 12 seconds** to remove the chill from them. (It is not necessary to pierce the yolks first.) Blend yolks and liqueur into chocolate mixture. Transfer to a large bowl.

3. In a separate bowl (copper if you have one), beat egg whites with an electric mixer until foamy. Gradually add sugar and beat until stiff. Gently stir ⅓ of whites into chocolate mixture. Add remaining whites and fold in carefully, just until whites disappear. Pour into a 2 quart glass serving bowl. Refrigerate until partially set, about 2 hours. Garnish (recipe follows). Chill until serving time.

Yield: 12 servings. Do not freeze.

Garnish for White Chocolate Mousse

1½ c. whipping cream (35%)
2 tbsp. icing sugar
2 tbsp. Amaretto liqueur
Chocolate-Dipped Strawberries (p. 364)
chocolate shavings

1. Whip cream. When nearly stiff, beat in icing sugar and Amaretto. Using a pastry bag and large star tip, decorate mousse. Prepare strawberries as directed; arrange a border of berries around the edge of the mousse, and place one large berry in the centre. Sprinkle with chocolate shavings. Refrigerate.

* Make sure that the bowl you use to whip the egg whites is grease-free and that no egg yolk gets into the white mixture.
* Tia Maria, Grand Marnier, Kirsch or Franjelica can be substituted for the Amaretto.
* Mousse can also be served in individual parfait glasses or Chocolate Cups (p. 366).

COMPANY CHOCOLATE MOUSSE

Prepare as for White Chocolate Mousse, but substitute 8 oz. semi-sweet or bittersweet chocolate for the white chocolate.

QUICK CHOCOLATE MOUSSE

A food processor and microwave make this marvelous mousse even quicker to prepare!

1 c. milk or light cream
2 c. chocolate chips (or 12 oz. bittersweet chocolate, broken into chunks)
3 eggs
¼ c. sugar
2 tbsp. Kahlua or Grand Marnier (or your favorite brandy)
whipped cream & grated chocolate, to garnish

1. MW milk uncovered on HIGH in a 2 cup Pyrex™ measure about **2 to 2½ minutes**, until boiling.

2. Steel Knife: Process chocolate until finely ground, about 25 to 30 seconds. Add hot milk through feed tube while machine is running. Process until blended. Add eggs, sugar and liqueur; process a few seconds longer to blend. Pour into 6 pretty dessert dishes. Chill 1 hour. Garnish with whipped cream and grated chocolate.

Yield: 6 servings. Can be frozen.

CHOCOLATE FONDUE

1 c. light cream or milk
2 tbsp. butter
12 oz. pkg. chocolate chips
2 tbsp. Kahlua or 2 tsp. vanilla

Dunkers:
strawberries
sliced bananas
marshmallows
cake cubes

1. Combine cream, butter, chocolate chips and liqueur in a microsafe ceramic fondue pot or serving bowl. **MW uncovered on HIGH for 2 minutes.** Stir well. **MW on HIGH 2 minutes longer,** stirring every minute. Fondue should be melted, smooth and glossy.

2. Keep warm over a fondue burner, or reheat briefly in the microwave as necessary, about **30 to 60 seconds at a time on MEDIUM (50%).** Use fondue forks to dip fruit, marshmallows and/or cake in melted chocolate.

Yield: 6 servings.

BLOW YOUR DIET CHOCOLATE TRIFLE

Stale cake or an overbaked disaster is ideal for this recipe! A favorite in my cooking classes....usually we eat the trifle immediately after making it and nobody ever complains! This is my son Steven's favorite recipe!

Home-Made Chocolate Pudding (p. 315) or packaged pudding mix
3 tbsp. Kahlua
3 c. chilled whipping cream
⅓ c. icing sugar
½ of a large chocolate cake, cut in 1″ chunks
grated semi-sweet chocolate

1. Prepare pudding as directed, but reduce milk by ½ cup. Cooking time will be about 1 minute less. (If you forget to use less milk, mixture won't be as firm, but will still be fine.) Add 1 tbsp. of the Kahlua to cooked pudding. Place wax paper directly on the surface of pudding to prevent a skin from forming. Cool completely.

2. Whip cream until nearly stiff. Beat in icing sugar. Remove ⅔ of whipped cream from bowl and reserve to garnish Trifle. Blend cooled chocolate pudding into remaining whipped cream in bowl. (May be prepared in advance and refrigerated until needed.)

3. Arrange half of cake chunks in the bottom of a 2 quart glass serving bowl. Sprinkle with 1 tbsp. liqueur. Pour in half of the pudding/cream mixture. Repeat once again. Top with reserved whipped cream. Garnish with grated chocolate. Chill several hours or overnight to blend flavors. (Can be made up to 2 days in advance.)

Yield: 10 to 12 servings. Do not freeze. Recipe may be doubled for a large crowd.

* If you don't have any leftover chocolate cake to make this recipe, a quick trick is to use your favorite chocolate cake recipe or a cake mix to make cupcakes. **Six cupcakes will take 2 to 2½ minutes on HIGH to microwave.** You will need about 1 dozen cupcakes for this recipe. Extra cupcakes can be frozen.
* I usually make this recipe with Easy Pareve Chocolate Cake (p. 293).

BLACK FOREST TRIFLE

Follow directions for Blow Your Diet Chocolate Trifle, but drain a 19 oz. can pitted Bing cherries and arrange over the pudding mixture. Chocolate Pastry Cream (p. 319) can be substituted for the pudding; Kirsch can be used instead of Kahlua.

DON'T TRIFLE WITH ME!

Follow directions for Blow Your Diet Chocolate Trifle, but use vanilla pudding, Grand Marnier and sponge cake. Sliced strawberries, kiwi, mandarin oranges or any fruit of your choice can be arranged over cake chunks.

EASY AS PIE

* **Microwaved pie crusts** will be flaky and tender, but pale in color because there is no heat to brown them. If you object to the color, use tea or coffee instead of water in your pastry recipe. Add 1 tsp. cinnamon and 1 tbsp. sugar for a spice crust. Whole wheat flour adds color. Otherwise, bake pie shells conventionally. (For 2-crust and crumb-topped fruit pies, see Combo-Cooking, below.)
* **A food processor** makes excellent pastry quickly. Once you add liquid to the dry ingredients, process with quick on/offs, just until dough holds together. Overprocessing makes pastry tough.
* **Roll dough equally in all directions** like the spokes of a wheel. This helps keep pastry round. Mend cracks as they form.
* **A pastry cloth** and stockinette rolling pin cover makes rolling out pastry easy as pie!
* **It only takes 5 to 6 minutes to microwave a pie shell**, until crust is dry and opaque. Press crust firmly against edges of pie plate to prevent crust from slipping down during cooking.
* **For one-crust microwaved pies (e.g. quiche)**, you must precook the crust before adding the filling. Then fill precooked crust and microwave according to recipe instructions.
* **PASTRY CUT-OUTS** can be used to decorate one-crust pies. Roll out leftover pastry and cut with cookie cutters into decorative shapes. Sprinkle with cinnamon-sugar; transfer carefully to wax paper. **MW for 2 to 4 minutes on HIGH**, until dry. Loosen while still warm. Arrange on microwaved pie.
* **To freeze pie crusts:** Prepare several pie crusts at a time, roll out and place in disposable aluminum foil pie plates. Stack and store tightly wrapped in the freezer. When needed, remove frozen crust from foil pie plate and transfer to a microsafe pie plate. (It should be the same size as the foil pie plate.) **It takes 1 minute on HIGH to defrost one pie crust.**
* **To defrost fruit pies:** If necessary, transfer to a microsafe pie plate. If plate is too big, fill extra space with crushed microsafe paper towels. **MW on MEDIUM (50%) for 8 to 12 minutes (allow about 5 to 6 minutes per lb.)** A wooden skewer should pass through centre of pie. Let stand 10 minutes to complete thawing.
* **To warm pies: a whole pie will take 1 to 1 ½ minutes on HIGH. One slice of pie will take about 20 seconds.** If you top the slice of pie with a scoop of ice cream, the filling will become hot and the ice cream will soften slightly.
* **COMBO-COOKING:** Two-crust and crumb-topped pies (e.g. apple) are excellent when cooked with a combination of microwaves and conventional baking. **MW on HIGH for 10 to 12 minutes**, until filling is hot and bubbling. Transfer pie to a preheated conventional oven and **bake at 425°F for 12 to 15 minutes**, until crust is golden. **Apple pie takes about 25 minutes by this method.**

BASIC PIE CRUST

If you don't have a food processor, don't freeze butter and shortening for this recipe. Use a pastry blender and follow the basic method described below to make and microwave the crust. If you have your own favorite recipe, use the cooking time below as a guide.

¼ lb. frozen butter (1 stick)
¼ c. frozen shortening
2 c. flour
½ tsp. salt
½ c. ice water

1. **Steel Knife:** Cut butter and shortening into 1″ pieces. Arrange around the bottom of the processor bowl. Add flour and salt. Use on/off turns, until mixture looks like coarse oatmeal.

2. Add water in a slow stream through feed tube while machine is running. Process just until dough gathers together, about 10 to 12 seconds after all the liquid is added. Divide in half and wrap each piece in plastic wrap. Chill for ½ hour or freeze for 15 minutes.

3. Roll out one piece at a time on a floured pastry cloth or wooden board into a large circle about 2″ larger than your pie plate. Fold in half, then in half again to make a pie-shaped wedge. Transfer to a 9″ Pyrex™ pie plate and unfold carefully. Trim dough, leaving ½″ overhang. Fold edge of dough under; flute edges and press firmly against pie plate.

4. Cover dough with a sheet of wax paper. Top with another pie plate to weigh down the pastry. Chill for 20 minutes. (If you don't have an extra microsafe pie plate, spread a layer of uncooked rice or ceramic pie weights on the wax paper.)

5. **MW on HIGH for 3 minutes**. Remove wax paper and pie plate. Rotate pie crust ¼ turn. **MW uncovered on HIGH 3 minutes longer**, or until crust is dry, opaque and slightly colored.

Yield: two 9″ or 10″ pie crusts. May be frozen. Refer to Easy as Pie (p. 325).

* **CONVECTION CYCLE:** Preheat oven to 400°F. Line pastry with aluminum foil; weigh it down with pie weights, uncooked rice or beans. Place on rack; **bake at 400°F for 8 minutes**, until slightly golden. Remove foil and pie weights. **Bake 5 minutes longer**, until crisp and golden. A metal pie plate can be used, if desired.

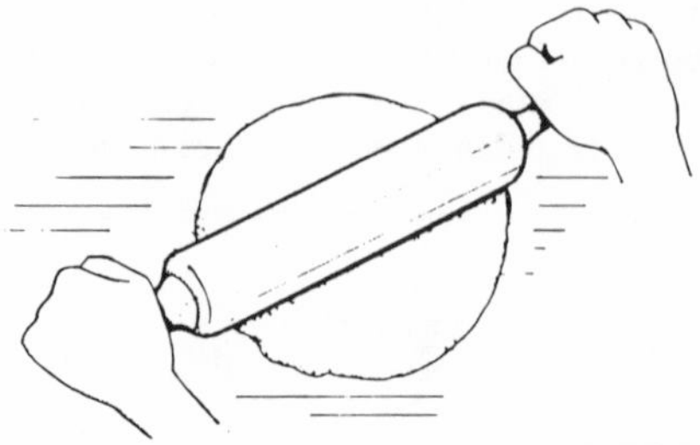

THAT'S THE WAY THE COOKIE CRUMBLES!

* **Cookie crumb crusts** cook quickly in the microwave. **They take only 2 minutes on HIGH**, and you never have to preheat a microwave oven!
* **Use the same microsafe pie plate** to melt the butter and bake the crust.
* **¼ cup finely chopped nuts** (hazelnuts, almonds, walnuts or pecans) may be substituted for ¼ cup of the cookie crumbs.
* **If you have a food processor**, butter does not need to be melted before mixing it with remaining ingredients.
* **Cookie crumb crusts** become soggy when cooked together with a very liquid filling. This is why I heat my cheesecake batter until thick before pouring it into the crust to complete the final cooking.

COOKIE CRUMB PIE CRUST

1 ½ c. cookie crumbs (see below)
3 tbsp. white or brown sugar
½ tsp. cinnamon
6 tbsp. butter or margarine, cut up

1. **Steel Knife:** Process all ingredients until the texture of wet sand, about 20 seconds. (If you don't have a food processor, place butter in 9″ glass pie plate or 10″ ceramic quiche dish. **MW uncovered on HIGH for 45 seconds** to melt. Combine with remaining ingredients and mix well.) Press into the bottom and up the sides of pie plate.

2. **MW uncovered on HIGH for 2 minutes** or until set, rotating plate ¼ **turn after 1 minute.**

Yield: one 9″ or 10″ crust.

* **CHOCOLATE WAFER CRUST:** Crush 28 to 30 chocolate wafers.
* **VANILLA WAFER CRUST:** Crush 36 vanilla wafers.
* **GRAHAM WAFER CRUST:** Crush 18 single graham wafers.
* **GINGERSNAP CRUST:** Crush 24 gingersnaps.
* **CORN FLAKE CRUMB CRUST:** Substitute 1 ½ cups corn flake crumbs for the cookie crumbs. (One cup corn flakes makes ¼ cup crumbs.) If using crust for a savory dish such as Quick Quiche (p. 128), omit sugar and cinnamon; season crumb mixture with a dash of salt and pepper.

STEEL KNIFE

LEMON MERINGUE PIE

Graham Wafer Crust (p. 327)
1 c. sugar
3 tbsp. flour
3 tbsp. cornstarch
dash salt
1 ½ c. boiling water
3 egg yolks
⅓ c. lemon juice
1 tsp. finely grated lemon zest
1 tbsp. butter or margarine

1. Prepare and microwave crust as directed. Let cool. Combine sugar, flour, cornstarch and salt in an 8 cup Pyrex™ measure or microsafe bowl. Slowly blend in water. **MW uncovered on HIGH for 3 to 4 minutes**, until thickened and boiling, stirring twice. Meanwhile, prepare Meringue (see below).

2. Combine egg yolks with lemon juice. Add a little of the hot mixture to yolks and mix well. Blend egg yolk mixture back into hot mixture. **MW uncovered on HIGH 1 to 2 minutes longer**, until boiling and thickened, stirring every minute. Add lemon zest and butter. Pour hot filling into baked crust.

3. Pile meringue onto hot filling, sealing meringue onto edge of crust. **MW uncovered on MEDIUM (50%) for 3 to 4 minutes**, until set when touched with your fingertips. If desired, brown under a preheated broiler in your conventional oven for 2 or 3 minutes, until golden. Watch carefully to prevent burning. Cool away from drafts to prevent weeping.

Yield: 6 to 8 servings. Do not freeze.

MERINGUE

3 egg whites
½ tsp. cream of tartar*
6 tbsp. sugar*

1. Beat egg whites with cream of tartar until foamy. Beat in sugar a tablespoon at a time and continue beating until stiff and glossy.

* Superfine or fruit sugar helps keep meringue from weeping.
* One teaspoon of lemon juice can be substituted for the cream of tartar.
* Instead of microwaving the meringue-topped pie, it can either be baked in a conventional oven or on the **CONVECTION** cycle of a combination oven. Preheat oven to 350°F. Place pie on rack. **Bake at 350°F for 8 to 10 minutes,** until golden.

LUSCIOUS LEMON CREAM PIE

If you love lemon, you'll adore this dessert! It's as light as a cloud.

9″ Graham Wafer Crust (p. 327)
¾ c. sugar
¼ c. cornstarch
1 c. water
1 tsp. grated lemon rind
⅓ c. lemon juice
2 egg yolks, lightly beaten
¼ lb. cream cheese*
2 egg whites
2 tbsp. additional sugar
1 c. whipping cream plus
2 tbsp. icing sugar, optional*
grated lemon rind

1. Prepare and microwave crust as directed. Let cool.

2. Combine ¾ c. sugar with cornstarch, water, lemon rind and lemon juice. Whisk to blend. Add egg yolks and mix well. **MW uncovered on HIGH for 4 to 5 minutes**, until thick and bubbling, whisking every 2 minutes. Remove from microwave.

3. Cut cream cheese into chunks and add to lemon mixture. Mix until cheese is melted and mixture is well blended. Place a piece of waxed paper directly on the surface to prevent a skin from forming; chill. (To speed up chilling, pour mixture into a shallow casserole. It will cool faster because more surface is exposed.)

4. Beat egg whites until they form soft peaks. Gradually add remaining 2 tbsp. sugar. Beat until stiff. Fold into chilled lemon mixture. Pour into crust. Refrigerate 2 to 3 hours, until set.

5. Whip cream until stiff. Blend in icing sugar. Pipe through a pastry bag and garnish dessert. Sprinkle with grated lemon rind.

Yield: 6 servings. Do not freeze.

* Dry cottage cheese (pot cheese) can be used instead of cream cheese if you are calorie-conscious. Whipped cream garnish can be omitted. Sprinkle top of pie lightly with graham wafer crumbs.
* Pie can be made up to 2 days ahead, but garnish with sweetened whipped cream same day you are serving it.
* Marshmallow Whipped Cream Garnish (below) may be used instead of whipped cream to decorate pie. Prepare it the day before you need it.

MARSHMALLOW WHIPPED CREAM GARNISH

1 c. miniature or cut-up marshmallows
1 c. whipping cream (35%)

1. Combine marshmallows with whipping cream. Cover and refrigerate overnight. Whip until double in volume. Use instead of Sweetened Whipped Cream to garnish dessert. Pipe through a pastry bag, using a star tube.

FRUIT FLAN

For this recipe, I prefer to bake the crust conventionally and make the filling and glaze in the microwave.

½ recipe Basic Pie Crust (p. 326)
Crème Pâtissière (p. 319)
1 c. strawberries, hulled & halved lengthwise
2 peaches, peeled & sliced
seedless green grapes, halved
1 kiwi, peeled & sliced
½ c. red currant jelly

1. Prepare pastry as directed. Roll out chilled pastry into a 12″ circle. Transfer to an 11″ metal flan pan with a removeable bottom. Roll rolling pin over the edges of the pan and the excess dough will be cut away. Line with aluminum foil and fill with uncooked rice or peas to weigh down pastry.

2. Preheat the **CONVECTION cycle (or your conventional oven)** to 400°F. Bake pastry on rack in middle of oven for **8 to 10 minutes**, until slightly golden. (Use shorter time for convection cooking.) Remove foil and rice or peas. **Bake 5 minutes longer**, until crisp and golden. Cool completely. (Can be done in advance.)

3. Prepare Crème Pâtissière; cool completely. Three hours before serving, fill pastry with chilled Crème Pâtissière. Arrange a border of strawberries around the outside edge of the flan, with the points facing towards the centre. Place grapes between points of strawberries. Arrange a circle of peaches, then fill centre with sliced kiwis.

4. **MW jelly uncovered on HIGH for 45 seconds**, until melted. Brush over fruit. Chill flan 2 to 3 hours before serving.

Yield: 8 servings. Do not freeze.

* Flan can be topped with canned, well-drained fruit when fresh fruits are unavailable (e.g. canned peaches, pears, apricots, mandarin oranges).

GRASSHOPPER PIE

24 large marshmallows (3 c.)
¼ c. milk
¼ c. green crème de menthe
2 tbsp. white crème de cacao
Chocolate Wafer Crust (p. 327)
1 c. chilled whipping cream (35%)
grated semi-sweet chocolate

1. Combine marshmallows and milk in a 3 quart microsafe bowl. **MW uncovered on HIGH for 2 to 3 minutes**, until puffy and melted, stirring once or twice. Stir in liqueurs. Chill for 20 minutes, or just until mixture mounds slightly when dropped from a spoon. Prepare and microwave crust while filling is chilling.

2. Whip cream until stiff. Fold into marshmallow mixture. Pour into crust. Refrigerate until set, about 3 to 4 hours, or wrap tightly and freeze (see notes below). Garnish with grated chocolate.

Yield: 8 servings. Freezes well.

* If desired, omit liqueurs; increase milk to ½ cup and add ½ tsp. peppermint extract and a few drops of green food coloring.
* This pie freezes very well. It can be served without thawing. Let stand at room temperature for 5 to 10 minutes before serving. When frozen, the taste is similar to an ice cream pie, whereas when refrigerated, it becomes more like a chiffon pie. Try it both ways!

GRASSHOPPER PARFAIT

Simply wonderful!

For a pretty parfait, prepare Grasshopper pie mixture as directed on p. 330, but omit crust. Layer marshmallow mixture with chocolate wafer crumbs in 6 or 8 parfait glasses. Chill 1 to 2 hours.

CHOCOLATE MARSHMALLOW PIE

24 large marshmallows (3 c.)
½ c. milk
2 oz. semi-sweet chocolate, cut up
Chocolate Wafer Crust (p. 327)
1 ½ c. chilled whipping cream
grated semi-sweet chocolate

1. Combine marshmallows, milk and chocolate in a 3 quart microsafe bowl. **MW uncovered on HIGH for 3 to 4 minutes,** until marshmallows and chocolate are melted, stirring twice. Stir until well mixed. Cool to room temperature. Prepare and microwave crust while filling is cooling.

2. Whip cream until stiff. Fold 2 cups of the whipped cream into marshmallow mixture. (Reserve remaining whipped cream to garnish pie.) Pour marshmallow mixture into crust. Refrigerate until set, about 3 to 4 hours, or wrap tightly and freeze (see notes below). Garnish with remaining whipped cream and grated chocolate.

Yield: 8 servings. Freezes well.

* If frozen, this pie can be served without thawing. Let stand at room temperature for 5 to 10 minutes before serving. When frozen, the taste is similar to an ice cream pie, whereas when refrigerated, it becomes more like a chiffon pie. Try it both ways!
* Also delicious with ½ cup toasted almonds added to the filling.

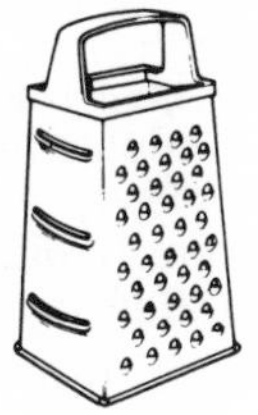

ROSE BERANBAUM'S PECAN PIE

My friend Rose knows I have a passion for pecans! She shared this recipe with me when I was on vacation in New York a few years ago. By heating the filling first in the microwave, then baking the pie conventionally, it's ready in half the usual time! Rose Beranbaum is the author of the best-selling cookbook "The Cake Bible".

¼ c. unsalted butter
4 egg yolks
⅓ c. Golden syrup (or corn syrup)
½ c. light brown sugar, packed
¼ c. heavy cream (35%)
pinch of salt
1 tsp. vanilla
1 ½ c. pecan halves
baked pie crust*

1. **MW butter uncovered on HIGH** in a microsafe bowl until melted, **about 1 minute**. Stir in egg yolks, syrup, sugar, cream and salt. **MW uncovered on HIGH for 2 minutes**, stirring every minute. If you have a probe, cook to 160°F. Otherwise, test temperature with a thermometer. Strain; stir in vanilla.
2. Preheat the **CONVECTION cycle** (or your conventional oven) to 350°F.
3. Arrange pecans in baked pie crust. Carefully pour filling over pecans. **Bake on rack in lower third of oven at 350°F for 20 to 25 minutes**, until puffy and golden. (Convection cooking takes less time than cooking in the conventional oven.)

Yield: 6 to 8 servings.

* Rose uses a 9 ½″ x 1″ metal quiche pan with a removeable bottom and bakes her crust conventionally to achieve a lovely golden crust. A microwaved pie crust will not be as attractive.

MMM-MUD PIE

This recipe takes time to assemble but is really quite simple. The results are worth it!

Chocolate Wafer Crust (p. 327)
3 c. coffee ice cream
15 caramel candies
1 tbsp. milk
6 oz. semi-sweet chocolate
¾ c. whipping cream (35%)
1 tbsp. Kahlua or Tia Maria
½ c. finely chopped almonds, if desired

1. Prepare crust in a deep 9″ glass pie plate and microwave as directed. Cool completely.
2. **MW ice cream for 1 minute on DEFROST (30%)**, until it can be spooned into cooled crumb crust. Spread evenly. Freeze until solid.
3. Combine caramels with milk in a small microsafe bowl. **MW uncovered on HIGH for 1 minute**, until smooth and melted. Stir well. Let cool. Pour over ice cream layer; freeze once again.
4. Combine chocolate with cream in a microsafe bowl. **MW uncovered on HIGH for 2 minutes. Stir. MW 1 minute longer**, or until smooth, melted and glossy. Stir in liqueur. Cool completely. Pour over caramel layer. When set, sprinkle with almonds; freeze until solid. Wrap well. Remove from freezer ½ hour before serving time and place in refrigerator to thaw slightly.

Yield: 6 servings. Store leftovers, if any, in the freezer.

BEST APPLE PIE

Basic Pie Crust (p. 326)
2 tbsp. bread crumbs
7 or 8 large apples, peeled, cored & sliced
½ c. sugar (to taste)
1 tsp. cinnamon
¼ c. flour
1 tbsp. water or milk
1 tbsp. additional sugar

1. Prepare pastry as directed. Roll out one portion into a large circle and place in an ungreased deep 9″ Pyrex™ pie plate or 10″ ceramic quiche dish. Trim off overhanging edges. Sprinkle with bread crumbs.

2. Combine apples with sugar, cinnamon and flour. Mix lightly. Place filling in pie shell. Roll out remaining dough and cut several slits. Place over filling. Trim away edges, leaving ½″ border all around. Tuck top crust under bottom crust. (This prevents the juices from leaking out during cooking.) Flute edges, pressing firmly to the edge of pie plate. Brush crust with water or milk. Sprinkle lightly with sugar.

3. Preheat conventional oven to 425°F. Meanwhile, **MW pie uncovered on HIGH for 10 to 12 minutes**, or until filling is bubbling. Transfer pie to middle rack of conventional oven and **bake at 425°F for 12 to 15 minutes**, until crust is golden.

Yield: 8 servings. Freezes well.

PEACH PIE: Substitute 8 peaches, peeled & sliced, for apples.

BLUEBERRY APPLE PIE: Use 3 apples, 1 ½ c. blueberries, ¾ cup sugar, ⅓ c. flour and 1 tsp. cinnamon for the filling.

RHUBARB PIE: Use 4 c. sliced rhubarb (or 2 c. sliced rhubarb and 2 c. sliced strawberries), 1 ¼ c. sugar and ⅓ c. flour for the filling.

CRUMBLY FRUIT PIE: Prepare any of the desired fruit pies, but omit top crust. Prepare topping for Easy Apple Crisp (p. 335) and sprinkle over fruit filling. Bake as directed in Step 3 of Best Apple Pie (above).

BLUEBERRY APPLE CRISP

This quick and easy recipe is perfect for novice microwavers. I teach it in my classes and my students love it.

Topping:
½ c. brown sugar, packed
¾ c. flour
½ c. cold butter, cut in chunks*
½ c. oatmeal or granola
1 tsp. cinnamon

Filling:
3 large apples, peeled & cored
2 c. fresh or frozen blueberries*
¼ c. flour
⅓ c. sugar
½ tsp. cinnamon

1. **Steel Knife:** Combine all ingredients for topping and process until crumbly, about 10 to 12 seconds. Empty contents of bowl onto a piece of waxed paper.

2. **Filling:** Slice apples. Combine with remaining filling ingredients and mix lightly. Spread evenly in an ungreased deep 9″ glass pie plate or 10″ ceramic quiche dish, depressing centre slightly. Spread topping over filling and pat gently. Dish will be very full but mixture will reduce during cooking.

3. **MW uncovered on HIGH for 12 to 14 minutes**, rotating dish ¼ turn halfway through cooking. Top will look cracked when done and fruit will be tender when pierced with a knife. Let stand for a few minutes before serving for topping to become more crisp. (Can be placed under the broiler briefly, if desired, but I never bother.) Serve warm or cold with a scoop of vanilla ice cream.

Yield: 6 servings.

* Margarine or oil can be used instead of butter. If you use oil, you will have less topping mixture, but the recipe will still work well.
* It is not necessary to defrost berries before cooking.
* Topping can be prepared and kept in a plastic bag in the freezer. No need to thaw before using! **A single serving** can be made in a 10 oz. glass custard cup and **will take about 3 minutes on HIGH to microwave.**
* If you prepare the Crisp earlier in the day, **it takes about 4 to 6 minutes uncovered on MEDIUM-HIGH (70%) to reheat.**
* Any sliced fresh fruits can be used instead of or added to the apples and blueberries (e.g. peaches, pears, nectarines).
* **One serving will take 30 seconds uncovered on HIGH to reheat.** If you top it with a scoop of ice cream before heating, fruit will be warm and ice cream will be slightly softened.

STEEL KNIFE

EASY APPLE CRISP

Easier than pie!

Filling:
6 medium apples, peeled, cored & sliced
3 tbsp. flour
¼ c. sugar
1 tsp. cinnamon

Topping:
1 c. flour
¼ lb. cold butter, cut in chunks
½ c. brown sugar, packed
2 tsp. cinnamon

1. Combine all ingredients for filling and mix well. Spread evenly in an ungreased deep 9″ glass pie plate or 10″ ceramic quiche dish, depressing centre slightly.

2. Steel Knife: Process all ingredients for topping for 8 to 10 seconds, until crumbly. Do not overprocess. Sprinkle over apple mixture; pat down evenly. **MW uncovered on HIGH for 10 to 12 minutes**, rotating dish ¼ turn at half time. Apples should be tender when pierced with a knife and top will be somewhat cracked. Delicious served with ice cream. Serve warm or cold.

Yield: 6 to 8 servings. Can be frozen.

* Read notes on Blueberry Apple Crisp (p. 334). The same rules apply.

PECAN APPLE CRISP

Prepare Easy Apple Crisp (above) as directed, but replace ½ cup flour with ½ c. finely chopped pecans in topping mixture.

EASY FRUIT CRISP

Substitute any of the fruits below for apples in Easy Apple Crisp (above) or Blueberry Apple Crisp (p. 334), or use a combination of several different fruits. **Microwave time will be 12 to 14 minutes on HIGH.** Rotate dish ¼ turn halfway through cooking.

EASY PEACH CRISP: Substitute 4 cups sliced peaches for apples; add 1 tsp. lemon juice.

EASY PEAR CRISP: Substitute 4 cups sliced pears for apples; add 1 tsp. lemon juice.

RHUBARB STRAWBERRY CRISP: Combine 2 c. sliced rhubarb with 2 c. sliced strawberries, 1 c. sugar and ¼ c. flour for the filling.

EASIEST CRISP OF ALL: Combine 4 cups of frozen blueberries with the remaining filling ingredients for Blueberry Apple Crisp (p. 334). There is no need to defrost berries before cooking, and besides, you never have to peel a blueberry!

BASIC BAKED APPLES

4 medium baking apples, cored (McIntosh, Cortland, Spartan)
4 tbsp. brown or white sugar
1 tsp. cinnamon

1. Either pierce skin of apples in several places with a fork or slice a band of skin ½ inch from the top of each apple in order for the steam to escape. Blend sugar and cinnamon. Fill centre of each apple with cinnamon-sugar. Arrange in a circle in a 9″ glass pie plate.

2. Cover with paper towel and **MW on HIGH for 5 to 6 minutes**, until apples are tender. **(Calculate 5 to 6 minutes per lb.)** Rotate plate ¼ turn halfway through cooking. Let stand covered for 3 to 4 minutes.

Yield: 4 servings.

* **1 medium apple will be cooked in approximately 2 to 3 minutes. 2 apples will take 3 to 4 minutes**, depending on size and type of apple. Fill each apple with 1 tsp. to 1 tbsp. sugar (to taste) and a pinch of cinnamon. Bake in a 10 oz. glass custard cup or microsafe dessert dish.
* Apples can be filled with any mixture of your choice. Some suggestions are: red cinnamon hearts; low-cal black cherry cola; brown sugar, butter, cinnamon & chopped nuts; maple syrup, raisins & chopped nuts.

RAY'S BEST BAKED APPLES

Ray is my friend Mimi's mother and she's so proud of her microwaved baked apples. She serves them to her card group and they love them. I loved them too when I tried them!

4 large baking apples
4 tbsp. raisins
4 tbsp. honey
4 tsp. orange juice
strawberry jam

1. Core apples. Pierce with a fork in several places to let steam escape. Place each apple in its own individual microsafe dessert dish. Fill with raisins and drizzle with honey and orange juice.

2. **MW uncovered on HIGH for 5 to 6 minutes**, or just until tender. Top each apple with a spoonful of strawberry jam (preferably the whole strawberry). Delicious hot or cold; even better with ice cream!

Yield: 4 servings.

6-7-8 APPLE SAUCE

When I first began to cook in the microwave, I never could remember how long anything took to cook. I named this recipe 6-7-8 Apple Sauce because 6 or 7 apples took 7 to 8 minutes to cook. Since 4 or 5 apples take 5 to 6 minutes, and 8 or 9 apples take 9 to 10 minutes, it could also be called 4-5-6 or 8-9-10 Apple Sauce!

6 or 7 medium apples, peeled & cored* (See Note)
¼ c. water or apple juice*
3 to 4 tbsp. sugar
1 tsp. cinnamon
1 tsp. lemon juice, if desired

1. Cut apples in chunks and place in a 2 quart microsafe casserole. Add remaining ingredients. Cover with vented plastic wrap or lid.

2. **MW on HIGH for 7 to 8 minutes**, or until apples are tender, stirring once or twice during cooking. Break up apples if desired or serve it chunky. Delicious hot or cold.

Yield: 6 servings. Freezes well.

* **Note:** If you have a food mill, apples may be cooked without peeling or coring. Wash apples and discard stems. Cut in chunks. Cook as directed above. Cool slightly and purée in a food mill. Color will be rosy pink.
* Use only 3 tbsp. sugar if using apple juice as the liquid. If using artificial sweetener, add after cooking.
* Any combination of fruit may be used (e.g. apples, pears, blueberries, peaches, plums, nectarines) for a delicious fruit dessert.
* If you are using plastic wrap to cover the casserole, you can stir the applesauce through the vented opening with a wooden chopstick.

POACHED PEARS

The pears will be rosy pink. Red wine can be used instead of cranberry juice, if desired.

1 c. cranberry juice cocktail
½ tsp. cinnamon
2 tbsp. honey, optional
4 firm, ripe pears

1. Combine cranberry juice, cinnamon and honey in a 1 quart covered microsafe casserole. **MW covered on HIGH for 3 to 4 minutes, until boiling.**

2. Meanwhile, peel pears; remove core from the bottom end. Do not remove stems. Place in hot juice, with the stem end pointing inwards. Cover and **MW on HIGH for 5 to 6 minutes**, turning pears over and rearranging them at half time. When done, pears will keep their shape but will be tender when pierced with a knife. Let cool, turning them over once or twice. Serve warm or chilled.

Yield: 4 servings.

DRIED FRUIT COMPOTE

1 ½ lb. dried mixed fruit (prunes, apricots, etc.)
1 c. raisins
1 orange, sliced
½ lemon, sliced
¼ c. sugar
½ tsp. cinnamon
3 c. water or orange juice

1. Combine all ingredients in an 8 cup microsafe bowl. Cover with plastic wrap, turning back one corner slightly to vent.

2. **MW covered on HIGH for 15 minutes**, stirring with a chopstick through the vented opening at half time. Let stand covered until cool. Fruit will plump as it stands. Refrigerate. Serve chilled. Keeps about a week to 10 days in the refrigerator.

Yield: 6 to 8 servings.

SUMMERTIME FRESH FRUIT COMPOTE

My daughter Jodi loves this recipe, even though it contains rhubarb, which is not one of her favorite fruits. My friend Seline adds a splash of raspberry liqueur to her chilled compote.

4 c. assorted fresh fruit (peaches, rhubarb, nectarines, plums, cherries, blueberries)
2 c. water
½ c. sugar (to taste)
1 tbsp. lemon juice

1. Peel peaches. Remove strings from rhubarb with a potato peeler. Remove pits from fruit. Cut larger fruits into chunks. Place in a 3 quart microsafe bowl. Cover with vented plastic wrap.

2. **MW on HIGH for 10 minutes; stir. MW on MEDIUM (50%) 7 to 8 minutes longer**, until tender. Let cool; refrigerate.

Yield: 6 to 8 servings.

GRAPEFRUIT

Cut grapefruit in half. Sprinkle each half with 1 tsp. brown sugar. Place in dessert dishes and **MW uncovered on HIGH for 1 to 1 ¼ minutes. Half a grapefruit will take about 45 seconds to heat.** Yummy!

STEWED PRUNES

An old-fashioned Jewish favorite which can be cooked and stored in the same bowl!

1 ½ lb. pitted prunes
1 c. Sultana raisins
3 c. water
¼ c. sugar
½ lemon, thinly sliced
½ orange, thinly sliced

1. Combine all ingredients in an 8 cup microsafe bowl. Cover with plastic wrap, turning back one corner slightly to vent.

2. **MW covered on HIGH for 15 minutes**, stirring with a chopstick through the vented opening at half time. Let stand covered until cool. Refrigerate. Serve chilled. Keeps a week to 10 days in the fridge.

Yield: 6 to 8 servings.

STEWED RHUBARB

4 c. sliced rhubarb
¼ c. orange juice or water
¾ c. sugar, or to taste
1 c. sliced strawberries, if desired

1. Combine all ingredients except strawberries in a 3 quart microsafe bowl. Cover with plastic wrap, turning back one corner slightly to vent. **MW covered on HIGH for 8 to 10 minutes**, until tender, stirring at half time. Stir in strawberries. Let stand covered until cool. Refrigerate.

Yield: 6 servings.

* Make sure to use a large enough bowl as rhubarb mixture can boil over during cooking.
* An easy way to stir the rhubarb is to use a wooden chopstick and insert it through the vented opening.

BLUEBERRY SAUCE

Delicious hot or cold. Serve over pancakes, cheese blintzes, ice cream, cheesecake or fruit salad.

2 c. fresh or frozen blueberries
½ c. sugar
2 tbsp. orange juice
½ c. water
2 tbsp. cornstarch
¼ c. additional water

1. Combine berries, sugar, orange juice and ½ cup water in a 2 quart microsafe bowl. **MW uncovered on HIGH for 5 minutes**, until bubbling.

2. Dissolve cornstarch in ¼ c. water. Stir into blueberry mixture. **MW on HIGH 2 to 3 minutes longer**, until thick and shiny, stirring once. Will keep about a week to 10 days in the refrigerator.

Yield: about 2 cups.

RASPBERRY SAUCE

10 oz. pkg. frozen raspberries
2 tsp. cornstarch
1 tbsp. lemon juice

1. Remove raspberries from package and place in a 1 quart microsafe bowl. **MW uncovered on HIGH for 2 to 3 minutes**, until almost defrosted. Stir to break up fruit. Put through a food mill and discard seeds. Return mixture back to bowl.

2. Add cornstarch and stir until dissolved. Add lemon juice and **MW uncovered on HIGH until clear and thick, about 2 minutes**, stirring every minute.

Yield: about 1 ¼ cups sauce. Strawberries can be substituted.

STRAWBERRY SAUCE

2 pints strawberries
¾ c. sugar
2 ½ tbsp. cornstarch
¾ c. cold water
1 tbsp. lemon juice
dash salt
2 tsp. butter or margarine

1. Wash strawberries under cold running water. Drain well and hull.

2. Place half the berries in the processor bowl. (Reserve remaining berries.) Process on the **Steel Knife** until crushed, about 10 seconds. Add sugar and process a few seconds longer to blend. Dissolve cornstarch in cold water in a 2 quart microsafe bowl. Stir in crushed strawberries.

3. **MW uncovered on HIGH for 6 to 8 minutes**, until thickened and boiling, stirring every 2 minutes. Cut reserved berries in half. Add to hot mixture along with remaining ingredients; mix well. Refrigerate.

Yield: about 4 cups. Serve over ice cream, cheese blintzes, cheesecake, crêpes or yogourt.

CHOCOLATE FUDGE SAUCE

½ c. milk
1 tbsp. butter
1 c. chocolate chips
1 tbsp. Kahlua or vanilla

1. Combine milk and butter in a 1 cup Pyrex™ measure. **MW on HIGH for 1 to 1 ¼ minutes**, until steaming hot.

2. **Steel Knife:** Meanwhile, process chocolate with 7 or 8 on/off turns, then let machine run until chocolate is finely chopped, about 30 seconds. Pour hot liquid through feed tube while machine is running. Add flavoring. Chocolate will melt instantly. Serve hot or chilled.

Yield: about 1 cup sauce.

* If you don't have a food processor, combine all ingredients in a 4 cup microsafe measure. **MW uncovered on HIGH for 1 ½ to 2 minutes**. Stir well. **MW on HIGH 1 minute longer**, or until chocolate is melted and mixture is shiny. Stir until smooth.
* Sauce will keep about 1 week in the refrigerator. It gets thick when cold. Serve over ice cream, poached pears or crêpes. Also makes delicious hot chocolate.
* Use the microwave to heat ready-made toppings and sauces right in their own jars. Be sure to remove metal lids and stir once or twice.

IN A JAM?

* **Be sure cooking container** is only 1/3 full when making jam; sugar mixtures have a tendency to boil over in the microwave.
* **Little stirring is needed** when microwaving jam, and it won't scorch! It's easy to make small batches at a time, when fruit is at its prime. Microwave time is about the same as in conventional cooking.
* **Jam may be stored** in a cool, dark pantry if you pour hot mixture into sterilized jars. Label, mark the date and store. Jam will keep a year or two. Discard any jars if they develop mold.
* **To sterilize jars, don't use the microwave!** Sterilize them on the stove while you microwave the jam. Fill jars 3/4 full of water and place in a large, shallow pan partly filled with water. Place lids under the water. Simmer for 20 minutes. Use tongs to remove jars and lids from water when ready to fill. Drain well.
* **Paraffin wax will not melt in the microwave**. Melt it in the top of a double-boiler. Pour a layer 1/8″ thick over slightly cooled jam. When paraffin hardens, seal jars and store.
* **Paraffin wax is not needed** when you use self-sealing jars with a 2-piece metal screw band lid. Follow manufacturer's directions.
* **Jam can also be frozen**. Make sure container is freezer-proof and leave about 2″ at the top to allow for expansion during freezing.
* **Refrigerated jam** keeps about 3 months. Frozen jam will keep about a year.
* **Frozen fruit** can be used instead of fresh fruit for jam-making. Allow 3/4 cup of sugar for every cup of berries. Cooking time may be 1 or 2 minutes longer for frozen fruit.
* **I never add pectin** to my jam, but you may, if your recipe calls for it. Powdered pectin should be added to the uncooked fruit along with the sugar. Liquid pectin should be added to the cooked jam. Cooking time will be shorter than the times indicated in my recipes; allow **8 to 9 minutes for 2 cups of fruit and 12 to 15 minutes for 4 cups of fruit.**
* **If you need to make a larger batch** than the recipe given, either cook jam conventionally or cook smaller batches one after the other in the microwave. Prepare fruit for next batch while first batch is cooking. Don't bother to wash out the cooking container between batches.

SMALL BATCH STRAWBERRY OR RASPBERRY JAM

This recipe is wonderful when you just need a small quantity of jam. It is perfect for gifts. My mother loves to make her jam in the microwave. After she cooks it, she spreads it on a plate, covers it loosely with wax paper and puts it on the countertop or windowsill to thicken for 24 hours, stirring it carefully once or twice. She calls this "Sunshine Jam".

2 c. ripe, firm strawberries or raspberries
1 tbsp. lemon juice
1 ½ c. granulated sugar

1. Wash berries under cold running water in a colander. Drain well. Hull and slice. Discard any bruised fruit. Be sure to include some berries that are a little green. Combine berries with sugar and lemon juice in a 2 or 3 quart microsafe bowl.

2. **MW uncovered on HIGH for 5 minutes**, until boiling. Stir well. **MW uncovered on HIGH for 5 to 7 minutes longer**, until juices are syrupy and slightly thickened. (**If mixture begins to boil over, reduce power to MEDIUM-HIGH (70%).**)

3. Skim off foam. Fill jars with jam. Cover tightly and refrigerate or freeze. If storing at room temperature, jars must be sterilized first. Read "In a Jam?" (p. 341).

Yield: about 1 ½ cups.

MEDIUM BATCH STRAWBERRY OR RASPBERRY JAM

4 c. ripe, firm strawberries or raspberries
2 tbsp. lemon juice
3 c. granulated sugar

1. Follow recipe for Small Batch Strawberry or Raspberry Jam, but use a 4 or 5 quart microsafe casserole to prevent boil-overs. **Total cooking time will be 20 to 22 minutes uncovered on HIGH**. Stir 2 or 3 times during cooking.

Yield: about 3 to 3 ½ cups jam.

SQUARES, COOKIES & CANDIES

MICRO-WAYS WITH SQUARES, COOKIES & CANDIES

- **Squares will bake more evenly** in the microwave in round pans, but then you can't call them squares!
- **Microsafe plastic pans** will cook foods about 20% faster than glass pans.
- **If using square pans** in the microwave, push batter higher into the corners to help prevent them from overcooking.
- **If baking pan is square**, rotate it every 2 minutes for more even cooking.
- **A turntable** helps squares cook more evenly and eliminates the need for rotating the baking dish during microwaving.
- **Elevate pan on a rack**, inverted pie plate or a portable turntable to help squares cook more evenly.
- **Most recipes for an 8″ square or round pan will microwave in about 4 to 7 minutes.**
- **To test if squares are cooked, touch top lightly.** No batter should cling to your fingertips.
- **Check bottom of glass baking pan** to see if squares are fully baked. Then let pan stand directly on the counter to complete cooking. Most recipes require 3 to 4 minutes of standing time.
- **Frostings or chopped nuts** will give a more attractive appearance to recipes that are light in color.
- **The bowl from your food processor** can be used to melt butter and/or chocolate if the bowl is microsafe. Test as directed on p. 21. The bowl from the Cuisinart and Robot Coupe food processors are microsafe. Do not put the **Steel Knife** into the microwave. One of my students melted the plastic on the blade from the high heat of melted butter and chocolate!
- **To bake squares on the CONVECTION cycle**, reduce conventional temperature by 25°F. Preheat oven. Place baking pan on rack recommended by your manufacturer for convection cooking. Reduce baking time slightly. Check at minimum time and add more time if needed.
- **I like to bake most of my cookie recipes** in my conventional oven or on the **CONVECTION** cycle of the **CONVECTION/MICROWAVE** oven. The cookie recipes in this section all work well in the microwave.
- **To bake cookies on the CONVECTION cycle of your CONVECTION/ MICROWAVE oven**, reduce usual temperature by 25 to 50°F. Preheat oven to required temperature (usually 325 or 350°F). Place cookies on a greased 12″ pizza pan or small aluminum cookie sheet. Place in oven on rack recommended by your manufacturer for convection cooking. Use the baking times given below as a guideline.
- **CONVECTION BAKING TIMES FOR COOKIES:** Shortbread and chocolate chip cookies take about 8 to 10 minutes at 350°F; peanut butter cookies take 10 to 12 minutes. Oatmeal cookies will take 12 to 15 minutes at 325°F. Check at minimum time and add more time if needed. Baking time is usually 25% less than in your conventional oven.
- **If you just want** to make a few cookies at a time for snacks and like to keep refrigerator-type cookie dough in your fridge, the microwave oven is ideal.

- **Line a flat dinner plate** or pie plate with a sheet of wax paper and arrange cookies 2″ apart in a circle around the outside of the dish. Place 2 or 3 cookies in the centre. **MW 2 to 3 minutes on HIGH for a batch of 6 to 9 cookies.**
- **If baking less than 6 cookies, MW 20 to 30 seconds per cookie on HIGH**, until no longer doughy.
- **Microwave cookies just until dry** and no raw, doughy spots remain. Watch carefully to prevent them from burning. Cookies will continue to cook for about 1 minute after removing them from the microwave. If overbaked, cookies will burn in the middle because of their high fat and sugar content.
- **Microwaved cookies will be softer** and will not brown. Dough will have to be stiffer to prevent spreading. Cookies should all be the same size for even baking.
- **Home-made or bought** chocolate chip cookies taste just-baked if you microwave them for **15 seconds per cookie on HIGH**, just until warm. Mmmmm!
- **Quicky cleanup:** If syrup hardens and sticks to the bowl when making candy and sugar syrups, fill bowl with hot water and microwave until boiling.

MICRO-WAYS WITH CHOCOLATE

"I love to melt chocolate in my microwave!" Julia Child.

- **Chocolate can develop white streaks** known as "bloom" if stored in a warm place. It is still fine to use; bloom will disappear when chocolate is melted.
- **Wrap chocolate well** to prevent it from absorbing odors. Store it in a cool, dark and dry place (65 to 70°F). It should not be kept in the fridge or freezer unless the weather is hot and humid.
- **I usually melt chocolate on HIGH, allowing about 1½ to 2 minutes for 1 or 2 squares (ounces) of chocolate**. Stir after 1 minute, then every 30 seconds, until barely melted. **Increase time by about 10 seconds for each additional square**.
- **If chocolate burns** in your microwave oven, it probably means that your oven has a hot spot. Instead of using **HIGH** power, **melt it on MEDIUM (50%) for 2 to 3 minutes**.
- **It is easy** to find out if there is a hot spot in your oven - chocolate will burn in one spot whereas it will barely be softened in another area.
- **Melting time may vary** with different brands of chocolate and from one brand of microwave oven to another.
- **Eight ounces to 1 lb. of chocolate will take 2½ to 3 minutes on HIGH, or 3 to 4 minutes on MEDIUM (50%)**. Stir after 2 minutes, then every minute.
- **Chocolate can burn in the microwave** if it reaches over 120°F. Once it has scorched, it cannot be used. Stirring chocolate helps it melt evenly and prevents scorching.
- **Never cover chocolate when melting it**. Condensation which forms on the covering can cause the chocolate to "seize" (become clumpy and lumpy) if a drop or two falls into the chocolate.
- **Make sure** that the measuring cup and mixing spoon are **completely dry** to prevent chocolate from seizing. If this happens, add vegetable shortening or oil (not butter or margarine) a teaspoon at a time to the seized chocolate. Stir until smooth.

- **Another remedy** for seized chocolate is to add an equal volume of hot liquid (cream, milk or coffee) plus a few drops of vanilla or liqueur - **PRESTO CHOCOLATE SAUCE!**
- **Semi-sweet and bittersweet chocolate bars** can be used instead of cooking chocolate if you run short.
- **Semi-sweet and bittersweet chocolate are interchangable** in recipes. Degree of sweetness can vary from one brand to another, so experiment to find the one you like best.
- **Couverture chocolate** is the best chocolate to use for dipping truffles and dried fruits because of its beautiful shine and its liquid consistency when melted and cooled.
- **White chocolate** is made from cocoa butter, sugar and milk powder. Since it contains no chocolate liquor, it is not considered real chocolate in Canada and the USA and is often called "coating". Good quality white chocolate is available in bars from several manufacturers. Do not confuse it with "summer coating", which contains palm kernel oil or vegetable oil rather than cocoa butter.
- **"Summer coating" or "confectioner's coating"** is artificially flavored chocolate. It comes in a multitude of colors and is usually shaped in discs. It does not need to be tempered and is easy and fun to use when making home-made candies. It is melted and poured into plastic molds which come in a variety of shapes and designs.
- **Since summer coating can burn easily** in the microwave, melt it on **MEDIUM (50%)** in glass jars and stir every minute. Leftovers can be stored and remelted right in the jar.
- **Chocolate molds** are available in specialty shops. They should be rinsed with hot water to clean; dry with a soft cloth. Do not wash plastic molds with soap or in the dishwasher.
- **Chocolate chips hold their shape when melted** and may look like they need more time in the microwave. Stir to check if they are melted.
- **I use semi-sweet chocolate chips** for my recipes (available in mini, regular and maxi sizes). I never use "chocolate-flavored chips".
- **One cup (a 6 oz. pkg.) of chocolate chips will melt in 1½ to 2 minutes uncovered on HIGH**. Stir after 1 minute, then every 30 seconds. **Use MEDIUM (50%)** if your microwave has a hot spot. Time will be **2 to 3 minutes**.
- **When cocoa is called for** in a recipe, it means unsweetened cocoa.
- **See Emergency Substitutions or Equivalents, p. 40.**
- **Chocolate contains phenylethylamine,** which is the same chemical produced by humans when in love. This is why many people binge on chocolate when suffering from a broken heart or are depressed!

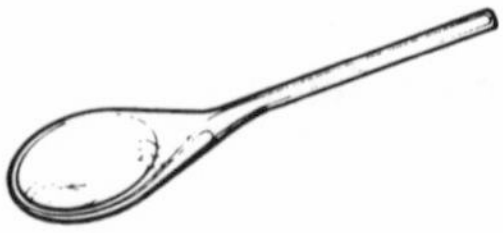

EASY FUDGE BROWNIES

2 oz. unsweetened chocolate
½ c. butter or margarine
1 c. sugar
2 eggs
¾ c. flour
½ tsp. baking powder
½ tsp. vanilla
dash of salt
½ c. chopped nuts, optional
½ c. chocolate chips, optional

1. In the bowl from your food processor (if microwave-safe*) or a large mixing bowl, combine chocolate and butter. **MW uncovered on HIGH for 2 minutes**, or just until melted, stirring once or twice.

2. Add remaining ingredients except nuts and/or chocolate chips. Mix just until smooth and blended (about 15 to 20 seconds on the food processor). Add nuts and/or chocolate chips. Process with 2 or 3 quick on/off turns, just until mixed.

3. Spread batter in an ungreased 8″ square Pyrex™ dish (refer to notes below). Push batter slightly higher in the corners; depress centre slightly. Elevate baking dish on a microsafe rack or inverted pie plate.

4. **MW uncovered on HIGH for 5 to 6 minutes**, rotating baking dish ¼ turn once or twice during cooking time. The top should be dry when touched and a toothpick inserted near the centre should come out almost clean.

5. Let stand directly on the countertop for 10 minutes. Cut in squares and serve while still warm with ice cream and hot Chocolate Fudge Sauce (p. 340). Also scrumptious if cooled completely and topped with either Chocolate Frosting (p. 295), Whipped Chocolate Ganache or Chocolate Truffle Glaze (p. 294).

Yield: 16 large or 25 small squares. These freeze well.

* To learn if your processor bowl is microsafe, do test on p. 21.
* If your microwave oven has an uneven cooking pattern, shield corners of baking dish with aluminum foil to prevent overcooking, or make Round Brownies (below). The centre will take slightly longer to bake if you use a square pan.
* To remove sticky batter easily from the **Steel Knife** of your processor, scrape most of batter from bowl into the baking dish with a rubber spatula, then place bowl and blade back on the base of your machine and turn it on for 2 seconds. The blade will spin itself clean!
* **CONVECTION METHOD:** Preheat oven to 325°F. Place Brownies on rack recommended by your manufacturer for convection cooking. **Bake on the CONVECTION cycle at 325°F for 25 minutes.** If not completely baked, leave them in the oven with the door closed for a few minutes to finish baking.
* **ROUND BROWNIES:** Bake Brownies in an ungreased 8″ round microsafe plastic or glass cake dish; microwave cooking time will be about 1 minute shorter in the plastic dish. Cut in 12 wedges to serve.
* **BROWNIE CUPCAKES:** Line microsafe muffin cups or custard cups with 2 paper cupcake liners. Spoon about 2 tbsp. batter into each one. **Six will take about 2 minutes uncovered on HIGH.** Rotate ¼ turn at half time.

CHOCOLATE MARSHMALLOW BROWNIES

1. Prepare and bake Easy Fudge Brownies (p. 347) as directed. Immediately upon removing them from the microwave, top with a single layer of miniature marshmallows or regular marshmallows which have been cut in half.

2. **MW uncovered on HIGH 1 minute longer**, until marshmallows are melted and puffy. Place pan directly on countertop and cool completely. Ice with Chocolate Frosting (p. 295). Cut in squares.

Yield: 25 squares. Freezes well.

MINT GLAZED BROWNIES

1. Prepare Easy Fudge Brownies (p. 347), but substitute ½ tsp. peppermint extract for the vanilla. Microwave as directed. Immediately upon removing them from the microwave, place about 2 dozen thin chocolate coated after-dinner mints on the hot Brownies.

2. **MW uncovered on HIGH for 1 minute longer**, until softened. Place pan directly on the countertop and spread chocolate evenly over Brownies with a spatula. When cool, cut in squares.

Yield: 25 squares. Freezes well.

CHOCO-MINT BROWNIES

1. Prepare Easy Fudge Brownies (p. 347) as directed. Cool completely. Prepare the following topping:

2 c. icing sugar
2 tbsp. milk
1 tsp. peppermint extract
¼ c. butter
few drops green food coloring
2 oz. semi-sweet chocolate

2. Combine all ingredients except chocolate. (Can be done in the food processor.) Mix until smooth and blended, about 10 to 15 seconds in the processor. Spread over cooled brownies.

3. **MW chocolate uncovered on HIGH for 1½ minutes**, just until melted, stirring after 1 minute. Drizzle chocolate over mint topping in a criss-cross design. When firm, cut into squares.

Yield: 25 squares. Freezes well.

SWEETENED CONDENSED MILK

6 tbsp. butter (¾ of a stick)
1 c. plus 2 tbsp. sugar
½ c. water
1½ c. instant skim milk powder

1. In a 3 quart microsafe bowl combine all ingredients and mix well. **MW uncovered on HIGH for 5 to 6 minutes**, until boiling and thickened. Stir once or twice during cooking, scraping down sides of bowl. Mixture will thicken upon standing. When cool, transfer to an airtight container and refrigerate until needed. Will keep several weeks.

Yield: the equivalent of a 14 oz. can of sweetened condensed milk.

SELINE'S FUDGY-WUDGY BROWNIES

These moist, rich, dark brownies are more like fudge than brownies! I tested them on a cooking class and they nibbled at them frozen, half thawed and completely defrosted! Instant success. This recipe is adapted from a conventional recipe given to me by my friend Seline, who is a chocolate addict!

1 lb. bittersweet or semi-sweet chocolate (Tobler, Poulain or Baker's)
½ lb. unsalted butter, cut up
1 tbsp. instant coffee
2 tbsp. boiling water
4 eggs
1 ½ c. sugar
½ c. flour
1 ½ c. pecans or walnuts

1. Break chocolate into chunks. Combine with butter in a large microsafe bowl. **MW uncovered on HIGH for 2 ½ to 3 ½ minutes**, until melted, stirring twice. Dissolve instant coffee in boiling water. Add to chocolate. Let cool.

2. **Steel Knife:** Process eggs with sugar until blended, about 2 minutes. Add chocolate mixture and blend in with on/off turns. Add flour and nuts and process with several on/off turns, until mixed. Scrape down sides of bowl 2 or 3 times during processing.

3. Spread batter evenly in an ungreased 7″ x 11″ Pyrex™™ baking dish. Push batter slightly higher in corners of dish; depress centre slightly. Elevate by placing casserole on a microsafe rack or inverted pie plate.

4. **MW uncovered on HIGH for 8 to 9 minutes**, rotating casserole ¼ turn halfway through cooking. When done, top should not stick to your fingertips when you touch it, but brownies will be very moist and fudgy, particularly in the centre. Edges will be set. If necessary, **MW on HIGH 1 to 2 minutes longer**.

5. Place directly on the countertop to cool for ½ hour. Cover and refrigerate overnight to set. Cut in squares. If desired, you can commit instant caloric suicide by icing these with Chocolate Truffle Glaze (p. 294)! Refrigerate.

Yield: 2 dozen small, sinfully rich squares. Equally delicious frozen or not!

* **CONVECTION METHOD:** Preheat oven to 325°F. Line a 9″ x 13″ pan with a double layer of aluminum foil, leaving a 2″ overhang on either end to act as handles. Butter foil-lined pan. Prepare batter as directed in Steps 1 and 2 above; spread evenly in pan. Place pan on rack recommended for convection cooking by your manufacturer. **Bake on the CONVECTION cycle at 325°F for 25 to 30 minutes**, or until the edges of the Brownies are set. The centre will still be moist. Cool for 30 minutes; refrigerate overnight. Invert onto a flat surface and peel off foil. Invert again and cut into squares.

PEANUT BUTTER CHOCOLATE CHIP BROWNIES

(Also known as "I think I'll have anutter peanut butter brownie!" A moist, chewy chocolate and peanut butter brownie studded with chocolate chips and topped with a yummy peanut butter frosting.)

¼ c. butter or margarine
1 c. chocolate chips, divided
1 c. sugar
¼ c. chunky or regular peanut butter
2 eggs
1 tsp. vanilla
¾ c. flour
½ tsp. baking powder
Peanut Butter Frosting (recipe follows)
½ c. chopped peanuts

1. In the bowl from your food processor (if microwave-safe) or a large mixing bowl, combine butter and **half** the chocolate chips. **MW on HIGH for 1 to 1½ minutes**, just until melted, stirring once or twice.

2. Add sugar, peanut butter, eggs, vanilla, flour and baking powder. Mix just until smooth and blended (about 30 seconds on the food processor). Sprinkle remaining chocolate chips over batter and process with 2 or 3 more quick on/off turns, just until mixed.

3. Spread batter in an ungreased 8″ square Pyrex™ dish (refer to notes below). Push batter slightly higher in corners of dish; depress centre slightly. Elevate baking dish on a microsafe rack or inverted pie plate.

4. **MW uncovered on HIGH for 5 to 6 minutes**, rotating baking dish ¼ turn once or twice during cooking time. The top should be dry when touched and a toothpick inserted near the centre should come out almost clean.

5. Let stand directly on the countertop for 10 minutes. When cool, frost with Peanut Butter Frosting; sprinkle with chopped peanuts. Cut in squares with a sharp knife. (Brownies will cut better if chilled first.)

Yield: 16 large or 25 small squares. These freeze well.

* These can also be microwaved in an 8″ round microsafe pan. If pan is plastic, microwave time will be about 1 minute shorter.
* **CONVECTION METHOD:** Preheat oven to 325°F. Place Brownies on rack recommended by your manufacturer for convection cooking. **Bake on the CONVECTION cycle at 325°F for 25 minutes**. If not completely baked, leave them in the oven with the door closed for a few minutes to finish baking.

PEANUT BUTTER FROSTING

1½ c. icing sugar
½ c. crunchy or regular peanut butter
¼ c. butter, cut in chunks
3 tbsp. milk

1. Combine all ingredients (can be done on the food processor). Mix until smooth and blended, about 12 to 15 seconds in the processor. Spread over cooled brownies.

NANAIMO BARS

Layer 1:
½ c. butter
¼ c. sugar
⅓ c. cocoa
1 egg
1 tsp. vanilla
1 ½ c. graham wafer crumbs
1 c. flaked coconut
½ c. chopped walnuts or pecans

Layer 2:
6 tbsp. soft butter
3 tbsp. vanilla pudding powder or custard powder
5 tbsp. milk
3 c. icing sugar

Glaze:
4 squares semi-sweet chocolate
2 tbsp. butter

1. **Layer 1:** Place butter in a large microsafe bowl. **MW uncovered on HIGH until melted, about 1 minute**. Blend in sugar, cocoa, egg and vanilla. **MW uncovered for 1 minute**, stirring after 30 seconds. Mixture will be slightly thickened, like custard. Add crumbs, coconut and nuts. Press evenly into a buttered 7″ x 11″ x 2″ pan.

2. **Layer 2:** Combine all ingredients and mix until smooth. (It will take about 20 seconds on the food processor.) Spread evenly over base. Chill while you prepare the Glaze.

3. **Glaze: MW chocolate with butter uncovered on HIGH for 1 ½ minutes**, or just until melted, stirring after 1 minute. Let cool 10 minutes. Pour glaze over Layer 2. Tilt pan back and forth so that glaze coats evenly. Refrigerate. Cut in squares.

Yield: 2 dozen. Freezes well.

PEPPERMINT NANAIMO BARS

Prepare Nanaimo Bars (above) as directed, but substitute ½ tsp. peppermint extract for the vanilla called for in the base. Add 1 tsp. peppermint extract and a few drops of green food coloring to Layer 2 to tint it very pale green.

RUM BALLS

2 c. almonds or filberts
4 c. stale chocolate or white cake
2 c. icing sugar
3 tbsp. cocoa
¼ c. butter
¼ c. milk
2 tbsp. rum

1. **Steel Knife:** Process nuts until finely ground, about 30 seconds. Empty bowl. Process chunks of stale cake until finely ground, about 30 seconds. Measure 4 cups.

2. Process icing sugar, cocoa, butter, milk and rum until blended, about 15 to 20 seconds. Add cake crumbs and ½ cup of the ground nuts; process until well mixed.

3. Roll mixture into 1″ balls. Roll in reserved nuts. Place on a foil-lined cookie sheet and refrigerate until firm. Serve in petit-four paper cups.

Yield: 5 dozen rum balls. These freeze well and can be eaten frozen. (Let them defrost for 5 minutes if you want to be polite!)

GOODBYE MOLLIES

A variation on "Hello Dollies" from "The Pleasures of your Processor".

¼ c. butter or margarine
1 c. graham wafer crumbs
2 ½ c. chocolate chips, divided
½ c. sliced almonds (or any nuts of your choice)
1 ¾ c. granola cereal (e.g. Great Granola, p. 238)
14 oz. can sweetened condensed milk (p. 348)

1. Place butter in an ungreased 7″ x 11″ Pyrex™ casserole. **MW uncovered on HIGH for 45 to 60 seconds**, until melted. Stir in crumbs and pat down evenly. Sprinkle with 1 cup chocolate chips, almonds and granola. Drizzle condensed milk evenly over chocolate/granola mixture.

2. **MW uncovered on HIGH for 6 to 7 minutes.** Mixture will be set, but the top may still be slightly sticky towards the centre when touched with your fingertips.

3. Top with remaining 1 ½ c. chocolate chips. **MW on HIGH 2 minutes longer**, until melted. (They will still hold their shape.) Place directly on the countertop and spread melted chocolate evenly with a spatula. Let stand until chocolate glaze is firm. Cut in squares with a sharp knife.

Yield: 2 dozen squares. May be frozen.

JOLLY MOLLIES

An even more chocolate variation of "Goodbye Mollies". Don't bother to count the calories!

5 tbsp. butter or margarine
1 ¼ c. chocolate wafer crumbs
3 c. chocolate chips, divided
1 ½ c. pecans, coarsely chopped
1 c. flaked coconut
14 oz. can sweetened condensed milk (p. 348)

1. Place butter in an ungreased 7″ x 11″ Pyrex™ casserole. **MW uncovered on HIGH for 45 to 60 seconds**, until melted. Stir in crumbs and pat down evenly. Sprinkle with 1 ½ cups chocolate chips. Sprinkle pecans and coconut over chocolate chips. Drizzle condensed milk evenly over chocolate/nut mixture.

2. **MW uncovered on HIGH for 7 to 8 minutes**. Mixture will be set, but the top may still be slightly sticky towards the centre when touched with your fingertips.

3. Top with remaining chocolate chips. **MW on HIGH 2 minutes longer**, until chocolate chips are melted. (They will still hold their shape.) Place directly on the countertop and spread melted chocolate evenly with a spatula. Let stand until chocolate glaze is firm. Cut in squares with a sharp knife.

Yield: 2 dozen squares. May be frozen.

DELICIOUS DATE SQUARES

This is a very old recipe that my friend Estelle Miller shared with me. It has been in her family for years. Their French-Canadian housekeeper brought it from her family. It converted easily to microwave method.

1 lb. pitted dates, cut up
½ c. sugar
1 c. water
1 ⅓ c. quick-cooking or rolled oats
¾ c. butter or margarine
1 ½ c. flour
1 c. brown sugar, lightly packed
¼ tsp. salt
1 tsp. baking powder

1. Combine dates with sugar and water in a 2 quart Pyrex™ measure. **MW uncovered on HIGH for 7 to 8 minutes**, until thick and smooth. Stir 2 or 3 times during cooking.

2. Combine oats, butter, flour, brown sugar, salt and baking powder. (May be done on the food processor.) Mix until crumbly, about 20 seconds on the processor. Pat half the mixture (about 2 cups) into the bottom of an ungreased 8″ square Pyrex™ pan.

3. Place on a microsafe rack or an inverted pie plate. **MW uncovered on MEDIUM (50%) for 4 to 5 minutes**, until set, rotating pan ¼ turn at half time. Spread cooked date mixture evenly over base. Sprinkle with reserved crumb mixture.

4. MW uncovered on HIGH for 6 to 8 minutes, or until slightly golden in color, rotating pan ¼ turn once or twice during cooking. Let stand directly on the countertop until cool. Cut into squares or bars.

Yield: about 24 squares or bars. Freezes well.

TOFFEE BARS

So yummy in your tummy!

1 tbsp. butter or margarine
9 or 10 graham wafer squares
¼ lb. butter or margarine
½ c. brown sugar, firmly packed
¾ c. slivered almonds or chopped pecans
6 oz. pkg. chocolate chips

1. Place 1 tbsp. butter in an 8″ square Pyrex™ casserole. **MW uncovered on HIGH for 30 seconds**, until melted. Spread evenly over the bottom and slightly up the sides of the casserole. Place graham wafers in a single layer in the bottom of the casserole. If necessary, cut wafers to fit.

2. Combine ¼ lb. butter with brown sugar in a 1 quart microsafe bowl. **MW uncovered on HIGH for 1 minute**. Beat with a whisk until smooth. **MW on HIGH 2 minutes longer**. Pour over graham wafers and spread evenly. Sprinkle with nuts.

3. MW uncovered on HIGH for 2 to 2 ½ minutes, or until bubbly and thick. Rotate casserole ¼ turn every minute.

4. Let stand for 2 minutes to cool slightly. Sprinkle with chocolate chips. When softened, spread chocolate evenly with a spatula. Let stand until set. Cut into bars with a sharp knife. Store in the refrigerator.

Yield: 24 bars. Can be frozen.

BUTTER COOKIES

The food processor and microwave team up to make short work of this yummy cookie.

½ c. butter, cut in chunks
½ c. brown sugar, packed
(or ½ c. granulated sugar)
1 egg
1 tsp. vanilla
1 ½ c. flour
¼ tsp. baking soda
1 tsp. orange zest

1. **Steel Knife:** Process butter, sugar, egg and vanilla for 2 minutes. Add remaining ingredients and process just until dough is mixed and begins to gather in a ball around the blades. Chill dough until firm, about ½ hour.

2. Use about 1 tsp. of dough for each cookie. Shape into 1″ balls. Line a dinner plate with wax paper. Arrange 9 cookies in a circle on the plate, placing 2 or 3 cookies in the centre. Cookies should be about 2″ apart.

3. **MW uncovered on HIGH for 2 to 3 minutes**, or until dry and no longer doughy. Let stand for 1 minute. Cookies will complete baking during standing time. Repeat with remaining cookies.

Yield: about 4 dozen. If desired, sprinkle baked cookies with icing sugar when cool. These freeze well.

* Leftover dough can be rolled into balls and stored in the fridge for 2 or 3 weeks. Just pop the cookies into the microwave when the cookie monster comes to visit. They'll be ready in minutes!
* **CONVECTION METHOD:** Preheat oven to 350°F. Place cookies 2″ apart on a lightly greased pizza pan or small aluminum cookie sheet. (Quantity you can bake at one time depends on size of pan.) Place on rack recommended by manufacturer for convection cooking. **Bake on the CONVECTION cycle at 350°F for 8 to 10 minutes**. Repeat with remaining cookies.

CHOCOLATE CHIP BUTTER COOKIES

Prepare Butter Cookies (above) as directed, but mix 1 cup chocolate chips into the dough. Shape and bake as directed above.

CINNAMON NUT BUTTER COOKIES

Butter Cookies (above)
⅔ c. walnuts or pecans
⅓ c. sugar
1 tsp. cinnamon

1. Prepare Butter Cookies as directed and shape into 1″ balls.

2. **Steel Knife:** Combine nuts, sugar and cinnamon. Process until nuts are fairly fine, about 15 seconds. Roll balls in nut mixture. Bake 9 at a time as directed. Any leftover nut mixture can be stored in the freezer.

SHORTBREAD

- **1 c. butter, cut in chunks**
- **½ c. icing sugar**
- **½ c. cornstarch**
- **1 ¾ c. flour**
- **½ tsp. vanilla**

1. **Steel Knife:** Process butter with icing sugar until well creamed, about 1 minute. Add remaining ingredients. Process with several on/off turns, just until dough is well mixed and begins to gather together in a ball around the blades.

2. Use about 1 tsp. of dough for each cookie. Shape into 1″ balls. Line a dinner plate with wax paper. Arrange 9 cookies in a circle on the plate, placing 2 or 3 cookies in the centre. Cookies should be about 2″ apart.

3. **MW uncovered on HIGH for 2 to 3 minutes**, or until dry and no longer doughy. Let stand for 1 minute. Cookies will complete baking during standing time. Repeat with remaining cookies.

Yield: about 4 dozen. If desired, sprinkle baked cookies with icing sugar when cool. These freeze well.

* **CONVECTION METHOD:** Preheat oven to 350°F. Place cookies 2″ apart on a lightly greased pizza pan or small aluminum cookie sheet. (Quantity you can bake at one time depends on size of pan.) Place on rack recommended by manufacturer for convection cooking. **Bake on CONVECTION cycle at 350°F for 8 to 10 minutes**. Repeat with remaining cookies.

CHOCOLATE MARSHMALLOW ROLL

My Mom always had these hidden in the freezer when I was a kid, but I always found them! Such a pretty addition to a plate of assorted squares.

- **4 oz. unsweetened chocolate**
- **1 tbsp. butter**
- **1 c. icing sugar**
- **1 egg**
- **3 c. miniature or cut-up marshmallows**
- **¾ c. chopped walnuts or pecans**
- **2 c. shredded coconut (or finely chopped nuts)**

1. Combine chocolate and butter in a large microsafe bowl. **MW uncovered on HIGH for 1 ½ to 2 minutes**, just until melted, stirring at half time. Blend in icing sugar and egg. Cool slightly. Mix in marshmallows and nuts so that marshmallows are coated with chocolate mixture.

2. Tear 3 sheets of aluminum foil about 12″ x 18″ each. Sprinkle a 2″ wide band of coconut down the length of the foil. Spoon ⅓ of the marshmallow mixture over the coconut. Sprinkle additional coconut over marshmallow mixture. Wrap up in foil to make a long roll, sealing well. Make 2 more rolls; wrap and freeze until firm. (Will keep up to 2 months in the freezer.)

3. Slice in ½″ thick slices. (Can be sliced and eaten directly from the freezer without any problem!) Place in colored cupcake papers to serve.

Yield: about 3 dozen. Store in the freezer.

GRANOLA RAISIN CLUSTERS

8 oz. semi-sweet chocolate
1 tbsp. oil
1 ¼ c. raisins
1 ¼ c. granola cereal (e.g. Great Granola, p. 238)

1. Place chocolate in a dry 1 quart microsafe bowl. **MW uncovered on HIGH for 2 ½ to 3 minutes**, just until melted, stirring twice. Blend in oil. Add raisins and granola and mix well.

2. Drop from a teaspoon onto a cookie sheet which has been lined with aluminum foil or wax paper. Refrigerate until firm, about 1 hour.

Yield: 2 dozen. These freeze well, if you hide them!

MARSHMALLOW RICE KRISPIE SQUARES

¼ c. butter or margarine
5 c. marshmallows (about 40)
5 c. rice krispies

1. Combine butter and marshmallows in a greased 9″ x 13″ Pyrex™ casserole. **MW uncovered on HIGH for 1 minute**. Stir well. **MW 1 to 2 minutes longer**, until marshmallows are puffed and melted.

2. Stir in cereal and mix well. Spread in casserole; wet your hands and pat down evenly. Refrigerate for ½ hour, just until set. (If refrigerated too long, they will be difficult to cut.) Cut in 1 ½″ squares with a sharp knife.

Yield: 4 dozen.

* **PEANUT BUTTER MARSHMALLOW SQUARES:** Blend ½ cup peanut butter into melted marshmallow mixture.
* **CHOCOLATE RICE KRISPIE SQUARES:** Add 1 cup chocolate chips and ½ cup chopped nuts along with the rice krispies to the melted marshmallow mixture. Heat of marshmallow mixture will melt the chocolate chips.

S'MORES

These are child's play. When you try them, you'll say "I want some more!"

graham wafers squares or chocolate or vanilla wafers
1 milk chocolate bar or chocolate chips
marshmallows, cut in half

1. Place a wafer on a paper plate or napkin. Top with a small piece of chocolate or 6 chocolate chips, then with half a marshmallow. **MW uncovered on HIGH for 15 to 20 seconds**. The marshmallow will puff up. Top with a second wafer and enjoy! **Add 15 seconds for each S'More.**

THREE MINUTE FUDGE

So easy, so good!

2 cups semi-sweet chocolate chips
2 squares unsweetened chocolate, halved
1 tbsp. butter
14 oz. can sweetened condensed milk*
1 ½ c. chopped nuts
1 tsp. vanilla

1. Combine all ingredients except nuts and vanilla in a 2 quart microsafe bowl. **MW uncovered on HIGH for 2 minutes**. Stir to blend. **MW on HIGH 1 minute longer**; stir once again. Chocolate should be melted and mixture should be smooth and shiny. Stir in nuts and vanilla.

2. Spread mixture evenly in a buttered 8″ square pan and chill until firm. Cut in 1″ squares. Serve in small paper cups.

Yield: about 1 ½ pounds.

* If desired, make your own Sweetened Condensed Milk (p. 348). Please note, this is not the same as evaporated milk!

ROCKY ROAD FUDGE

Prepare Three Minute Fudge as directed in Step 1. Cool mixture slightly. Stir in 2 cups miniature or cut-up marshmallows. Spread in a buttered 8″ square pan and refrigerate. Cut in 1″ squares.

VANILLA FUDGE

Your family will say "Here comes the fudge!"

2 c. brown sugar
¾ c. evaporated milk
¾ c. butter
16 marshmallows (about 2 cups)
1 c. icing sugar
1 tsp. vanilla
¾ c. chopped nuts

1. Combine brown sugar, evaporated milk and butter in an 8 cup Pyrex™ measuring cup; mix well. **MW uncovered on HIGH for 10 minutes**, stirring at half time. Stir in marshmallows until melted. Add remaining ingredients and beat until smooth. Spread evenly in a buttered 8″ square pan. Refrigerate. Cut in squares.

Yield: 25 pieces, about 3 lb.

AS YOU LIKE IT FUDGE

Follow recipe for Vanilla Fudge (above) but omit icing sugar. Stir 1 ½ cups chocolate, peanut butter or butterscotch chips into fudge mixture along with marshmallows.

POPCORN

* **Microwave manufacturers** do not generally recommend popping popcorn in a paper bag because the bag could ignite due to the high temperatures reached by the kernels. The exception is specially packaged microwave popcorn.
* **Microwave popcorn** is packaged in a microsafe bag. Some brands pop better than others.
* **Do not exceed** the popcorn manufacturer's recommended times for microwave popcorn. It usually takes about 3 minutes. Usually, no popping occurs during the first minute or so. The popcorn is done when the popping slows down to every 2 or 3 seconds. Wait a few minutes before opening bag to prevent steam burns.
* **Do not leave microwave oven unattended** when popping corn. If overdone, popcorn can scorch.
* **Do not reheat unpopped kernels.** Do not re-use the bag from packaged microwave popcorn.
* **If you wish to make popcorn** from scratch, use a special microwave corn popper. Do not add oil. Follow manufacturer's directions. Usually some kernels will remain unpopped, especially if popcorn is not fresh.
* **Popcorn should be very fresh.** Buy small quantities and store in an airtight container.
* **Do not attempt** to make popcorn in your microwave unless your oven has a minimum of 600 watts. However, there are brands of microwave popcorn which can be made in an oven with as low as 450 watts. Refer to package directions.

PEANUT BRITTLE

1 c. sugar
½ c. corn syrup
1 ½ c. roasted salted peanuts
1 tbsp. butter
1 tsp. vanilla
1 tsp. baking soda

1. Combine sugar and corn syrup in a 3 quart heat-resistant, plastic microsafe bowl. **MW uncovered on HIGH for 5 minutes.**

2. Stir in peanuts. **MW on HIGH 2 to 3 minutes longer**, or until peanuts and syrup are lightly browned. Add butter, vanilla and baking soda; mix until light and foamy. (Be careful, syrup is very hot.)

3. Pour quickly onto a buttered cookie sheet and spread to desired thickness. When cool, break into pieces.

Yield: about 1 lb.

* Read Sugar Mixtures in the Microwave Oven (p. 25) and High Temperature Resistant Cookware (p. 25).

NUTS ABOUT POPCORN

Caramel-coated popcorn and nuts. What could be better? Read boxed notes following Almond Buttercrunch (below).

¼ c. butter or margarine
½ c. honey
½ c. sugar
3 c. mixed nuts (whole almonds, pecans, filberts and/or peanuts)
5 c. popped popcorn

1. Combine butter, honey and sugar in a 3 quart heat-resistant, plastic microsafe bowl. **MW uncovered on HIGH for 5 minutes**, until boiling and golden. Stir in nuts and **MW on HIGH 4 to 5 minutes longer**, stirring twice. Mixture will be amber in color and nuts will be crisp and toasted. Combine with popcorn and mix well.

2. Spread in a single layer on a buttered sheet of aluminum foil. Let stand until cool. Break into chunks and store in an airtight container.

Yield: About 2 quarts.

ALMOND BUTTERCRUNCH

Fabulous! Makes a great gift (for yourself or someone else!) Nothing's as lovin' as something from my micro-oven!

1 c. butter
1 c. sugar
1 tbsp. corn syrup
4 tbsp. water
1 ½ c. finely chopped almonds
6 oz. pkg. chocolate chips

1. Combine butter, sugar, corn syrup and water in a 3 quart heat-resistant, plastic microsafe bowl. **MW uncovered on HIGH for 12 to 14 minutes**, stirring twice during cooking. (**Watch carefully**, temperature rises quickly during the last minute or two of cooking and sugar can burn!) Mixture will be caramel-colored and 290°F on a candy thermometer * (hard-crack stage).

2. While mixture is cooking, spread ⅔ of nuts on a sheet of ungreased aluminum foil to cover a 9″ x 12″ area. Quickly pour hot caramel mixture evenly over nuts. Sprinkle immediately with chocolate chips. When softened, spread chocolate evenly with a spatula. Sprinkle with remaining nuts. Refrigerate. When hard, break into pieces.

Yield: 1 ½ lb. candy.

* If using a conventional candy thermometer, it can not be left in the microwave during cooking, whereas a microwave candy thermometer can.
* Soak measuring cup in hot water after cooking to dissolve any candy mixture which sticks.
* If you are making this for gifts, hide it or the candy monster will make it disappear!
* Read Sugar Mixtures in the Microwave Oven (p. 25) and High Temperature Resistant Cookware (p. 25).

ALMOND BARK

1 ¼ lb. semi-sweet chocolate or summer coating chocolate*

2 c. toasted unblanched almonds (or any nuts you like)

1. Line a cookie sheet with aluminum foil. Place broken-up chocolate in a dry 8 cup Pyrex™ measure. **MW uncovered on MEDIUM for 2 minutes; stir. MW 1 to 2 minutes longer**, stirring every minute, until chocolate is melted. Stir in almonds. Spread in a thin layer on foil. Freeze for 15 minutes, until hard. Break into chunks. Store in refrigerator.

Yield: about 1 ½ lb.

* Summer coating, also known as confectioner's coating, is used for amateur candymaking because it stays shiny and glossy. It may burn if melted on **HIGH** power and requires more frequent stirring than real chocolate.
* For a pretty effect, melt ¼ lb. white chocolate on **MEDIUM (50%) for 2 minutes**, stirring every minute. Drizzle over dark chocolate in a zig-zag fashion. Chill until hard. Break into chunks.

SPEEDY TURTLES

4 dozen pecan halves
12 caramels

8 oz. semi-sweet chocolate
2 tbsp. oil

1. Line a cookie sheet with wax paper. Arrange pecans in groups of 4 on the cookie sheet so that they resemble the feet of a turtle. Flatten each caramel into a 1 ½″ square. Press a caramel gently onto each set of "feet". These will be the turtle's body.

2. Place broken-up chocolate in a dry microsafe bowl. **MW uncovered on MEDIUM (50%) for 2 minutes. Stir. MW 1 to 2 minutes longer**, stirring every minute, just until smooth and melted. Stir in oil. Spoon chocolate over caramels, leaving tips of pecans showing. Refrigerate until set.

Yield: 1 dozen. Store them in a cool dry place.

CARAMEL NUT CHEWS

14 oz. pkg. caramels
2 tbsp. water

3 c. pecans or mixed nuts
½ lb. milk or semi-sweet chocolate, if desired

1. Combine caramels and water in a 4 cup Pyrex™ measure. **MW uncovered on HIGH for 3 minutes**, until melted, stirring twice. Reserve ½ cup nuts as a garnish. Stir remaining nuts into melted caramel mixture; spread evenly in a buttered 9″ square pan.

2. Place chocolate in a dry microsafe bowl; **MW uncovered on HIGH for 2 minutes. Stir. MW 1 to 2 minutes longer**, until melted, stirring every minute. Spread over caramel nut mixture. Top with chopped nuts. Let stand until firm. Cut in 1 ½″ squares.

Yield: 3 dozen.

CHOCOLATE TRUFFLES

Absolutely decadent!

6 oz. whipping cream (35%)*
2 tbsp. unsalted butter*
8 oz. semi-sweet or bittersweet chocolate, broken into chunks*
1 tbsp. Kahlua, Grand Marnier, raspberry liqueur or rum
¼ c. cocoa
2 tbsp. icing sugar

1. Combine cream and butter in a 2 cup Pyrex™ measure. **MW uncovered on HIGH for 1½ minutes**, or until almost boiling.

2. Steel Knife: Process chocolate with several on/off turns to start, then let machine run until chocolate is fine, about 30 seconds. Pour hot cream/butter mixture through the feed tube while the machine is running. Process just until chocolate is melted and mixture is smooth. **(If you don't have a processor, melt chocolate in the microwave for 2½ to 3 minutes uncovered on HIGH**; stir every minute. Slowly stir in hot cream.) Add liqueur.

3. Refrigerate mixture until firm, about 3 hours or overnight (or freeze in an 8″ square pan about 1 hour, stirring several times.) Mix cocoa and icing sugar together in a small bowl. Drop 1″ mounds of chocolate into cocoa mixture. Roll into balls, coating truffles completely with cocoa mixture. Wash and dry your hands as necessary. (Licking is not allowed!) Place truffles in paper candy cups. Refrigerate or freeze. Serve chilled as they soften quite quickly at room temperature.

Yield: about 3 dozen. These will keep about 1 week in the refrigerator or 1 month in the freezer.

* English Devon Cream (48% butterfat) can be used instead of whipping cream to make extra-rich truffles. To remove cream easily from its glass jar, **MW uncovered on HIGH for 30 seconds**. Then transfer cream to a 2 cup measure. Reduce butter to 1 tbsp. and add to Devon Cream. **MW 1¼ minutes longer on HIGH.**.
* The finer the quality of chocolate you use, the better the truffle! I like to use a good quality eating chocolate such as Tobler, although nobody has ever refused to eat my truffles made with semi-sweet baking chocolate!
* If you wish to use milk chocolate to make truffles, increase the quantity to 9 ounces or truffles will be too soft.
* Place truffles in a sieve after coating with cocoa to give them a textured look as well as removing excess cocoa.
* Truffles can be rolled in chocolate sprinkles or finely chopped nuts instead of cocoa/icing sugar mixture.

WHITE CHOCOLATE TRUFFLES

½ c. whipping (35%) cream
2 tbsp. butter
8 oz. white chocolate, cut in chunks
1 tbsp. Amaretto, Franjelica or Grand Marnier
¾ c. almonds or filberts (hazelnuts), finely ground

1. Combine cream and butter in a 2 cup Pyrex™ measure. **MW uncovered on HIGH for 1 to 1 ¼ minutes**, or until almost boiling.

2. Steel Knife: Process chocolate with several on/off turns to start, then let machine run until chocolate is fine, about 30 seconds. Pour hot cream through the feed tube while the machine is running. Process just until chocolate is melted and mixture is smooth. Blend in liqueur. Chill until firm, about 3 hours or overnight.

3. Drop 1″ mounds of chocolate into ground nuts. Roll into balls, coating truffles completely with nuts. Wash and dry your hands as necessary. (No licking allowed!) Place truffles in paper candy cups. Refrigerate or freeze. Serve chilled as they soften quite quickly at room temperature.

Yield: about 2 dozen. These will keep about 1 week in the refrigerator or 1 month in the freezer.

DIPPED TRUFFLES

1. Break up 1 lb. chocolate and place in a dry 4 cup Pyrex™ measure. **MW uncovered on HIGH for 3 to 4 minutes (or MEDIUM (50%) for 4 to 6 minutes)**, stirring every minute, until melted. Cool to 88°F for bittersweet or semi-sweet chocolate and 84°F for milk or white chocolate. Stir chocolate often while cooling. If it is too warm, it will melt the truffle centres. Check temperature with a chocolate thermometer, if possible.

2. Place bowl containing melted, cooled chocolate on a hot tray or a heating pad set at low and covered with a towel. This will keep chocolate from cooling and thickening. Stir occasionally. Dip chilled truffle in chocolate; let excess drip back into the bowl.

3. Place dipped truffles into a pie plate filled with 1 cup cocoa, preferably Dutch-processed such as Droste's. Spoon cocoa over truffle to coat.

4. Place truffles carefully in a foil-lined rectangular storage container. Let set for 15 minutes at room temperature. Cover and refrigerate or freeze until needed. Serve in paper candy cups.

* Couverture chocolate, available in specialty shops, is excellent for dipping as it gives a thin coating which is very shiny.

* To use semi-sweet or bittersweet chocolate without tempering it (see p. 363), add 2 tbsp. vegetable oil to 6 to 8 oz. melted chocolate. For milk chocolate and white chocolate, add 2 tsp. oil to every 6 to 8 oz. This is faster than tempering chocolate and results in a very shiny product which is excellent for dipping.

TEMPERING CHOCOLATE IN THE MICROWAVE

1 ¼ lb. bittersweet, semi-sweet or milk chocolate

1. Chop 1 lb. of the chocolate coarsely. Reserve ¼ lb. in a solid piece. Place chopped chocolate in a dry microsafe bowl. **MW uncovered on MEDIUM (50%) for 2 minutes**. Stir.

2. **MW on MEDIUM (50%) 2 to 4 minutes longer**, until completely melted, stirring every minute. Check temperature with a chocolate thermometer. The temperature must be 110 to 115°F, but no higher; otherwise, chocolate may scorch or turn grainy. This temperature melts all the cocoa butter crystals. Let cool for 5 minutes, stirring occasionally.

3. Add reserved ¼ lb. piece of chocolate and stir slowly and steadily in order not to form air bubbles. When it reaches 84 to 91°F depending on the type of chocolate being tempered (see below), remove any remaining unmelted chocolate. (It can be saved for baking or nibbling!)

4. Place bowl on a hot tray or a heating pad set at low and covered with a towel. This will maintain the temperature of the tempered chocolate. Stir occasionally and check the temperature. **If necessary, reheat on MEDIUM (50%) for 10 seconds**, or just until it reaches the required temperature below. Don't let temperature of melted chocolate exceed 91°F.

Recommended Temperatures for Dipping, Molding or Coating

Bittersweet or semi-sweet chocolate	**86 to 91°F**
Milk or white chocolate	**84 to 86°F**
Summer Coating	**100°F**

* Tempering is necessary for chocolate that will be used to coat truffles and other dipped delights, to make chocolate decorations such as leaves and curls that will be served at room temperature.
* Tempering ensures the development of stable cocoa butter crystals which are evenly distributed throughout the chocolate, keeping it shiny and glossy when set, without gray streaks. When real chocolate is melted, it requires special care to return it to its "good temper".
* A chocolate thermometer which registers from 80 to 130°F is invaluable when learning to temper chocolate. Your kitchen should be cool and dry, not warmer than 68 to 70°F for best results. It will take about 15 to 20 minutes to complete the tempering process.
* **LEFTOVERS:** Spread on a baking sheet covered with wax paper; cool until set. Break up and store tightly wrapped in a cool, dry place. Chocolate will have to be tempered again for dipping, molding or coating. It does not require retempering when used for cakes, cookies, frostings and desserts.

CHOCOLATE-DIPPED STRAWBERRIES

1 dozen large or 2 dozen medium strawberries, (about 1 pint)
4 oz. semi-sweet or white chocolate
finely chopped nuts, if desired

1. Wash strawberries; do not remove stems. Gently pat dry with paper towels. Let stand to air-dry for 20 minutes. (It is important that the berries are completely dry before you dip them in chocolate, or the chocolate will thicken and clump.) Line a large plate with wax paper or foil.

2. Chop chocolate. In a dry microsafe bowl, **MW chocolate uncovered on HIGH for 2 minutes**, or until melted, stirring every minute to prevent it from burning. **(If your microwave oven has a tendency to burn chocolate, MW on MEDIUM (50%) and increase time to 3 to 4 minutes**, stirring every minute.) Let cool to just below body temperature, about 90°F., stirring occasionally.

3. Dip pointed end of strawberry ¾ of the way into the melted chocolate. Allow excess chocolate to drip back into bowl. If desired, roll in chopped nuts. Place strawberry on waxed paper. Repeat with remaining berries. If chocolate thickens, return it to the microwave and **MW on MEDIUM (50%) 30 seconds at a time** to melt it.

4. Refrigerate berries about 20 minutes, or until set. (Can be prepared up to 4 hours before serving time.) Use as a garnish for White Chocolate Mousse (p. 322), or serve in small paper cups to very special guests.

Yield: 1 dozen.

* Recipe can be doubled successfully. However, melting time for double the quantity of chocolate will only be **30 to 60 seconds longer on HIGH, or 1 to 2 minutes on MEDIUM (50%)**. Summer coating chocolate can be used.
* **RIBBON-DIPPED STRAWBERRIES:** Prepare as for Chocolate-Dipped Strawberries, but first dip berries ⅔ of the way into melted white chocolate. (You will need 4 oz. of white chocolate and 4 oz. of semi-sweet chocolate.) Refrigerate berries for 20 minutes, or until set. Then melt semi-sweet chocolate. Dip bottom ⅓ of berries into melted semi-sweet chocolate. Omit nuts. Refrigerate berries until set.

FROZEN CHOCOLATE-DIPPED BANANAS

4 bananas, peeled & halved crosswise
8 wooden coffee stirrers
1 c. chocolate chips
2 tbsp. butter
chopped nuts or granola cereal (e.g. Great Granola, p. 238)

1. Insert sticks into bananas. Freeze 2 hours, until frozen.

2. Combine chocolate chips and butter in a microsafe bowl. **MW uncovered on HIGH for 1½ to 2 minutes**, until melted, stirring every minute. Spoon melted chocolate over bananas, letting excess chocolate drip back into the bowl. Sprinkle with chopped nuts or granola. Freeze until firm.

Yield: 8 servings. Leftovers, if any, can be wrapped and frozen.

QUICK CHOCOLATE CURLS

1. **MW 1 square** of semi-sweet chocolate or a piece of chocolate bar on wax paper **on HIGH for 15 to 20 seconds** to soften chocolate slightly.

2. Hold chocolate with the wax paper to prevent it from melting onto your fingers. Using a potato peeler, peel curls from the flat side of the chocolate, pressing firmly. (Do not handle curls or they may melt from the warmth of your hand. Let curls drop directly onto the cake you are garnishing, or onto wax paper.)

GIANT CHOCOLATE CURLS

4 oz. semi-sweet chocolate, chopped
2 tsp. vegetable oil

1. In a dry microsafe bowl, **MW chocolate with oil uncovered on HIGH for 2 minutes**, or until barely melted, stirring each minute to prevent chocolate from burning. (**If your microwave has a tendency to burn chocolate, melt on MEDIUM (50%) about 3 minutes**, stirring every minute.)

2. Meanwhile cut twelve 5″ squares of heavy aluminum foil. Spoon about 1 tbsp. of melted chocolate mixture on foil to make a 3″ rectangle or circle of chocolate. Spread evenly with the back of the spoon. Refrigerate for 3 to 4 minutes, just until chocolate is set but not hard.

3. Bring sides of foil together so edges of chocolate form a horn shape. Leave top end open; do not overlap chocolate. Crimp foil to seal. Refrigerate for 30 minutes, until firm. Carefully peel off foil. Refrigerate or freeze in an airtight container. Will keep about 1 month in the freezer.

Yield: 12 curls.

CHOCOLATE CUT-OUTS

1. **MW 2 to 3 oz. semi-sweet chocolate uncovered on HIGH in a dry microsafe bowl for 2 minutes (or on MEDIUM (50%) for 2 ½ to 3 minutes)**, stirring every minute, until melted. Cool to just below body temperature, about 90°F, stirring occasionally.

2. Spread chocolate to ⅛″ thickness on wax paper. When barely set, use a cookie cutter and cut out shapes. If chocolate is too firm, it will crack when you try to cut it. Refrigerate briefly. Do not try to move cut-outs until they have set.

3. Carefully lift cut-outs off wax paper with a flexible metal spatula and transfer to cake you are garnishing (or store tightly wrapped in freezer until needed). Scraps or broken cut-outs can be remelted or nibbled!

CHOCOLATE LEAVES

lemon, rose or gardenia leaves*

4 oz. semi-sweet, milk or white chocolate, cut-up

1. Wash leaves. Dry thoroughly. Discard any that have holes.

2. **MW chocolate uncovered on HIGH in a dry microsafe bowl for 2 to 2 ½ minutes (or on MEDIUM (50%) for 3 to 4 minutes)**, stirring every minute, until melted. Cool to just below body temperature, about 90°F, stirring occasionally.

3. Hold the leaf by the stem and use your finger under the leaf as a support. Using a small metal spatula or artist's brush, spread melted chocolate on the underside of leaf to a thickness of ⅛″. If chocolate is too thin, it will break when you try to peel away the leaf. Do not get any chocolate on the other side of the leaf. Set on a tray lined with wax paper.

4. Refrigerate for 10 to 15 minutes, until set. Beginning at the stem end, gently peel leaf off from chocolate. Use as a garnish for cakes and tortes. Can be stored in the fridge or freezer in a tightly covered container.

* Don't use leaves that are toxic (e.g. mistletoe, poinsettia, lily of the valley). Leaves that are safe to use could also be dangerous if they have been sprayed with insecticides. If in doubt, consult your Department of Agriculture.

CHOCOLATE CUPS

4 oz. semi-sweet chocolate

foil or paper cupcake liners

1. **MW cut-up chocolate uncovered on HIGH in a dry microsafe bowl for 2 to 2 ½ minutes (or on MEDIUM (50%) for 3 to 4 minutes)**, stirring every minute, until melted. Let cool to just below body temperature, about 90°F, stirring occasionally.

2. Arrange paper cups on a tray. Use the back of a spoon and brush a thin layer of melted chocolate up and around the inside of each paper cup. Refrigerate 10 minutes, or until set.

3. Repeat coating process once again. (You will probably have to remelt chocolate in bowl. **MW briefly on MEDIUM (50%), about 30 seconds**, just until melted.) Refrigerate chocolate cups until set. (May be stored in the refrigerator in a tightly closed container until needed.) Carefully peel away paper liners and fill (e.g. mousse, ice, cream, fresh fruit).

Yield: about 1 ½ to 2 dozen cups, depending on size.

PASSOVER RECIPES & ALPHABETICAL INDEX

MICRO-WAYS FOR PASSOVER

- **To Kosher a microwave oven for Passover:** Wash all surfaces thoroughly; wipe dry. Do not use for 24 hours. **MW 2 cups water uncovered on HIGH for 10 minutes.** Wipe oven dry.
- **Line the bottom of microwave oven** with cooking parchment. It is microsafe; it withstands temperatures to about 400°F.
- **During Passover,** all meals are prepared at home, unless you are lucky enough to be invited to family or friends! The microwave oven and food processor can help you return to the joys of Jewish cuisine with less fuss.
- **Many recipes throughout this book** can be adapted for Passover use. Use ingredients marked "Kosher l'Pesach", or substitute appropriate ingredients (e.g. matzo meal for bread crumbs). Sephardic and Ashkenazic Jews follow different guidelines as to which foods are allowed. When in doubt, consult your Rabbi.
- **If a recipe from another chapter** suggests serving the cooked dish with a vegetable or side dish not allowed for Passover (e.g. noodles, grains, peas, corn, beans, legumes or their derivatives), substitute an approved food.
- **Availability of Kosher l'Pesach products varies regionally;** e.g. whipping cream, cheeses (Mozzerella, Cheddar), icing sugar.
- **Use potato starch** to thicken gravies, sauces and puddings. Substitute 1 tbsp. potato starch for 1 tbsp. of cornstarch or 2 tbsp. of flour.
- **For bread crumbs or cracker crumbs,** substitute an equal amount of matzo meal. Ground mandlen gives a nice golden color when used to coat chicken. For graham cracker crumbs or cookie crumbs, use ground Passover cookies (e.g. egg kichel or mandel bread). Grind on the **Steel Knife** with quick on/off turns, until fine.
- **Passover mayonnaise** is available commercially, or use the recipe on p. 88, but omit mustard.
- **Use any mild gratable Passover cheese** instead of Mozzerella.
- **If Passover chocolate chips** are not available, substitute 6 oz. of coarsely chopped bittersweet Passover chocolate bar.
- **For 1 square unsweetened chocolate,** use 3 tbsp. cocoa plus 1 tbsp. oil.
- **Substitute an equal amount** of white sugar for brown sugar.
- **For vanilla,** substitute an equal amount of Kosher Passover liqueur (e.g. Sabra) or scrape inside of a split vanilla bean.
- **Use oval, round or ring-shaped pans** for best cooking results. Pyrex™, Corning Ware™ and porcelain casseroles are excellent.
- **Do not use dishes with gold or silver trim** in the microwave; they will arc and spark. You will think it is the 4th of July instead of Passover!
- **Many Passover recipes** depend on egg whites for lightness and volume. They rise beautifully in the microwave, but deflate as flat as a pancake when the microwave shuts off because they need hot, dry air to set their structure.
- **Vegetable dishes and most casseroles** are naturals for the microwave. To brown, transfer to a **400°F oven for 10 to 15 minutes,** or sprinkle with paprika or crushed mandlen.
- **Fruit dishes** can be topped with cinnamon, chopped nuts or a streusel-type topping.

MATZO BALLS

We felt as round as matzo balls when my friend Bella Borts and I finally concluded (after numerous testings) that the maximum quantity we could microwave at one time was based on ½ cup matzo meal. Even my dog turned her nose up at some of our failures! These are tasty and easy.

2 eggs
2 tbsp. oil
1 tbsp. water, chicken broth or club soda
½ c. matzo meal
¼ tsp. salt
dash of onion & garlic powder
4 c. hot water + ½ tsp. salt

1. Combine eggs, oil, 1 tbsp. liquid, matzo meal and seasonings; mix well. (These can be made using the **Steel Knife** of your food processor.) Freeze mixture for 15 minutes or refrigerate for ½ hour. Wet hands and form mixture into twelve 1″ balls.

2. Combine remaining water with salt in a 2 quart microsafe bowl. (You need a large container to allow the matzo balls to expand.) **MW uncovered on HIGH about 7 to 8 minutes,** until water is at a full rolling boil. Carefully add matzo balls. Cover tightly. (If using plastic wrap, turn back one corner ⅛″ to vent.)

3. MW on HIGH for 12 to 14 minutes. Do not uncover during cooking. Let stand covered for 5 minutes. Remove from water with a slotted spoon. Serve in chicken soup.

Yield: 12 matzo balls. These freeze well.

* For extra light matzo balls, add ¼ tsp. baking powder to the matzo meal mixture. There is a brand of baking powder available for Passover.
* Matzo balls may be cooked conventionally on the stove-top while you are cooking your soup in the microwave (or vice versa). Drop balls into 3 quarts boiling salted water. Cover tightly and cook on medium heat for 25 to 30 minutes. Do not peek! Remove from water with a slotted spoon.
* Freeze matzo balls in chicken soup. They defrost and reheat beautifully!

MATZO BALLS FROM A MIX

1 envelope Matzo Ball Mix
4 c. hot water
½ tsp. salt

1. Prepare mixture as directed on package. Cook in boiling salted water as directed in the recipe for Matzo Balls (above).

* Do not double recipe in the microwave. If cooking for a crowd, cook Matzo Balls conventionally.

EASY CHICKEN DUMPLING SOUP

4 ½ c. home-made or canned chicken soup
1 egg
½ c. water
¼ tsp. salt
½ c. matzo meal

1. Place soup in a 2 quart microsafe bowl. **MW uncovered on HIGH until boiling, about 10 minutes,** stirring at half time.

2. Meanwhile, combine remaining ingredients and mix well. Let stand for 5 minutes to thicken slightly. Remove soup from microwave. Drop dumpling mixture a teaspoonful at a time into hot soup. (If you dip the spoon into soup each time, the dumplings will slide right off!)

3. Place soup back in microwave. **MW uncovered on HIGH for 4 to 5 minutes,** until dumplings float to the top.

Yield: 3 to 4 servings.

CHICKEN GEFILTE FISH

Stock:
2 onions, sliced
2 carrots, sliced
2 tsp. salt
¼ tsp. pepper
½ tsp. sugar
6 c. hot water

1. Combine all ingredients for stock in a large microsafe bowl or 5 quart Corning Ware™ casserole. **MW covered on HIGH for 20 minutes.** Meanwhile, prepare chicken mixture.

Chicken Mixture:
2 medium onions
1 carrot
4 single chicken breasts, skinned & boned (1 ¼ lb.)
2 eggs
¼ c. matzo meal
¾ tsp. salt
⅛ tsp. pepper
½ tsp. sugar

2. Cut onions, carrot and chicken into chunks. Process onions and carrot on the **Steel Knife** until finely minced, about 15 seconds. Add chicken and process until finely ground, about 30 seconds, scraping down sides of processor bowl as necessary. Add remaining ingredients for chicken mixture and process until well mixed, about 20 seconds longer.

3. Moisten your hands with cold water to facilitate shaping of chicken. Shape into 10 balls and add to hot stock. Balls should be completely covered with liquid. Cover casserole with lid or vented plastic wrap.

4. **MW on MEDIUM (50%) for 10 to 12 minutes.** Let stand covered for 10 to 15 minutes. Carefully remove from broth and transfer to a large platter. Garnish with cooked carrot slices. Chill. Serve with horseradish.

Yield: 10 balls.

* Leftover stock can be used to make a tasty vegetable soup. Add 4 cups of chopped vegetables (e.g. potatoes, carrots, celery, zucchini, broccoli). **MW covered on HIGH for 25 to 30 minutes,** until vegetables are tender.

PASSOVER QUICHE

This recipe is an adaptation of one developed by Jeannie Rader of St. Louis, Missouri. It's easy and it's good.

Crust:
6 tbsp. butter or margarine
1 ½ c. matzo meal
pinch of salt & pepper

1. **Crust:** Place butter in a 1 quart microsafe bowl. **MW uncovered on HIGH for 1 minute,** until melted. Stir in remaining ingredients for crust and mix well. Press into the bottom and up the sides of a deep 9″ Pyrex™ pie plate or 10″ ceramic quiche dish. **MW uncovered on HIGH for 2 minutes,** until set, rotating dish ¼ turn after 1 minute. Wash and dry bowl.

Filling:
1 medium onion, chopped
½ c. sliced mushrooms
3 tbsp. butter or margarine
2 eggs, lightly beaten
⅔ c. milk
1 c. grated cheese (Cheddar, Swiss or Farmer)
½ tsp. salt
dash pepper & nutmeg

2. **Filling:** Combine onions, mushrooms and butter in a 1 quart microsafe bowl. **MW uncovered on HIGH for 4 minutes,** until tender, stirring once. Cool slightly. Add remaining ingredients for filling; mix well. Pour mixture into baked crust.

3. **Bake conventionally at 375°F for 25 to 30 minutes,** until golden brown. If using the **CONVECTION CYCLE,** no preheating is required; place quiche on rack recommended by oven manufacturer.

Yield: 6 servings.

* 3 matzos can be substituted for the matzo meal. Break matzos into chunks. Process on the **Steel Knife** until fine crumbs are formed, about 30 to 40 seconds.

MATZO PIZZA

1 matzo
2 to 3 tbsp. tomato sauce
2 oz. sliced Mozzerella or Farmer cheese
1 tbsp. green pepper, chopped
thinly sliced mushrooms, if desired

1. Spread matzo with sauce. Top with cheese, green pepper and mushrooms. Place on a microsafe paper towel and **MW uncovered on MEDIUM (50%) for 2 to 2 ½ minutes,** until cheese is melted.

Yield: 1 serving.

* This recipe takes 10 minutes at 375°F in a conventional oven!
* Miniatures can be made on round matzo crackers. **One dozen miniatures will take about 2 to 2 ½ minutes on MEDIUM (50%).**

PASSOVER LASAGNA

2 cloves garlic, minced
1 onion, chopped
1 green pepper, chopped
1 c. mushrooms, sliced
2 tbsp. oil
3 c. Passover Tomato Sauce with Mushrooms*
4 matzos
2 c. cottage cheese
3 c. grated Mozzerella cheese*

1. Combine garlic, onion, green pepper, mushrooms and oil in a medium microsafe bowl. **MW uncovered on HIGH for 4 minutes,** until tender.

2. Spread 1 cup of sauce in the bottom of a 7″ x 11″ oblong glass casserole. Spread half the vegetables over the sauce. Trim matzos to fit dish; arrange a layer of matzos over sauce. Spread 1 cup of cottage cheese over matzos. Top with 1 cup grated cheese.

3. Repeat layers once more. Top lasagna with remaining sauce. Reserve remaining grated cheese. Cover lasagna with waxed paper, then microsafe plastic wrap, turning back one corner slightly to vent. Elevate casserole on a microsafe rack or inverted pie plate.

4. MW on MEDIUM (50%) for 10 minutes. Rotate casserole ½ turn. **MW on MEDIUM 8 to 10 minutes longer,** until bubbling hot. Uncover and sprinkle with reserved cheese. Let stand for 10 minutes. If necessary, **MW uncovered on HIGH for 2 minutes,** just until cheese is completely melted. Cut in squares to serve. Serve with a large tossed salad.

Yield: 6 servings.

* There is also a vegetarian spaghetti sauce available for Passover, or you could substitute 3 cups of Quick Tomato Sauce (p. 89).
* Grated Farmer or Cheddar cheese (or any cheese that can be grated) can be substituted for Mozzerella cheese if it is not available in your area.

FRIED MATZO

2 matzos
2 eggs, lightly beaten
salt & pepper, to taste
2 tbsp. butter

1. Soak matzos briefly under warm running water. Break into large pieces and add to beaten eggs. Add seasoning; stir well.

2. MW butter uncovered on HIGH in a 9″ Pyrex™ pie plate or 10″ ceramic quiche dish **for 2 minutes,** until melted and golden brown. Tip pan to coat all surfaces with butter.

3. Add matzo mixture and spread in an even layer. **MW uncovered on HIGH for 1 minute.** Turn pieces over. **MW 30 to 60 seconds** longer, until barely set. Let stand for 1 to 2 minutes to complete cooking.

Yield: 1 serving.

PASSOVER ROAST CHICKEN

2 chickens (3 lb. each), cut up
2 cloves garlic, crushed
1 tsp. paprika
¼ tsp. pepper
3 tbsp. honey
2 tbsp. oil
2 stalks celery, sliced
2 medium onions, sliced
¼ c. Kosher sweet red wine
½ c. orange juice or chicken broth
paprika
salt & pepper, to taste

1. Wash chicken pieces; pat dry. Combine garlic, paprika, pepper, honey and oil to make a paste. Rub over chicken. Put vegetables in the bottom of a 9″ x 13″ Pyrex™ casserole. Place chicken skin-side down over vegetables, with the thicker, meatier pieces towards the outside of the dish. Add wine and juice or broth; sprinkle with paprika.

2. Cover with cooking parchment or vented plastic wrap. **MW on HIGH for 15 minutes.** Uncover carefully to prevent steam burns. Turn chicken over and re-arrange so that more cooked portions are towards the centre of the dish. Baste with pan juices. Meanwhile, preheat conventional oven to 400°F.

3. **Cover chicken and MW on HIGH 15 minutes longer.** Remove from microwave, uncover carefully and add salt and pepper to taste; sprinkle with paprika.

4. Transfer immediately to conventional oven. **Roast uncovered at 400°F for 10 minutes.** Turn chicken pieces over, baste with pan juices and **roast 10 minutes longer,** until golden. Serve with Honey Glazed Carrots (p. 375).

Yield: 6 to 8 servings. Reheats well.

* This recipe also works well with chicken breasts. You should have about 8 large single chicken breasts.
* Microwave cooking time to partially cook chicken will be **5 minutes per lb. on HIGH.**
* Carrots can be microwaved while chicken is browning in the conventional oven.
* If you have a combination **CONVECTION/MICROWAVE** oven, chicken can be microwaved as directed above to the end of Step 3. Remove from oven and insert rack recommended by manufacturer for **CONVECTION CYCLE. Roast chicken uncovered at 375°F for 10 minutes.** Turn chicken over, baste with pan juices and **roast 10 minutes longer,** until golden.

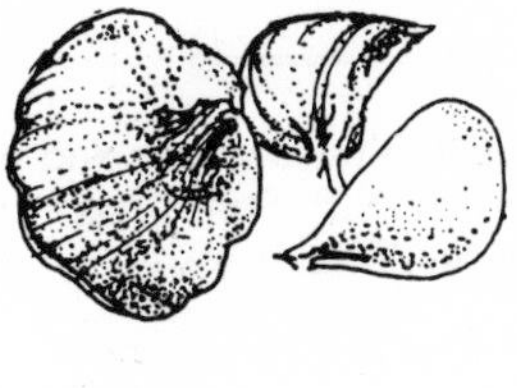

PASSOVER SWEET & SOUR MEATBALLS

Meat Mixture:
2 lb. ground beef or veal
2 eggs
1 tsp. salt
¼ tsp. pepper
¼ tsp. garlic powder
½ c. matzo meal

Sauce:
2 - 10 oz. cans Passover Tomato Sauce with Mushrooms
½ c. sugar or honey (to taste)
1 to 2 tbsp. lemon juice (to taste)
2 tbsp. red wine, if desired

1. Shape meat mixture into 1″ meatballs, adding ¼ cup of the sauce mixture to the meatball mixture for more flavor, if desired. Arrange meatballs in a single layer in an ungreased 3 quart oval or rectangular microsafe casserole.

2. MW **uncovered 10 to 12 minutes on HIGH,** re-arranging at half time. Meatballs should lose their pink color. Let stand 3 or 4 minutes. Drain off any pan juices. Pour sauce over cooked meatballs and mix well. (May be prepared in advance up to this point and refrigerated until needed.)

3. MW **covered** with casserole lid or waxed paper **on HIGH for 10 to 12 minutes,** stirring once or twice. Let stand covered for 3 or 4 minutes.

Yield: 4 to 6 servings as a main course and 6 to 8 servings as an appetizer. Freezes well. Flavor is even better the next day.

PASSOVER MOCK KISHKA

2 medium onions
2 carrots, peeled & trimmed
1 stalk celery
½ green pepper
2 eggs
½ c. oil
1 c. matzo meal
1 c. cake meal
3 tbsp. water or chicken broth
1 tsp. salt
¼ tsp. pepper, garlic powder & paprika

1. Cut vegetables in chunks. Process on the **Steel Knife** until fine, about 15 seconds. Add eggs and process 5 seconds longer. Add remaining ingredients and process until well mixed.

2. Empty mixture into a 9″ pie plate and shape into a ring about 3″ in diameter. Wet your hands for easier handling. Cover with waxed paper, tucking ends under the dish.

3. **MW on HIGH for 6 to 8 minutes,** until dry to the touch. Let stand covered for 2 minutes. Slice into 12 to 16 pieces. Serve with gravy from brisket or roast chicken.

Yield: 6 to 8 servings. Freezes well.

* **TURKEY STUFFING:** Double all ingredients and prepare as directed in Step 1. Use as a stuffing for turkey. N.B. Stuff turkey just before cooking. Read Stuffing Poultry (The Right Stuff!) on p. 137.

HONEY GLAZED CARROTS

An easy and delicious holiday favorite.

2 lb. carrots, peeled & trimmed
½ c. orange juice
½ tsp. salt
dash pepper
½ c. honey
2 tbsp. potato starch
¼ c. orange juice or cold water
1 tbsp. margarine or oil

1. **Slicer:** Cut carrots to fit feed tube. Slice, using medium pressure. You should have 6 cups sliced carrots. Combine carrots with ½ cup orange juice, salt, pepper and honey in a 2 quart oval or round microsafe casserole. Mix very well. Cover with vented plastic wrap or casserole lid.

2. **MW on HIGH for 16 to 18 minutes,** until tender, stirring once or twice. If mixture bubbles over, **reduce power to MEDIUM (50%) and double the remaining cooking time.**

3. Blend potato starch with orange juice or cold water. Stir into carrots. Add margarine. (May be prepared in advance up to this point and refrigerated until serving time.)

4. **Cover once again and MW on HIGH for 4 to 6 minutes,** until hot and thickened, stirring twice. Let stand covered for 5 minutes.

Yield: 8 servings. May be frozen.

FRUIT & VEGETABLE TSIMMIS

In Jewish, a tsimmis means much ado about nothing. This Tsimmis is really something!

2 large sweet potatoes, peeled
8 carrots, peeled & trimmed*
½ c. raisins
½ c. pitted prunes
½ c. dates, pitted & cut up
½ c. apricots, cut up
1 seedless orange, peeled
1 tbsp. lemon juice
½ c. honey
2 tbsp. water
½ tsp. salt
dash pepper

1. **Slicer:** Cut sweet potatoes and carrots to fit feed tube. Slice, using medium pressure. You should have about 8 cups. Add raisins, prunes, dates and apricots.

2. **Steel Knife:** Process peeled orange until finely ground. Add with remaining ingredients to vegetables and mix well. Place in an ungreased 3 quart deep round casserole. Cover with casserole lid or vented plastic wrap.

3. **MW on HIGH for 20 to 25 minutes,** until tender, stirring at half time. Uncover, mix gently but thoroughly; cover with lid or a dinner plate. Let stand covered for 10 minutes. Freezes well.

Yield: 8 to 10 servings.

* 1 medium squash, peeled & sliced, may be substituted for half the carrots.

SPINACH VEGETABLE KUGEL

If you have a processor, use it to prepare the vegetables quickly for this colorful kugel. The conventional recipe was given to me by an excellent cook, Doris Lacovetsky of Winnipeg. I adapted it easily for the microwave.

10 oz. pkg. fresh spinach
2 onions, chopped
2 stalks celery, chopped
½ green pepper, chopped
3 medium carrots, grated
3 tbsp. oil
½ c. mushrooms, sliced
4 eggs
¾ tsp. salt
¼ tsp. pepper
1 c. matzo meal

1. Remove stems from spinach. Wash very well, but do not dry. Place in a 2 quart microsafe casserole. Cover with casserole lid or vented plastic wrap. **MW on HIGH for 4 minutes,** until wilted. Let stand covered for 3 minutes. Uncover and let cool. Remove from casserole and squeeze dry.

2. Place onions, celery, green pepper, carrots and oil in casserole. **MW uncovered on HIGH for 4 minutes,** until tender-crisp. Stir in mushrooms; **MW uncovered on HIGH 2 minutes longer.**

3. Coarsely chop spinach (can be done on the **Steel Knife**). Combine all ingredients and mix well. Pour into a lightly greased 10″ ceramic quiche dish. Cover with waxed paper or cooking parchment.

4. Elevate casserole on a microsafe rack or inverted pie plate. **MW covered on HIGH for 10 to 12 minutes,** rotating casserole ¼ turn halfway through cooking. When done, edges will be set and a knife inserted in the centre of the kugel will come out almost dry. Let stand covered for 10 minutes. It will complete its cooking during the standing time.

Yield: 6 to 8 servings. Freezes well.

* A deep 9″ pie plate can be used to cook the kugel. You will have best results if the sides are fairly straight rather than sloped.
* Spinach mixture can also be made into miniature kugels. Line compartments of a microsafe muffin pan with paper cupcake liners. Fill half full. **Six will take about 2 to 2½ minutes on HIGH, or 40 seconds for one.** Rotate pan ¼ turn halfway through cooking. Let stand 2 minutes. Repeat with remaining spinach mixture.

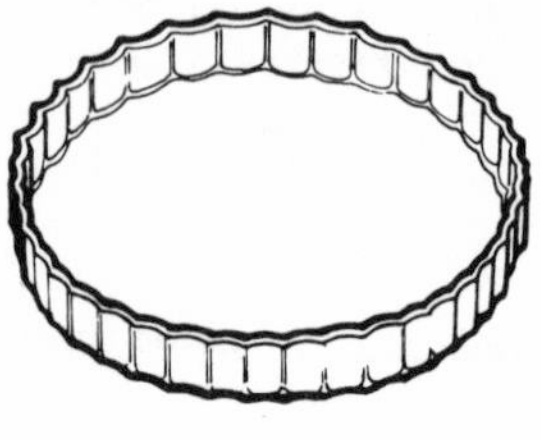

PASSOVER FARFEL & BROCCOLI KUGEL

This recipe is cooked using both the microwave and conventional oven. It's sure to be a hit with your guests.

5 c. matzo farfel
3 ½ c. hot chicken soup
¾ lb. broccoli, chopped
2 onions, chopped
1 red or green pepper, chopped
3 tbsp. oil
1 c. mushrooms, sliced
1 ½ tsp. salt
¼ tsp. pepper
5 eggs
paprika to garnish

1. Combine farfel and chicken soup and let stand for 10 minutes, until liquid is absorbed. Preheat conventional oven to 375°F. (If completing recipe in a combination oven, do not preheat.)

2. Meanwhile, place broccoli in a medium-sized microsafe bowl. Cover with vented plastic wrap. **MW on HIGH for 4 to 5 minutes,** until tender-crisp. Let stand covered for 1 minute. Uncover and let cool.

3. Combine onions and peppers with oil in a 3 quart oval or rectangular microsafe/heatproof casserole. **MW uncovered on HIGH for 4 minutes.** Stir in mushrooms and **MW on HIGH 2 minutes longer.**

4. Combine all ingredients with vegetables in the casserole and mix well. Spread evenly and sprinkle with paprika. **Bake in the conventional oven at 375°F for 45 to 55 minutes.** (If using a combination oven, insert rack recommended by manufacturer and **bake uncovered on CONVECTION CYCLE at 325°F for 35 to 45 minutes.)** When done, kugel will be golden and crusty. Check at minimum time for doneness.

Yield: 12 servings. May be frozen.

* **For 8 servings,** use a 2 quart casserole. Use 3 cups farfel, 2 cups chicken broth, 3 eggs and 1 ¼ tsp. salt. If desired, broccoli can be omitted. Baking time will be about 35 to 45 minutes.
* To heat chicken soup, **allow 1 ½ minutes on HIGH for each cup of soup.**

PASSOVER BUTTERCRUNCH

Absolutely Addictive!

½ c. butter or margarine
½ c. honey
½ c. sugar
3 c. matzo farfel
½ c. whole or sliced almonds
½ c. pecan halves

1. Combine butter, honey and sugar in a large heat resistant plastic bowl which can withstand high temperatures*. **MW uncovered on HIGH for 5 to 6 minutes,** until boiling and golden. Stir once or twice during cooking. Add farfel and nuts and mix well.

2. **MW uncovered on HIGH 4 to 5 minutes longer,** stirring every 2 minutes. Mixture should be golden brown; if you drop a small amount in cold water it will turn crisp.

3. Spread in a single layer on a buttered sheet of aluminum foil. Cool slightly. Wet your hands with cold water and press down firmly on warm mixture to flatten. Let stand until firm. Break into small pieces. Store in an airtight container.

Yield: about 1 ½ lb. It was hard to tell exactly because I sampled it several times to test for doneness before I remembered to weigh it!

PASSOVER GRANOLA

A delicious breakfast cereal loved by children of all ages. This will make a welcome Passover treat. Make sure you use a specially tempered bowl which can resist high temperatures without shattering. If you don't have the proper cooking container, follow method for Great Granola (p. 238).

¼ c. oil
¾ c. honey
3 c. matzo farfel
½ c. coarsely chopped almonds
½ c. coarsely chopped pecans
½ c. coconut
1 tsp. cinnamon
½ c. raisins, if desired

1. Combine oil and honey in a large heat resistant plastic bowl which can withstand high temperatures*. **MW uncovered on HIGH for 2 to 3 minutes,** stirring once or twice, until boiling. Add remaining ingredients except for raisins. Mix well to coat with honey mixture.

2. **MW uncovered on HIGH for 6 to 7 minutes,** stirring every 2 minutes. Granola mixture will be golden brown, but will still be sticky when you remove it from the microwave. It will crisp upon standing.

3. Let cool, stirring 2 or 3 times to break up mixture. Stir in raisins. Store in an airtight container.

Yield: 6 cups.

* Use plastic cookware specially designed to use in both conventional and microwave ovens and which can withstand temperatures up to 400°F.

* Read High Temperature-Resistant Cookware (p. 25) and Sugar Mixtures in the Microwave Oven (p. 25). It will help you choose the correct cookware for microwaving sugar mixtures with temperatures exceeding 250°F.

UPSY-DOWNSY CRUMB CRUST

This versatile crumb mixture can be used either as a topping for a fruit crisp or used as a pie crust!

1 ¾ oz. pkg. soup mandlen (3 cups mandlen)*
1 c. pecans
¼ c. oil
½ c. sugar
1 ¼ tsp. cinnamon

Method for Fruit Crisp Topping

1. **Steel Knife:** Process mandlen until finely crushed, about 12 to 15 seconds. Add pecans and process until coarsely chopped, about 8 to 10 seconds. Add remaining ingredients and process for 8 to 10 seconds to blend.
2. Use as a topping for fruit crisps (see Passover Pecan Apple Crisp, below). Crumb mixture can be prepared in advance and stored in a plastic bag in the refrigerator or freezer until needed.

Method for Pie Crust

1. **Steel Knife:** Process mandlen until finely crushed, about 12 to 15 seconds. Empty bowl. Process pecans until finely crushed, about 25 seconds. Longer processing time will release oil from the nuts and help to bind the crumb mixture. Add mandlen crumbs, oil, sugar and cinnamon. Process for 8 to 10 seconds to blend.
2. Press mixture into the bottom and up the sides of an ungreased 9″ Pyrex™ pie plate. **MW uncovered on HIGH for 2 minutes,** until set, rotating dish ¼ turn after 1 minute. Cool. Fill as desired.

* Passover cookies such as mandel bread or egg kichel can be used instead of soup mandlen. You will need about 1 ¼ cups crumbs.

PASSOVER PECAN APPLE CRISP

Upsy-Downsy Crumb Crust (above)
4 to 5 large apples, peeled, cored & sliced
1 tsp. lemon juice
3 tbsp. matzo cake meal
¼ cup sugar
1 tsp. cinnamon

1. Prepare crumb mixture for Upsy-Downsy Pie Crumb, using Method for Fruit Crisp Topping. Set aside.
2. Sprinkle apples with lemon juice. Combine with cake meal, sugar and cinnamon; mix well. Place in an ungreased 10″ ceramic quiche dish or deep 9″ pie plate. Sprinkle with crumb mixture.
3. **MW uncovered on HIGH for 10 to 12 minutes,** rotating dish ¼ turn halfway through cooking. Apples should be tender when pierced with a knife in the centre of the dish. Enjoy warm or at room temperature. Refrigeration is not necessary.

Yield: 8 servings.

Note: Other fruits may be used instead of apples (e.g. blueberries, sliced pears, peaches, strawberries, plums).

PASSOVER LEMON MERINGUE PIE

Upsy-Downsy Crumb Crust (p. 379)
1 c. sugar
4 tbsp. + 1 tsp. potato starch
1 ½ c. boiling water*
3 egg yolks
⅓ c. fresh lemon juice
2 tsp. grated lemon rind
1 tbsp. butter or margarine

1. Prepare crumb mixture for Upsy-Downsy Crumb Crust, using Method for Pie Crust. Microwave crust as directed. Cool.

2. Combine sugar with potato starch in a 2 quart microsafe measure or bowl. Slowly whisk in boiling water. **MW uncovered on HIGH for 2 to 3 minutes,** until thick and boiling, whisking twice.

3. Combine yolks with lemon juice. Add ½ cup of the hot mixture to yolks and mix well. Blend egg yolk mixture back into hot mixture. **MW uncovered on HIGH 1 to 2 minutes longer,** or until boiling and thickened, whisking every minute. Add lemon rind and butter. Pour hot filling into baked crust.

4. Prepare Meringue (below). Immediately pile meringue onto hot filling, sealing meringue onto edge of crust. **MW uncovered on MEDIUM (50%) for 3 minutes,** until set when touched with your fingertips. If desired, brown in a **preheated 425°F oven for 2 or 3 minutes,** until golden. Watch carefully. Cool away from drafts to prevent weeping.

Yield: 8 servings. Do not freeze.

Meringue

3 egg whites
1 tsp. fresh lemon juice
6 tbsp. sugar

1. Using an electric mixer, beat egg whites with lemon juice until foamy. Beat in sugar a tablespoon at a time and continue beating until stiff and glossy.

* **Water may be boiled in the microwave on HIGH, about 4 minutes.**
* Lemon filling may be used to fill cream puffs.
* Instead of microwaving the meringue-topped pie, it can either be baked in a conventional oven or on the **CONVECTION CYCLE** of a combination oven. **Preheat oven to 350°F.** If using **CONVECTION CYCLE,** place pie on rack recommended by oven manufacturer. **Bake at 350°F for 8 to 10 minutes,** until golden. Watch carefully to prevent burning.

CHOCOLATE MARSHMALLOW FARFEL SQUARES

This recipe is sure to become a favorite.

¼ c. butter or margarine
5 c. Passover marshmallows (about 40)
5 c. matzo farfel
¾ tsp. cinnamon
1 c. chocolate chips*
1 c. chopped nuts (pecans, walnuts or almonds)

Glaze:
1 c. chocolate chips*
1 tbsp. oil

1. Place butter and marshmallows in a greased 9″ x 13″ Pyrex™ casserole. **MW uncovered on HIGH for 2 to 3 minutes,** until melted, stirring every minute.

2. Add farfel, cinnamon, chocolate chips and half the nuts. Mix well. Spread evenly in casserole. Wet hands and pat down evenly.

3. **Glaze:** Combine chocolate chips and oil in a 1 cup Pyrex™ measuring cup. **Melt uncovered on HIGH for 2 minutes,** stirring at half time. Spread over farfel mixture. Sprinkle with reserved nuts.

4. Refrigerate ½ hour, just until chocolate is set. Cut in 1 ½″ squares with a sharp knife. (If you wait too long, it will be difficult to slice.)

Yield: 4 dozen squares. Can be frozen, but slice first.

* You can use either regular or coconut covered marshmallows.
* If Passover chocolate chips are not available in your area, substitute 12 oz. of bittersweet Passover chocolate bars, broken up, in the squares and the Glaze.
* Do not substitute margarine or butter for oil in the glaze, or the chocolate will seize (get clumpy and lumpy).

PASSOVER BROWNIES

Easy and good!

2 eggs
1 c. sugar
½ c. oil
½ c. cocoa
½ c. cake meal*
1 tbsp. potato starch
1 tbsp. orange juice
¾ c. chopped nuts

1. **Steel Knife:** Beat eggs, sugar and oil until light, about 1 minute. Add cocoa, cake meal, potato starch and juice. Process 20 seconds longer, until smooth. Add nuts; process with quick on/off turns, just until mixed.

2. Line the bottom of an 8″ square Pyrex™ baking dish with waxed paper. Spread mixture evenly in pan, pushing it slightly higher in the corners. Work quickly; mixture will become thick. Let stand for 5 minutes.

3. Elevate baking dish on an inverted pie plate. **MW on HIGH for 4½ to 6 minutes,** rotating dish ¼ turn every 2 minutes. If batter begins to overcook in the corners, shield with flat pieces of aluminum foil. When done, top will be set and won't stick to your fingertips. A toothpick will come out clean when inserted into the centre of the brownies.

4. Let stand directly on the counter to cool. Cut in 1½″ squares and remove from pan carefully with a flexible metal spatula. Be careful not to cut through waxed paper.

Yield: 25 squares. Can be frozen.

* Recipe can also be made with matzo meal, but process the mixture for 45 seconds in Step 1 to make the matzo meal less coarse.

INDEX

INDEX

The recipes in MicroWays have been written for regular microwave cookery. For those who own combination Convection/Microwave ovens, the following options are also given:-

* Recipes involving Convection cookery are indicated by "**C**".
* Recipes involving Convection/Microwave cookery are indicated by "**CM**".

– A –

– B –

– D –

- N -

- O -

– P –

– Q –

– R –